Annual Editions:
Anthropology,
Thirty-Eighth Edition

Elvio Angeloni

http://create.mheducation.com

ISBN-10: 1259242633   ISBN-13: 9781259242632

Contents

Preface

This thirty-eighth edition of *Annual Editions: Anthropology* contains a variety of articles on contemporary issues in social and cultural anthropology. In contrast to the broad range of topics with minimum depth that is typical of standard textbooks, this anthology provides an opportunity to read first-hand accounts by anthropologists of their own research. In allowing scholars to speak for themselves about the issues in which they are experts, we are better able to understand the kinds of questions anthropologists ask, the ways in which they ask them, and how they go about searching for answers. Indeed, where there is disagreement among anthropologists, this format allows the readers to draw their own conclusions. Given the very broad scope of anthropology—in time, space, and subject matter—the present collection of highly readable articles has been selected according to a certain criteria. The articles have been chosen from both professional and nonprofessional publications for the purpose of supplementing standard textbooks that are used in introductory courses. Some of the articles are considered classics in the field, while others have been selected for their timely relevance.

Finally, it should be pointed out that an *Author's Note* is available for several classic articles that have been in this book since they were originally published. These updates consist of fresh perspectives on important issues, written by the authors themselves exclusively for this book.

Included in this volume are a number of features that are designed to make it useful for students, researchers, and professionals in the field of anthropology. While the articles are arranged along the lines of broadly unifying themes, the *Topic Guide* can be used to establish specific reading assignments tailored to the needs of a particular course of study. In addition, each unit is preceded by an overview, which provides a background for informed reading of the articles and emphasizes critical issues. *Learning Outcomes* accompany each article and outline the key concepts that students should focus on as they are reading the material. *Critical Thinking* questions, found at the end of each article, allow students to test their understanding of the key points of the article. The *Internet References* section can be used to further explore the topics online.

Instructors will appreciate a password-protected online *Instructor's Resource Guide* and students will find online quizzing to further test their understanding of the material. These tools are available at www.mhhe.com/createcentral.

Those involved in producing this volume wish to make the next one as useful and effective as possible. Your criticism and advice are always welcome. Any anthology can be improved. This continues to be—annually.

Editor

Elvio Angeloni received his BA from UCLA in 1963, MA in anthropology from UCLA in 1965, and MA in communication arts from Loyola Marymount University in 1976. He has produced several films, including *Little Warrior,* winner of the Cinemedia VI Best Bicentennial Theme, and *Broken Bottles*, shown on PBS. He served as an academic adviser on the instructional television series *Faces of Culture*. He received the Pasadena City College Outstanding Teacher Award in 2006 and has since retired from teaching. He is also the academic editor of *Annual Editions: Physical Anthropology, Classic Edition Sources: Anthropology* co-editor of *Roundtable Viewpoints Physical Anthropology*, and co-editor of *Annual Editions: Archaeology*. His primary area of interest has been indigenous peoples of the American Southwest. evangeloni@gmail.com

Academic Advisory Board

Members of the Academic Advisory Board are instrumental in the final selection of articles for the *Annual Editions* series. Their review of the articles for content, level, and appropriateness provides critical direction to the editor(s) and staff. We think that you will find their careful consideration reflected in this book.

Lauren Arenson
Pasadena City College

Victoria Bernal
University of California–Irvine

Mary Jill Brody
Louisiana State University

Daniel Cring
University of Louisiana–Lafayette

Christina Dames
Lindenwood University

Ronald Enders
Ashland Community Technical College

Beverly Fogelson
Oakland University

Josephine Fritts
Ozarks Technical Community College

Jeremy L. Goldstein
St. George's School

Carol Hayman
Austin Community College

Elias S. Kary
Monterey Peninsula College

Diane A. Lichtenstein
Baldwin-Wallace College and Cleveland Institute of Art

Heather Smith Mode
Gaston College

Sabina Trumble
University of Phoenix and Ashford University

Tim Vermande
Art Institute of Indianapolis

Mary Vermilion
Saint Louis University

John D. Wilkins
Grand Canyon University

Correlation Guide

The *Annual Editions* series provides students with convenient, inexpensive access to current, carefully selected articles from the public press. **Annual Editions: Anthropology, 38/e** is an easy-to-use reader that presents articles on important topics such as *cultural diversity, gender, social change*, and many more. For more information on other *McGraw-Hill Create™* titles and collections, visit www.mcgrawhillcreate.com.

This convenient guide matches the articles in **Annual Editions: Anthropology, 38/e** with **Culture, 2/e** by Kottak/Gezon.

Culture, 2/e	Annual Editions: Anthropology, 38/e
Chapter 1: What Is Anthropology?	Tricking and Tripping: Fieldwork on Prostitution in the Era of AIDS
Chapter 2: Culture	Body Ritual among the Nacirema Breastfeeding and Culture Eating Christmas in the Kalahari The Berdache Tradition Why Manners Matter
Chapter 3: Doing Anthropology	Eating Christmas in the Kalahari Shakespeare in the Bush The September 11 Effect on Anthropology Tricking and Tripping: Fieldwork on Prostitution in the Era of AIDS
Chapter 4: Language and Communication	How Language Shapes Thought Strong Language Lost in Translation: You Talkin' to Me? Vanishing Languages War of Words
Chapter 5: Making a Living	Being Indigenous in the 21st Century The Inuit Paradox Tricking and Tripping: Fieldwork on Prostitution in the Era of AIDS When Brothers Share a Wife: Among Tibetans, the Good Life Relegates Many Women to Spinsterhood
Chapter 6: Political Systems	The Evolution of Inequality The Secrets of Haiti's Living Dead
Chapter 7: Families, Kinships, and Marriage	Arranging a Marriage in India Kidnapping Women: Discourses of Emotion and Social Change in the Kyrgyz Republic The Invention of Marriage When Brothers Share a Wife: Among Tibetans, the Good Life Relegates Many Women to Spinsterhood Who Needs Love! In Japan, Many Couples Don't
Chapter 8: Gender	Meghalaya: Where Women Call the Shots Rising Number of Dowry Deaths in India The Berdache Tradition The Hijras: An Alternative Gender in India Where Fat Is a Mark of Beauty
Chapter 9: Religion	Body Ritual among the Nacirema Five Myths of Terrorism The Adaptive Value of Religious Ritual The Berdache Tradition Understanding Islam
Chapter 10: The World System and Colonialism	Blood in the Jungle Ecuador's Paradise Lost Ruined Saving Our Identity: an Uphill Battle for the Tuva of China The Evolution of Inequality Understanding Islam

Culture, 2/e	Annual Editions: Anthropology, 38/e
Chapter 11: Ethnicity and Race	Armor against Prejudice The Americanization of Mental Illness The Arrow of Disease The Inuit Paradox
Chapter 12: Applying Anthropology	The Americanization of Mental Illness The Arrow of Disease Ruined
Chapter 13: Anthropology's Role in a Globalizing World	Being Indigenous in the 21st Century The Americanization of Mental Illness The Inuit Paradox The September 11 Effect on Anthropology Understanding Islam

This convenient guide matches the articles in **Annual Editions: Anthropology, 38/e** with the corresponding chapters in **Cultural Anthropology: Appreciating Cultural Diversity, 16/e** by Kottak.

Cultural Anthropology: Appreciating Cultural Diversity, 16/e	Annual Editions: Anthropology, 38/e
Chapter 1: What Is Anthropology?	Tricking and Tripping: Fieldwork on Prostitution in the Era of AIDS
Chapter 2: Culture	Body Ritual among the Nacirema Breastfeeding and Culture Eating Christmas in the Kalahari The Berdache Tradition Why Manners Matter
Chapter 3: Method and Theory in Cultural Anthropology	Eating Christmas in the Kalahari Shakespeare in the Bush The September 11 Effect on Anthropology Tricking and Tripping: Fieldwork on Prostitution in the Era of AIDS
Chapter 4: Applying Anthropology	Ruined The Americanization of Mental Illness The Arrow of Disease
Chapter 5: Language and Communication	How Language Shapes Thought My Two Minds Strong Language Lost in Translation: You Talkin' to Me? War of Words
Chapter 6: Ethnicity and Race	Armor against Prejudice The Americanization of Mental Illness The Arrow of Disease The Inuit Paradox
Chapter 7: Making a Living	Being Indigenous in the 21st Century The Inuit Paradox Tricking and Tripping: Fieldwork on Prostitution in the Era of AIDS When Brothers Share a Wife: Among Tibetans, the Good Life Relegates Many Women to Spinsterhood
Chapter 8: Political Systems	Meghalaya: Where Women Call the Shots No More Angel Babies on the Alto do Cruzeiro The Evolution of Inequality The Secrets of Haiti's Living Dead
Chapter 9: Gender	Meghalaya: Where Women Call the Shots Rising Number of Dowry Deaths in India The Berdache Tradition The Hijras: An Alternative Gender in India Where Fat Is a Mark of Beauty

Cultural Anthropology: Appreciating Cultural Diversity, 16/e	Annual Editions: Anthropology, 38/e
Chapter 10: Families, Kinship, and Descent	Arranging a Marriage in India Kidnapping Women: Discourses of Emotion and Social Change in the Kyrgyz Republic The Invention of Marriage When Brothers Share a Wife: Among Tibetans, the Good Life Relegates Many Women to Spinsterhood Who Needs Love! In Japan, Many Couples Don't
Chapter 11: Marriage	Arranging a Marriage in India Kidnapping Women: Discourses of Emotion and Social Change in the Kyrgyz Republic Rising Number of Dowry Deaths in India The Invention of Marriage Who Needs Love! In Japan, Many Couples Don't
Chapter 12: Religion	Body Ritual among the Nacirema Five Myths of Terrorism The Adaptive Value of Religious Ritual The Berdache Tradition Understanding Islam
Chapter 13: Arts, Media, and Sports	Cell Phones, Sharing, and Social Status in an African Society
Chapter 14: The World System and Colonialism	Blood in the Jungle Ecuador's Paradise Lost Saving Our Identity: an Uphill Battle for the Tuva of China The Arrow of Disease The Evolution of Inequality
Chapter 15: Anthropology's Role in a Globalizing World	Being Indigenous in the 21st Century Ruined The Americanization of Mental Illness The September 11 Effect on Anthropology Understanding Islam

This convenient guide matches the articles in **Annual Editions: Anthropology, 38/e** with the corresponding chapters in **Mirror for Humanity: A Concise Introduction to Cultural Anthropology, 9/e** by Kottak.

Mirror for Humanity: A Concise Introduction to Cultural Anthropology, 9/e	Annual Editions: Anthropology, 38/e
Chapter 1: What Is Anthropology?	Tricking and Tripping: Fieldwork on Prostitution in the Era of AIDS
Chapter 2: Culture	Body Ritual among the Nacirema Breastfeeding and Culture Eating Christmas in the Kalahari The Berdache Tradition Why Manners Matter
Chapter 3: Doing Anthropology	Eating Christmas in the Kalahari Shakespeare in the Bush The September 11 Effect on Anthropology Tricking and Tripping: Fieldwork on Prostitution in the Era of AIDS
Chapter 4: Language and Communication	How Language Shapes Thought My Two Minds Strong Language Lost in Translation: You Talkin' to Me? War of Words
Chapter 5: Making a Living	Being Indigenous in the 21st Century The Inuit Paradox Tricking and Tripping: Fieldwork on Prostitution in the Era of AIDS When Brothers Share a Wife: Among Tibetans, the Good Life Relegates Many Women to Spinsterhood

Mirror for Humanity: A Concise Introduction to Cultural Anthropology, 9/e	Annual Editions: Anthropology, 38/e
Chapter 6: Political Systems	Meghalaya: Where Women Call the Shots No More Angel Babies on the Alto do Cruzeiro The Evolution of Inequality The Secrets of Haiti's Living Dead
Chapter 7: Families, Kinship, and Marriage	Arranging a Marriage in India Kidnapping Women: Discourses of Emotion and Social Change in the Kyrgyz Republic The Invention of Marriage When Brothers Share a Wife: Among Tibetans, the Good Life Relegates Many Women to Spinsterhood Who Needs Love! In Japan, Many Couples Don't
Chapter 8: Gender	Meghalaya: Where Women Call the Shots Rising Number of Dowry Deaths in India The Berdache Tradition The Hijras: An Alternative Gender in India Where Fat Is a Mark of Beauty
Chapter 9: Religion	Body Ritual among the Nacirema Five Myths of Terrorism The Adaptive Value of Religious Ritual The Berdache Tradition Understanding Islam
Chapter 10: Ethnicity and Race	Armor against Prejudice The Americanization of Mental Illness The Arrow of Disease The Inuit Paradox
Chapter 11: Applying Anthropology	The Americanization of Mental Illness The Arrow of Disease The Inuit Paradox
Chapter 12: The World System and Colonialism	Blood in the Jungle Ecuador's Paradise Lost Saving Our Identity: an Uphill Battle for the Tuva of China The Americanization of Mental Illness The Arrow of Disease
Chapter 13: Anthropology's Role in a Globalizing World	Being Indigenous in the 21st Century The Americanization of Mental Illness The September 11 Effect on Anthropology Understanding Islam

Topic Guide

This topic guide suggests how the selections in this book relate to the subjects covered in your course. **All the articles that relate to each topic are listed below the bold-faced term.**

Acculturation

Being Indigenous in the 21st Century
Breastfeeding and Culture
Cell Phones, Sharing, and Social Status in an African Society
Ecuador's Paradise Lost
My Two Minds
Saving Our Identity: an Uphill Battle for the Tuva of China
The Americanization of Mental Illness
The Arrow of Disease
The Price of Progress
The September 11 Effect on Anthropology
Understanding Islam
Vanishing Languages
War of Words
Who Needs Love! In Japan, Many Couples Don't

Aggression

Blood in the Jungle
Ecuador's Paradise Lost
Five Myths of Terrorism
Kidnapping Women: Discourses of Emotion and Social Change in the Kyrgyz Republic
Rising Number of Dowry Deaths in India
The Arrow of Disease
Understanding Islam

Altruism

Eating Christmas in the Kalahari

Child care

Breastfeeding and Culture
No More Angel Babies on the Alto do Cruzeiro
Where Fat Is a Mark of Beauty

Children

Breastfeeding and Culture
No More Angel Babies on the Alto do Cruzeiro
Where Fat Is a Mark of Beauty

Communication

Armor against Prejudice
Cell Phones, Sharing, and Social Status in an African Society
How Language Shapes Thought
Saving Our Identity: an Uphill Battle for the Tuva of China
Shakespeare in the Bush
Strong Language Lost in Translation: You Talkin' to Me?
Understanding Islam
Vanishing Languages
War of Words

Cross-cultural experience

Arranging a Marriage in India
Eating Christmas in the Kalahari
Saving Our Identity: an Uphill Battle for the Tuva of China
Shakespeare in the Bush

The Americanization of Mental Illness
The Inuit Paradox
Understanding Islam
Vanishing Languages

Cultural change

Breastfeeding and Culture
Cell Phones, Sharing, and Social Status in an African Society
Ecuador's Paradise Lost
Meghalaya: Where Women Call the Shots
No More Angel Babies on the Alto do Cruzeiro
Population Seven Billion
Rising Number of Dowry Deaths in India
Ruined
Saving Our Identity: an Uphill Battle for the Tuva of China
The Americanization of Mental Illness
The Arrow of Disease
The Evolution of Inequality
The Inuit Paradox
The Invention of Marriage
The Price of Progress
Vanishing Languages
War of Words
Who Needs Love! In Japan, Many Couples Don't

Cultural diversity

Armor against Prejudice
Arranging a Marriage in India
How Language Shapes Thought
Meghalaya: Where Women Call the Shots
Saving Our Identity: an Uphill Battle for the Tuva of China
The Americanization of Mental Illness
The Berdache Tradition
Understanding Islam
Vanishing Languages
War of Words

Cultural identity

Armor against Prejudice
Being Indigenous in the 21st Century
Ecuador's Paradise Lost
Saving Our Identity: an Uphill Battle for the Tuva of China
The Adaptive Value of Religious Ritual
The Inuit Paradox
Understanding Islam
Vanishing Languages
War of Words
Where Fat Is a Mark of Beauty

Cultural relativity

Arranging a Marriage in India
Eating Christmas in the Kalahari
How Language Shapes Thought
Meghalaya: Where Women Call the Shots
The Americanization of Mental Illness
The Inuit Paradox
Understanding Islam
Vanishing Languages

Medicine

Body Ritual among the Nacirema
The Americanization of Mental Illness

Participant observation

Eating Christmas in the Kalahari
Shakespeare in the Bush
Tricking and Tripping: Fieldwork on Prostitution
in the Era of AIDS

Patriarchy

Kidnapping Women: Discourses of Emotion and Social
Change in the Kyrgyz Republic
Who Needs Love! In Japan, Many Couples Don't

Political systems

Ecuador's Paradise Lost
Five Myths of Terrorism
The Arrow of Disease
The Price of Progress
Understanding Islam
When Brothers Share a Wife: Among Tibetans, the Good Life
Relegates Many Women to Spinsterhood

Poverty

Population Seven Billion

Race

Armor against Prejudice
The Americanization of Mental Illness
The Arrow of Disease
The Inuit Paradox

Rituals

The Adaptive Value of Religious Ritual
Body Ritual among the Nacirema
Kidnapping Women: Discourses of Emotion and
Social Change in the Kyrgyz Republic
The Great New England Vampire Panic
The Hijras: An Alternative Gender in India
The Secrets of Haiti's Living Dead
Understanding Islam
Where Fat Is a Mark of Beauty
Why Manners Matter

Sexuality

The Berdache Tradition
The Hijras: An Alternative Gender in India
When Brothers Share a Wife: Among Tibetans, the Good Life
Relegates Many Women to Spinsterhood
Who Needs Love! In Japan, Many Couples Don't

Social change

Being Indigenous in the 21st Century
Breastfeeding and Culture
Ecuador's Paradise Lost
Meghalaya: Where Women Call the Shots
No More Angel Babies on the Alto do Cruzeiro
Population Seven Billion
Rising Number of Dowry Deaths in India
Ruined
Saving Our Identity: an Uphill Battle for the Tuva of China
The Americanization of Mental Illness
The Arrow of Disease
The Evolution of Inequality
The Invention of Marriage
The Price of Progress
Understanding Islam
Vanishing Languages
War of Words
Who Needs Love! In Japan, Many Couples Don't

Social equality

Armor against Prejudice
Rising Number of Dowry Deaths in India
Saving Our Identity: an Uphill Battle for the Tuva of China
The Price of Progress
Who Needs Love! In Japan, Many Couples Don't

Social relationships

Armor against Prejudice
Arranging a Marriage in India
Cell Phones, Sharing, and Social Status in an African Society
Eating Christmas in the Kalahari
Meghalaya: Where Women Call the Shots
Rising Number of Dowry Deaths in India
Saving Our Identity: an Uphill Battle for the Tuva of China
Strong Language Lost in Translation: You Talkin' to Me?
The Adaptive Value of Religious Ritual
The Evolution of Inequality
The Hijras: An Alternative Gender in India
The Invention of Marriage
The Secrets of Haiti's Living Dead
Tricking and Tripping: Fieldwork on Prostitution in the Era of AIDS
Understanding Islam
Who Needs Love! In Japan, Many Couples Don't

Violence

Blood in the Jungle
Ecuador's Paradise Lost
Five Myths of Terrorism
No More Angel Babies on the Alto do Cruzeiro
Rising Number of Dowry Deaths in India
Saving Our Identity: an Uphill Battle for the Tuva of China
Understanding Islam

World Map

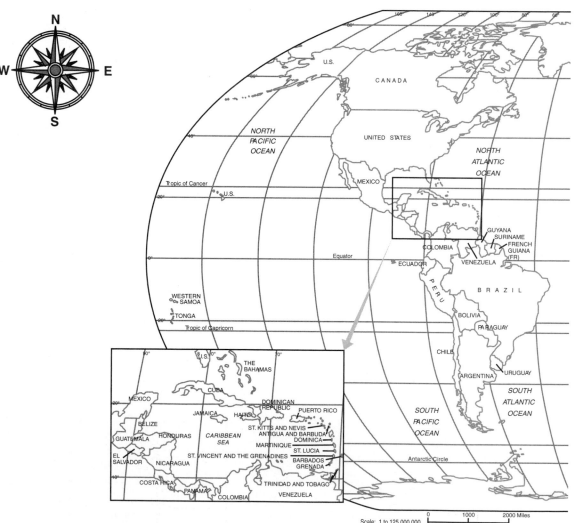

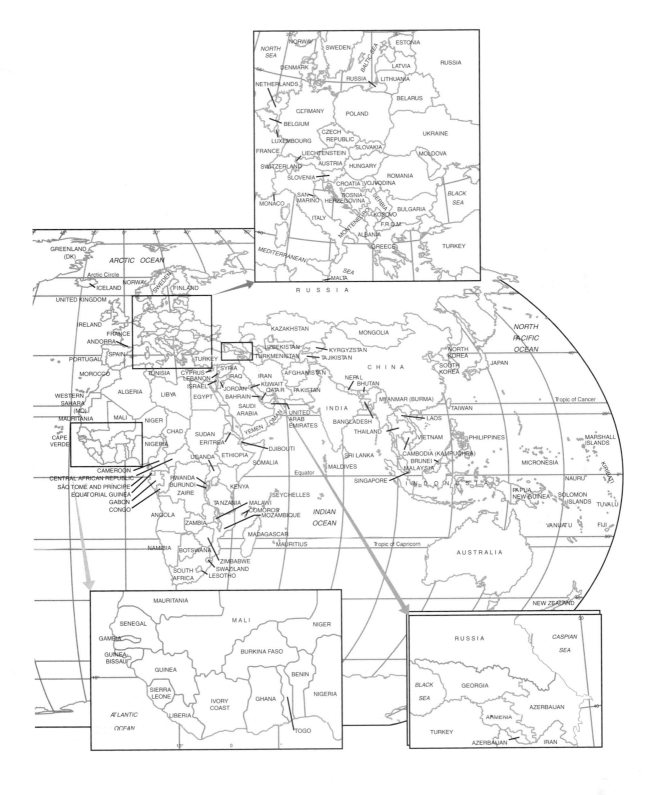

Unit 1

UNIT

Prepared by: Elvio Angeloni, *Pasadena City College*

Anthropological Perspectives

For at least a century, the goals of anthropology have been to describe societies and cultures throughout the world and to compare and contrast the differences and similarities among them. Anthropologists study in a variety of settings and situations, ranging from small hamlets and villages to neighborhoods and corporate offices of major urban centers throughout the world. They study hunters and gatherers, peasants, farmers, labor leaders, politicians, and bureaucrats. They examine religious life in Latin America as well as revolutionary movements.

Wherever practicable, anthropologists take on the role of "participant observer." Through active involvement in the life ways of people, they hope to gain an insider's perspective without sacrificing the objectivity of the trained scientist. Sometimes the conditions for achieving such a goal seem to form an almost insurmountable barrier, but anthropologists call on persistence, adaptability, and imagination to overcome the odds against them.

The diversity of focus in anthropology means that it is earmarked less by its particular subject matter than by its perspective. Although the discipline relates to both the biological and social sciences, anthropologists know that the boundaries drawn between disciplines are highly artificial. For example, while in theory it is possible to examine only the social organization of a family unit or the organization of political power in a nation-state, in reality it is impossible to separate the biological from the social, from the economic, from the political. The importance of the cultural aspects of our being can be stated very simply in the anthropology axiom: Biology is not destiny.

One might get the impression while reading about some of the anthropological field experience that the field has had primarily to do with the exotic and the unusual and, therefore, is not particularly relevant to the larger world in which most of us live. On the contrary, much is at stake in our attempts to achieve a more objective understanding of the diversity of peoples' ways. The more we understand why others do as they do, the more we come to appreciate why we are as we are and vice versa. After all, the purpose of anthropology is not only to describe and explain, but also to develop a special vision of the world in which cultural alternatives (past, present, and future) can be measured against one another and used as guides for human action.

Prepared by: Elvio Angeloni, *Pasadena City College*

The September 11 Effect on Anthropology

LARA DEEB AND JESSICA WINEGAR

Learning Outcomes

After reading this article, you will be able to:

- Understand the effects of September 11 on the field of anthropology.

Conventional wisdom among scholars of the Middle East is that the September 11, 2001 attacks left behind a threatening professional environment. Graduate students and faculty alike speak of hostile infiltrators in their classrooms, inevitably bitter tenure battles and the self-censorship that both can produce. At the same time, in the aftermath of September 11 Middle East scholars anticipated that the perennially spotty job market might improve.

Our research for *Anthropology's Politics,* a book project under contract with Stanford University Press, thus far confirms that scholars have in fact gained new "opportunities" during the past decade, but with government agencies or NGOs rather than in academe, where tenure-track jobs (as in most fields) have become scarcer. Our data also shows that scholars employed at universities, particularly those without tenure, labor under greater surveillance and suspicion. While trepidation about this climate is general to Middle East anthropologists regardless of specialty, the vast majority of actual incidents have been related to scholars' analysis of the conflict in Israel-Palestine.

Time and time again, in our interviews with anthropologists of the Middle East, they describe their jobs as "a minefield." They may have problems explaining research on politically sensitive topics to their universities' institutional review boards; they may see their grant funding denied or withdrawn; they may encounter prejudice among colleagues on hiring and tenure committees; and they may experience conflict with students when presenting critical perspectives on the US-led "war on terror." Whether or not their difficulties were expressly tied to politics, faculty frequently linked their personal stories to the political climate. One person described the resulting fear as "knowing that people who fall on the wrong side can suffer in their careers."

Scholars are increasingly worried about losing access to field sites and control over the use of their work. The new "security"

orientation of the study of the Middle East and Islam has led to more frequent invitations from government agencies, Washington think tanks and military subcontractors. These invitations often make anthropologists nervous, as they do not want to be identified with US Middle East policy or have their insights employed in its formulation.

But when it comes to tangibly negative effects on careers and academic freedom, Palestine—not the "war on terror"—is the enduring issue. "The word on the street" in graduate school, many anthropologists say, is that "if you work on Palestine you will never get a job," at least not in the United States. Indeed, Palestine frequently rose as a specter in anthropologists' job interviews in the 2000s. In the words of one Palestine scholar, "It's not what I said, it's the subject I work on. . . . People don't want to open themselves up to controversy—once the word Palestine is there, people say, 'Why do we want to make everyone upset?' " Even scholars who research other countries were often questioned about their politics on Palestine during campus visits, sometimes point blank.

Quantitatively, we have found that Palestine is the number-one cause of persecution of faculty in the classroom, despite anthropologists' assumption that everyone is at risk in the post-September 11 political climate. Many whose research does not focus on Palestine avoid it in their teaching, in part because they feel "on less sure ground," but also due to worries about classroom consequences. Well-publicized right-wing attacks—from inside and outside the discipline—foment this atmosphere of apprehension. On Campus Watch, the most robust of the conservative websites that collects reports on scholars of the Middle East, the vast majority of the articles about Middle East anthropology or anthropologists concern Israel-Palestine. The question of Palestine also dominates the websites Discover the Network and Students for Academic Freedom, both sponsored by right-wing activist David Horowitz. This focus is not a post-September 11 phenomenon, but a continuation of decades of concerted agitation against those speaking out about Palestinian rights. There does, however, seem to be a difference in the scale and organization of the attacks, which are facilitated by the Internet and other new media, and have been strengthened by the deeper Islamophobia of the post-September 11 era.

Nevertheless, there were in fact more job opportunities for Middle East anthropologists in the 2000s than in the preceding decade. Our quantitative analysis shows, however, that the increase paled in comparison to increases in fields such as history, political science and religious studies—presumably because those disciplines are thought to provide birds-eye views of the region or explanations for the September 11 events. At the same time, the US government has presumed that anthropology is able to provide on-the-ground information useful for counter-terrorism, and thus anthropologists are heavily recruited to staff "Human Terrain Systems" or other military projects that depend on local knowledge. The recruitment efforts have met with little success, as they run up against the anthropological Code of Ethics and anthropologists' political sensibilities, both of which prohibit such collaboration. The 2009 version of the Code of Ethics, currently under revision, clearly states that it is a set of guidelines for anthropologists rather than a binding document that adjudicates violations for its members. It states that "anthropological researchers must ensure that they do not harm the safety, dignity or privacy of the people with whom they work, conduct research or perform other professional activities, or who might reasonably be thought to be affected by their research." The vast majority of anthropologists understand providing information to the US military to contradict this tenet of the code.

September 11 affected scholarly life by pushing many scholars to speak publicly about the Middle East and Islam. In this regard, the "war on terror" is viewed as both opportunity and danger-filled obligation, an ambivalence perfectly captured in one anthropologist's phrase, "poisoned chalice." While a few resisted sipping from this cup, explaining that their scholarly work was not so conventionally political, most felt that they faced an ethical imperative to correct stereotypes and dispel misunderstandings—even if they became subject to slander and libel.

September 11 also shaped scholars' choices of field site and topic. Many anthropologists continue to shy away from Israel-Palestine. Some have begun to work on US military engagement in the region. Others have moved toward studies of Islam, although many anthropologists express concern that religion has come to stand in for the Middle East in the academy as it has in public discourse. It remains to be seen what impact the "Arab spring" might have on this trend.

In general, Middle East anthropologists share other Middle East scholars' sense that American institutions of higher education have become battlegrounds pitting defenders of academic freedom against defenders of various state policies, particularly those of Israel. The explosion of media outlets and the corporatization of universities in the 2000s have created a feeling that off-campus forces have more power today than in the past to shape scholarly discourse. Even scholars with tenure often find civic engagement unpleasant, not because they do not want to speak to the public, but because uninformed political opinion often trumps fact-based discussion in these forums. Those without tenure, especially those whose specialties or views generate controversy, have to fear for their job security as well. Those who call for eliminating tenure would do well to recognize that such a move might diminish the supply of in-depth knowledge of the Middle East to the American public.

Critical Thinking

1. What has been the conventional wisdom among scholars of the Middle East as a result of the September 11, 2001 attacks?
2. What did the authors' discover as a result of their research?
3. Why do anthropologists of the Middle East describe their jobs as "a minefield"? Why they are increasingly worried?
4. What is the "enduring issue" and why? Why is there a difference in the scale and organization of the attacks on anthropologists since September 11 even though this has been a decades-long issue?
5. How do the authors assess the job opportunities for Middle East anthropologists compared to other fields?
6. Why have recruitment efforts met with little success?
7. Why has the "war on terror" been viewed as both an opportunity and a danger-filled obligation?
8. How has September 11 shaped scholars' choices of field site and topic?
9. In what respects have American institutions of higher education become battlegrounds? What might be the result of eliminating tenure?

Create Central

www.mhhe.com/createcentral

Internet References

Anthropology Links
http://anthropology.gmu.edu

Archaeology and Anthropology Computing and Study Skills
www.isca.ox.ac.uk/index.html

Introduction to Fieldwork and Ethnography
http://web.mit.edu/dumit/www/syl-anth.html

The Institute for Intercultural Studies
www.interculturalstudies.org/main.html

Lara Deeb, an editor of this magazine, teaches anthropology at Scripps College. **Jessica Winegar** teaches anthropology at Northwestern University.

Article   Prepared by: Elvio Angeloni, *Pasadena City College*

Eating Christmas in the Kalahari

RICHARD BORSHAY LEE

Learning Outcomes

After reading this article, you will be able to:

- Describe some of the unique research strategies of anthropological fieldwork.

- Explain how anthropologists who become personally involved with a community through participant observation maintain their objectivity as scientists.

- Explain the ways in which the results of fieldwork depend on the kinds of questions asked.

The !Kung Bushmen's knowledge of Christmas is third-hand. The London Missionary Society brought the holiday to the southern Tswana tribes in the early nineteenth century. Later, native catechists spread the idea far and wide among the Bantu-speaking pastoralists, even in the remotest corners of the Kalahari Desert. The Bushmen's idea of the Christmas story, stripped to its essentials, is "praise the birth of white man's god-chief"; what keeps their interest in the holiday high is the Tswana-Herero custom of slaughtering an ox for his Bushmen neighbors as an annual goodwill gesture. Since the 1930s, part of the Bushmen's annual round of activities has included a December congregation at the cattle posts for trading, marriage brokering, and several days of trance-dance feasting at which the local Tswana headman is host.

As a social anthropologist working with !Kung Bushmen, I found that the Christmas ox custom suited my purposes. I had come to the Kalahari to study the hunting and gathering subsistence economy of the !Kung, and to accomplish this it was essential not to provide them with food, share my own food, or interfere in any way with their food-gathering activities. While liberal handouts of tobacco and medical supplies were appreciated, they were scarcely adequate to erase the glaring disparity in wealth between the anthropologist, who maintained a two-month inventory of canned goods, and the Bushmen, who rarely had a day's supply of food on hand. My approach, while paying off in terms of data, left me open to frequent accusations of stinginess and hard-heartedness. By their lights, I was a miser.

The Christmas ox was to be my way of saying thank you for the cooperation of the past year; and since it was to be our last Christmas in the field, I determined to slaughter the largest, meatiest ox that money could buy, insuring that the feast and trance-dance would be a success.

Through December I kept my eyes open at the wells as the cattle were brought down for watering. Several animals were offered, but none had quite the grossness that I had in mind. Then, ten days before the holiday, a Herero friend led an ox of astonishing size and mass up to our camp. It was solid black, stood five feet high at the shoulder, had a five-foot span of horns, and must have weighed 1,200 pounds on the hoof. Food consumption calculations are my specialty, and I quickly figured that bones and viscera aside, there was enough meat—at least four pounds—for every man, woman, and child of the 150 Bushmen in the vicinity of /ai/ai who were expected at the feast.

Having found the right animal at last, I paid the Herero £20 ($56) and asked him to keep the beast with his herd until Christmas day. The next morning word spread among the people that the big solid black one was the ox chosen by /ontah (my Bushman name; it means, roughly, "whitey") for the Christmas feast. That afternoon I received the first delegation. Ben!a, an outspoken sixty-year-old mother of five, came to the point slowly.

"Where were you planning to eat Christmas?"

"Right here at /ai/ai," I replied.

"Alone or with others?"

"I expect to invite all the people to eat Christmas with me."

"Eat what?"

"I have purchased Yehave's black ox, and I am going to slaughter and cook it."

"That's what we were told at the well but refused to believe it until we heard it from yourself."

"Well, it's the black one," I replied expansively, although wondering what she was driving at.

"Oh, no!" Ben!a groaned, turning to her group. "They were right." Turning back to me she asked, "Do you expect us to eat that bag of bones?"

"Bag of bones! It's the biggest ox at /ai/ai."

"Big, yes, but old. And thin. Everybody knows there's no meat on that old ox. What did you expect us to eat off it, the horns?"

Everybody chuckled at Ben!a's one-liner as they walked away, but all I could manage was a weak grin.

That evening it was the turn of the young men. They came to sit at our evening fire. /gaugo, about my age, spoke to me man-to-man.

"/ontah, you have always been square with us," he lied. "What has happened to change your heart? That sack of guts and bones of Yehave's will hardly feed one camp, let alone all the Bushmen around ai/ai." And he proceeded to enumerate the seven camps in the /ai/ai vicinity, family by family. "Perhaps you have forgotten that we are not few, but many. Or are you too blind to tell the difference between a proper cow and an old wreck? That ox is thin to the point of death."

"Look, you guys," I retorted, "that is a beautiful animal, and I'm sure you will eat it with pleasure at Christmas."

"Of course we will eat it; it's food. But it won't fill us up to the point where we will have enough strength to dance. We will eat and go home to bed with stomachs rumbling."

That night as we turned in, I asked my wife, Nancy: "What did you think of the black ox?"

"It looked enormous to me. Why?"

"Well, about eight different people have told me I got gypped; that the ox is nothing but bones."

"What's the angle?" Nancy asked. "Did they have a better one to sell?"

"No, they just said that it was going to be a grim Christmas because there won't be enough meat to go around. Maybe I'll get an independent judge to look at the beast in the morning."

Bright and early, Halingisi, a Tswana cattle owner, appeared at our camp. But before I could ask him to give me his opinion on Yehave's black ox, he gave me the eye signal that indicated a confidential chat. We left the camp and sat down.

"/ontah, I'm surprised at you: you've lived here for three years and still haven't learned anything about cattle."

"But what else can a person do but choose the biggest, strongest animal one can find?" I retorted.

"Look, just because an animal is big doesn't mean that it has plenty of meat on it. The black one was a beauty when it was younger, but now it is thin to the point of death."

"Well I've already bought it. What can I do at this stage?"

"Bought it already? I thought you were just considering it. Well, you'll have to kill it and serve it, I suppose. But don't expect much of a dance to follow."

My spirits dropped rapidly. I could believe that Ben!a and /gaugo just might be putting me on about the black ox, but Halingisi seemed to be an impartial critic. I went around that day feeling as though I had bought a lemon of a used car.

In the afternoon it was Tomazo's turn. Tomazo is a fine hunter, a top trance performer . . . and one of my most reliable informants. He approached the subject of the Christmas cow as part of my continuing Bushman education.

"My friend, the way it is with us Bushmen," he began, "is that we love meat. And even more than that, we love fat. When we hunt we always search for the fat ones, the ones dripping with layers of white fat: fat that turns into a clear, thick oil in the cooking pot, fat that slides down your gullet, fills your stomach and gives you a roaring diarrhea," he rhapsodized.

"So, feeling as we do," he continued, "it gives us pain to be served such a scrawny thing as Yehave's black ox. It is big, yes, and no doubt its giant bones are good for soup, but fat is what we really crave and so we will eat Christmas this year with a heavy heart."

The prospect of a gloomy Christmas now had me worried, so I asked Tomazo what I could do about it.

"Look for a fat one, a young one . . . smaller, but fat. Fat enough to make us //gom ('evacuate the bowels'), then we will be happy."

My suspicions were aroused when Tomazo said that he happened to know of a young, fat, barren cow that the owner was willing to part with. Was Tomazo working on commission, I wondered? But I dispelled this unworthy thought when we approached the Herero owner of the cow in question and found that he had decided not to sell.

The scrawny wreck of a Christmas ox now became the talk of the /ai/ai water hole and was the first news told to the outlying groups as they began to come in from the bush for the feast. What finally convinced me that real trouble might be brewing was the visit from u!au, an old conservative with a reputation for fierceness. His nickname meant spear and referred to an incident thirty years ago in which he had speared a man to death. He had an intense manner; fixing me with his eyes, he said in clipped tones:

"I have only just heard about the black ox today, or else I would have come here earlier. /ontah, do you honestly think you can serve meat like that to people and avoid a fight?" He paused, letting the implications sink in. "I don't mean fight you, /ontah; you are a white man. I mean a fight between Bushmen. There are many fierce ones here, and with such a small quantity of meat to distribute, how can you give everybody a fair share? Someone is sure to accuse another of taking too much or hogging all the choice pieces. Then you will see what happens when some go hungry while others eat."

The possibility of at least a serious argument struck me as all too real. I had witnessed the tension that surrounds the distribution of meat from a kudu or gemsbok kill, and had documented many arguments that sprang up from a real or imagined slight in meat distribution. The owners of a kill may spend up to two hours arranging and rearranging the piles of meat under the gaze of a circle of recipients before handing them out. And I also knew that the Christmas feast at /ai/ai would be bringing together groups that had feuded in the past.

Convinced now of the gravity of the situation, I went in earnest to search for a second cow; but all my inquiries failed to turn one up.

The Christmas feast was evidently going to be a disaster, and the incessant complaints about the meagerness of the ox had already taken the fun out of it for me. Moreover, I was getting bored with the wisecracks, and after losing my temper a few times, I resolved to serve the beast anyway. If the meat fell short, the hell with it. In the Bushmen idiom, I announced to all who would listen:

"I am a poor man and blind. If I have chosen one that is too old and too thin, we will eat it anyway and see if there is enough meat there to quiet the rumbling of our stomachs."

On hearing this speech, Ben!a offered me a rare word of comfort. "It's thin," she said philosophically, "but the bones will make a good soup."

At dawn Christmas morning, instinct told me to turn over the butchering and cooking to a friend and take off with Nancy to spend Christmas alone in the bush. But curiosity kept me from retreating. I wanted to see what such a scrawny ox looked like on butchering and if there *was* going to be a fight, I wanted to catch every word of it. Anthropologists are incurable that way.

The great beast was driven up to our dancing ground, and a shot in the forehead dropped it in its tracks. Then, freshly cut branches were heaped around the fallen carcass to receive the meat. Ten men volunteered to help with the cutting. I asked /gaugo to make the breast bone cut. This cut, which begins the butchering process for most large game, offers easy access for removal of the viscera. But it also allows the hunter to spot-check the amount of fat on the animal. A fat game animal carries a white layer up to an inch thick on the chest, while in a thin one, the knife will quickly cut to bone. All eyes fixed on his hand as /gaugo, dwarfed by the great carcass, knelt to the breast. The first cut opened a pool of solid white in the black skin. The second and third cut widened and deepened the creamy white. Still no bone. It was pure fat; it must have been two inches thick.

"Hey /gau," I burst out, "that ox is loaded with fat. What's this about the ox being too thin to bother eating? Are you out of your mind?"

"Fat?" /gau shot back, "You call that fat? This wreck is thin, sick, dead!" And he broke out laughing. So did everyone else. They rolled on the ground, paralyzed with laughter. Everybody laughed except me; I was thinking.

I ran back to the tent and burst in just as Nancy was getting up. "Hey, the black ox. It's fat as hell! They were kidding about it being too thin to eat. It was a joke or something. A put-on. Everyone is really delighted with it!"

"Some joke," my wife replied. "It was so funny that you were ready to pack up and leave /ai/ai."

If it had indeed been a joke, it had been an extraordinarily convincing one, and tinged, I thought, with more than a touch of malice as many jokes are. Nevertheless, that it was a joke lifted my spirits considerably, and I returned to the butchering site where the shape of the ox was rapidly disappearing under the axes and knives of the butchers. The atmosphere had become festive. Grinning broadly, their arms covered with blood well past the elbow, men packed chunks of meat into the big cast-iron cooking pots, fifty pounds to the load, and muttered and chuckled all the while about the thinness and worthlessness of the animal and /ontah's poor judgment.

We danced and ate that ox two days and two nights; we cooked and distributed fourteen potfuls of meat and no one went home hungry and no fights broke out.

But the "joke" stayed in my mind. I had a growing feeling that something important had happened in my relationship with the Bushmen and that the clue lay in the meaning of the joke. Several days later, when most of the people had dispersed back to the bush camps, I raised the question with Hakekgose, a Tswana man who had grown up among the !Kung, married a !Kung girl, and who probably knew their culture better than any other non-Bushman.

"With us whites," I began, "Christmas is supposed to be the day of friendship and brotherly love. What I can't figure out is why the Bushmen went to such lengths to criticize and belittle the ox I had bought for the feast. The animal was perfectly good and their jokes and wisecracks practically ruined the holiday for me."

"So it really did bother you," said Hakekgose. "Well, that's the way they always talk. When I take my rifle and go hunting with them, if I miss, they laugh at me for the rest of the day. But even if I hit and bring one down, it's no better. To them, the kill is always too small or too old or too thin; and as we sit down on the kill site to cook and eat the liver, they keep grumbling, even with their mouths full of meat. They say things like, 'Oh this is awful! What a worthless animal! Whatever made me think that this Tswana rascal could hunt!' "

"Is this the way outsiders are treated?" I asked.

"No, it is their custom; they talk that way to each other too. Go and ask them."

/gaugo had been one of the most enthusiastic in making me feel bad about the merit of the Christmas ox. I sought him out first.

"Why did you tell me the black ox was worthless, when you could see that it was loaded with fat and meat?"

"It is our way," he said smiling. "We always like to fool people about that. Say there is a Bushman who has been hunting. He must not come home and announce like a braggard, 'I have killed a big one in the bush!' He must first sit down in silence until I or someone else comes up to his fire and asks, 'What did you see today?' He replies quietly, 'Ah, I'm no good for hunting. I saw nothing at all [pause] just a little tiny one.' Then I smile to myself," /gaugo continued, "because I know he has killed something big."

"In the morning we make up a party of four or five people to cut up and carry the meat back to the camp. When we arrive at the kill we examine it and cry out, 'You mean to say you have dragged us all the way out here in order to make us cart home your pile of bones? Oh, if I had known it was this thin I wouldn't have come.' Another one pipes up, 'People, to think I gave up a nice day in the shade for this. At home we may be hungry but at least we have nice cool water to drink.' If the horns are big, someone says, 'Did you think that somehow you were going to boil down the horns for soup?'

"To all this you must respond in kind. 'I agree,' you say, 'this one is not worth the effort; let's just cook the liver for strength and leave the rest for the hyenas. It is not too late to hunt today and even a duiker or a steenbok would be better than this mess.'

"Then you set to work nevertheless; butcher the animal, carry the meat back to the camp and everyone eats," /gaugo concluded.

Things were beginning to make sense. Next, I went to Tomazo. He corroborated /gaugo's story of the obligatory insults over a kill and added a few details of his own.

"But," I asked, "why insult a man after he has gone to all that trouble to track and kill an animal and when he is going to share the meat with you so that your children will have something to eat?"

"Arrogance," was his cryptic answer.

"Arrogance?"

"Yes, when a young man kills much meat he comes to think of himself as a chief or a big man, and he thinks of the rest of us as his servants or inferiors. We can't accept this. We refuse one who boasts, for someday his pride will make him kill somebody. So we always speak of his meat as worthless. This way we cool his heart and make him gentle."

"But why didn't you tell me this before?" I asked Tomazo with some heat.

"Because you never asked me," said Tomazo, echoing the refrain that has come to haunt every field ethnographer.

The pieces now fell into place. I had known for a long time that in situations of social conflict with Bushmen I held all the cards. I was the only source of tobacco in a thousand square miles, and I was not incapable of cutting an individual off for non-cooperation. Though my boycott never lasted longer than a few days, it was an indication of my strength. People resented my presence at the water hole, yet simultaneously dreaded my leaving. In short I was a perfect target for the charge of arrogance and for the Bushmen tactic of enforcing humility.

I had been taught an object lesson by the Bushmen; it had come from an unexpected corner and had hurt me in a vulnerable area. For the big black ox was to be the one totally generous, unstinting act of my year at /ai/ai, and I was quite unprepared for the reaction I received.

As I read it, their message was this: There are no totally generous acts. All "acts" have an element of calculation. One black ox slaughtered at Christmas does not wipe out a year of careful manipulation of gifts given to serve your own ends. After all, to kill an animal and share the meat with people is really no more than Bushmen do for each other every day and with far less fanfare.

In the end, I had to admire how the Bushmen had played out the farce—collectively straight-faced to the end. Curiously, the episode reminded me of the *Good Soldier Schweik* and his marvelous encounters with authority. Like Schweik, the Bushmen had retained a thorough-going skepticism of good intentions. Was it this independence of spirit, I wondered, that had kept them culturally viable in the face of generations of contact with more powerful societies, both black and white? The thought that the Bushmen were alive and well in the Kalahari was strangely comforting. Perhaps, armed with that independence and with their superb knowledge of their environment, they might yet survive the future.

Critical Thinking

1. To what extent do the Bushmen typically celebrate Christmas?

2. Why did Lee wish to slaughter an ox for the Bushmen?

3. What was it about the Bushman ways of life and Lee's role as an anthropologist that led to their reactions to his generosity?

4. Why was the Bushman reaction "strangely comforting" to Lee in the final analysis?

Create Central

www.mhhe.com/createcentral

Internet References

Anthropology Links
  http://anthropology.gmu.edu
Archaeology and Anthropology Computing and Study Skills
  www.isca.ox.ac.uk/index.html
Introduction to Fieldwork and Ethnography
  http://web.mit.edu/dumit/www/syl-anth.html
The Institute for Intercultural Studies
  www.interculturalstudies.org/main.html

Richard Borshay Lee is a full professor of anthropology at the University of Toronto. He has done extensive fieldwork in southern Africa, is coeditor of *Man the Hunter* (1968) and *Kalahari Hunter-Gatherers* (1976), and author of *The !Kung San: Men, Women, and Work in a Foraging Society.*

Lee, Richard Borshay. From *Natural History*, December 1969, pp. 14–22, 60–64. Copyright © 1969 by Natural History Magazine. Reprinted by permission.

Article

Prepared by: Elvio Angeloni, *Pasadena City College*

Tricking and Tripping
Fieldwork on Prostitution in the Era of AIDS

CLAIRE E. STERK

Learning Outcomes

After reading this article, you will be able to:

- Explain how anthropologists who become personally involved with a community through participant observation maintain their objectivity as scientists.

- Give examples of the kind of ethical obligations fieldworkers have toward their informants.

S tudents often think of anthropological fieldwork as requiring travel to exotic tropical locations, but that is not necessarily the case. This reading is based on fieldwork in the United States—on the streets in New York City as well as Atlanta. Claire Sterk is an anthropologist who works in a school of public health and is primarily interested in issues of women's health, particularly as it relates to sexual behavior. In this selection, an introduction to a recent book by the same title, she describes the basic fieldwork methods she used to study these women and their communities. Like most cultural anthropologists, Sterk's primary goal was to describe "the life" of prostitution from the women's own point of view. To do this, she had to be patient, brave, sympathetic, trustworthy, curious, and nonjudgmental. You will notice these characteristics in this selection; for example, Sterk begins her book with a poem written by one of her informants. Fieldwork is a slow process, because it takes time to win people's confidence and to learn their language and way of seeing the world. In this regard, there are probably few differences between the work of a qualitative sociologist and that of a cultural anthropologist (although anthropologists would not use the term "deviant" to describe another society or a segment of their own society).

Throughout the world, HIV/AIDS is fast becoming a disease found particularly in poor women. Sex workers or prostitutes have often been blamed for AIDS, and they have been further stigmatized because of their profession. In reality, however, entry into prostitution is not a career choice; rather, these women and girls are themselves most often victims of circumstances such as violence and poverty. Public health officials want to know why sex workers do not always protect their health by making men wear condoms. To answer such questions, we must know more about the daily life of these women.

The way to do that, the cultural anthropologist would say, is to ask and to listen.

As you read this selection, ask yourself the following questions:

- What happens when Sterk says, "I'm sorry for you" to one of her informants? Why?
- Why do you think fieldwork might be a difficult job?
- Do you think that the fact that Sterk grew up in Amsterdam, where prostitution is legal, affected her research?
- Which of the six themes of this work, described at the end of the article, do you think is most important?

O ne night in March of 1987 business was slow. I was hanging out on a stroll with a group of street prostitutes. After a few hours in a nearby diner/coffee shop, we were kicked out. The waitress felt bad, but she needed our table for some new customers. Four of us decided to sit in my car until the rain stopped. While three of us chatted about life, Piper wrote this poem. As soon as she read it to us, the conversation shifted to more serious topics—pimps, customers, cops, the many hassles of being a prostitute, to name a few. We decided that if I ever finished a book about prostitution, the book would start with her poem.

This book is about the women who work in the lower echelons of the prostitution world. They worked in the streets and other public settings as well as crack houses. Some of these women viewed themselves primarily as prostitutes, and a number of them used drugs to cope with the pressures of the life. Others identified themselves more as drug users, and their main reason for having sex for money or other goods was to support their own drug use and often the habit of their male partner. A small group of women interviewed for this book had left prostitution, and most of them were still struggling to integrate their past experiences as prostitutes in their current lives.

The stories told by the women who participated in this project revealed how pimps, customers, and others such as police officers and social and health service providers treated them as "fallen" women. However, their accounts also showed their strengths and the many strategies they developed to challenge these others. Circumstances, including their drug use, often forced them to sell sex, but they all resisted the notion that they might be selling themselves. Because they engaged in an illegal profession, these women had little status: their working conditions were poor, and their work was physically and mentally exhausting. Nevertheless, many women described the ways in which they gained a sense of control over their lives. For instance, they learned how to manipulate pimps, how to control the types of services and length of time bought by their customers, and how to select customers. While none of these schemes explicitly enhanced their working conditions, they did make the women feel stronger and better about themselves.

In this book, I present prostitution from the point of view of the women themselves. To understand their current lives, it was necessary to learn how they got started in the life, the various processes involved in their continued prostitution careers, the link between prostitution and drug use, the women's interactions with their pimps and customers, and the impact of the AIDS epidemic and increasing violence on their experiences. I also examined the implications for women. Although my goal was to present the women's thoughts, feelings, and actions in their own words, the final text is a sociological monograph compiled by me as the researcher. Some women are quoted more than others because I developed a closer relationship with them, because they were more able to verbalize and capture their circumstances, or simply because they were more outspoken.

The Sample

The data for this book are qualitative. The research was conducted during the last ten years in the New York City and Atlanta metropolitan areas. One main data source was participant observation on streets, in hotels and other settings known for prostitution activity, and in drug-use settings, especially those that allowed sex-for-drug exchanges. Another data source was in-depth, life-history interviews with 180 women ranging in age from 18 to 59 years, with an average age of 34. One in two women was African-American and one in three white; the remaining women were Latina. Three in four had completed high school, and among them almost two-thirds had one or more years of additional educational training. Thirty women had graduated from college.

Forty women worked as street prostitutes and did not use drugs. On average, they had been prostitutes for 11 years. Forty women began using drugs an average of three years after they began working as prostitutes, and the average time they had worked as prostitutes was nine years. Forty women used drugs an average of five years before they became prostitutes, and on the average they had worked as prostitutes for eight years. Another forty women began smoking crack and exchanging sex for crack almost simultaneously, with an average of four years in the life. Twenty women who were interviewed were ex-prostitutes.

Comments on Methodology

When I tell people about my research, the most frequent question I am asked is how I gained access to the women rather than what I learned from the research. For many, prostitution is an unusual topic of conversation, and many people have expressed surprise that I, as a woman, conducted the research. During my research some customers indeed thought I was a working woman, a fact that almost always amuses those who hear about my work. However, few people want to hear stories about the women's struggles and sadness. Sometimes they ask questions about the reasons why women become prostitutes. Most of the time, they are surprised when I tell them that the prostitutes as well as their customers represent all layers of society. Before presenting the findings, it seems important to discuss the research process, including gaining access to the women, developing relationships, interviewing, and then leaving the field.[1]

Locating Prostitutes and Gaining Entree

One of the first challenges I faced was to identify locations where street prostitution took place. Many of these women worked on strolls, streets where prostitution activity is concentrated, or in hotels known for prostitution activity. Others, such as the crack prostitutes, worked in less public settings such as a crack house that might be someone's apartment.

I often learned of well-known public places from professional experts, such as law enforcement officials and health care providers at emergency rooms and sexually transmitted disease clinics. I gained other insights from lay experts, including taxi drivers, bartenders, and community representatives such as members of neighborhood associations. The contacts universally mentioned some strolls as the places where many women worked, where the local police focused attention, or where residents had organized protests against prostitution in their neighborhoods.

As I began visiting various locales, I continued to learn about new settings. In one sense, I was developing ethnographic maps of street prostitution. After several visits to a specific area, I also was able to expand these maps by adding information about the general atmosphere on the stroll, general characteristics of the various people present, the ways in which the women and customers connected, and the overall flow of action. In addition, my visits allowed the regular actors to notice me.

I soon learned that being an unknown woman in an area known for prostitution may cause many people to notice you, even stare at you, but it fails to yield many verbal interactions. Most of the time when I tried to make eye contact with one of the women, she quickly averted her eyes. Pimps, on the other hand, would stare at me straight on and I ended up being the one to look away. Customers would stop, blow their horn, or wave me over, frequently yelling obscenities when I ignored them. I realized that gaining entree into the prostitution world was not going to be as easy as I imagined it. Although I lacked such training in any of my qualitative methods classes, I decided to move slowly and not force any interaction. The most I said during the initial weeks in a new area was limited to "how are you" or "hi." This strategy paid off during my first visits to one of the strolls in Brooklyn, New York. After several appearances, one of the women walked up to me and sarcastically asked if I was looking for something. She caught me off guard, and all the answers I had practiced did not seem to make sense. I mumbled something about just wanting to walk around. She did not like my answer, but she did like my accent. We ended up talking about the latter and she was especially excited when I told her I came from Amsterdam. One of her friends had gone to Europe with her boyfriend, who was in the military. She understood from her that prostitution and drugs were legal in the Netherlands. While explaining to her that some of her friend's impressions were incorrect, I was able to show off some of my knowledge about prostitution. I mentioned that I was interested in prostitution and wanted to write a book about it.

Despite the fascination with my background and intentions, the prostitute immediately put me through a Streetwalker 101 test, and apparently I passed. She told me to make sure to come back. By the time I left, I not only had my first conversation but also my first connection to the scene. Variations of this entry process occurred on the other strolls. The main lesson I learned in these early efforts was the importance of having some knowledge of the lives of the people I wanted to study, while at the same time refraining from presenting myself as an expert.

Qualitative researchers often refer to their initial connections as gatekeepers and key respondents. Throughout my fieldwork I learned that some key respondents are important in providing initial access, but they become less central as the research evolves. For example, one of the women who introduced me to her lover, who was also her pimp, was arrested and disappeared for months. Another entered drug treatment soon after she facilitated my access. Other key respondents provided access to only a segment of the players on a scene. For example, if a woman worked for a pimp, [she] was unlikely . . . to introduce me to women working for another pimp. On one stroll my initial contact was with a pimp whom nobody liked. By associating with him, I almost lost the opportunity to meet other pimps. Some key respondents were less connected than promised—for example, some of the women who worked the street to support their drug habit. Often their connections were more frequently with drug users and less so with prostitutes.

Key respondents tend to be individuals central to the local scene, such as, in this case, pimps and the more senior prostitutes. Their function as gatekeepers often is to protect the scene and to screen outsiders. Many times I had to prove that I was not an undercover police officer or a woman with ambitions to become a streetwalker. While I thought I had gained entree, I quickly learned that many insiders subsequently wondered about my motives and approached me with suspicion and distrust.

Another lesson involved the need to proceed cautiously with self-nominated key respondents. For example, one of the women presented herself as knowing everyone on the stroll. While she did know everyone, she was not a central figure. On the contrary, the other prostitutes viewed her as a failed streetwalker whose drug use caused her to act unprofessionally. By associating with me, she hoped to regain some of her status. For me, however, it meant limited access to the other women because I affiliated myself with a woman who was marginal to the scene. On another occasion, my main key respondent was a man who claimed to own three crack houses in the neighborhood. However, he had a negative reputation, and people accused him of cheating on others. My initial alliance with him delayed, and almost blocked, my access to others in the neighborhood. He intentionally tried to keep me from others on the scene, not because he would gain something from that transaction but because it made him feel powerful. When I told him I was going to hang out with some of the other people, he threatened me until one of the other dealers stepped in and told him to stay away. The two of them argued back and forth, and finally I was free to go. Fortunately, the dealer who had spoken up for me was much more central and positively associated with the local scene. Finally, I am unsure if I would have had success in gaining entrance to the scene had I not been a woman.

Developing Relationships and Trust

The processes involved in developing relationships in research situations amplify those involved in developing relationships in general. Both parties need to get to know each other, become aware and accepting of each other's roles, and engage in a reciprocal relationship. Being supportive and providing practical assistance were the most visible and direct ways for me as the researcher to develop a relationship. Throughout the years, I have given countless rides, provided child care on numerous occasions, bought groceries, and listened for hours to stories that were unrelated to my initial research questions. Gradually, my role allowed me to become part of these women's lives and to build rapport with many of them.

Over time, many women also realized that I was uninterested in being a prostitute and that I genuinely was interested in learning as much as possible about their lives. Many felt flattered that someone wanted to learn from them and that they had knowledge to offer. Allowing women to tell their stories and engaging in a dialogue with them probably were the single most important techniques that allowed me to develop relationships with them. Had I only wanted to focus on the questions I had in mind, developing such relationships might have been more difficult.

At times, I was able to get to know a woman only after her pimp endorsed our contact. One of my scariest experiences occurred before I knew to work through the pimps, and one such man had some of his friends follow me on my way home one night. I will never know what plans they had in mind for me because I fortunately was able to escape with only a few bruises. Over a year later, the woman acknowledged that her pimp had gotten upset and told her he was going to teach me a lesson.

On other occasions, I first needed to be screened by owners and managers of crack houses before the research could continue. Interestingly, screenings always were done by a man even if the person who vouched for me was a man himself. While the women also were cautious, the ways in which they checked me out tended to be much more subtle. For example, one of them would tell me a story, indicating that it was a secret about another person on the stroll. Although I failed to realize this at the time, my field notes revealed that frequently after such a conversation, others would ask me questions about related topics. One woman later acknowledged that putting out such stories was a test to see if I would keep information confidential.

Learning more about the women and gaining a better understanding of their lives also raised many ethical questions. No textbook told me how to handle situations in which a pimp abused a woman, a customer forced a woman to engage in unwanted sex acts, a customer requested unprotected sex from a woman who knew she was HIV infected, or a boyfriend had realistic expectations regarding a woman's earnings to support his drug habit. I failed to know the proper response when asked to engage in illegal activities such as holding drugs or money a woman had stolen from a customer. In general, my response was to explain that I was there as a researcher. During those occasions when pressures became too severe, I decided to leave a scene. For example, I never returned to certain crack houses because pimps there continued to ask me to consider working for them.

Over time, I was fortunate to develop relationships with people who "watched my back." One pimp in particular intervened if he perceived other pimps, customers, or passersby harassing me. He also was the one who gave me my street name: Whitie (indicating my racial background) or Ms. Whitie for those who disrespected me. While this was my first street name, I subsequently had others. Being given a street name was a symbolic gesture of acceptance. Gradually, I developed an identity that allowed me to be both an insider and an outsider. While hanging out on the strolls and other gathering places, including crack houses, I had to deal with some of the same uncomfortable conditions as the prostitutes, such as cold or warm weather, lack of access to a rest room, refusals from owners for me to patronize a restaurant, and of course, harassment by customers and the police.

I participated in many informal conversations. Unless pushed to do so, I seldom divulged my opinions. I was more open with my feelings about situations and showed empathy. I learned quickly that providing an opinion can backfire. I agreed that one of the women was struggling a lot and stated that I felt sorry for her. While I meant to indicate my "genuine concern for her, she heard that I felt sorry for her because she was a failure. When she finally, after several weeks, talked with me again, I was able to explain to her that I was not judging her, but rather felt concerned for her. She remained cynical and many times asked me for favors to make up for my mistake. It took me months before I felt comfortable telling her that I felt I had done enough and that it was time to let go. However, if she was not ready, she needed to know that I would no longer go along. This was one of many occasions when I learned that although I wanted to facilitate my work as a researcher, that I wanted people to like and trust me, I also needed to set boundaries.

Rainy and slow nights often provided good opportunities for me to participate in conversations with groups of women. Popular topics included how to work safely, what to do about condom use, how to make more money. I often served as a health educator and a supplier of condoms, gels, vaginal douches, and other feminine products. Many women were very worried about the

AIDS epidemic. However, they also were worried about how to use a condom when a customer refused to do so. They worried particularly about condom use when they needed money badly and, consequently, did not want to propose that the customer use one for fear of rejection. While some women became experts at "making" their customers use a condom—for example, "by hiding it in their mouth prior to beginning oral sex—others would carry condoms to please me but never pull one out. If a woman was HIV positive and I knew she failed to use a condom, I faced the ethical dilemma of challenging her or staying out of it.

Developing trusting relationships with crack prostitutes was more difficult. Crack houses were not the right environment for informal conversations. Typically, the atmosphere was tense and everyone was suspicious of each other. The best times to talk with these women were when we bought groceries together, when I helped them clean their homes, or when we shared a meal. Often the women were very different when they were not high than they were when they were high or craving crack. In my conversations with them, I learned that while I might have observed their actions the night before, they themselves might not remember them. Once I realized this, I would be very careful to omit any detail unless I knew that the woman herself did remember the event.

In-Depth Interviews

All interviews were conducted in a private setting, including women's residences, my car or my office, a restaurant of the women's choice, or any other setting the women selected. I did not begin conducting official interviews until I developed relationships with the women. Acquiring written informed consent prior to the interview was problematic. It made me feel awkward. Here I was asking the women to sign a form after they had begun to trust me. However, often I felt more upset about this technicality than the women themselves. As soon as they realized that the form was something the university required, they seemed to understand. Often they laughed about the official statements, and some asked if I was sure the form was to protect them and not the school.[2] None of the women refused to sign the consent form, although some refused to sign it right away and asked to be interviewed later.

In some instances the consent procedures caused the women to expect a formal interview. Some of them were disappointed when they saw I only had a few structured questions about demographic characteristics, followed by a long list of open-ended questions. When this disappointment occurred, I reminded the women that I wanted to learn from them and that the best way to do so was by engaging in a dialogue rather than interrogating them. Only by letting the women identify their salient issues and the topics they wanted to address was I able to gain an insider's perspective. By being a careful listener and probing for additional information and explanation, I as the interviewer, together with the women, was able to uncover the complexities of their lives. In addition, the nature of the interview allowed me to ask questions about contradictions in a woman's story. For example, sometimes a woman would say that she always used a condom. However, later on in the conversation she would indicate that if she needed drugs she would never use one. By asking her to elaborate on this, I was able to begin developing insights into condom use by type of partner, type of sex acts, and social context.

The interviewer becomes much more a part of the interview when the conversations are in-depth than when a structured questionnaire is used. Because I was so integral to the process, the way the women viewed me may have biased their answers. On the one hand, this bias might be reduced because of the extent to which both parties already knew each other; on the other, a woman might fail to give her true opinion and reveal her actions if she knew that these went against the interviewer's opinion. I suspected that some women played down the ways in which their pimps manipulated them once they knew that I was not too fond of these men. However, some might have taken more time to explain the relationship with their pimp in order to "correct" my image.

My background, so different from that of these women, most likely affected the nature of the interviews. I occupied a higher socioeconomic status. I had a place to live and a job. In contrast to the nonwhite women, I came from a different racial background. While I don't know to what extent these differences played a role, I acknowledge that they must have had some effect on this research.

Leaving the Field

Leaving the field was not something that occurred after completion of the fieldwork, but an event that took place daily. Although I sometimes stayed on the strolls all night or hung out for several days, I always had a home to return to. I had a house with electricity, a warm shower, a comfortable bed, and a kitchen. My house sat on a street where I had no fear of being shot on my way there and where I did not find condoms or syringes on my doorstep.

During several stages of the study, I had access to a car, which I used to give the women rides or to run errands together. However, I will never forget the cold night when everyone on the street was freezing, and I left to go home. I turned up the heat in my car, and tears streamed down my cheeks. I appreciated the heat, but I felt more guilty about that luxury than ever before. I truly felt like an outsider, or maybe even more appropriate, a betrayer.

Throughout the years of fieldwork, there were a number of times when I left the scene temporarily. For example, when so many people were dying from AIDS, I was unable to ignore the devastating impact of this disease. I needed an emotional break.

Physically removing myself from the scene was common when I experienced difficulty remaining objective. Once I became too involved in a woman's life and almost adopted her and her family. Another time I felt a true hatred for a crack house owner and was unable to adhere to the rules of courteous interactions. Still another time, I got angry with a woman whose steady partner was HIV positive when she failed to ask him to use a condom when they had sex.

I also took temporary breaks from a particular scene by shifting settings and neighborhoods. For example, I would invest most of my time in women from a particular crack house for several weeks. Then I would shift to spending more time on one of the strolls, while making shorter and less frequent visits to the crack house. By shifting scenes, I was able to tell people why I was leaving and to remind all of us of my researcher role.

While I focused on leaving the field, I became interested in women who had left the life. It seemed important to have an understanding of their past and current circumstances. I knew some of them from the days when they were working, but identifying others was a challenge. There was no gathering place for ex-prostitutes. Informal networking, advertisements in local newspapers, and local clinics and community settings allowed me to reach twenty of these women. Conducting interviews with them later in the data collection process prepared me to ask specific questions. I realized that I had learned enough about the life to know what to ask. Interviewing ex-prostitutes also prepared me for moving from the fieldwork to writing.

It is hard to determine exactly when I left the field. It seems like a process that never ends. Although I was more physically removed from the scene, I continued to be involved while analyzing the data and writing this book. I also created opportunities to go back, for example, by asking women to give me feedback on parts of the manuscript or at times when I experienced writer's block and my car seemed to automatically steer itself to one of the strolls. I also have developed other research projects in some of the same communities. For example, both a project on intergenerational drug use and a gender-specific intervention project to help women remain HIV negative have brought me back to the same population. Some of the women have become key respondents in these new projects, while others now are members of a research team. For example, Beth, one of the women who has left prostitution, works as an outreach worker on another project.

Six Themes in the Ethnography of Prostitution

The main intention of my work is to provide the reader with a perspective on street prostitution from the point of view of the women themselves. There are six fundamental aspects of the women's lives as prostitutes that must be considered. The first concerns the women's own explanations for their involvement in prostitution and their descriptions of the various circumstances that led them to become prostitutes. Their stories include justifications such as traumatic past experiences, especially sexual abuse, the lack of love they experienced as children, pressures by friends and pimps, the need for drugs, and most prominently, the economic forces that pushed them into the life. A number of women describe these justifications as excuses, as reflective explanations they have developed after becoming a prostitute.

The women describe the nature of their initial experiences, which often involved alienation from those outside the life. They also show the differences in the processes between women who work as prostitutes and use drugs and women who do not use drugs. ·

Although all these women work either on the street or in drug-use settings, their lives do differ. My second theme is a typology that captures these differences, looking at the women's prostitution versus drug-use identities. The typology distinguishes among (a) streetwalkers, women who work strolls and who do not use drugs; (b) hooked prostitutes, women who identify themselves mainly as prostitutes but who upon their entrance into the life also began using drugs; (c) prostituting addicts, women who view themselves mainly as drug users and who became prostitutes to support their drug habit; and (d) crack prostitutes, women who trade sex for crack.

This typology explains the differences in the women's strategies for soliciting customers, their screening of customers, pricing of sex acts, and bargaining for services. For example, the streetwalkers have the most bargaining power, while such power appears to be lacking among the crack prostitutes.

Few prostitutes work in a vacuum. The third theme is the role of pimps, a label that most women dislike and for which they prefer to substitute "old man" or "boyfriend." Among the pimps, one finds entrepreneur lovers, men who mainly employ streetwalkers and hooked prostitutes and sometimes prostituting addicts. Entrepreneur lovers engage in the life for business reasons. They treat the women as their employees or their property and view them primarily as an economic commodity. The more successful a woman is in earning them money, the more difficult it is for that woman to leave her entrepreneur pimp.

Most prostituting addicts and some hooked prostitutes work for a lover pimp, a man who is their steady partner but who also lives off their earnings. Typically, such pimps employ only one woman. The dynamics in the relationship between a prostitute and her lover pimp become more complex when both partners use drugs. Drugs often become the glue of the relationship.

For many crack prostitutes, their crack addiction serves as a pimp. Few plan to exchange sex for crack when they first begin using; often several weeks or months pass before a woman who barters sex for crack realizes that she is a prostitute.

Historically, society has blamed prostitutes for introducing sexually transmitted diseases into the general population. Similarly, it makes them scapegoats for the spread of HIV/AIDS. Yet their pimps and customers are not held accountable. The fourth theme in the anthropological study of prostitution is the impact of the AIDS epidemic on the women's lives. Although most are knowledgeable about HIV risk behaviors and the ways to reduce their risk, many misconceptions exist. The women describe the complexities of condom use, especially with steady partners but also with paying customers. Many women have mixed feelings about HIV testing, wondering how to cope with a positive test result while no cure is available. A few of the women already knew their HIV-infected status, and the discussion touches on their dilemmas as well.

The fifth theme is the violence and abuse that make common appearances in the women's lives. An ethnography of prostitution must allow the women to describe violence in their neighborhoods as well as violence in prostitution and drug-use settings. The most common violence they encounter is from customers. These men often assume that because they pay for sex they buy a woman. Apparently, casual customers pose more of a danger than those who are regulars. The types of abuse the women encounter are emotional, physical, and sexual. In addition to customers, pimps and boyfriends abuse the women. Finally, the women discuss harassment by law enforcement officers.

When I talked with the women, it often seemed that there were no opportunities to escape from the life. Yet the sixth and final theme must be the escape from prostitution. Women who have left prostitution can describe the process of their exit from prostitution. As ex-prostitutes they struggle with the stigma of their past, the challenges of developing a new identity, and the impact of their past on current intimate relationships. Those who were also drug users often view themselves as ex-prostitutes and recovering addicts, a perspective that seems to create a role conflict. Overall, most ex-prostitutes find that their past follows them like a bad hangover.

Notes

1. For more information about qualitative research methods, see, for example, Patricia Adler and Peter Adler, *Membership Roles in Field Research* (Newbury Park: Sage, 1987); Michael Agar, *The Professional Stranger* (New York: Academic Press, 1980) and *Speaking of Ethnography* (Beverly Hills: Sage, 1986); Howard Becker and Blanche Geer, "Participant Observation and Interviewing: A Comparison," *Human Organization* 16 (1957): 28–32; Norman Denzin, *Sociological Methods: A Sourcebook* (Chicago: Aldine, 1970); Barney Glaser and Anselm Strauss, *The Discovery of Grounded Theory: Strategies for Qualitative Research* (Chicago: Aldine, 1967); Y. Lincoln and E. Guba, *Naturalistic Inquiry* (Beverly Hills: Sage, 1985); John Lofland, "Analytic Ethnography: Features, Failings, and Futures," *Journal of Contemporary Ethnography* 24 (1996): 30–67; and James Spradley, *The Ethnographic Interview* (New York: Holt, Rinehart and Winston, 1979) and *Participant Observation* (New York: Holt, Rinehart and Winston, 1980).

2. For a more extensive discussion of informed consent procedures and related ethical issues, see Bruce L. Berg, *Qualitative Research Methods for the Social Sciences,* 3rd edition, Chapter 3: "Ethical Issues" (Boston: Allyn and Bacon, 1998).

Critical Thinking

1. How do prostitutes gain a sense of control over their lives?

2. How does the author describe the women in her study?

3. How does the author describe people's reactions when she tells them what her research is about?

4. How and where did she find places of prostitution?

5. What was the main lesson she learned in her early efforts?

6. How does she describe "key respondents"?

7. How did she manage to develop relationships with prostitutes? What was the single most important technique?

8. How did the author handle situations involving ethical questions?

9. Describe the author's interview techniques and the rationale behind them.

10. How did the author feel about being able to "leave the field" daily?

11. Under what circumstances would she leave a scene temporarily?

12. What explanations do the women themselves give for their involvement in prostitution?

13. What is the author's typology regarding prostitutes? What kinds of strategies are thereby explained? Which has the most bargaining power? Which has the least?

14. How does the author describe the different kinds of pimps?

15. Who is historically held responsible for the spread of HIV/AIDS? Who is not held responsible?

16. How does the author describe the violence and abuse suffered by prostitutes and who is likely to inflict it?

17. With what do ex-prostitutes come to struggle?

Create Central

www.mhhe.com/createcentral

Internet References

Anthropology Links
http://anthropology.gmu.edu

Archaeology and Anthropology Computing and Study Skills
www.isca.ox.ac.uk/index.html

Introduction to Anthropological Fieldwork and Ethnography
http://web.mit.edu/dumit/www/syl-anth.html

Women Watch
www.un.org/womenwatch/about

Article Prepared by: Elvio Angeloni, *Pasadena City College*

Why Manners Matter

Valerie Curtis

Learning Outcomes

After reading this article, you will be able to:

- Discuss the importance of manners as an evolutionary adaptation.
- Describe and explain the "disgust system" as a psychological adaptation.
- Explain why manners have become particularly important in recent human history.

You wake up in the morning. Your partner burps and drags on a smelly dressing gown. You can't find your toothbrush so you use his and then wipe some muck off the floor with it. Leaving the house, you step over a turd deposited by a neighbour, then drive into a traffic jam caused by everyone ignoring the lights. In your office, everyone interrupts each other until a spitting match breaks out. Leaving work, ill-groomed strangers press up against you in the lift and one sneezes in your face.

What a grim picture. A world without manners hardly seems worth living in. Yet manners are so ingrained in our lives that we hardly notice them.

I believe that they are too important to ignore. We need to better understand manners for two reasons: first, because they are a principal weapon in the war on disease, and second, because manners underpin our ability to function as a cooperative species. In my new book on the evolution of disgust, *Don't Look, Don't Touch,* I argue that, far from being an old-fashioned set of rules about which fork to use, manners are so important that they should be up there with fire and the invention of language as a prime candidate for what makes us human.

The first, and most ancient, function of manners is to solve the problem of how to be social without getting sick. Imagine that you and I encounter each other. Although I'd like to hang around in case you have information or goods to exchange, it might be more sensible if I ran away because, to me, you are a walking bag of microbes. With every exhalation you might emit millions of influenza viruses, and your handshake might transfer salmonella bacteria or scabies mites. More intimate contact could give me hepatitis, syphilis, or worse. Your proximity to me is potentially deadly. You too, of course, make the same subconscious calculation. So how can we get close enough to share benefits but avoid sharing our microbes? This is the job of manners.

Manners dictate that if I want to interact with you I should stay at a safe distance; far enough away not to spray you with microbe-laden saliva. They tell me that I should clean and cover my body, especially the smelly bits where microbes might lurk, and to share my food with you, but not any leftovers that I have already bitten into. And manners tell me to invite you to my dwelling, but only once I've cleaned it of my bodily wastes. I do all of this because I cannot afford to disgust you. If I fail in my manners, you may reject and ostracise me and refuse further collaboration. Worse, you may gossip about my lapses in hygiene and tarnish my reputation, denying me access to the benefits of life as a member of an intensely social species.

This ability to be mannerly is supported by two psychological adaptations. One is the disgust system, which motivates us to recognize and avoid potential pathogen hot zones. The other is the ability to feel shame, which, I hypothesise, evolved to help us learn to avoid becoming disgusting to others. A study by Roger Giner-Sorolla at the University of Kent, UK, confirmed that we feel shame if someone looks at us with a disgusted expression. And research from Richard Stevenson's lab at Macquarie University in Sydney, Australia, suggests that parents use disgust expressions to teach hygiene behaviour to their children. Indeed, I suspect that one of the reasons we evolved the ability to communicate disgust via its characteristic facial and vocal expression is to teach others good manners. By pulling a face and exclaiming "Eeeugh!" we demonstrate disgust for another person's poor hygiene. This elicits shame in the target, and as a result, they modify their manners, which protects us.

But manners have acquired another function besides disease avoidance. As group sizes grew from related individuals, to clans, tribes and beyond, the problem of how to cooperate with unrelated others became more serious. Individuals who tried to get the benefits of social life without paying their share of the costs could derail the whole cooperative enterprise. Humans became adept at looking for clues as to who was likely to cooperate and who was not. Manners provided an indicator. Those who were careful with hygiene were good candidates, as were those who demonstrated that they put the interests of others before themselves. The child who passes a plate of food before serving herself is showing that she can control her selfish tendencies. In effect, she is saying: "Look how well my mother taught me. If I can show such self-control now, how useful a member of this society I will be in the future. In the meantime, you can safely do business with my family." The child taught restraint with cake now by her mother would be likely to receive a greater total of cooperative cake in her lifetime.

Those who master manners are set to reap the many benefits that come from living in a highly cooperative ultra-society. Manners are therefore a sort of proto-morality, a set of behaviors that we make "second nature" early in life so that we can avoid disgusting others with our parasites and antisocial behavior.

There are, of course, exceptions to these rules. A study on manners that my team at the London School of Hygiene and Tropical Medicine has just completed in Nepal showed that rules of hygiene are often suspended for close family members. This is probably because sharing saliva-contaminated food with someone who is already an intimate is unlikely to have disease consequences. We also saw that courtesy manners are suspended as guests become more familiar, probably because in an established cooperative relationship there is less need to signal cooperative intent. Of course, in intimate relationships, hygiene manners can be suspended entirely. Perhaps we find kissing attractive because it signifies that one's partner is serious, so much so that they will contemplate sharing our pathogens.

We play out a mannerly dance every day, getting close, but not too close, offering tokens of goodwill, but not giving away too much, in every social interaction. Yet we do the dance largely unaware of why we do it. We don't rationally calculate how to avoid inflicting our pathogens on others, nor do we consciously calculate that a small courtesy now might lead us to a big trading opportunity later. Instead, we have vague intuitions that it would be better not to disgust a guest by appearing unkempt or by offering them a dirty towel, and we follow the rules of politeness that were drummed into us as children. When we fail in these civilities, the disgust shown by our interlocutor provokes shame and teaches us not to repeat the offence.

My team is now investigating whether we can use manners to encourage better hygienic behavior, for example, in campaigns to prevent disease by improving hand washing and food hygiene in Nepal and Zambia. But it may be that understanding manners can bring us an even bigger prize.

The acquisition of manners was one of the first baby steps humans took on the road to large-scale cooperation, and cooperation, underpinned by our moral sense, was the great leap forward that allowed humans to become a hyper-social species. We have since worked together to achieve technical dominance of the planet. If we can better understand how microbes gave us manners and manners then shaped our morality, it might hold clues for our future as a species.

Critical Thinking

1. Discuss the role of manners for human beings and what they specifically dictate.
2. Describe and explain the psychological adaptations related to the "disgust system."
3. Why have manners become particularly important as group sizes have increased in human history?
4. Discuss the circumstances in which the rules of hygiene are suspended.

Create Central

www.mhhe.com/createcentral

Internet References

Everyday Health
   www.everydayhealth.com/
Good Health
   www.goodhealth.com.au

VALERIE CURTIS is a disgustologist and director of the Hygiene Centre at the London School of Hygiene and Tropical Medicine. This essay is based on her new book, *Don't Look, Don't Touch: The science behind revulsion* (Oxford University Press/University of Chicago Press).

Unit 2

UNIT

Prepared by: Elvio Angeloni, *Pasadena City College*

Culture and Communication

Anthropologists are interested in all aspects of human behavior and how they interrelate. Language is a form of such behavior (albeit, primarily verbal behavior) and, therefore, worthy of study. Although it changes over time, language is culturally patterned and passed down from one generation to the next through learning, not instinct. In keeping with the idea that language is integral to human social interactions, it has long been recognized that human communication through language is, by its nature, different from the communication found among other animals. Central to this difference is the fact that humans communicate abstractly, with symbols that have meaning independent of the immediate sensory experiences of either the sender or the receiver of the message. Thus, for instance, humans are able to refer to the future and the past and not just the present.

Recent experiments have shown that anthropoid apes can be taught a small portion of Ameslan or American Sign Language. It must be remembered, however, that their very rudimentary ability has to be tapped by painstaking human effort and that the degree of difference between apes and humans serves only to emphasize the peculiar need of humans for, and development of, language.

Just as the abstract quality of symbols lifts our thoughts beyond our immediate sense perceptions, so also it inhibits our ability to think about and convey the full meaning of our personal experience. No categorical term can do justice to its referents—the variety of forms to which the term refers. The degree to which this is an obstacle to clarity of thought and communication relates to the degree of abstraction involved in the symbols. The word "chair," for instance, would not present much difficulty, as it has objective referents. However, consider the trouble we have in thinking and communicating with words whose referents are not tied to immediate sense perception—words such as "freedom," "democracy," and "justice." At best, the likely result is *symbolic confusion:* an inability to think or communicate in objectively definable symbols. At worst, language may be used to purposefully obfuscate.

A related issue has to do with the fact that languages differ as to what is relatively easy to express within the restrictions of their particular vocabularies and grammatical structure. Thus, although a given language may not have enough words to cope with a new situation or a new field of activity, the typical solution is to invent words or to borrow them. In this way, it has been claimed that any language can be used to say anything.

While we often become frustrated with the ways in which symbolic confusion cause misunderstandings between individuals or groups, we should also pause to admire the beauty and wonder inherent in this uniquely human form of communication—in all of its linguistic diversity—and the tremendous potential of recent research to enhance effective communication among all of us.

Article   Prepared by: Elvio Angeloni, *Pasadena City College*

War of Words

MARK PAGEL

Learning Outcomes

After reading this article, you will be able to:

- Discuss the origins and functions of linguistic diversity in human societies.

- Discuss the future of linguistic diversity in terms of its direction and causes.

For anyone interested in languages, the north-eastern coastal region of Papua New Guinea is like a well-stocked sweet shop. Korak speakers live right next to Brem speakers, who are just up the coast from Wanambre speakers, and so on. I once met a man from that area and asked him whether it is true that a different language is spoken every few kilometres. "Oh no," he replied, "they are far closer together than that."

Around the world today, some 7,000 distinct languages are spoken. That's 7,000 different ways of saying "good morning" or "it looks like rain"—more languages in one species of mammal than there are mammalian species. What's more, these 7,000 languages probably make up just a fraction of those ever spoken in our history. To put human linguistic diversity into perspective, you could take a gorilla or chimpanzee from its troop and plop it down anywhere these species are found, and it would know how to communicate. You could repeat this with donkeys, crickets or goldfish and get the same outcome.

This highlights an intriguing paradox at the heart of human communication. If language evolved to allow us to exchange information, how come most people cannot understand what most other people are saying? This perennial question was famously addressed in the Old Testament story of the Tower of Babel, which tells of how humans developed the conceit that they could use their shared language to cooperate in the building of a tower that would take them to heaven. God, angered at this attempt to usurp his power, destroyed the tower and to ensure it would not be rebuilt he scattered the people and confused them by giving them different languages. The myth leads to the amusing irony that our separate languages exist to prevent us from communicating. The surprise is that this might not be far from the truth.

The origins of language are difficult to pin down. Anatomical evidence from fossils suggests that the ability to speak arose in our ancestors sometime between 1.6 million and 600,000 years ago (*New Scientist*, 24 March, p. 34). However, indisputable evidence that this speech was conveying complex ideas comes only with the cultural sophistication and symbolism associated with modern humans. They emerged in Africa perhaps 200,000 to 160,000 years ago, and by 60,000 years ago had migrated out of the continent—eventually to occupy nearly every region of the world. We should expect new languages to arise as people spread out and occupy new lands because as soon as groups become isolated from one another their languages begin to drift apart and adapt to local needs (*New Scientist*, 10 December 2011, p. 34). But the real puzzle is that the greatest diversity of human societies and languages arises not where people are most spread out, but where they are most closely packed together.

Papua New Guinea is a classic case. That relatively small land mass—only slightly larger than California—is home to between 800 and 1,000 distinct languages, or around 15 per cent of all languages spoken on the planet. This linguistic diversity is not the result of migration and physical isolation of different populations. Instead, people living in close quarters seem to have chosen to separate into many distinct societies, leading lives so separate that they have become incapable of talking to one another. Why?

Thinking about this, I was struck by an uncanny parallel between linguistic and biological diversity. A well-known phenomenon in ecology called Rapoport's rule states that the greatest diversity of biological species is found near to the equator, with numbers tailing off as you approach the poles. Could this be true for languages too? To test the idea, anthropologist Ruth Mace from University College London and I looked at the distribution of around 500 Native American tribes before the arrival of Europeans and used this to plot the number of different language groups per unit area at each degree of latitude (*Nature*, vol 428, p. 275). It turned out that the distribution matched Rapoport's rule remarkably well.

The congruity of biological species and cultures with distinct languages is probably not an accident. To survive the harsh polar landscape, species must range far and wide, leaving little opportunity for new ones to arise. The same is true of human groups in the far northern regions. They too must cover wide geographical areas to find sufficient food, and this tends to blend languages and cultures. At the other end of the spectrum, just as the bountiful, sun-drenched tropics are a cradle of biological speciation, so this rich environment has allowed humans to thrive and splinter into a profusion of societies.

Of course that still leaves the question of why people would want to form into so many distinct groups. For the myriad biological species in the tropics, there are advantages to being different because it allows each to adapt to its own ecological niche. But humans all occupy the same niche, and splitting into distinct cultural and linguistic groups actually brings disadvantages, such as slowing the movement of ideas, technologies and people. It also makes societies more vulnerable to risks and plain bad luck. So why not have one large group with a shared language?

An answer to this question is emerging with the realisation that human history has been characterised by continual battles. Ever since our ancestors walked out of Africa, beginning around 60,000 years ago, people have been in conflict over territory and resources. In my book *Wired for Culture* (Norton/Penguin, 2012) I describe how, as a consequence, we have acquired a suite of traits that help our own particular group to outcompete the others. Two traits that stand out are "groupishness"—affiliating with people with whom you share a distinct identity—and xenophobia, demonising those outside your group and holding parochial views towards them. In this context, languages act as powerful social anchors of our tribal identity. How we speak is a continual auditory reminder of who we are and, equally as important, who we are not. Anyone who can speak your particular dialect is a walking, talking advertisement for the values and cultural history you share. What's more, where different groups live in close proximity, distinct languages are an effective way to prevent eavesdropping or the loss of important information to a competitor.

In support of this idea, I have found anthropological accounts of tribes deciding to change their language, with immediate effect, for no other reason than to distinguish themselves from neighbouring groups. For example, a group of Selepet speakers in Papua New Guinea changed its word for "no" from *bia* to *bune* to be distinct from other Selepet speakers in a nearby village. Another group reversed all its masculine and feminine nouns—the word for he became she, man became woman, mother became father, and so on. One can only sympathise with anyone who had been away hunting for a few days when the changes occurred.

The use of language as identity is not confined to Papua New Guinea. People everywhere use language to monitor who is a member of their "tribe." We have an acute, and sometimes obsessive, awareness of how those around us speak, and we continually adapt language to mark out our particular group from others. In a striking parallel to the Selepet examples, many of the peculiar spellings that differentiate American English from British—such as the tendency to drop the "u" in words like colour—arose almost overnight when Noah Webster produced the first American Dictionary of the English Language at the start of the 19th century. He insisted that: "As an independent nation, our honor [sic] requires us to have a system of our own, in language as well as government."

Use of language to define group identity is not a new phenomenon. To examine how languages have diversified over the course of human history, my colleagues and I drew up family trees for three large language groups—Indo-European languages, the Bantu languages of Africa, and Polynesian languages from Oceania (*Science,* vol 319, p. 588). These "phylogenies," which trace the history of each group back to a common ancestor, reveal the number of times a contemporary language has split or "divorced" from related languages. We found that some languages have a history of many divorces, others far fewer.

When languages split, they often experience short episodes during which they change rapidly. The same thing happens during biological evolution, where it is known as punctuational evolution (*Science,* vol 314, p. 119). So the more divorces a language has had, the more its vocabulary differs from its ancestral language. Our analysis does not say why one language splits into two. Migration and isolation of groups is one explanation, but it also seems clear that bursts of linguistic change have occurred at least in part to allow speakers to assert their own identities. There really has been a war of words going on.

So what of the future? The world we live in today is very different from the one our ancestors inhabited. For most of our history, people would have encountered only their own cultural group and immediate neighbours. Globalisation and electronic communication mean we have become far more connected and culturally homogenised, making the benefits of being understood more apparent. The result is a mass extinction of languages to rival the great biological extinctions in Earth's past.

Although contemporary languages continue to evolve and diverge from one another, the rate of loss of minority languages now greatly exceeds the emergence of new languages. Between 30 and 50 languages are disappearing every year as the young people of small tribal societies adopt majority languages. As a percentage of the total, this rate of loss equals or exceeds the decline in biological species diversity through loss of habitat and climate change. Already a mere 15 of the Earth's 7,000 languages account for about 40 per cent of the world's speakers, and most languages have very few speakers.

Still, this homogenisation of languages and cultures is happening at a far slower pace than it could, and that is because of the powerful psychological role language plays in marking out our cultural territories and identities. One consequence of this is that languages resist "contamination" from other languages, with speakers often treating the arrival of foreign words with a degree of suspicion—witness the British and French grumblings about so-called Americanisms. Another factor is the role played by nationalistic agendas in efforts to save dying languages, which can result in policies such as compulsory Welsh lessons for schoolchildren up to the age of 16 in Wales.

Linguistic Creativity

This resistance to change leaves plenty of time for linguistic diversity to pop up. Various street and hip-hop dialects, for example, are central to the identity of specific groups, while mass communication allows them easily to reach their natural constituencies. Another interesting example is Globish, a pared-down form of English that uses just 1,000 or so words and simplified language structures. It has spontaneously evolved among people who travel extensively, such as diplomats and international business people. Amusingly, native English speakers can be disadvantaged around Globish because they use words and grammar that others cannot understand.

In the long run, though, it seems virtually inevitable that a single language will replace all others. In evolutionary terms, when otherwise equally good solutions to a problem compete, one of them tends to win out. We see this in the near worldwide standardisation of ways of telling time, measuring weights and distance, CD and DVD formats, railway gauges, and the voltages and frequencies of electricity supplies. It may take a very long time, but languages seem destined to go the same way—all are equally good vehicles of communication, so one will eventually replace the others. Which one will it be?

Today, around 1.2 billion people—about 1 in 6 of us—speak Mandarin. Next come Spanish and English with about 400 million speakers each, and Bengali and Hindi follow close behind. On these counts Mandarin might look like the favourite in the race to be the world's language. However, vastly more people learn English as a second language than any other. Years ago, in a remote part of Tanzania, I was stopped while attempting to speak Swahili to a local person who held up his hand and said: "My English is better than your Swahili." English is already the worldwide lingua franca, so if I had to put money on one language eventually to replace all others, this would be it.

In the ongoing war of words, casualties are inevitable. As languages become extinct we are not simply losing different ways of saying "good morning," but the cultural diversity that has arisen around our thousands of distinct tribal societies. Each language plays a powerful role in establishing a cultural identity—it is the internal voice that carries the memories, thoughts, hopes and fears of a particular group of people. Lose the language and you lose that too.

Nevertheless, I suspect a monolinguistic future may not be as bad as doomsayers have suggested. There is a widely held belief that the language you speak determines the way you think, so that a loss of linguistic diversity is also a loss of unique styles of thought. I don't believe that. Our languages determine the words we use but they do not limit the concepts we can understand and perceive. Besides, we might draw another, more positive, moral from the story of Babel: With everyone speaking the same language, humanity can more easily cooperate to achieve something monumental. Indeed, in today's world it is the countries with the least linguistic diversity that have achieved the most prosperity.

Critical Thinking

1. Discuss the linguistic diversity among humans in comparison to animal communication.

2. What is the "intriguing paradox" at the heart of human communication?

3. How does the author explain the original diversity of human languages?

4. Where on earth is the greatest diversity of human languages and why?

5. How do *groupishness* and *xenophobia* both play a role in linguistic diversity? Be familiar with the evidence cited by the author in support of this idea.

6. What are the factors involved in why a language splits into two?

7. What is the future for linguistic diversity and why? Why is the pace of "homogenization" slower than it could be?

8. In what contexts does linguistic diversity continue to pop up?

9. What does the author see as the future for linguistic diversity? Why might a "monolinguistic future" not be as bad as doomsayers have suggested?

Create Central

www.mhhe.com/createcentral

Internet References

Exploratorium Magazine: "The Evolution of Languages"
  www.exploratorium.edu/exploring/language
Language and Culture
  http://anthro.palomar.edu/language/default.htm
Language Extinction
  www.colorado.edu/iec
Showcase Anthropology
  www.anthropology.wisc.edu

Article
Prepared by: Elvio Angeloni, *Pasadena City College*

How Language Shapes Thought

The languages we speak affect our perceptions of the world.

LERA BORODITSKY

Learning Outcomes

After reading this article, you will be able to:

- Explain how language can restrict our thought processes.
- Explain the cultural differences with respect to people's perceptions of space and time.

I am standing next to a five-year-old girl in Pormpuraaw, a small Aboriginal community on the western edge of Cape York in northern Australia. When I ask her to point north, she points precisely and without hesitation. My compass says she is right. Later, back in a lecture hall at Stanford University, I make the same request of an audience of distinguished scholars—winners of science medals and genius prizes. Some of them have come to this very room to hear lectures for more than 40 years. I ask them to close their eyes (so they don't cheat) and point north. Many refuse; they do not know the answer. Those who do point take a while to think about it and then aim in all possible directions. I have repeated this exercise at Harvard and Princeton and in Moscow, London and Beijing, always with the same results.

A five-year-old in one culture can do something with ease that eminent scientists in other cultures struggle with. This is a big difference in cognitive ability. What could explain it? The surprising answer, it turns out, may be language.

The notion that different languages may impart different cognitive skills goes back centuries. Since the 1930s it has become associated with American linguists Edward Sapir and Benjamin Lee Whorf, who studied how languages vary and proposed ways that speakers of different tongues may think differently. Although their ideas met with much excitement early on, there was one small problem: a near complete lack of evidence to support their claims. By the 1970s many scientists had become disenchanted with the Sapir-Whorf hypothesis, and it was all but abandoned as a new set of theories claiming that language and thought are universal muscled onto the scene. But now, decades later, a solid body of empirical evidence showing how languages shape thinking has finally emerged. The evidence overturns the long-standing dogma about universality and yields fascinating insights into the origins of knowledge and the construction of reality. The results have important implications for law, politics and education.

Under the Influence

Around the world people communicate with one another using a dazzling array of languages—7,000 or so all told—and each language requires very different things from its speakers. For example, suppose I want to tell you that I saw *Uncle Vanya* on 42nd Street. In Mian, a language spoken in Papua New Guinea, the verb I used would reveal whether the event happened just now, yesterday or in the distant past, whereas in Indonesian, the verb wouldn't even give away whether it had already happened or was still coming up. In Russian, the verb would reveal my gender. In Mandarin, I would have to specify whether the titular uncle is maternal or paternal and whether he is related by blood or marriage, because there are different words for all these different types of uncles and then some (he happens to be a mother's brother, as the Chinese translation clearly states). And in Pirahã, a language spoken in the Amazon, I couldn't say "42nd," because there are no words for exact numbers, just words for "few" and "many."

Languages differ from one another in innumerable ways, but just because people talk differently does not necessarily mean they think differently. How can we tell whether speakers of Mian, Russian, Indonesian, Mandarin or Pirahã actually end up attending to, remembering and reasoning about the world in different ways because of the languages they speak? Research in my lab and in many others has been uncovering how language shapes even the most fundamental dimensions of human experience: space, time, causality and relationships to others.

Let us return to Pormpuraaw. Unlike English, the Kuuk Thaayorre language spoken in Pormpuraaw does not use relative spatial terms such as left and right. Rather Kuuk Thaayorre speakers talk in terms of absolute cardinal directions (north, south, east, west, and so forth). Of course, in English we also use cardinal direction terms but only for large spatial scales. We would not say, for example, "They set the salad forks southeast of the dinner forks—the philistines!" But in Kuuk

Thaayorre cardinal directions are used at all scales. This means one ends up saying things like "the cup is southeast of the plate" or "the boy standing to the south of Mary is my brother." In Pormpuraaw, one must always stay oriented, just to be able to speak properly.

Moreover, groundbreaking work conducted by Stephen C. Levinson of the Max Planck Institute for Psycholinguistics in Nijmegen, the Netherlands, and John B. Haviland of the University of California, San Diego, over the past two decades has demonstrated that people who speak languages that rely on absolute directions are remarkably good at keeping track of where they are, even in unfamiliar landscapes or inside unfamiliar buildings. They do this better than folks who live in the same environments but do not speak such languages and in fact better than scientists thought humans ever could. The requirements of their languages enforce and train this cognitive prowess.

People who think differently about space are also likely to think differently about time. For example, my colleague Alice Gaby of the University of California, Berkeley, and I gave Kuuk Thaayorre speakers sets of pictures that showed temporal progressions—a man aging, a crocodile growing, a banana being eaten. We then asked them to arrange the shuffled photographs on the ground to indicate the correct temporal order.

We tested each person twice, each time facing in a different cardinal direction. English speakers given this task will arrange the cards so that time proceeds from left to right. Hebrew speakers will tend to lay out the cards from right to left. This shows that writing direction in a language influences how we organize time. The Kuuk Thaayorre, however, did not routinely arrange the cards from left to right or right to left. They arranged them from east to west. That is, when they were seated facing south, the cards went left to right. When they faced north, the cards went from right to left. When they faced east, the cards came toward the body, and so on. We never told anyone which direction they were facing—the Kuuk Thaayorre knew that already and spontaneously used this spatial orientation to construct their representations of time.

Representations of time vary in many other ways around the world. For example, English speakers consider the future to be "ahead" and the past "behind." In 2010 Lynden Miles of the University of Aberdeen in Scotland and his colleagues discovered that English speakers unconsciously sway their bodies forward when thinking about the future and back when thinking about the past. But in Aymara, a language spoken in the Andes, the past is said to be in front and the future behind. And the Aymara speakers' body language matches their way of talking: in 2006 Raphael Núñez of U.C.S.D. and Eve Sweetser of U.C. Berkeley found that Aymara gesture in front of them when talking about the past and behind them when discussing the future.

Remembering Whodunit

Speakers of different languages also differ in how they describe events and, as a result, how well they can remember who did what. All events, even split-second accidents, are complicated and require us to construe and interpret what happened. Take, for example, former vice president Dick Cheney's quail-hunting accident, in which he accidentally shot Harry Whittington. One could say that "Cheney shot Whittington" (wherein Cheney is the direct cause), or "Whittington got shot by Cheney" (distancing Cheney from the outcome), or "Whittington got peppered pretty good" (leaving Cheney out altogether). Cheney himself said "Ultimately I'm the guy who pulled the trigger that fired the round that hit Harry," interposing a long chain of events between himself and the outcome. President George Bush's take—"he heard a bird flush, and he turned and pulled the trigger and saw his friend get wounded"—was an even more masterful exculpation, transforming Cheney from agent to mere witness in less than a sentence.

Speakers of different languages differ in how well they can remember who did what.

The American public is rarely impressed with such linguistic wiggling because nonagentive language sounds evasive in English, the province of guilt-shirking children and politicians. English speakers tend to phrase things in terms of people doing things, preferring transitive constructions like "John broke the vase" even for accidents. Speakers of Japanese or Spanish, in contrast, are less likely to mention the agent when describing an accidental event. In Spanish one might say *"Se rompió el florero,"* which translates to "the vase broke" or "the vase broke itself."

My student Caitlin M. Fausey and I have found that such linguistic differences influence how people construe what happened and have consequences for eyewitness memory. In our studies, published in 2010, speakers of English, Spanish and Japanese watched videos of two guys popping balloons, breaking eggs and spilling drinks either intentionally or accidentally. Later we gave them a surprise memory test. For each event they had witnessed, they had to say which guy did it, just like in a police line-up. Another group of English, Spanish and Japanese speakers described the same events. When we looked at the memory data, we found exactly the differences in eyewitness memory predicted by patterns in language. Speakers of all three languages described intentional events agentively, saying things such as "He popped the balloon," and all three groups remembered who did these intentional actions equally well. When it came to accidents, however, interesting differences emerged. Spanish and Japanese speakers were less likely to describe the accidents agentively than were English speakers, and they correspondingly remembered who did it less well than English speakers did. This was not because they had poorer memory overall—they remembered the agents of intentional events (for which their languages would naturally mention the agent) just as well as English speakers did.

Not only do languages influence what we remember, but the structures of languages can make it easier or harder for us to learn new things. For instance, because the number words in some languages reveal the underlying base-10 structure more transparently than do the number words in English (there are no troublesome teens like 11 or 13 in Mandarin, for instance), kids learning those languages are able to learn the base-10 insight sooner. And depending on how many syllables the number words have, it will be easier or harder to keep a phone number in mind or to do mental calculation. Language can even affect how quickly children figure out whether they are male or female. In 1983 Alexander Guiora of the University of Michigan at Ann Arbor compared three groups of kids growing up with Hebrew, English or Finnish as their native language. Hebrew marks gender prolifically (even the word "you" is different depending on gender), Finnish has no gender marking and English is somewhere in between. Accordingly, children growing up in a Hebrew-speaking environment figure out their own gender about a year earlier than Finnish-speaking children; English-speaking kids fall in the middle.

What Shapes What?

These are just some of the many fascinating findings of cross-linguistic differences in cognition. But how do we know whether differences in language create differences in thought, or the other way around? The answer, it turns out, is both—the way we think influences the way we speak, but the influence also goes the other way. The past decade has seen a host of ingenious demonstrations establishing that language indeed plays a causal role in shaping cognition. Studies have shown that changing how people talk changes how they think. Teaching people new color words, for instance, changes their ability to discriminate colors. And teaching people a new way of talking about time gives them a new way of thinking about it.

Another way to get at this question is to study people who are fluent in two languages. Studies have shown that bilinguals change how they see the world depending on which language they are speaking. Two sets of findings published in 2010 demonstrate that even something as fundamental as who you like and do not like depends on the language in which you are asked. The studies, one by Oludamini Ogunnaike and his colleagues at Harvard and another by Shai Danziger and his colleagues at Ben-Gurion University of the Negev in Israel, looked at Arabic-French bilinguals in Morocco, Spanish-English bilinguals in the U.S. and Arabic-Hebrew bilinguals in Israel, in each case testing the participants' implicit biases. For example, Arabic-Hebrew bilinguals were asked to quickly press buttons in response to words under various conditions. In one condition if they saw a Jewish name like "Yair" or a positive trait like "good" or "strong," they were instructed to press "M,"; if they saw an Arab name like "Ahmed" or a negative trait like "mean" or "weak," they were told to press "X." In another condition the pairing was reversed so that Jewish names and negative traits shared a response key, and Arab names and positive traits shared a response key. The researchers measured how quickly subjects were able to respond under the two conditions. This task has been widely used to measure involuntary or automatic biases—how naturally things such as positive traits and ethnic groups seem to go together in people's minds.

Surprisingly, the investigators found big shifts in these involuntary automatic biases in bilinguals depending on the language in which they were tested. The Arabic-Hebrew bilinguals, for their part, showed more positive implicit attitudes toward Jews when tested in Hebrew than when tested in Arabic.

People communicate using a multitude of languages that vary considerably in the information they convey.

Scholars have long wondered whether different languages might impart different cognitive abilities.

In recent years empirical evidence for this causal relation has emerged, indicating that one's mother tongue does indeed mold the way one thinks about many aspects of the world, including space and time.

The latest findings also hint that language is part and parcel of many more aspects of thought than scientists had previously realized.

Language also appears to be involved in many more aspects of our mental lives than scientists had previously supposed. People rely on language even when doing simple things like distinguishing patches of color, counting dots on a screen or orienting in a small room: my colleagues and I have found that limiting people's ability to access their language faculties fluently—by giving them a competing demanding verbal task such as repeating a news report, for instance—impairs their ability to perform these tasks. This means that the categories and distinctions that exist in particular languages are meddling in our mental lives very broadly. What researchers have been calling "thinking" this whole time actually appears to be a collection of both linguistic and nonlinguistic processes. As a result, there may not be a lot of adult human thinking where language does not play a role.

A hallmark feature of human intelligence is its adaptability, the ability to invent and rearrange conceptions of the world to suit changing goals and environments. One consequence of this flexibility is the great diversity of languages that have emerged around the globe. Each provides its own cognitive toolkit and encapsulates the knowledge and worldview developed over thousands of years within a culture. Each contains a way of perceiving, categorizing and making meaning in the world, an invaluable guidebook developed and honed by our ancestors. Research into how the languages we speak shape the way we think is helping scientists to unravel how we create knowledge and construct reality and how we got to be as smart and sophisticated as we are. And this insight, in turn, helps us understand the very essence of what makes us human.

More to Explore

Language Changes Implicit Associations between Ethnic Groups and Evaluation in Bilinguals. Shai Danziger and Robert Ward in *Psychological Science,* vol. 21, no. 6, pages 799–800; June 2010.

Constructing Agency: The Role of Language. Caitlin M. Fausey et al. in *Frontiers in Cultural Psychology,* vol. 1, Article 162. Published online October 15, 2010.

Remembrances of Times East: Absolute Spatial Representations of Time in an Australian Aboriginal Community. Lera Boroditsky and Alice Gaby in *Psychological Science,* vol. 21, no. 11, pages 1635–1639; November 2010.

Critical Thinking

1. How is it that a 5-year-old in the Pormpuraaw community of northern Australia has a better sense of direction than many trained scientists in the United States?

2. Be familiar with the examples cited as to how people differ cross-culturally in terms of their perceptions of space and time.

3. What are some of the cultural differences in terms of how people describe events, especially in terms of agency?

4. What evidence is there that languages affect people's perceptions of color? How they learn? Who they like and don't like? That they need language in order to perform certain mental tasks?

Create Central

www.mhhe.com/createcentral

Internet References

Language and Culture Center for Nonverbal Studies
www.library.kent.edu/resource.php?id=2800
Language and Culture
http://anthro.palomar.edu/language/default.htm
Nonverbal Behavior
www.usal.es/~nonverbal/researchcenters.htm

LERA BORODITSKY is an assistant professor of cognitive psychology at Stanford University and editor in chief of *Frontiers in Cultural Psychology*. Her lab conducts research around the world, focusing on mental representation and the effects of language on cognition.

Article   Prepared by: Elvio Angeloni, *Pasadena City College*

Armor against Prejudice

ED YONG

Learning Outcomes

After reading this article, you will be able to:

- Discuss the impact of negative stereotypes on many minorities.

- Discuss the effect of "stereotype threat" on individual performance.

- Explain the interventionist approach to stereotype threat and its possible positive outcome.

Neil deGrasse Tyson, the renowned science communicator, earned his PhD in astrophysics from Columbia University in 1991. About 4,000 astrophysicists resided in the country at the time. Tyson brought the total number of African-Americans among them to a paltry seven. In a convocation address, he spoke openly about the challenges he faced: "In the perception of society, my academic failures are expected and my academic successes are attributed to others." Tyson said. "To spend most of my life fighting these attitudes levies an emotional tax that is a form of intellectual emasculation. It is a tax that I would not wish upon my enemies."

Tyson's words speak to a broad truth: negative stereotypes impose an intellectual burden on many minorities and on others who think that the people around them perceive them as inferior in some way. In many different situations—at school, at work or in sports stadiums—these individuals worry that they will fail in a way that affirms derogatory stereotypes. Young white athletes fear that they will not perform as well as their black peers, for example, and women in advanced math classes worry that they will earn lower grades than the men. This anxiety—Tyson's "emotional tax"—is known as stereotype threat. Hundreds of studies have confirmed that stereotype threat undermines performance, producing the very failure they dread. Sometimes, people become trapped in a vicious cycle in which poor performance leads to more worry, which further impedes performance.

In recent years, psychologists have greatly improved their understanding of how stereotype threat affects individuals, why it happens and, most important, how to prevent it. Although the threat is real, some researchers question how well some of the relevant laboratory studies mirror anxiety in real-world settings; they also note that it is just one of many factors that contribute to social and academic inequality. Yet it is also one of the factors that can be easily changed. In studies conducted in actual schools, relatively simple interventions—such as self-esteem-boosting writing exercises completed in less than an hour—have produced dramatic and long-lasting effects, shrinking achievement gaps, and expelling stereotype threat from the classroom and students' minds. Some educators are working on ways to scale up these interventions to statewide education programs.

Identifying the Threat

Two psychologists, Claude Steele of Stanford University and Joshua Aronson, then also at Stanford, coined the term "stereotype threat" in 1995. Then, as now, black students across the U.S. earned worse grades on average than their peers and were more likely to drop out early at all levels of education. The various explanations for this gap included the pernicious idea that black students were innately less intelligent. Steele and Aronson were not convinced. Instead, they reasoned, the very existence of this negative stereotype might impair a student's performance.

In a now classic experiment, they presented more than 100 college students with a frustrating test. When they told the students that the exam would not measure their abilities, black and white students with comparable SAT scores did equally well. When Steele and Aronson told the students that the test would assess their intellectual ability, however, the black students' scores fell, but those of their white peers did not. Simply asking the students to record their race beforehand had the same effect.

The study was groundbreaking. Steele and Aronson showed that standardized tests are far from standardized. When presented in a way that invokes stereotype threat, even subtly, they put some students at an automatic disadvantage. "There was a lot of skepticism at first, but it's reducing with time," Aronson says. "In the beginning, even I didn't believe how strong the effects were. I thought, 'Somebody else has to replicate this.'"

Many researchers have. To date, hundreds of studies have found evidence of stereotype threat in all manner of groups. It afflicts students from poorer backgrounds in academic tests and men in tasks of social sensitivity. White students suffer from it when pitted against Asian peers in math tests or against black peers in sports. In many of these studies, the strongest students suffer the greatest setbacks. The ones who are most invested in succeeding are most likely to be bothered by a negative stereotype and most likely to underperform as a result. Stereotype threat is nothing if not painfully ironic.

Exactly how pervasive stereotype threat is in real-world settings remains somewhat unclear, however, largely because the relevant studies face the same problems that plague much of social psychology. Most were conducted with small numbers of college students—which increases the chances of statistical flukes—and not all studies found a strong effect. Some critics also note that laboratory experiments are often a poor substitute for the real world. Paul Sackett of the University of Minnesota has argued that outside the lab, stereotype threat could be less common and more easily overcome. Last year Gijsbert Stoet, then at the University of Leeds in England, and David C. Geary of the University of Missouri—Columbia examined every study that looked for stereotype threat among women taking math tests—a phenomenon that Steele and his colleagues first identified in 1999. Out of 20 that repeated the 1999 experiment, only 11 concluded that women performed worse than men. Geary is not ready to discount stereotype threat, but he thinks it may not be as strong as it is sometimes portrayed.

Ann Marie Ryan of Michigan State University has identified some plausible reasons for such inconsistent conclusions. In 2008 she and Hanna-Hanh Nguyen, then at California State University, Long Beach, compared the results of 76 different studies on stereotype threat in high schoolers and undergraduates. They found that in the lab, scientists are able to detect the threat only under certain conditions, such as when they give volunteers an especially difficult test or when they work with people who strongly identify with their social group.

In the past decade, psychologists have shifted from showing that stereotype threat exists to understanding how it works. Researchers have demonstrated that the threat operates in the same way across different groups of people. Anxiety arrives; motivation falls; expectations lower. Building on these findings, Toni Schmader of the University of British Columbia surmised that the threat preys on something fundamental. The most obvious culprit was working memory—the collection of cognitive skills that allows us to temporarily hold and manipulate information in our mind. This suite of skills is a finite resource, and stereotype threat can drain it. Individuals might psychologically exhaust themselves by worrying about other people's prejudices and thinking about how to prove them wrong. To test this idea, Schmader gave 75 volunteers a difficult working memory test, during which they had to memorize a list of words while solving mathematical equations. She told some volunteers that the test would assess their memory skills and that men and women may have inborn differences in their abilities. Sure enough, women who were told of this supposed discrepancy kept fewer words in mind, whereas their male colleagues had no such problems.

This depletion of working memory creates various stumbling blocks to success. People tend to overthink actions that would otherwise be automatic and become more sensitive to cues that might indicate discrimination. An ambiguous expression can be misread as a sneer, and even one's own anxiety can become a sign of imminent failure. Minds also wander, and self-control weakens. When Schmader stopped women in the middle of a math test and asked them what they were thinking of, those under stereotype threat were more likely to be daydreaming.

Expelling Stereotypes

Most recently, researchers have moved the study of stereotype threat out of the lab and into schools and lecture halls, where they try to dispel or prevent the threat altogether. "I see three waves of research," Schmader says. "The first was identifying the phenomenon and how far it travels. The second was looking at who experiences the effect and its mechanisms. The third wave is now to translate these results into interventions."

Geoffrey Cohen, also at Stanford, has achieved particularly impressive results. His method is disarmingly simple: he asks people to consider what is important to them, be it popularity or musical ability, and write about why it matters. The 15-minute exercise acts like a mental vaccine that boosts students' self-confidence, helping them combat any future stereotype threat.

In 2003 Cohen visited racially diverse middle schools in California and put his exercise through a randomized controlled trial—the gold-standard test in medicine that checks if an intervention works by pitting it against a placebo. Cohen administered his exercise to seventh graders: half wrote about their own values, and the rest wrote about things that were unimportant to them. The trial was double-blinded, meaning that neither Cohen nor the students knew who was in which group.

At the end of the term, black students who completed the exercise had closed a 40 percent academic gap between them and their white peers. Best of all, the students at the bottom of the class benefited most. Over the next two years, the same students took two or three booster versions of the original exercise. Only 5 percent of the poorest students who wrote about their values ended up in remedial classes or repeated a grade, compared with 18 percent of those in the control group. Ultimately, the black students' grade point averages rose by a quarter of a point and by 0.4 point among the worst performers.

A few fractions of a point here and there might not seem like a huge improvement, but even small changes in confidence—whether positive or negative—have a cumulative effect. Children who do poorly at first can quickly lose self-confidence or a teacher's attention; conversely, signs of modest progress can motivate far greater success. By intervening early on, Cohen asserts, educators can turn vicious cycles into virtuous ones.

Cohen's task is so simple that Ryan and others are not entirely convinced by his results. "It was hard for us to believe, but we've replicated it since," Cohen says. In the past five years ,he has used his exercise to swing the fortunes of black students in three different middle schools and to largely close the gender gap in a college-level physics class. Skeptics, though, still hope that independent researchers will try to replicate these studies.

Meanwhile Cohen is seeking new ways to help students. He has collaborated with Greg Walton, also at Stanford, to counter a kind of isolation that stereotype threat often induces. Many minorities worry that their academic peers will not fully accept them. Walton combated these worries with survey statistics and quotes from older students showing that such feelings are common to everyone regardless of race and that they disappear with time. "It makes them reframe their own experiences through the lens of this message, rather than of race," Walton explains.

Walton and Cohen tested their hour-long exercise with college students in their first spring term. Three years later, when the students graduated, the achievement gap between blacks and whites had been halved. The black students were also happier and healthier than their peers who did not take part in Walton's exercise. In the past three years, they had made fewer visits to the doctor. Walton acknowledges that such a simple exercise may look trivial to an outsider. But, he says, for students who are "actively worried about whether they fit in, the knowledge that those concerns are shared and temporary is actually very powerful."

Cohen and Walton are now scaling up their simple and inexpensive interventions from individual schools to entire states. The pair—as well as Carol Dweck and Dave Paunesku—both also at Stanford, created PERTS (the Project for Education Research That Scales), which allows them to rapidly administer their interventions online. They can also combine the programs or pit them against one another to see which have the greatest effects.

Even if the programs work as planned, researchers who study stereotype threat admit that undoing it is not a panacea against inequality. Cohen, for example, tested his initial writing exercise only in schools with mixed ethnicities, and he is unsure if it would work in predominantly minority schools. "There are many reasons why we have achievement gaps—inequality of resources, bad schools, less well-trained teachers," Walton adds. "There doesn't seem to be much hope of addressing these structural barriers. What's exciting about stereotype threat is that we can make headway in the face of those things."

Recent work on the phenomenon not only offers realistic hope for alleviating some truly tenacious problems—it also upends pervasive beliefs. By thwarting stereotype threat, researchers have shown that the stereotypes themselves are unfounded. Performance gaps between black and white students or between male and female scientists do not indicate differences in ability; rather they reflect prejudices that we can change. "The things we thought were so intractable 15 years ago aren't," Aronson says, "and that's a hugely positive message."

Critical Thinking

1. In what ways do negative stereotypes impose an intellectual burden on many minorities?

2. Discuss the effect of "stereotype threat" on performance and how it can be changed.

3. How did the experiment by Steele and Aronson illustrate the effects of stereotype threat?

4. Discuss the findings of the various studies on stereotype threat.

5. Why has it been difficult to assess the effects of stereotype threat outside the lab settings?

6. How does Ann Marie Ryan explain the inconsistent conclusions?

7. Discuss the ways in which stereotype threat actually works.

8. Discuss the interventionist methods of Geoffrey Cohen and Greg Walton and why they seem to reduce the effects of stereotype threat.

9. Explain why undoing stereotype threat is not a panacea and yet offers a realistic hope.

Create Central

www.mhhe.com/createcentral

Internet References

Language and Culture

http://anthro.palomar.edu/language/default.htm

Linguistic Society of America

www.linguisticsociety.org/resource/sociolinguistics

Understanding Prejudice

http://www.understandingprejudice.org/apa/

ED YONG is a science writer based in England. He has written for *Nature, Wired, National Geographic* and *New Scientist,* among other publications.

Article Prepared by: Elvio Angeloni, *Pasadena City College*

Shakespeare in the Bush

LAURA BOHANNAN

Learning Outcomes

After reading this article, you will be able to:

- Describe the relationship between a people's language, culture, and interaction with their environment.

- Give examples of the ways in which communication is difficult in a cross-cultural situation.

Just before I left Oxford for the Tiv in West Africa, conversation turned to the season at Stratford. "You Americans," said a friend, "often have difficulty with Shakespeare. He was, after all, a very English poet, and one can easily misinterpret the universal by misunderstanding the particular."

I protested that human nature is pretty much the same the whole world over; at least the general plot and motivation of the greater tragedies would always be clear—everywhere—although some details of custom might have to be explained and difficulties of translation might produce other slight changes. To end an argument we could not conclude, my friend gave me a copy of *Hamlet* to study in the African bush: it would, he hoped, lift my mind above its primitive surroundings, and possibly I might, by prolonged meditation, achieve the grace of correct interpretation.

It was my second field trip to that African tribe, and I thought myself ready to live in one of its remote sections—an area difficult to cross even on foot. I eventually settled on the hillock of a very knowledgeable old man, the head of a homestead of some hundred and forty people, all of whom were either his close relatives or their wives and children. Like the other elders of the vicinity, the old man spent most of his time performing ceremonies seldom seen these days in the more accessible parts of the tribe. I was delighted. Soon there would be three months of enforced isolation and leisure, between the harvest that takes place just before the rising of the swamps and the clearing of new farms when the water goes down. Then, I thought, they would have even more time to perform ceremonies and explain them to me.

I was quite mistaken. Most of the ceremonies demanded the presence of elders from several homesteads. As the swamps rose, the old men found it too difficult to walk from one homestead to the next, and the ceremonies gradually ceased. As the swamps rose even higher, all activities but one came to an end.

The women brewed beer from maize and millet. Men, women, and children sat on their hillocks and drank it.

People began to drink at dawn. By midmorning the whole homestead was singing, dancing, and drumming. When it rained, people had to sit inside their huts: there they drank and sang or they drank and told stories. In any case, by noon or before, I either had to join the party or retire to my own hut and my books. "One does not discuss serious matters when there is beer. Come, drink with us." Since I lacked their capacity for the thick native beer, I spent more and more time with *Hamlet*. Before the end of the second month, grace descended on me. I was quite sure that *Hamlet* had only one possible interpretation, and that one universally obvious.

Early every morning, in the hope of having some serious talk before the beer party, I used to call on the old man at his reception hut—a circle of posts supporting a thatched roof above a low mud wall to keep out wind and rain. One day I crawled through the low doorway and found most of the men of the homestead sitting huddled in their ragged cloths on stools, low plank beds, and reclining chairs, warming themselves against the chill of the rain around a smoky fire. In the center were three pots of beer. The party had started.

The old man greeted me cordially. "Sit down and drink." I accepted a large calabash full of beer, poured some into a small drinking gourd, and tossed it down. Then I poured some more into the same gourd for the man second in seniority to my host before I handed my calabash over to a young man for further distribution. Important people shouldn't ladle beer themselves.

"It is better like this," the old man said, looking at me approvingly and plucking at the thatch that had caught in my hair. "You should sit and drink with us more often. Your servants tell me that when you are not with us, you sit inside your hut looking at a paper."

The old man was acquainted with four kinds of "papers": tax receipts, bride price receipts, court fee receipts, and letters. The messenger who brought him letters from the chief used them mainly as a badge of office, for he always knew what was in them and told the old man. Personal letters for the few who had relatives in the government or mission stations were kept until someone went to a large market where there was a letter writer and reader. Since my arrival, letters were brought to me to be read. A few men also brought me bride price receipts, privately, with requests to change the figures to a higher sum. I found moral arguments were of no avail, since in-laws are fair game, and the technical hazards of forgery difficult to explain to an illiterate people. I did not wish them to think me silly enough to look at any such papers for days on end, and I hastily explained that my "paper" was one of the "things of long ago" of my country.

"Ah," said the old man. "Tell us."

I protested that I was not a storyteller. Story telling is a skilled art among them; their standards are high, and the audiences critical—and vocal in their criticism. I protested in vain. This morning they wanted to hear a story while they drank. They threatened to tell me no more stories until I told them one of mine. Finally, the old man promised that no one would criticize my style "for we know you are struggling with our language." "But," put in one of the elders, "you must explain what we do not understand, as we do when we tell you our stories." Realizing that here was my chance to prove *Hamlet* universally intelligible, I agreed.

The old man handed me some more beer to help me on with my storytelling. Men filled their long wooden pipes and knocked coals from the fire to place in the pipe bowls; then, puffing contentedly, they sat back to listen. I began in the proper style, "Not yesterday, not yesterday, but long ago, a thing occurred. One night three men were keeping watch outside the homestead of the great chief, when suddenly they saw the former chief approach them."

"Why was he no longer their chief?"

"He was dead," I explained. "That is why they were troubled and afraid when they saw him."

"Impossible," began one of the elders, handing his pipe on to his neighbor, who interrupted, "Of course it wasn't the dead chief. It was an omen sent by a witch. Go on."

Slightly shaken, I continued. "One of these three was a man who knew things"—the closest translation for scholar, but unfortunately it also meant witch. The second elder looked triumphantly at the first. "So he spoke to the dead chief saying, 'Tell us what we must do so you may rest in your grave,' but the dead chief did not answer. He vanished, and they could see him no more. Then the man who knew things—his name was Horatio—said this event was the affair of the dead chief's son, Hamlet."

There was a general shaking of heads round the circle. "Had the dead chief no living brothers? Or was this son the chief?"

"No," I replied. "That is, he had one living brother who became the chief when the elder brother died."

The old men muttered: such omens were matters for chiefs and elders, not for youngsters; no good could come of going behind a chief's back; clearly Horatio was not a man who knew things.

"Yes, he was," I insisted, shooing a chicken away from my beer. "In our country the son is next to the father. The dead chief's younger brother had become the great chief. He had also married his elder brother's widow only about a month after the funeral."

"He did well," the old man beamed and announced to the others, "I told you that if we knew more about Europeans, we would find they really were very like us. In our country also," he added to me, "the younger brother marries the elder brother's widow and becomes the father of his children. Now, if your uncle, who married your widowed mother, is your father's full brother, then he

will be a real father to you. Did Hamlet's father and uncle have one mother?"

His question barely penetrated my mind; I was too upset and thrown too far off balance by having one of the most important elements of *Hamlet* knocked straight out of the picture. Rather uncertainly I said that I thought they had the same mother, but I wasn't sure—the story didn't say. The old man told me severely that these genealogical details made all the difference and that when I got home I must ask the elders about it. He shouted out the door to one of his younger wives to bring his goatskin bag.

Determined to save what I could of the mother motif, I took a deep breath and began again. "The son, Hamlet, was very sad because his mother had married again so quickly. There was no need for her to do so, and it is our custom for a widow not to go to her next husband until she has mourned for two years."

"Two years is too long," objected the wife, who had appeared with the old man's battered goatskin bag. "Who will hoe your farms for you while you have no husband?"

"Hamlet," I retorted without thinking, "was old enough to hoe his mother's farms himself. There was no need for her to remarry." No one looked convinced. I gave up. "His mother and the great chief told Hamlet not to be sad, for the great chief himself would be a father to Hamlet. Furthermore, Hamlet would be the next chief: therefore he must stay to learn the things of a chief. Hamlet agreed to remain, and all the rest went off to drink beer."

While I paused, perplexed at how to render Hamlet's disgusted soliloquy to an audience convinced that Claudius and Gertrude had behaved in the best possible manner, one of the younger men asked me who had married the other wives of the dead chief.

"He had no other wives," I told him.

"But a chief must have many wives! How else can he brew beer and prepare food for all his guests?"

I said firmly that in our country even chiefs had only one wife, that they had servants to do their work, and that they paid them from tax money.

It was better, they returned, for a chief to have many wives and sons who would help him hoe his farms and feed his people; then everyone loved the chief who gave much and took nothing—taxes were a bad thing.

I agreed with the last comment, but for the rest fell back on their favorite way of fobbing off my questions: "That is the way it is done, so that is how we do it."

I decided to skip the soliloquy. Even if Claudius was here thought quite right to marry his brother's widow, there remained the poison motif, and I knew they would disapprove of fratricide. More hopefully I resumed, "That night Hamlet kept watch with the three who had seen his dead father. The dead chief again appeared, and although the others were afraid, Hamlet followed his dead father off to one side. When they were alone, Hamlet's dead father spoke."

"Omens can't talk!" The old man was emphatic.

"Hamlet's dead father wasn't an omen. Seeing him might have been an omen, but he was not." My audience looked as confused as I sounded. "It *was* Hamlet's dead father. It was a thing we call a 'ghost.'" I had to use the English word, for unlike many of the neighboring tribes, these people didn't believe in the survival after death of any individuating part of the personality.

"What is a 'ghost?' An omen?"

"No, a 'ghost' is someone who is dead but who walks around and can talk, and people can hear him and see him but not touch him."

They objected. "One can touch zombis."

"No, no! It was not a dead body the witches had animated to sacrifice and eat. No one else made Hamlet's dead father walk. He did it himself."

"Dead men can't walk," protested my audience as one man.

I was quite willing to compromise. "A 'ghost' is the dead man's shadow."

But again they objected. "Dead men cast no shadows."

"They do in my country," I snapped.

The old man quelled the babble of disbelief that arose immediately and told me with that insincere, but courteous, agreement one extends to the fancies of the young, ignorant, and superstitious, "No doubt in your country the dead can also walk without being zombis." From the depths of his bag he produced a withered fragment of kola nut, bit off one end to show it wasn't poisoned, and handed me the rest as a peace offering.

"Anyhow," I resumed, "Hamlet's dead father said that his own brother, the one who became chief, had poisoned him. He wanted Hamlet to avenge him. Hamlet believed this in his heart, for he did not like his father's brother." I took another swallow of beer. "In the country of the great chief, living in the same homestead, for it was a very large one, was an important elder who was often with the chief to advise and help him. His name was Polonius. Hamlet was courting his daughter, but her father and her brother . . . [I cast hastily about for some tribal analogy] warned her not to let Hamlet visit her when she was alone on her farm, for he would be a great chief and so could not marry her."

"Why not?" asked the wife, who had settled down on the edge of the old man's chair. He frowned at her for asking stupid questions and growled, "They lived in the same homestead."

"That was not the reason," I informed them. "Polonius was a stranger who lived in the homestead because he helped the chief, not because he was a relative."

"Then why couldn't Hamlet marry her?"

"He could have," I explained, "but Polonius didn't think he would. After all, Hamlet was a man of great importance who ought to marry a chief's daughter, for in his country a man could have only one wife. Polonius was afraid that if Hamlet made love to his daughter, then no one else would give a high price for her."

"That might be true," remarked one of the shrewder elders, "but a chief's son would give his mistress's father enough presents and patronage to more than make up the difference. Polonius sounds like a fool to me."

"Many people think he was," I agreed. "Meanwhile Polonius sent his son Laertes off to Paris to learn the things of that country, for it was the homestead of a very great chief indeed. Because he was afraid that Laertes might waste a lot of money on beer and women and gambling, or get into trouble by fighting, he sent one of his servants to Paris secretly, to spy out what Laertes was doing. One day Hamlet came upon Polonius's daughter Ophelia. He behaved so oddly he frightened

her. Indeed"—I was fumbling for words to express the dubious quality of Hamlet's madness—"the chief and many others had also noticed that when Hamlet talked one could understand the words but not what they meant. Many people thought that he had become mad." My audience suddenly became much more attentive. "The great chief wanted to know what was wrong with Hamlet, so he sent for two of Hamlet's age mates [school friends would have taken long explanation] to talk to Hamlet and find out what troubled his heart. Hamlet, seeing that they had been bribed by the chief to betray him, told them nothing. Polonius, however, insisted that Hamlet was mad because he had been forbidden to see Ophelia, whom he loved."

"Why," inquired a bewildered voice, "should anyone bewitch Hamlet on that account?"

"Bewitch him?"

"Yes, only witchcraft can make anyone mad, unless, of course, one sees the beings that lurk in the forest."

I stopped being a storyteller, took out my notebook and demanded to be told more about these two causes of madness. Even while they spoke and I jotted notes, I tried to calculate the effect of this new factor on the plot. Hamlet had not been exposed to the beings that lurk in the forests. Only his relatives in the male line could bewitch him. Barring relatives not mentioned by Shakespeare, it had to be Claudius who was attempting to harm him. And, of course, it was.

For the moment I staved off questions by saying that the great chief also refused to believe that Hamlet was mad for the love of Ophelia and nothing else. "He was sure that something much more important was troubling Hamlet's heart."

"Now Hamlet's age mates," I continued, "had brought with them a famous storyteller. Hamlet decided to have this man tell the chief and all his homestead a story about a man who had poisoned his brother because he desired his brother's wife and wished to be chief himself. Hamlet was sure the great chief could not hear the story without making a sign if he was indeed guilty, and then he would discover whether his dead father had told him the truth."

The old man interrupted, with deep cunning, "Why should a father lie to his son?" he asked.

I hedged: "Hamlet wasn't sure that it really was his dead father." It was impossible to say anything, in that language, about devil-inspired visions.

"You mean," he said, "it actually was an omen, and he knew witches sometimes send false ones. Hamlet was a fool not to go to one skilled in reading omens and divining the truth in the first place. A man-who-sees-the-truth could have told him how his father died, if he really had been poisoned, and if there was witchcraft in it; then Hamlet could have called the elders to settle the matter."

The shrewd elder ventured to disagree. "Because his father's brother was a great chief, one-who-sees-the-truth might therefore have been afraid to tell it. I think it was for that reason that a friend of Hamlet's father—a witch and an elder—sent an omen so his friend's son would know. Was the omen true?"

"Yes," I said, abandoning ghosts and the devil; a witch-sent omen it would have to be. "It was true, for when the storyteller was telling his tale before all the homestead, the great chief rose in fear. Afraid that Hamlet knew his secret he planned to have him killed."

The stage set of the next bit presented some difficulties of translation. I began cautiously. "The great chief told Hamlet's mother to find out from her son what he knew. But because a woman's children are always first in her heart, he had the important elder Polonius hide behind a cloth that hung against the wall of Hamlet's mother's sleeping hut. Hamlet started to scold his mother for what she had done."

There was a shocked murmur from everyone. A man should never scold his mother.

"She called out in fear, and Polonius moved behind the cloth. Shouting, 'A rat!' Hamlet took his machete and slashed through the cloth." I paused for dramatic effect. "He had killed Polonius!"

The old men looked at each other in supreme disgust. "That Polonius truly was a fool and a man who knew nothing! What child would not know enough to shout, 'It's me!'" With a pang, I remembered that these people are ardent hunters, always armed with bow, arrow, and machete; at the first rustle in the grass an arrow is aimed and ready, and the hunter shouts "Game!" If no human voice answers immediately, the arrow speeds on its way. Like a good hunter Hamlet had shouted, "A rat!"

I rushed in to save Polonius's reputation. "Polonius did speak. Hamlet heard him. But he thought it was the chief and wished to kill him earlier that evening. . . ." I broke down, unable to describe to these pagans, who had no belief in individual afterlife, the difference between dying at one's prayers and dying "unhousell'd, disappointed, unaneled."

This time I had shocked my audience seriously. "For a man to raise his hand against his father's brother and the one who has become his father—that is a terrible thing. The elders ought to let such a man be bewitched."

I nibbled at my kola nut in some perplexity, then pointed out that after all the man had killed Hamlet's father.

"No," pronounced the old man, speaking less to me than to the young men sitting behind the elders. "If your father's brother has killed your father, you must appeal to your father's age mates; *they* may avenge him. No man may use violence against his senior relatives." Another thought struck him. "But if his father's brother had indeed been wicked enough to bewitch Hamlet and make him mad that would be a good story indeed, for it would be his fault that Hamlet, being mad, no longer had any sense and thus was ready to kill his father's brother."

There was a murmur of applause. *Hamlet* was again a good story to them, but it no longer seemed quite the same story to me. As I thought over the coming complications of plot and motive, I lost courage and decided to skim over dangerous ground quickly.

"The great chief," I went on, "was not sorry that Hamlet had killed Polonius. It gave him a reason to send Hamlet away, with his two treacherous mates, with letters to a chief of a far country, saying that Hamlet should be killed. But Hamlet changed the writing on their papers, so that the chief killed his age mates instead." I encountered a reproachful glare from one of the men whom I had told undetectable forgery was not merely immoral but beyond human skill. I looked the other way.

"Before Hamlet could return, Laertes came back for his father's funeral. The great chief told him Hamlet had killed Polonius. Laertes swore to kill Hamlet because of this, and because his sister Ophelia, hearing her father had been killed by the man she loved, went mad and drowned in the river."

"Have you already forgotten what we told you?" The old man was reproachful. "One cannot take vengeance on a madman; Hamlet killed Polonius in his madness. As for the girl, she not only went mad, she was drowned. Only witches can make people drown. Water itself can't hurt anything. It is merely something one drinks and bathes in."

I began to get cross. "If you don't like the story, I'll stop."

The old man made soothing noises and himself poured me some more beer. "You tell the story well, and we are listening. But it is clear that the elders of your country have never told you what the story really means. No, don't interrupt! We believe you when you say your marriage customs are different, or your clothes and weapons. But people are the same everywhere; therefore, there are always witches and it is we, the elders, who know how witches work. We told you it was the great chief who wished to kill Hamlet, and now your own words have proved us right. Who were Ophelia's male relatives?"

"There were only her father and her brother." *Hamlet* was clearly out of my hands.

"There must have been many more; this also you must ask of your elders when you get back to your country. From what you tell us, since Polonius was dead, it must have been Laertes who killed Ophelia, although I do not see the reason for it."

We had emptied one pot of beer, and the old men argued the point with slightly tipsy interest. Finally one of them demanded of me, "What did the servant of Polonius say on his return?"

With difficulty I recollected Reynaldo and his mission. "I don't think he did return before Polonius was killed."

"Listen," said the elder, "and I will tell you how it was and how your story will go, then you may tell me if I am right. Polonius knew his son would get into trouble, and so he did. He had many fines to pay for fighting, and debts from gambling. But he had only two ways of getting money quickly. One was to marry off his sister at once, but it is difficult to find a man who will marry a woman desired by the son of a chief. For if the chief's heir commits adultery with your wife, what can you do? Only a fool calls a case against a man who will someday be his judge. Therefore Laertes had to take the second way: he killed his sister by witchcraft, drowning her so he could secretly sell her body to the witches."

I raised an objection. "They found her body and buried it. Indeed Laertes jumped into the grave to see his sister once more—so, you see, the body was truly there. Hamlet, who had just come back, jumped in after him."

"What did I tell you?" The elder appealed to the others. "Laertes was up to no good with his sister's body. Hamlet prevented him, because the chief's heir, like a chief, does not wish any other man to grow rich and powerful. Laertes would be angry, because he would have killed his sister without benefit to himself. In our country he would try to kill Hamlet for that reason. Is this not what happened?"

"More or less," I admitted. "When the great chief found Hamlet was still alive, he encouraged Laertes to try to kill

Hamlet and arranged a fight with machetes between them. In the fight both the young men were wounded to death. Hamlet's mother drank the poisoned beer that the chief meant for Hamlet in case he won the fight. When he saw his mother die of poison, Hamlet, dying, managed to kill his father's brother with his machete."

"You see, I was right!" exclaimed the elder.

"That was a very good story," added the old man, "and you told it with very few mistakes. There was just one more error, at the very end. The poison Hamlet's mother drank was obviously meant for the survivor of the fight, whichever it was. If Laertes had won, the great chief would have poisoned him, for no one would know that he arranged Hamlet's death. Then, too, he need not fear Laertes' witchcraft; it takes a strong heart to kill one's only sister by witchcraft.

"Sometime," concluded the old man, gathering his ragged toga about him, "you must tell us some more stories of your country. We, who are elders, will instruct you in their true meaning, so that when you return to your own land your elders will see that you have not been sitting in the bush, but among those who know things and who have taught you wisdom."

Critical Thinking

1. What attitude did Laura Bohannan have about cross-cultural translation of Shakespeare before visiting the Tiv?

2. What differences in custom and belief hampered her telling of "Hamlet" and how?

3. Was there a difference between Laura Bohannan and the Tiv in terms of what they got out of this experience? Explain.

Create Central

www.mhhe.com/createcentral

Internet References

Hypertext and Ethnography
www.umanitoba.ca/anthropology

International Communication Association
www.icahdq.org

LAURA BOHANNAN is a former professor of anthropology at the University of Illinois, at Chicago.

Bohannan, Laura. From *Natural History*, August/September 1966. Copyright © 1966 by Laura Bohannan. Reprinted by permission of the author.

Article   Prepared by: Elvio Angeloni, *Pasadena City College*

Strong Language Lost in Translation: You Talkin' to Me?

CAROLINE WILLIAMS

Learning Outcomes

After reading this article, you will be able to:

- Discuss body language in terms of what it can actually tell us about a person.

- Discuss the relationship between body language and sexual attraction.

- Discuss the ways in which body language can be used to increase success and influence how we feel.

When Tom Cruise and Katie Holmes announced their divorce last year, tabloid journalists fell over themselves to point out that they had seen it coming. "Just look at their body language!" the headlines screamed, above shots of Holmes frowning while holding Cruise at arm's length. "Awkward!" And when Barack Obama lost last year's first US presidential debate to Republican nominee Mitt Romney, some commentators blamed it on his "low-energy" body language and tendency to look down and purse his lips, which made him come across as "lethargic and unprepared."

Popular culture is full of such insights. After all, it is fun to speculate on the inner lives of the great and the good. But anyone with a sceptical or logical disposition cannot fail to notice the thumping great elephant in the room—the assumption that we can read a person's thoughts and emotions by watching how they move their body. With so many myths surrounding the subject, it is easy to think we understand the coded messages that others convey, but what does science have to say about body language? Is there anything more in it than entertainment value? If so, which movements and gestures speak volumes and which are red herrings? And, knowing this, can we actually alter our own body language to manipulate how others perceive us?

A good place to start looking for answers is the oft-quoted statistic that 93 percent of our communication is non-verbal, with only 7 percent based on what we are actually saying. This figure came from research in the late 1960s by Albert Mehrabian, a social psychologist at the University of California, Los Angeles. He found that when the emotional message conveyed by tone of voice and facial expression differed from the word being spoken (for example, saying the word "brute" in a positive tone and with a smile), people tended to believe the non-verbal cues over the word itself. From these experiments. Mehrabian calculated that perhaps only 7 percent of the emotional message comes from the words we use, with 38 percent coming from tone and the other 55 percent from non-verbal cues.

Mehrabian has spent much of the past four-and-a-bit decades pointing out that he never meant this formula to be taken as some kind of gospel and that it only applies to very specific circumstances—when someone is talking about their likes and dislikes. He now says that "unless a communicator is talking about their feelings or attitudes, these equations are not applicable" and that he cringes every times he hears his theory applied to communication in general.

So the oldest stat in the body language book isn't quite what it seems, and the man who came up with the formula would like everyone to please stop going on about it. After all, if we really could understand 93 percent of what people are saying without recourse to words, we wouldn't need to learn foreign languages and no one would ever get away with a lie.

Clearly, people can lie successfully. And, generally, though it is useful to lie occasionally, we would rather that others could not. Which is why a lot of the interest in body language concerns detecting lies. Legend has it that liars give themselves away with physical "tells", such as looking to the right, fidgeting, holding their own hands or scratching their nose. How much of this stacks up?

The first item is easy to dispatch. A study published last year, the first to scientifically test the "liars look right" assertion, found no evidence to back it up. A team led by psychologist Richard Wiseman from the University of Hertfordshire in Hatfield, UK, observed the eye movements of volunteers telling lies in lab-based experiments. They also studied footage of people at police press conferences for missing persons, where some of the emotional pleas for information came from individuals who turned out to be involved in the disappearance. In neither case did the liars look to the right any more than in other directions (*PLoS One,* vol. 7, p. e40259).

As for other tells, a meta-analysis of more than 100 studies found that the only bodily signs found in liars significantly more often than in truth-tellers were dilated pupils and certain kinds of fidgeting—fiddling with objects and scratching, but not rubbing their face or playing with their hair. The best way to spot a liar, the study found, was not to watch a person's body language but to listen to what they were saying. Liars tended to talk with a higher-pitched voice, gave fewer details in their accounts of events, were more negative and tended to repeat words.

Overall, the researchers concluded, subjective measures—or a gut feeling—might be more effective for lie detection than any available scientific measure. The problem with relying on body language is that while liars may be slightly more likely to exhibit a few behaviors, people who are telling the truth do the same things. In fact, the signals you might think of as red flags for lying, like fidgeting and avoiding eye contact, tend to be signs of emotional discomfort in general, and a non-liar is more likely to express them under the pressure of questioning. This is perhaps why, despite having a vested interest in spotting liars, we are generally pretty bad at it. In fact, US psychologist Paul Ekman has found that most people perform no better than would be expected by chance. And the success rate of judges, police, forensic psychiatrists, and FBI agents is only marginally higher.

So it might be best not to go around accusing people of lying based on their body language. And there are lots of other examples in which our preconceptions of non-verbal communication are off-beam or even totally misleading. Take crossed arms. Most people believe that when someone folds their arms they are being defensive or trying to fend off another individual or their opinions. This may be true. "But the same arm-cross can mean the opposite if the torso is super-erect, bent back somewhat—then it conveys invulnerability," says David McNeill, who studies gestures at the University of Chicago. Besides, an arm crosser might simply be cold, trying to get comfortable, or just lacking pockets.

McNeill is also not convinced by claims trotted out by public-speaking consultants about the importance of hand gestures. It is often said, for example, that "steepling" your fingers, makes you look authoritative and an open hand signals honesty. He says that these are examples of metaphorical gestures that have the meanings that people in management perceive, but they are not limited to these meanings. In other words, these well-known "rules" of body language are arbitrary. An open hand, for example might be a metaphor for trustworthiness, but it could just as easily signal holding the weight of something. The gesture is ambiguous without context and cues from spoken language.

So far, our scientific approach has provided little support for those who claim to speak fluent body-ese, but it turns out there are some gestures everyone understands. At the 2008 Olympic and Paralympic Games, athletes from all cultures made the same postures when they won: arms up in a high V, with the chin raised. The same was true for athletes who had been blind from birth, suggesting that the victory pose is innate, not learned by observation. Defeat postures seemed to be universal too. Almost everyone hunches over with slumped shoulders when they lose.

In fact, if you are hunting for signs of victory or defeat, the body may be a better place to look than the face. Hillel Aviezer at Princeton University and colleagues revealed last year that the facial expressions of professional tennis players when they won or lost an important point were so similar that people struggled to tell them apart. However, the body language was easy to read even when the face was blanked out (*Science,* vol. 338, p. 1225).

Other recent studies indicate that we can glean important clues about people from the way they move. Men judge a woman's walk and dance as significantly sexier when she is in the most fertile part of her menstrual cycle, suggesting that a woman's body language sends out the message that she is ready to mate, whether or not she—or the men around her—realise it. Meanwhile, women and heterosexual men rate the dances of stronger men more highly than those of weaker men, which might be an adaptation for women to spot good mates and men to assess potential opponents.

Using body language to assess sexual attraction can be risky, though. Karl Grammer at the University of Vienna in Austria found support for the popular notion that women signal interest in a man by flipping their hair, tidying their clothes, nodding, and making eye contact. But he also discovered that they make the same number of encouraging signals in the first minute of meeting a man whether they fancy him or not. Such flirting is only a sign of real interest if it keeps going after the first four minutes or so. Grammer interprets this as women using body language to keep a man talking until they can work out whether he is worth getting to know.

Even when there is general agreement about how to interpret body language, we can be wrong, as has been revealed in new research on gait. Psychologist John Thoresen at the University of Durham, UK, filmed people walking and then converted the images to point-light displays to highlight the moving limbs while removing distracting information about body shape. He found that almost everyone judged a swaggering walk to signal an adventurous, extroverted, warm, and trustworthy person. A slow, loose and relaxed walk, on the other hand, was associated with a calm, unflappable personality. However, when the researchers compared the actual personalities of the walkers to the assumptions other people made about them, they found no correlation (*Cognition,* vol. 124, p. 2621).

Arguably, it doesn't really matter what your body language actually reveals about you. What matters is what other people think it is telling them. So can it be faked?

Fake It to Make It

Thoresen says that it should certainly be possible to fake a confident walk. "I have no data to back this up," he says, "but I do believe people can be trained to change perceived personality." There are other corporeal tricks that may help in impression management, too. For example, people in job interviews who sit still, hold eye contact, smile, and nod along with the conversation are more likely to be offered a job. Those whose gaze wanders or who avoid eye contact, keep their head still and don't change their expression much are more likely to be rejected. If it doesn't come naturally, consciously adopting a confident strut, a smile and nod and some extra eye contact probably won't hurt—unless you overdo it and come across as a bit scary.

Faking calmness and confidence may change the way others perceive us, but psychologist Dana Carney at the University of California, Berkeley, believes that it can do far more than that. She says we can use our body language to change ourselves. Carney and her colleagues asked volunteers to hold either a "high-power" or "low-power" pose for two minutes. The former were expansive, including sitting with legs on a desk and hands behind the head and standing with legs apart and hands on hips, while the latter involved hunching and taking up little space. Afterward, they played a gambling game where the odds of winning were 50:50, and the researchers took saliva samples to test the levels of testosterone and cortisol—the "power" and stress hormones, respectively—in their bodies. Those who had held high-power poses were significantly more likely to gamble than those who held low-power poses (86 percent compared with 60 percent). Not only that, willingness to gamble was linked to physiological changes. High-power posers had a 20 percent increase in testosterone and a 25 percent decrease in cortisol, while low-power posers showed a 10 percent decrease in testosterone and a 15 percent increase in cortisol (*Psychological Science,* vol. 21, p. 1463).

"We showed that you can actually change your physiology," says Carney. "This goes beyond just emotion—there is something deeper happening here." The feeling of power is not just psychological: increased testosterone has been linked with increased pain tolerance, so power posing really can make us more powerful.

And this is not the only way body language can influence how you feel. Carney points to studies showing that sitting up straight leads to positive emotions, while sitting with hunched shoulders leads to feeling down. There is also plenty of evidence that faking a smile makes you feel happier, while frowning has the opposite effect. In fact, there is evidence that people who have Botox injections that prevent them from frowning feel generally happier.

Despite these interesting results, if science has shown us anything it is that we should always question our preconceptions about body language. Even when people from diverse cultures are in agreement about the meaning of a particular movement or gesture, we may all be wrong. As the evidence accumulates, there could come a time when we can tailor our body language to skillfully manipulate the messages we send out about ourselves. For now, at least our popular conceptions can be modified with a little evidence-based insight. Or as Madonna almost put it: "Don't just stand there, let's get to it, strike a pose. There's something to it."

Critical Thinking

1. Discuss the source of the notion that 93 percent of our communications is non-verbal, with only 7 percent based on what we are actually saying. What is the truth of the matter?

2. Discuss the evidence regarding the various methods proposed for detecting lies.

3. Discuss the meaning of such body language as arm-crossing, arms up in a high V, defeat postures, and facial expression when losing or winning.

4. What is the evidence regarding body language and sexual attraction?

5. Is there any relationship between the way a person walks and one's personality?

6. How can one increase the likelihood of a successful job interview?

7. Discuss the evidence for the idea that body language can influence how you feel.

Create Central

www.mhhe.com/createcentral

Internet References

Center for Nonverbal Studies
    www.library.kent.edu/resource.php?id = 2800
Nonverbal Behavior
    www.usal.es/~nonverbal/researchcenters.htm

CAROLINE WILLIAMS is a writer based in Surrey, UK.

Article   Prepared by: Elvio Angeloni, *Pasadena City College*

Vanishing Languages

Russ Rymer

Learning Outcomes

After reading this article, you will be able to:

- Explain the importance of the variety of human languages in today's world.
- Discuss the different ways in which languages highlight the varieties of human experience.

Tuvan
The Compassion of Khoj Özeeri

One morning in early fall Andrei Mongush and his parents began preparations for supper, selecting a black-faced, fat-tailed sheep from their flock and rolling it onto its back on a tarp outside their livestock paddock. The Mongush family's home is on the Siberian taiga, at the edge of the endless steppes, just over the horizon from Kyzyl, the capital of the Republic of Tuva, in the Russian Federation. They live near the geographic center of Asia, but linguistically and personally, the family inhabits a borderland, the frontier between progress and tradition. Tuvans are historically nomadic herders, moving their *aal*—an encampment of yurts—and their sheep and cows and reindeer from pasture to pasture as the seasons progress. The elder Mongushes, who have returned to their rural aal after working in the city, speak both Tuvan and Russian. Andrei and his wife also speak English, which they are teaching themselves with pieces of paper labeled in English pasted onto seemingly every object in their modern kitchen in Kyzyl. They work as musicians in the Tuvan National Orchestra, an ensemble that uses traditional Tuvan instruments and melodies in symphonic arrangements. Andrei is a master of the most characteristic Tuvan music form: throat singing, or *khöömei*.

When I ask university students in Kyzyl what Tuvan words are untranslatable into English or Russian, they suggest khöömei, because the singing is so connected with the Tuvan environment that only a native can understand it, and also *khoj özeeri*, the Tuvan method of killing a sheep. If slaughtering livestock can be seen as part of humans' closeness to animals, khoj özeeri represents an unusually intimate version. Reaching through an incision in the sheep's hide, the slaughterer severs a vital artery with his fingers, allowing the animal to quickly slip away without alarm, so peacefully that one must check its eyes to see if it is dead. In the language of the Tuvan people, khoj özeeri means not only slaughter but also kindness, humaneness, a ceremony by which a family can kill, skin, and butcher a sheep, salting its hide and preparing its meat and making sausage with the saved blood and cleansed entrails so neatly that the whole thing can be accomplished in two hours (as the Mongushes did this morning) in one's good clothes without spilling a drop of blood. Khoj özeeri implies a relationship to animals that is also a measure of a people's character. As one of the students explained, "If a Tuvan killed an animal the way they do in other places"—by means of a gun or knife—"they'd be arrested for brutality."

Tuvan is one of the many small languages of the world. The Earth's population of seven billion people speaks roughly 7,000 languages, a statistic that would seem to offer each living language a healthy one million speakers, if things were equitable. In language, as in life, things aren't. Seventy-eight percent of the world's population speaks the 85 largest languages, while the 3,500 smallest languages share a mere 8.25 million speakers. Thus, while English has 328 million first-language speakers, and Mandarin 845 million, Tuvan speakers in Russia number just 235,000. Within the next century, linguists think, nearly half of the world's current stock of languages may disappear. More than a thousand are listed as critically or severely endangered—teetering on the edge of oblivion.

In an increasingly globalized, connected, homogenized age, languages spoken in remote places are no longer protected by national borders or natural boundaries from the languages that dominate world communication and commerce. The reach of Mandarin and English and Russian and Hindi and Spanish and Arabic extends seemingly to every hamlet, where they compete with Tuvan and Yanomami and Altaic in a house-to-house battle. Parents in tribal villages often encourage their children to move away from the insular language of their forebears and toward languages that will permit greater education and success.

Who can blame them? The arrival of television, with its glamorized global materialism, its luxury-consumption pros-elytizing, is even more irresistible. Prosperity, it seems, speaks English. One linguist, attempting to define what a language is, famously (and humorously) said that a language is a dia-lect with an army. He failed to note that some armies are better equipped than others. Today any language with a television sta-tion and a currency is in a position to obliterate those without, and so residents of Tuva must speak Russian and Chinese if they hope to engage with the surrounding world. The incursion of dominant Russian into Tuva is evident in the speaking competencies of the generation of Tuvans who grew up in the mid-20th century, when it was the fashion to speak, read, and write in Russian and not their native tongue.

Yet Tuvan is robust relative to its frailest counterparts, some of which are down to a thousand speakers, or a mere handful, or even one individual. Languages like Wintu, a native tongue in California, or Siletz Dee-ni, in Oregon, or Amurdak, an Aboriginal tongue in Australia's Northern Territory, retain only one or two fluent or semifluent speakers. A last speaker with no one to talk to exists in unspeakable solitude.

Increasingly, as linguists recognize the magnitude of the modern language die-off and rush to catalog and decipher the most vulnerable tongues, they are confronting underlying questions about languages' worth and utility. Does each language have boxed up within it some irreplaceable beneficial knowledge? Are there aspects of cultures that won't survive if they are translated into a dominant language? What unexpected insights are being lost to the world with the collapse of its linguistic variety?

Fortunately, Tuvan is not among the world's endangered languages, but it could have been. Since the breakup of the Soviet Union, the language has stabilized. It now has a well-equipped army—not a television station, yet, or a currency, but a newspaper and a respectable 264,000 total speakers (including some in Mongolia and China). Yet Tofa, a neighboring Siberian language, is down to some 30 speakers. Tuvan's importance to our understanding of disappearing languages lies in another question linguists are struggling to answer: What makes one language succeed while another dwindles or dies?

Aka
The Respect of Mucrow

I witnessed the heartrending cost of broken languages among the Aka people in Palizi, a tiny, rustic hamlet perched on a mountainside in Arunachal Pradesh, India's rugged northeastern most state. It is reachable by a five-hour drive through palm and hardwood jungles on single-track mountain roads. Its one main street is lined with unpainted board-faced houses set on stilts and roofed with thatch or metal. Villagers grow their own rice, yams, spinach, oranges, and ginger; slaughter their own hogs and goats; and build their own houses. The tribe's isolation has bred a radical self-sufficiency, evidenced in an apparent lack of an Aka word for job, in the sense of salaried labor.

The Aka measure personal wealth in mithan, a breed of Himalayan cattle. A respectable bride price in Palizi, for instance, is expressed as eight mithan. The most cherished Aka possession is the precious *tradzy* necklace—worth two mithan—made from yellow stones from the nearby river, which is passed down to their children. The yellow stones for the tradzy necklaces can no longer be found in the river, and so the only way to have a precious necklace is to inherit one.

Speaking Aka—or any language—means immersing oneself in its character and concepts. "I'm seeing the world through the looking glass of this language," said Father Vijay D'Souza, who was running the Jesuit school in Palizi at the time of my visit. The Society of Jesus established the school in part because it

was concerned about the fragility of the Aka language and culture and wanted to support them (though classes are taught in English). D'Souza is from southern India, and his native language is Konkani. When he came to Palizi in 1999 and began speaking Aka, the language transformed him.

"It alters your thinking, your worldview," he told me one day in his headmaster's office, as children raced to classes through the corridor outside. One small example: *mucrow*. A similar word in D'Souza's native language would be an insult, meaning "old man." In Aka "mucrow" means something more. It is a term of respect, deference, endearment. The Aka might address a woman as mucrow to indicate her wisdom in civic affairs, and, says D'Souza, "an Aka wife will call her husband mucrow, even when he's young," and do so affectionately.

American linguists David Harrison and Greg Anderson have been coming to Arunachal Pradesh to study its languages since 2008. They are among the scores of linguists worldwide engaged in the study of vanishing languages. Some have academic and institutional affiliations (Harrison and Anderson are both connected with National Geographic's Enduring Voices Project), while others may work for Bible societies that translate Scripture into new tongues. The authoritative index of world languages is *Ethnologue,* maintained by SIL International, a faith-based organization. The researchers' intent may be hands-off, to record a grammar and lexicon before a language is lost or contaminated, or it may be interventionist, to develop a written accompaniment for the oral language, compile a dictionary, and teach native speakers to write.

Linguists have identified a host of language hotspots (analogous to biodiversity hotspots) that have both a high level of linguistic diversity and a high number of threatened languages. Many of these are in the world's least reachable, and often least hospitable, places—like Arunachal Pradesh. Aka and its neighboring languages have been protected because Arunachal Pradesh has long been sealed off to outsiders as a restricted border region. Even other Indians are not allowed to cross into the region without federal permission, and so its fragile microcultures have been spared the intrusion of immigrant labor, modernization—and linguists. It has been described as a black hole of linguistics because its incredible language variety remains so little explored.

Much of public life in Palizi is regulated through the repetition of mythological stories used as forceful fables to prescribe behavior. Thus a money dispute can draw a recitation about a spirit whose daughters are eaten by a crocodile, one by one, as they cross the river to bring him dinner in the field. He kills the crocodile, and a priest promises to bring the last daughter back to life but overcharges so egregiously that the spirit seeks revenge by becoming a piece of ginger that gets stuck in the greedy priest's throat.

Such stories were traditionally told by the elders in a highly formal version of Aka that the young did not yet understand and according to certain rules, among them this: Once an elder begins telling a story, he cannot stop until the story is finished. As with linguistic literacy, disruption is disaster. Yet Aka's young people no longer follow their elders in learning the formal version of the language and the stories that have governed daily life. Even in this remote region, young people are seduced away from their mother tongue by Hindi on the television and

English in the schools. Today Aka's speakers number fewer than 2,000, few enough to put it on the endangered list.

One night in Palizi, Harrison, Anderson, an Indian linguist named Ganesh Murmu, and I sat cross-legged around the cooking fire at the home of Pario Nimasow, a 25-year-old teacher at the Jesuit school. A Palizi native, Nimasow loved his Aka culture even as he longed to join the outside world. In his sleeping room in an adjacent hut was a television waiting for the return of electricity, which had been out for many months thanks to a series of landslides and transformer malfunctions. After dinner Nimasow disappeared for a moment and came back with a soiled white cotton cloth, which he unfolded by the flickering light of the cooking fire. Inside was a small collection of ritual items: a tiger's jaw, a python's jaw, the sharp-toothed mandible of a river fish, a quartz crystal, and other objects of a shaman's sachet. This sachet had belonged to Nimasow's father until his death in 1991.

"My father was a priest," Nimasow said, "and his father was a priest." And now? I asked. Was he next in line? Nimasow stared at the talismans and shook his head. He had the kit, but he didn't know the chants; his father had died before passing them on. Without the words, there was no way to bring the artifacts' power to life.

Linguistics has undergone two great revolutions in the past 60 years, on seemingly opposite ends of the discipline. In the late 1950s Noam Chomsky theorized that all languages were built on an underlying universal grammar embedded in human genes. A second shift in linguistics—an explosion of interest in small and threatened languages—has focused on the variety of linguistic experience. Field linguists like David Harrison are more interested in the idiosyncrasies that make each language unique and the ways that culture can influence a language's form. As Harrison points out, some 85 percent of languages have yet to be documented. Understanding them can only enrich our comprehension of what is universal to all languages.

Different languages highlight the varieties of human experience, revealing as mutable aspects of life that we tend to think of as settled and universal, such as our experience of time, number, or color. In Tuva, for example, the past is always spoken of as ahead of one, and the future is behind one's back. "We could never say, I'm looking forward to doing something," a Tuvan told me. Indeed, he might say, "I'm looking forward to the day before yesterday." It makes total sense if you think of it in a Tuvan sort of way: If the future were ahead of you, wouldn't it be in plain view?

Smaller languages often retain remnants of number systems that may predate the adoption of the modern world's base-ten counting system. The Pirahã, an Amazonian tribe, appear to have no words for any specific numbers at all but instead get by with relative words such as "few" and "many." The Pirahã's lack of numerical terms suggests that assigning numbers may be an invention of culture rather than an innate part of human cognition. The interpretation of color is similarly varied from language to language. What we think of as the natural spectrum of the rainbow is actually divided up differently in different tongues, with many languages having more or fewer color categories than their neighbors.

Language shapes human experience—our very cognition—as it goes about classifying the world to make sense of the circumstances at hand. Those classifications may be broad—Aka divides the animal kingdom into animals that are eaten and those that are not—or exceedingly fine-tuned. The Todzhu reindeer herders of southern Siberia have an elaborate vocabulary for reindeer; an *iyi düktüg myiys,* for example, is a castrated former stud in its fourth year.

If Aka, or any language, is supplanted by a new one that's bigger and more universally useful, its death shakes the foundations of the tribe. "Aka is our identity," a villager told me one day as we walked from Palizi down the path that wound past the rice fields to the forests by the river. "Without it, we are the general public." But should the rest of the world mourn too? The question would not be an easy one to frame in Aka, which seems to lack a single term for world. Aka might suggest an answer, though, one embodied in the concept of mucrow—a regard for tradition, for long-standing knowledge, for what has come before, a conviction that the venerable and frail have something to teach the callow and the strong that they would be lost without.

Critical Thinking

1. In what respects does the Mongush family "inhabit a borderland"?

2. Why are some Tuvan words untranslatable?

3. How many languages are there in the world? Why are so many of them disappearing?

4. What are some of the underlying questions about languages' worth and utility? How is the language of Tuvan important to our understanding of disappearing languages?

5. In what ways does the Aka language reflect Aka culture?

6. What is the difference between a linguist's "hands-off" approach versus an "interventionist approach"?

7. In what respects is the Aka language located in a "language hotspot"? How have they been protected?

8. Why are Aka youth no longer learning the stories that have governed daily life?

9. How does the author illustrate the fact that different languages highlight the varieties of human experience?

Create Central

www.mhhe.com/createcentral

Internet References

Intute: Anthropology
www.intute.ac.uk/anthropology

RUSS RYMER is the author of *Genie: A Scientific Tragedy,* the story of an abused child whose case helped scientists study the acquisition of language.

Article   Prepared by: Elvio Angeloni, *Pasadena City College*

My Two Minds

CATHERINE DE LANGE

Learning Outcomes

After reading this article, you will be able to:

- Discuss the origins of human linguistic diversity.
- Discuss the advantages of being bilingual.

When I was just a newborn baby, my mother gazed down at me in her hospital bed and did something that was to permanently change the way my brain developed. Something that would make me better at learning, multitasking and solving problems. Eventually, it might even protect my brain against the ravages of old age. Her trick? She started speaking to me in French.

At the time, my mother had no idea that her actions would give me a cognitive boost. She is French and my father English, so they simply felt it made sense to raise me and my brothers as bilingual. Yet as I've grown up, a mass of research has emerged to suggest that speaking two languages may have profoundly affected the way I think.

Cognitive enhancement is just the start. According to some studies, my memories, values, even my personality, may change depending on which language I happen to be speaking. It is almost as if the bilingual brain houses two separate minds. All of which highlights the fundamental role of language in human thought. "Bilingualism is quite an extraordinary microscope into the human brain," says neuroscientist Laura Ann Petitto of Gallaudet University in Washington DC.

The view of bilingualism has not always been this rosy. For many parents like mine, the decision to raise children speaking two languages was controversial. Since at least the 19th century, educators warned that it would confuse the child, making them [sic] unable to learn either language properly. At best, they thought the child would become a jack-of-all-trades and master of none. At worst, they suspected it might hinder other aspects of development, resulting in a lower IQ.

These days, such fears seem unjustified. True, bilingual people tend to have slightly smaller vocabularies in each language than their monolingual peers, and they are sometimes slower to reach for the right word when naming objects. But a key study in the 1960s by Elizabeth Peal and Wallace Lambert at McGill University in Montreal, Canada, found that the ability to speak two languages does not stunt overall development. On the contrary, when controlling for other factors which might also affect performance, such as socioeconomic status and education, they found that bilinguals outperformed monolinguals in 15 verbal and non-verbal tests (*Psychological Monographs,* vol 76, no 27, p. 1).

Unfortunately, their findings were largely overlooked. Although a trickle of research into the benefits of bilingualism followed their study, most researchers and educators continued to cling to the old ideas. It is only within the last few years that bilingualism has received the attention it deserves. "For 30 years I've been sitting in my little dark room doing my thing and suddenly in the last five years it's like the doors have swung open," says Ellen Bialystok, a psychologist at York University in Toronto, Canada.

In part, the renewed interest comes from recent technological developments in neuroscience, such as functional near-infrared spectroscopy (fNIRS)—a form of brain imaging that acts as a silent and portable monitor, peering inside the brains of babies as they sit on their parents' laps. For the first time, researchers can watch young babies' brains in their initial encounters with language.

Using this technique, Petitto and her colleagues discovered a profound difference between babies brought up speaking either one or two languages. According to popular theory, babies are born "citizens of the world," capable of discriminating between the sounds of any language. By the time they are a year old, however, they are thought to have lost this ability, homing in exclusively on the sounds of their mother tongue. That seemed to be the case with monolinguals, but Petitto's study found that bilingual children still showed increased neural activity in response to completely unfamiliar languages at the end of their first year (*Brain and Language,* vol 121, p. 130).

She reckons the bilingual experience "wedges open" the window for learning language. Importantly, the children still reached the same linguistic milestones, such as their first word, at roughly the same time as monolingual babies, supporting the idea that bilingualism can invigorate rather than hinder a child's development. This seems to help people like me acquire new languages throughout our lives. "It's almost like the monolingual brain is on a diet, but the bilingual brain shows us the full, plump borders of the language tissue that are available," says Petitto.

Indeed, the closer the researchers looked, the more benefits they discovered, some of which span a broad range of skills.

Bialystok first stumbled upon one of these advantages while asking children to spot whether various sentences were grammatically correct. Both monolinguals and bilinguals could see the mistake in phrases such as "apples growed on trees," but differences arose when they considered nonsensical sentences such as "apples grow on noses." The monolinguals, flummoxed by the silliness of the phrase, incorrectly reported an error, whereas the bilinguals gave the right answer (*Developmental Psychology,* vol 24, p. 560).

Bialystok suspected that rather than reflecting expertise in grammar, their performance demonstrated improvement in what is called the brain's "executive system," a broad suite of mental skills that centre on the ability to block out irrelevant information and concentrate on a task at hand. In this case, they were better able to focus on the grammar while ignoring the meaning of words. Sure enough, bilingual kids in subsequent studies aced a range of problems that directly tested the trait. Another executive skill involves the ability to switch between different tasks without becoming confused, and bilinguals are better at these kinds of challenges too. When categorising objects, for instance, they can jump from considering the shape to the colour without making errors (*Bilingualism: Language and Cognition,* vol 13, p. 253).

A Second Viewpoint

These traits are critical to almost everything we do, from reading and mathematics to driving. Improvements therefore result in greater mental flexibility, which may explain why the bilingual people performed so well in Peal and Lambert's tests, says Bialystok.

Its virtues may even extend to our social skills. Paula Rubio-Fernández and Sam Glucksberg, both psychologists at Princeton University, have found that bilinguals are better at putting themselves in other people's shoes to understand their side of a situation. This is because they can more easily block out what they already know and focus on the other viewpoint (*Journal of Experimental Psychology: Learning, Memory and Cognition,* vol 38, p. 211).

So what is it about speaking two languages that makes the bilingual brain so flexible and focused? An answer comes from the work of Viorica Marian at Northwestern University in Evanston, Illinois, and colleagues, who used eye-tracking devices to follow the gaze of volunteers engaged in various activities. In one set-up, Marian placed an array of objects in front of Russian-English bilinguals and asked them to "pick up the marker," for example.

The twist is that the names of some of the objects in the two languages sound the same but have different meanings. The Russian word for stamp sounds like "marker," for instance, which in English can mean *pen.* Although the volunteers never misunderstood the question, the eye-tracker showed that they would quickly glance at the alternative object before choosing the correct one (*Bilingualism: Language and Cognition,* vol 6, p. 97).

This almost-imperceptible gesture gives away an important detail about the workings of the bilingual brain, revealing that the two languages are constantly competing for attention in the back of our minds. As a result, whenever we bilinguals speak, write, or listen to the radio, our brain is busy choosing the right word while inhibiting the same term from the other language. It is a considerable test of executive control—just the kind of cognitive workout, in fact, that is common in many commercial "brain-training" programs, which often require you to ignore distracting information while tackling a task.

It did not take long for scientists to wonder whether these mental gymnastics might help the brain resist the ravages of ageing. After all, there is plenty of evidence to suggest that other forms of brain exercise can create "cognitive reserve," a kind of mental padding that cushions the mind against age-related decline. To find out, Bialystok and her colleagues collected data from 184 people diagnosed with dementia, half of whom were bilingual. The results, published in 2007, were startling—symptoms started to appear in the bilingual people four years later than in their monolingual peers (*Neuropsychologia,* vol 45, p. 459). Three years later, they repeated the study with a further 200 people showing signs of Alzheimer's disease. Again, there was around a five-year delay in the onset of symptoms in bilingual patients (*Neurology,* vol 75, p. 1726). The results held true even after factors such as occupation and education were taken into account. "I was as surprised as anyone that we found such large effects," Bialystok says.

Besides giving us bilinguals a brain boost, speaking a second language may have a profound effect on behaviour.

Neuroscientists and psychologists are coming to accept that language is deeply entwined with thought and reasoning, leading some to wonder whether bilingual people act differently depending on which language they are speaking. That would certainly tally with my experience. People often tell me that I seem different when I speak English compared with when I speak French.

Such effects are hard to characterise, of course, since it is not easy to pull apart the different strands of yourself. Susan Ervin-Tripp, now at the University of California, Berkeley, found an objective way to study the question in the 1960s, when she asked Japanese-English bilinguals to complete a set of unfinished sentences in two separate sessions—first in one language, then the other. She found that her volunteers consistently used very different endings depending on the language. For example, given the sentence "Real friends should" a person using Japanese replied "help each other out," yet in English opted for "be very frank." Overall, the responses seemed to reflect how monolinguals of either language tended to complete the task. The findings led Ervin-Tripp to suggest that bilinguals use two mental channels, one for each language, like two different minds.

Her theory would seem to find support in a number of recent studies. David Luna from Baruch College in New York City and colleagues, for example, recently asked bilingual English-Spanish volunteers to watch TV adverts featuring women—first in one language and then six months later in the other—and then rate the personalities of the characters involved. When the volunteers viewed the ads in Spanish, they tended to rate the women as independent and extrovert, but when they saw the advert in English they described the same characters as hopeless and dependent (*Journal of Consumer Research,* vol 35, p. 279). Another study found that Greek-English bilinguals reported very different emotional reactions to the same story depending on the language—finding themselves "indifferent" to the character in one version, but feeling "concerned" for his progress in the other, for example (*Journal of Multilingual and Multicultural Development,* vol 25, p. 124).

One explanation is that each language brings to mind the values of the culture we experienced while learning it, says Nairán Ramírez-Esparza, a psychologist at the University of Washington in Seattle. She recently asked bilingual Mexicans to rate their personality in English and Spanish questionnaires. Modesty is valued more highly in Mexico than it is in the US, where assertiveness gains respect, and the language of the questions seemed to trigger these differences. When questioned in Spanish, each volunteer was more humble than when the survey was presented in English.

Some of the behavioural switches may be intimately linked to the role of language as a kind of scaffold that supports and structures our memories. Many studies have found that we are more likely to remember an object if we know its name, which may explain why we have so few memories of early childhood. There is even some evidence that the grammar of a language can shape your memory. Lera Boroditsky at Stanford University in California recently found that Spanish speakers are worse at remembering who caused an accident than English speakers, perhaps because they tend to use impersonal phrases like "Se rompió el florero" ("the vase broke itself") that do not state the person behind the event (*Psychonomic Bulletin Review,* vol 18, p. 150).

The result seems to be that a bilingual person's recollections will change depending on the language they are [sic] speaking. In a clever but simple experiment, Marian and Margarita Kaushanskaya, then at Northwestern University, asked Mandarin-English bilinguals a general knowledge question, first in one language then the other. For instance, they were asked to "name a statue of someone standing with a raised arm while looking into the distance." They found people were more likely to recall the Statue of Liberty when asked in English, and a statue of Mao when asked in Mandarin (*Psychonomic Bulletin & Review,* p. 14, vol 925). The same seems to occur when bilinguals recall personal, autobiographical memories. "So childhood memories will come up faster and more often when you are reinstating that language," Marian says.

Despite the recent progress, the researchers may just be seeing the tip of the iceberg when it comes to the impact of bilingualism, and many questions remain. Chief among them will be the question of whether any monolingual person could cash in on the benefits. If so, what better incentive to bolster language education in schools, which is flagging in both the UK and US.

Much has been made of the difficulties of learning a new language later in life, but the evidence so far suggests the effort should pay off. "You can learn another language at any age, you can learn it fluently, and you can see benefits to your cognitive system," says Marian. Bialystok agrees that late language-learners gain an advantage, even if the performance boost is usually less pronounced than in bilingual speakers. "Learn a language at any age, not to become bilingual, but just to remain mentally stimulated," she says. "That's the source of cognitive reserve."

As it is, I'm grateful that particular challenge is behind me. My mother could never have guessed the extent to which her words would change my brain and the way I see my world, but I'm certain it was worth the effort. And for all that I just have to say: Merci!

Critical Thinking

1. What was the view of educators regarding bilingualism from the 19th century until recently?
2. What has recent evidence shown regarding bilinguals?
3. How has new technology sparked renewed interest in this subject?
4. What has been the popular theory regarding babies learning language? How do bilingual babies compare with monolingual babies with respect to acquiring new languages? With respect to spotting grammatical correctness in sentences?
5. What skill differences have been showing up in further tests?
6. In what ways do these skills extend beyond the linguistic?
7. What do such studies reveal about "executive control" in bilinguals?
8. What appears to be the relationship between "gymnastic abilities" and resistance to the ravages of aging?
9. What is the evidence that bilinguals are affected by the language they speak in terms of their values, how they perceive others, and what they remember?
10. Why should people be encouraged to learn a language at any age?

Create Central

www.mhhe.com/createcentral

Internet References

Exploratorium Magazine: "The Evolution of Languages"
www.exploratorium.edu/exploring/language
Linguistic Inquiry and Word Count
www.liwc.net

Unit 3

UNIT

Prepared by: Elvio Angeloni, *Pasadena City College*

The Organization of Society and Culture

Human beings do not interact with one another or think about their world in random fashion. They engage in structured and recurrent physical and mental activities. Such patterns of behavior and thought—referred to here as the organization of society and culture—may be seen in a number of different contexts, from the mating preferences of hunter-gatherer bands to whether a mother breastfeeds her child to the decisions made by neighboring tribes as to whether they shall go to war or establish peaceful relations with each other.

Of special importance are the ways in which people make a living—in other words, the production, distribution, and consumption of goods and services. It is only by knowing the basic subsistence systems that we can hope to gain insight into other levels of social and cultural phenomena, for they are all inextricably bound together. Noting the various aspects of a sociocultural system in harmonious balance, however, does not imply an anthropological seal of approval. To understand infanticide

(killing of the newborn) in the manner that it is practiced among some peoples is neither to condone nor condemn it. The adaptive patterns that have been in existence for a great length of time, such as many of the patterns of hunters and gatherers, probably owe their existence to their contributions to long-term human survival.

Anthropologists, however, are not content with the data derived from their individual experiences with others. On the contrary, personal descriptions must become the basis for sound anthropological theory. Otherwise, they remain meaningless, isolated relics of culture in the manner of museum pieces. In other words, while anthropological accounts of field are to some extent descriptive, they should also serve to challenge both the academic and "commonsense" notions about why people behave and think the way they do. They remind us that assumptions are never really safe and if anthropologists are kept on their toes, it is the field as a whole that benefits.

Article

Prepared by: Elvio Angeloni, *Pasadena City College*

The Evolution of Inequality

DEBORAH ROGERS

Learning Outcomes

After reading this article, you will be able to:

- Discuss the egalitarian nature of our hunter-gatherer ancestors before 5,000 years ago.

- Discuss the transition from egalitarian hunter-gatherer societies to the distinctive inequality that exists in modern times.

Humans lived as egalitarians for tens of thousands of years. As unequal society arose, its instability caused it to spread, argues anthropologist Deborah Rogers.

For 5000 years, humans have grown accustomed to living in societies dominated by the privileged few. But it wasn't always this way. For tens of thousands of years, egalitarian hunter-gatherer societies were widespread. And as a large body of anthropological research shows, long before we organised ourselves into hierarchies of wealth, social status and power, these groups rigorously enforced norms that prevented any individual or group from acquiring more status, authority or resources than others.

Decision-making was decentralised and leadership ad hoc; there weren't any chiefs. There were sporadic hot-blooded fights between individuals, of course, but there was no organised conflict between groups. Nor were there strong notions of private property and therefore any need for territorial defence. These social norms affected gender roles as well; women were important producers and relatively empowered, and marriages were typically monogamous.

Keeping the playing field level was a matter of survival. These small-scale, nomadic foraging groups didn't stock up much surplus food, and given the high-risk nature of hunting—the fact that on any given day or week you may come back empty-handed—sharing and cooperation were required to ensure everyone got enough to eat. Anyone who made a bid for higher status or attempted to take more than their share would be ridiculed or ostracised for their audacity. Suppressing our primate ancestors' dominance hierarchies by enforcing these egalitarian norms was a central adaptation of human evolution, argues social anthropologist Christopher Boehm. It enhanced cooperation and lowered risk as small, isolated bands of humans spread into new habitats and regions across the world, and was likely crucial to our survival and success.

How, then, did we arrive in the age of institutionalised inequality? That has been debated for centuries. Philosopher Jean-Jacques Rousseau reasoned in 1754 that inequality was rooted in the introduction of private property. In the mid-19th century, Karl Marx and Friedrich Engels focused on capitalism and its relation to class struggle. By the late 19th century, social Darwinists claimed that a society split along class lines reflected the natural order of things—as British philosopher Herbert Spencer put it, "the survival of the fittest." (Even into the 1980s there were some anthropologists who held this to be true—arguing that dictators' success was purely Darwinian, providing estimates of the large numbers of offspring sired by the rulers of various despotic societies as support.)

Birth of Hierarchy

But by the mid-20th century a new theory began to dominate. Anthropologists including Julian Steward, Leslie White and Robert Carneiro offered slightly different versions of the following story: Population growth meant we needed more food, so we turned to agriculture, which led to surplus and the need for managers and specialised roles, which in turn led to corresponding social classes. Meanwhile, we began to use up natural resources and needed to venture ever further afield to seek them out. This expansion bred conflict and conquest, with the conquered becoming the underclass.

More recent explanations have expanded on these ideas. One line of reasoning suggests that self-aggrandising individuals who lived in lands of plenty ascended the social ranks by exploiting their surplus—first through feasts or gift-giving, and later by outright dominance. At the group level, argue anthropologists Peter Richerson and Robert Boyd, improved coordination and division of labour allowed more complex societies to outcompete the simpler, more equal societies. From a mechanistic perspective, others argued that once inequality took hold—as when uneven resource-distribution benefited one family more than others—it simply became evermore entrenched. The advent of agriculture and trade resulted in private property, inheritance, and larger trade networks, which perpetuated and compounded economic advantages.

It is not hard to imagine how stratification could arise, or that self-aggrandisers would succeed from time to time. But none of these theories quite explain how those aiming to dominate would have overcome egalitarian norms of nearby communities, or why the earliest hierarchical societies would stop enforcing these norms in the first place. Many theories about the spread of stratified society begin with the idea that inequality is somehow a beneficial cultural trait that imparts efficiencies, motivates innovation and increases the likelihood of survival. But what if the opposite were true?

In a demographic simulation that Omkar Deshpande, Marcus Feldman and I conducted at Stanford University, California, we found that, rather than imparting advantages to the group, unequal access to resources is inherently destabilising and greatly raises the chance of group extinction in stable environments. This was true whether we modelled inequality as a multitiered class society, or as what economists call a Pareto wealth distribution—in which, as with the 1 percent, the rich get the lion's share.

Counterintuitively, the fact that inequality was so destabilising caused these societies to spread by creating an incentive to migrate in search of further resources. The rules in our simulation did not allow for migration to already-occupied locations, but it was clear that this would have happened in the real world, leading to conquests of the more stable egalitarian societies— exactly what we see as we look back in history.

In other words, inequality did not spread from group to group because it is an inherently better system for survival, but because it creates demographic instability, which drives migration and conflict and leads to the cultural—or physical— extinction of egalitarian societies. Indeed, in our future research we aim to explore the very real possibility that natural selection itself operates differently under regimes of equality and inequality. Egalitarian societies may have fostered selection on a group level for cooperation, altruism and low fertility (which leads to a more stable population), while inequality might exacerbate selection on an individual level for high fertility, competition, aggression, social climbing and other selfish traits.

So what can we learn from all this? Although dominance hierarchies may have had their origins in ancient primate social behaviour, we human primates are not stuck with an evolutionarily determined, survival-of-the-fittest social structure. We cannot assume that because inequality exists, it is somehow beneficial. Equality—or inequality—is a cultural choice.

Critical Thinking

1. In what respects were hunter-gatherers egalitarian before 5,000 years ago and why?

2. What have been the various theories of the past that have been put forth to explain inequality? What was the opposing theory developed by the mid-20th century?

3. How did agriculture perpetuate and compound economic advantages for some?

4. Why did inequality spread from group to group in spite of the fact that it is inherently destabilizing?

5. How do egalitarian societies contrast with those with inequality with regard to the process of selection?

6. What can we learn from all of this, according to the author?

Create Central

www.mhhe.com/createcentral

Internet References

Living Links
www.emory.edu/LIVING_LINKS/dewaal.html
Society for Historical Archaelogy
www.sha.org

DEBORAH ROGERS is an affiliated researcher at Stanford University's Institute for Research in the Social Sciences and directs the Initiative for Equality.

Article

Prepared by: Elvio Angeloni, *Pasadena City College*

Meghalaya: Where Women Call the Shots

Many Indian women cry out for equality, but a matrilineal culture thrives with little parallel in the northeast.

SUBIR BHAUMIK

Learning Outcomes

After reading this article, you will be able to:

- Describe the matrilineal kinship system of the tribes of Meghalaya.

- Contrast marriage as a modern institution with traditional practices.

- Discuss the ways in which the political system contrasts with the economic system in Meghalaya.

In a far corner of India, a country where women usually cry out for equality, respect, and protection, there's a state where men are asking for more rights.

Meghalaya—"Home of Clouds"—is picturesque state with its capital Shillong a regional hub for education and the trendsetter for the Westernised culture that's accepted by most tribes in the country's northeast.

The two major tribes of Meghalaya, Khasis and Jaintias, are matrilineal with a vengeance. Children take the mother's surname, daughters inherit the family property with the youngest getting the lion's share, and most businesses are run by women.

Known as the "Khatduh", the youngest daughter anchors the family, looking after elderly parents, giving shelter and care to unmarried brothers and sisters, and watching over property.

The Khasi Social Custom of Lineage Act protects the matrilineal structure.

Some trace the origins of the system to Khasi and Jaintia kings, who preferred to entrust the household to their queens when they went to battle. This custom has continued to provide women the pride of place in the tribal society.

"Matriliny safeguards women from social ostracism when they remarry because their children, no matter who the father was, would be known by the mother's clan name. Even if a woman delivered a child out of wedlock, which is quite common, there is no social stigma attached to the woman in our society," says Patricia Mukhim, a national award-winning social activist who edits the *Shillong Times* newspaper.

Mukhim says her society will not succumb to the dominant patriarchial system in most of India.

"We have interfaced with several cultures and our women have married people from other Indian provinces and from outside India. But very few Khasi women have given up their culture," says Mukhim. "Most have transmitted the culture to their children born out of wedlock with non-Khasis."

Matrilineal Culture

Anirban Roy, a Bengali married to a Jaintia woman whom he met as a fellow student in a veterinary college, says he faced no problem adjusting to the matrilineal culture of his wife's family.

"Everyone in the wife's clan made it a point to come and introduce themselves and invite me to their houses either for lunch or for dinner to know each other better. Whenever we face a problem, the members of my wife's clan rushed to our help," said Roy. "As a groom, I enjoyed great respect and privilege."

But many Khasi and Jaintia men complain, and some formed the equivalent of a "men's liberation group" called Syngkhong Rympei Thymai (SRT) back in 1990.

"Our men now have no roles as fathers or uncles. Since ancient times, fathers have been the protector and bread-earner, but this notion is not so much of a reality in our society now," says Keith Pariat, SRT's founder.

"In our society, there is applause and celebration when a girl is born, but the birth of a boy is just taken in the stride," Pariat says.

Some tribal families have been switching over to patrilieany, where the father assumes leadership of the family, Pariat says. But he admits that such cases are rare.

SRT has only about 3,000 members, but most are silent members who are too nervous to publicly challenge matrilineal traditions of the Khasi-Jaintia society.

"We hope things will change and we will get a more meaningful role to play in our society. But we cannot force a change," says Anthony Kharkhongor, an SRT member.

C Joshua Thomas, regional director of the Indian Council of Social Science Research, says religious beliefs also help perpetuate the matrilineal system. Thomas is based in Shillong and has closely watched the tribal societies in Meghalaya in his long career as a social scientist.

"This system will survive because the people zealously guard this system. It has support from many quarters, including the indigenous religious systems Seng Khasi and also from the mainline Christian churches both from the Catholics and Protestant orders. The NGOs in Meghalaya also support this system," he says.

Khasi-Jaintia women, meanwhile, say the men have enough of a role to play in society—if they want to.

"Even in our matrilineal society, we treat the fathers as the head of the family, and they take important family decisions. Men are given due recognition even in major family decisions," says Iwbih Nylla Tariang, a female employee with Meghalaya's animal husbandry department.

But Tariang is keen that the present matrilineal system stays as is.

"Unlike elsewhere in India, we have followed a unique matrilineal society for centuries. Our society in Meghalaya always gave respect to women. The children taking mother's family name is the biggest respect," she says.

"Disgruntled Individuals"

The social activist Mukhim calls the SRT a "bunch of disgruntled individuals."

"Khasis, as a whole, do not find any problem with matriliny. It is a small group of urban males who seem dissatisfied having to live with the wife's family," Mukhim says.

"Khasi men were known to be polygamous and marriages are brittle. Marriage as an institution came about only after Christianity and is practised only among Christians. Those who follow the indigenous faith, or who are outside the purview of any religion, still practise cohabitation or living together. So our system works."

In India, where women often become victims of "honour killings" if seen with a male from another caste, Khasi-Jaintia women enjoy remarkable social mobility and can accompany any men without taboo.

Unlike elsewhere in India where the bride's family is generally required to pay a dowry to the groom's family, the women of Khasi-Jaintia society do not.

Nor are there any arranged marriages.

Khasi women are enterprising and run small businesses well. In Shillong's oldest market, the Lewduh, women operate almost all businesses.

Many Khasi political leaders are apprehensive about outsiders coming to settle in Meghalaya and marrying local women.

In 2007, the Khasi Hills Autonomous District Council (KHADC), which gives the tribes self-governance, declared a policy of encouraging Khasi women to have more children.

Some Khasi mothers who had given birth to 15 or more offspring were handed out cash rewards.

"We have a lot of land but migrants from other parts of India and neighbouring Bangladesh are coming into Meghalaya in some numbers," says KHADC chief HS Shylla, justifying cash rewards in a country where the federal government advocates strict family planning.

"We may be swamped by them, like neighbouring Tripura or Assam, if we don't grow in numbers."

One crucial area exists, however, where women are not the dominant figures. The Dorbar Shnong—or the grassroots political institution of the tribes—debars women from holding office and remains a male-centric institution.

"Women would be represented at the Dorbar by male members of the family such as their husbands, brothers, or uncles. These days women attend the Dorbar but cannot hold office as executive members, and certainly not as the headman," says Thomas.

The 60-member Meghalaya state assembly also has only four women lawmakers—an unusual situation in a society where social and economic powers rest with females.

"This is one reason why women in Meghalaya have been uncertain about entering electoral politics. There is an inherent feeling that politics is a male domain," says Mukhim.

Critical Thinking

1. Describe the matrilineal social system of the tribes of Meghalaya.
2. Discuss the claims and counterclaims with respect to the discontent expressed by some men.
3. How does marriage as a modern institution contrast with the traditional practice?
4. How does the experience of women in Meghalaya contrast with that of women in the rest of India?

5. Discuss the concerns of Khasi political leaders regarding the influx of outsiders.

6. How does the political system contrast with the economic system in Meghalaya?

Create Central

www.mhhe.com/createcentral

Internet References

Kinship and Social Organization
www.umanitoba.ca/anthropology

Sex and Marriage
http://anthro.palomar.edu/marriage/default.htm

Article

Prepared by: Elvio Angeloni, *Pasadena City College*

Breastfeeding and Culture

KATHERINE DETTWYLER

Learning Outcomes

After reading this article, you will be able to:

- Discuss the benefit of breastfeeding for child, mother, and society.

- Discuss the factors that affect the practices of breastfeeding in various cultures.

In a perfect world—one where child health and cognitive development were optimal—all children would be breast-fed for as long as they wanted. As large-bodied, highly intelligent primates, that would be for a minimum of 2.5 years and as long as 6 or 7 years, or longer. In a perfect world, all mothers would know how to breastfeed and be supported in their efforts to do so by health care providers, spouses, friends, neighbors, co-workers, and the general beliefs of their culture. Breastfeeding is, first and foremost, a way to provide protective immunities and health-promoting factors to children. Breast milk should be the primary source of nutrition for the first two years of life, complemented by appropriate solid foods around six months of age. Breast milk provides important immunities and nutrients, especially for growing brains, for as long as the child is breastfed. It is a source of physical and emotional comfort to a child, and for the mother it is the wellspring of the important mothering hormones, prolactin and oxytocin.

Ordinarily, childbirth is followed by breastfeeding, with its flood of prolactin, the "mothering hormone," and oxytocin, "the hormone of love." Both hormones elicit caretaking, affective, and protective behaviors by the mother towards her child. If the mother does not breastfeed, her body interprets this as "the baby died," and enters a state of hormonal grieving, preparing for a new attempt at reproduction. The mother, however, still has to cope with a newborn, and later a toddler, without the calming and nurturing influence of prolactin and oxytocin.

Like childbirth, however, breastfeeding is influenced by a variety of cultural beliefs, some directly related to breastfeeding itself, and others pertaining to a woman's role in society, to the proper relationship between mother and child, to the proper relationship between mother and father, and even to beliefs about breasts themselves.

One way of thinking about cultural influences on breastfeeding initiation and duration is based on the Demographic Transition, in which societies move from a pre-transition state of high birth and death rates, through a transitional stage of high birth but low death rates (resulting in rapid population growth), and eventually into a post-transition stage of low birth and death rates. Margaret Mead was the first to recognize an "Infant Feeding Transition." A culture begins in a pre-transition state of almost everyone breastfeeding for several years, then moves through a transitional stage of bottle-feeding. Three main forces conspire to move women away from breastfeeding: (1) the separation of their productive labor and their reproductive labor, as societies shift from subsistence-based economies to wage labor-based economies, and/or women are taken away from both productive and reproductive work to be their husband's social partners; (2) increasing confidence in the power of science to provide "better living through chemistry" coupled with decreasing confidence in the ability of women's bodies to function normally, and (3) the rise of commercial interests intent on making a profit by convincing women that breastfeeding is less healthy, difficult, primitive, and/or shameful. The transition is initiated by women with more education and higher incomes turning to shorter and shorter durations of breastfeeding, and eventually only wet-nursing (in previous centuries) or bottle-feeding (in the 20th and 21st centuries) from birth.

As time goes by, women with less education and lower income levels emulate their social superiors and adopt bottle-feeding as well. By the time the last of the lower classes have adopted bottle-feeding as being "modern and scientific," the well-educated upper-class women are returning to breastfeeding, first for short periods, and then for increasing durations. They have moved on to the post-transition stage. The return to breastfeeding by well-educated upper-class women is fueled by several factors, including research during the last few decades clearly documenting the superiority of breastfeeding over formula in terms of maternal and child health and child cognitive development, feminism's insistence that women's reproductive powers are of great value, and a general backlash against the infant formula companies for promoting their products in unethical ways. Primarily, in the United States it has been well-educated middle- and upper-class women who have fought for legislation to protect the rights of mothers to breastfeed in public, and for better maternity care and on-site child care facilities.

In the late 1950s, anthropologist Margaret Mead urged researchers to: "Find out how we can get from the working class mothers who breastfeed to the upper middle-class women who also breastfeed, without a generation of bottle feeders in between" (Raphael 1979). We still haven't figured out how to do this.

There are still a number of "pre-transition" cultures in the world, in which all women breastfeed each child for several years, but Western influence—particularly in the form of aggressive infant formula marketing strategies and the export of Western cultural beliefs about breasts as sex objects—is affecting even the remotest regions of the world. Korea, for example, is in the early stages of the transition from universal long-term breastfeeding to the adoption of bottles. Survey data reveal a decline in breastfeeding incidence and duration from the 1960s to the 1990s, led by upper-class, well-educated urban Korean women. China, likewise, has begun the transition to bottle-feeding, experiencing a rapid decline in the prevalence of breastfeeding in urban and periurban areas. Not surprisingly, China has been targeted by the infant formula companies as the next great market for their products.

Cuba is at the beginning of the infant feeding transition, with mothers of higher educational levels having the shortest duration of breastfeeding. Cuba seems to be well ahead of the United States in meeting established goals for maternal and child health through breastfeeding, with national strategies for supporting and promoting breastfeeding, including having all government hospitals participate in the World Health Organization's Baby-Friendly Hospital Initiative, and developing educational programs for day care centers and elementary and secondary schools to try to create a breastfeeding-friendly culture among both males and females from an early age. Cuba may be able to avoid a complete switch to bottle-feeding.

The Arabian Gulf countries (Bahrain, Kuwait, Oman, Qatar, Saudi Arabia, and the United Arab Emirates) are fully into the transitional phase, with middle- and upper-class women seldom breastfeeding, or only for a few weeks, and older women nursing longer than younger women. The influence of oil revenues on the lifestyles of these women, including the common employment of foreign housemaids and nannies, who bottle-feed the children, is fascinating and disturbing. The transition from full breastfeeding to almost full bottle-feeding has been particularly swift in this part of the world. "Westernized" hospital practices have been especially harmful, with hospital personnel and private clinics being used to promote the use of formula.

Australia, Canada, and the United States represent societies farthest along this "Infant Feeding Transition," with women of higher incomes and more education initiating breastfeeding in great numbers, and with increasing durations as well. This trend began in the 1970s, but was helped by the 1997 statement by the American Academy of Pediatrics that all children in the United States should be nursed for a minimum of one year (and thereafter as long as both mother and child wish), as well as by recent research showing that formula-fed children have lower IQs than their breastfed counterparts. In the United States, breastfeeding to the age of three years or beyond is becoming more and more common, as is breastfeeding siblings of different ages, known as "tandem nursing" (Dettwyler 2001). In the last decades, the

biggest leaps in initiating breastfeeding in the United States have been among WIC clients (women, infants, and children), who tend to be poor and less well-educated, indicating a trickle-down effect of breastfeeding from the upper classes, as well as the success of WIC Peer Counselor training programs.

Exactly how a particular region responds to influence from the Western industrialized nations and from the multinational infant formula companies depends on many different social, political, and economic factors. This makes it difficult to predict how the infant feeding transition will look in a specific region, or how long the bottle-feeding stage will last.

Cultural beliefs affect breastfeeding in other ways as well. Among the Bambara of Mali, people believe that because breast milk is made from a woman's blood, the process of breastfeeding creates a special relationship between a child and the woman who breastfeeds that child, whether or not she is the child's biological mother. In addition, breastfeeding creates a bond among all of the children who nurse from the same woman, whether or not they are biological siblings.

Having milk-siblings expands one's kinship network, providing more people one can call on for help in times of need. However, these kinship ties also prohibit marriage between the related children. In order to reduce the impact on potential marriage partners, women try to breastfeed other women's children only if they would already be excluded as marriage partners. Thus, a woman might wet-nurse the children of her co-wives, the children of her husband's brothers, or her grandchildren, while avoiding breastfeeding the children of her best friend, who she hopes will grow up to marry her own children. Similar beliefs about the "milk tie" are found among people in Haiti, Papua New Guinea, the Balkans, Burma, and among the Badawin of Kuwait and Saudi Arabia. In cultures where everyone is breastfed, or where everyone is bottle-fed, one's identity does not hinge on how one was fed. But in cultures entering or leaving the transition, feeding practices can be very important to one's identity. In a culture just entering the transition, to be bottle-fed is to have high status and be wealthy and modern. In a culture entering the final stage, to be breastfed is to have high status and be wealthy and modern.

In a wide variety of cultures, males are breastfed longer than females, sometimes much longer. These practices are supported by a variety of cultural beliefs, including the ideas that earlier weaning for girls insures a much-desired earlier menopause (Taiwan), that boys must be nursed longer so they will be willing to take care of their aged parents (Ireland), and that breast milk is the conduit for machismo, something boys need, but girls do not (Ecuador). Additionally, a number of societies have noted that males are physiologically weaker than females, more prone to illness and early death, so mothers nurse their sons longer to help ensure their survival.

Cultural beliefs about birth can have a profound influence on the success or failure of breastfeeding. Breastfeeding works best when the mother and baby are un-drugged at delivery, when they are kept together after birth, when the baby is not washed, when the baby is fed at the first cue (long before crying), when breastfeeding occurs early and often, when free formula samples and other gifts are not given to the mother, and when all those who surround the mother are knowledgeable and supportive of breastfeeding. Where the culture of birthing meets most or all of these criteria, we find higher rates of breastfeeding as well as longer durations. The World Health Organization's Baby-Friendly Hospital Initiative provides both a blueprint for optimal breastfeeding conditions and references to support their recommendations.

Cultural beliefs about how often children should breastfeed can help or hinder the process. The composition of human milk, as well as studies of human populations where children are allowed to breastfeed on demand, suggests that the natural frequency of breastfeeding is several times an hour for a few minutes each time, rather than according to a schedule, with longer feedings separated by several hours. Infrequent feeding in the early days and weeks of breastfeeding can permanently affect a mother's milk supply. As control of breast milk production gradually shifts from primarily endocrine (prolactin) to primarily autocrine (based on breast fullness) during the first few months postpartum, women who have been nursing on a three- to four-hour schedule may find that they no longer have sufficient milk to meet their babies' needs. A simple strategy of unrestricted breastfeeding from birth onwards would prevent this supply problem.

Perhaps the most pernicious cultural belief affecting breastfeeding is the one found in the United States and a small number of other (mostly Western) cultures—the belief that women's breasts are naturally erotic. American culture is obsessed with the sexual nature of women's breasts and their role in attracting and keeping male attention, as well as their role in providing sexual pleasure. This is reflected by the "normal" circumstances under which breasts are exposed in the United States (*Playboy* centerfolds, low-cut evening gowns, bikinis), by the phenomenon of breast augmentation surgery, by the association of breasts with sexual pleasure, and by the reactions of some people when they see women breastfeeding (embarrassment, horror, disgust, disapproval). In fact, the cultural belief that breasts are intrinsically erotic is just that, a cultural belief of limited distribution—one that has devastating consequences for women who want to breastfeed their children.

The mammary glands play no role in sexual behavior in any species other than humans. Among humans, the cross-cultural evidence clearly shows that most cultures do not define the breasts as sex objects. Extensive cross-cultural research in the 1940s and 1950s, published by Ford and Beach, found that, of 190 cultures surveyed, only 13 viewed women's breasts as sexually attractive. Likewise, 13 cultures out of 190 involved women's breasts in sexual activity. Of these latter 13, only three are also listed among the 13 where breasts are considered sexually attractive.

In most cultures, breasts are viewed solely as functional body parts, used to feed children—similar to how the typical American male views women's elbows, as devices to bend arms. Thus, in most cultures, it doesn't matter whether they are covered or not, or how big they are; husbands do not feel jealous of their nursing children, and women are never accused of breastfeeding for their own sexual pleasure. In the United States, and increasingly where Western ideas about breasts as sex objects are taking hold, women find that they must be extremely discreet about where and how they breastfeed. They may get little support for breastfeeding, or even active resistance from jealous husbands; they may receive dirty looks or rude comments or be asked to go elsewhere (often the bathroom) to nurse. Still others are accused of sexually abusing their children for breastfeeding them longer than a year (Dettwyler 2001).

The evolution of cultural beliefs about breasts is difficult to pin down. Carolyn Latteier and Marilyn Yalom provide the most thorough research on the history of Western culture's obsession with breasts. The rise of both the infant formula industry and commercial pornography following World War II contributed to modern views of breasts as sex objects, rather than glands for producing milk for children.

Among health care providers themselves, a culture of denial about the health risks of formula contributes to the persistence of bottle-feeding. Many physicians view bottle-feeding as "almost as good" in spite of overwhelming research to the contrary. It is estimated that for every 1,000 deaths of infants in the United States, four of those deaths can be directly attributed to the use of infant formula. Additionally, children who are formula-fed have higher rates of many illnesses during childhood including diabetes, ear infections, gastrointestinal and upper respiratory infections, lymphoma, Sudden Infant Death Syndrome, and allergies. They continue to have higher rates of illnesses throughout life, including heart disease, some types of cancer, and multiple sclerosis. Children who are formula-fed likewise have lower average scores on intelligence tests and lower grades in school. Mothers who breastfeed their children, especially for longer durations, have lower rates of reproductive cancers (especially breast cancer), and lower rates of osteoporosis.

Unfortunately, obstetricians often view infant nutrition as the responsibility of the pediatrician, while the pediatrician claims that by the time the child is born, the mother has long since made up her mind about how she will feed her child. Many health care professionals say that they hesitate to discuss the dangers of formula for fear of "making women feel guilty." This is patronizing of parents and robs them of their chance to make an informed decision about this important area of child care.

In a perfect world, all cultural beliefs would support breastfeeding. The World Health Organization's Baby-Friendly Hospital Initiative and the Coalition for Improving Maternity Services' Mother-Friendly Childbirth Initiative are two attempts to clarify the best cultural practices for initiating breastfeeding. The Internet has also had a major impact on the culture of breastfeeding support. LactNet is an e-mail list for professionals who work in the lactation field. Kathleen Bruce and Kathleen Auerbach, both lactation consultants in the United States, began the list in March of 1995. It has grown to include more than 3,000 individuals from 38 countries who share ideas, beliefs, research studies, and clinical experience. Documents such as the Baby-Friendly Hospital Initiative and the Mother-Friendly Childbirth Initiative, and resources such as LactNet, are creating and sustaining a global culture of breastfeeding support.

Additional Resources

For Internet links related to this chapter, please visit our website at www.mhhe.com/dettwyler,

Ford, C. S., and F. A. Beach. *Patterns of Sexual Behavior.* New York: Harper & Row, 1951.

Giuliani, Rudolph W. (Introduction) and the editors of LIFE Magazine. *One Nation: America Remembers September 11, 2001.* New York: Little Brown & Company, 2001.

Kear, Adrian, and Deborah Lynn Steinberg, eds. *Mourning Diana: Nation, Culture and the Performance of Grief.* New York: Routledge, 1999.

Latteier, C. *Breasts: The Women's Perspective on an American Obsession.* Binghamton, NY: Haworth Press, 1998.

Podolefsky, Aaron, and Peter J. Brown, eds. *Applying Anthropology: An Introductory Reader.* 7th ed. New York: McGraw-Hill Higher Education, 2002.

Raphael, D. "Margaret Mead—A Tribute." *The Lactation Review* 4, no. 1 (1979), pp. 1–3.

Simopoulos, A. P., J. E. Dutra de Oliveira, and I. D. Desai, eds. *Behavioral and Metabolic Aspects of Breastfeeding: International Trends. World Review of Nutrition and Dietetics, Volume 78.* Basel, Switzerland: S. Karger, 1995.

Stuart-Macadam, Patricia, and Katherine A. Dettwyler, eds. *Breastfeeding: Biocultural Perspectives.* New York: Aldine de Gruyter Publishers, 1995.

Walker, M. "A Fresh Look at the Hazards of Artificial Infant Feeding, II." 1998. Available from the International Lactation Consultants Association.

Yalom, M. *A History of the Breast.* New York: Random House, Inc., 1997.

Critical Thinking

1. Discuss the importance of breastfeeding for both mother and child.
2. What kinds of cultural factors influence breastfeeding?
3. Discuss the main forces that move women away from breastfeeding.
4. What factors have fueled the return to breastfeeding?
5. How has Western influence brought about bottle-feeding in countries that are undergoing a transition? Why might Cuba be an exception in this regard?
6. Why are the Arabian Gulf countries "fully into the transitional phase"?
7. Describe the "Infant Feeding Transition" and why it is occurring.
8. How do cultural beliefs affect breastfeeding?
9. Why are males breastfed more often than females?
10. What are some of the detrimental effects of not breastfeeding?

Create Central

www.mhhe.com/createcentral

Internet References

Journal of Human Lactation
http://jhl.sagepub.com

American Anthropological Association Children and Childhood Interest Group
http://aaacig.usu.edu

Dettwyler, Katherine. From *Reflections on Anthropology: A Four-Field Reader,* McGraw-Hill, 2003, pp. 21–27. Copyright © 2003 by Katherine Dettwyler. Reprinted by permission of the author.

Article

Prepared by: Elvio Angeloni, *Pasadena City College*

The Inuit Paradox

How can people who gorge on fat and rarely see a vegetable be healthier than we are?

PATRICIA GADSBY

Learning Outcomes

After reading this article, you will be able to:

- Describe some healthful habits we can learn by studying hunter-gatherers.

- Identify the traditional Inuit (Eskimo) practices that are important for their survival in the circumstances they live in and contrast them with the values professed by the society you live in.

Patricia Cochran, an Inupiat from Northwestern Alaska, is talking about the native foods of her childhood: "We pretty much had a subsistence way of life. Our food supply was right outside our front door. We did our hunting and foraging on the Seward Peninsula and along the Bering Sea."

"Our meat was seal and walrus, marine mammals that live in cold water and have lots of fat. We used seal oil for our cooking and as a dipping sauce for food. We had moose, caribou, and reindeer. We hunted ducks, geese, and little land birds like quail, called ptarmigan. We caught crab and lots of fish—salmon, whitefish, tomcod, pike, and char. Our fish were cooked, dried, smoked, or frozen. We ate frozen raw whitefish, sliced thin. The elders liked stinkfish, fish buried in seal bags or cans in the tundra and left to ferment. And fermented seal flipper, they liked that too."

Cochran's family also received shipments of whale meat from kin living farther north, near Barrow. Beluga was one she liked; raw muktuk, which is whale skin with its underlying blubber, she definitely did not. "To me it has a chew-on-a-tire consistency," she says, "but to many people it's a mainstay." In the short subarctic summers, the family searched for roots and greens and, best of all from a child's point of view, wild blueberries, crowberries, or salmonberries, which her aunts would mix with whipped fat to make a special treat called *akutuq*—in colloquial English, Eskimo ice cream.

Now Cochran directs the Alaska Native Science Commission, which promotes research on native cultures and the health and environmental issues that affect them. She sits at her keyboard in Anchorage, a bustling city offering fare from Taco Bell to French cuisine. But at home Cochran keeps a freezer filled with fish, seal, walrus, reindeer, and whale meat, sent by her family up north, and she and her husband fish and go berry picking—"sometimes a challenge in Anchorage," she adds, laughing. "I eat fifty-fifty," she explains, half traditional, half regular American.

No one, not even residents of the northernmost villages on Earth, eats an entirely traditional northern diet anymore. Even the groups we came to know as Eskimo—which include the Inupiat and the Yupiks of Alaska, the Canadian Inuit and Inuvialuit, Inuit Greenlanders, and the Siberian Yupiks—have probably seen more changes in their diet in a lifetime than their ancestors did over thousands of years. The closer people live to towns and the more access they have to stores and cash-paying jobs, the more likely they are to have westernized their eating. And with westernization, at least on the North American continent, comes processed foods and cheap carbohydrates—Crisco, Tang, soda, cookies, chips, pizza, fries. "The young and urbanized," says Harriet Kuhnlein, director of the Centre for Indigenous Peoples' Nutrition and Environment at McGill University in Montreal, "are increasingly into fast food." So much so that type 2 diabetes, obesity, and other diseases of Western civilization are becoming causes for concern there too.

Today, when diet books top the best-seller list and nobody seems sure of what to eat to stay healthy, it's surprising to learn how well the Eskimo did on a high-protein, high-fat diet. Shaped by glacial temperatures, stark landscapes, and protracted winters, the traditional Eskimo diet had little in the way of plant food, no agricultural or dairy products, and was unusually low in carbohydrates. Mostly people subsisted on what they hunted and fished. Inland dwellers took advantage of caribou feeding on tundra mosses, lichens, and plants too tough for humans to stomach (though predigested vegetation in the animals' paunches became dinner as well). Coastal people exploited the sea. The main nutritional challenge was avoiding starvation in late winter if primary meat sources became too scarce or lean.

These foods hardly make up the "balanced" diet most of us grew up with, and they look nothing like the mix of grains, fruits, vegetables, meat, eggs, and dairy we're accustomed to seeing in conventional food pyramid diagrams. How could such a diet possibly be adequate? How did people get along on little else but fat and animal protein?

The diet of the far north shows that there are no essential foods—only essential nutrients.

What the diet of the Far North illustrates, says Harold Draper, a biochemist and expert in Eskimo nutrition, is that there are no essential foods—only essential nutrients. And humans can get those nutrients from diverse and eye-opening sources.

One might, for instance, imagine gross vitamin deficiencies arising from a diet with scarcely any fruits and vegetables. What furnishes vitamin A, vital for eyes and bones? We derive much of ours from colorful plant foods, constructing it from pigmented plant precursors called carotenoids (as in carrots). But vitamin A, which is oil soluble, is also plentiful in the oils of cold-water fishes and sea mammals, as well as in the animals' livers, where fat is processed. These dietary staples also provide vitamin D, another oil-soluble vitamin needed for bones. Those of us living in temperate and tropical climates, on the other hand, usually make vitamin D indirectly by exposing skin to strong sun—hardly an option in the Arctic winter—and by consuming fortified cow's milk, to which the indigenous northern groups had little access until recent decades and often don't tolerate all that well.

As for vitamin C, the source in the Eskimo diet was long a mystery. Most animals can synthesize their own vitamin C, or ascorbic acid, in their livers, but humans are among the exceptions, along with other primates and oddballs like guinea pigs and bats. If we don't ingest enough of it, we fall apart from scurvy, a gruesome connective-tissue disease. In the United States today we can get ample supplies from orange juice, citrus fruits, and fresh vegetables. But vitamin C oxidizes with time; getting enough from a ship's provisions was tricky for early 18th- and 19th-century voyagers to the polar regions. Scurvy—joint pain, rotting gums, leaky blood vessels, physical and mental degeneration—plagued European and U.S. expeditions even in the 20th century. However, Arctic peoples living on fresh fish and meat were free of the disease.

Impressed, the explorer Vilhjalmur Stefansson adopted an Eskimo-style diet for five years during the two Arctic expeditions he led between 1908 and 1918. "The thing to do is to find your antiscorbutics where you are," he wrote. "Pick them up as you go." In 1928, to convince skeptics, he and a young colleague spent a year on an Americanized version of the diet under medical supervision at Bellevue Hospital in New York City. The pair ate steaks, chops, organ meats like brain and liver, poultry, fish, and fat with gusto. "If you have some fresh meat in your diet every day and don't overcook it," Stefansson declared triumphantly, "there will be enough C from that source alone to prevent scurvy."

In fact, all it takes to ward off scurvy is a daily dose of 10 milligrams, says Karen Fediuk, a consulting dietitian and former graduate student of Harriet Kuhnlein's who did her master's thesis on vitamin C. (That's far less than the U.S. recommended daily allowance of 75 to 90 milligrams— 75 for women, 90 for men.) Native foods easily supply those 10 milligrams of scurvy prevention, especially when organ meats—preferably raw—are on the menu. For a study published with Kuhnlein in 2002, Fediuk compared the vitamin C content of 100-gram (3.55-ounce) samples of foods eaten by Inuit women living in the Canadian Arctic: Raw caribou liver supplied almost 24 milligrams, seal brain close to 15 milligrams, and raw kelp more than 28 milligrams. Still higher levels were found in whale skin and muktuk.

As you might guess from its antiscorbutic role, vitamin C is crucial for the synthesis of connective tissue, including the matrix of skin. "Wherever collagen's made, you can expect vitamin C," says Kuhnlein. Thick skinned, chewy, and collagen rich, raw muktuk can serve up an impressive 36 milligrams in a 100-gram piece, according to Fediuk's analyses. "Weight for weight, it's as good as orange juice," she says. Traditional Inuit practices like freezing meat and fish and frequently eating them raw, she notes, conserve vitamin C, which is easily cooked off and lost in food processing.

Hunter-gatherer diets like those eaten by these northern groups and other traditional diets based on nomadic herding or subsistence farming are among the older approaches to human eating. Some of these eating plans might seem strange to us— diets centered around milk, meat, and blood among the East African pastoralists, enthusiastic tuber eating by the Quechua living in the High Andes, the staple use of the mongongo nut in the southern African !Kung—but all proved resourceful adaptations to particular eco-niches. No people, though, may have been forced to push the nutritional envelope further than those living at Earth's frozen extremes. The unusual makeup of the far-northern diet led Loren Cordain, a professor of evolutionary nutrition at Colorado State University at Fort Collins, to make an intriguing observation.

Four years ago, Cordain reviewed the macronutrient content (protein, carbohydrates, fat) in the diets of 229 hunter-gatherer groups listed in a series of journal articles collectively known as the Ethnographic Atlas. These are some of the oldest surviving human diets. In general, hunter-gatherers tend to eat more animal protein than we do in our standard Western diet, with its reliance on agriculture and carbohydrates derived from grains and starchy plants. Lowest of all in carbohydrate, and highest in combined fat and protein, are the diets of peoples living in the Far North, where they make up for fewer plant foods with extra fish. What's equally striking, though, says Cordain, is that these meat-and-fish diets also exhibit a natural "protein ceiling." Protein accounts for no more than 35 to 40 percent of their total calories, which suggests to him that's all the protein humans can comfortably handle.

Wild-animal fats are different from other fats. Farm animals typically have lots of highly saturated fat.

This ceiling, Cordain thinks, could be imposed by the way we process protein for energy. The simplest, fastest way to make energy is to convert carbohydrates into glucose, our body's primary fuel. But if the body is out of carbs, it can burn fat, or if necessary, break down protein. The name given to the convoluted business of making glucose from protein is gluconeogenesis. It takes place in the liver, uses a dizzying slew of enzymes, and creates nitrogen waste that has to be converted into urea and disposed of through the kidneys. On a truly traditional diet, says Draper, recalling his studies in the 1970s, Arctic people had plenty of protein but little carbohydrate, so they often relied on gluconeogenesis. Not only did they have bigger livers to handle the additional work but their urine volumes were also typically larger to get rid of the extra urea. Nonetheless, there appears to be a limit on how much protein the human liver can safely cope with: Too much overwhelms the liver's waste-disposal system, leading to protein poisoning—nausea, diarrhea, wasting, and death.

Whatever the metabolic reason for this syndrome, says John Speth, an archaeologist at the University of Michigan's Museum of Anthropology, plenty of evidence shows that hunters through the ages avoided protein excesses, discarding fat-depleted animals even when food was scarce. Early pioneers and trappers in North America encountered what looks like a similar affliction, sometimes referred to as rabbit starvation because rabbit meat is notoriously lean. Forced to subsist on fat-deficient meat, the men would gorge themselves, yet wither away. Protein can't be the sole source of energy for humans, concludes Cordain. Anyone eating a meaty diet that is low in carbohydrates must have fat as well.

Stefansson had arrived at this conclusion, too, while living among the Copper Eskimo. He recalled how he and his Eskimo companions had become quite ill after weeks of eating "caribou so skinny that there was no appreciable fat behind the eyes or in the marrow." Later he agreed to repeat the miserable experience at Bellevue Hospital, for science's sake, and for a while ate nothing but defatted meat. "The symptoms brought on at Bellevue by an incomplete meat diet [lean without fat] were exactly the same as in the Arctic . . . diarrhea and a feeling of general baffling discomfort," he wrote. He was restored with a fat fix but "had lost considerable weight." For the remainder of his year on meat, Stefansson tucked into his rations of chops and steaks with fat intact. "A normal meat diet is not a high-protein diet," he pronounced. "We were really getting three-quarters of our calories from fat." (Fat is more than twice as

calorie dense as protein or carbohydrate, but even so, that's a lot of lard. A typical U.S diet provides about 35 percent of its calories from fat.)

Stefansson dropped 10 pounds on his meat-and-fat regimen and remarked on its "slenderizing" aspect, so perhaps it's no surprise he's been co-opted as a posthumous poster boy for Atkins-type diets. No discussion about diet these days can avoid Atkins. Even some researchers interviewed for this article couldn't resist referring to the Inuit way of eating as the "original Atkins." "Superficially, at a macronutrient level, the two diets certainly look similar," allows Samuel Klein, a nutrition researcher at Washington University in St. Louis, who's attempting to study how Atkins stacks up against conventional weight-loss diets. Like the Inuit diet, Atkins is low in carbohydrates and very high in fat. But numerous researchers, including Klein, point out that there are profound differences between the two diets, beginning with the type of meat and fat eaten.

Fats have been demonized in the United States, says Eric Dewailly, a professor of preventive medicine at Laval University in Quebec. But all fats are not created equal. This lies at the heart of a paradox—the Inuit paradox, if you will. In the Nunavik villages in northern Quebec, adults over 40 get almost half their calories from native foods, says Dewailly, and they don't die of heart attacks at nearly the same rates as other Canadians or Americans. Their cardiac death rate is about half of ours, he says. As someone who looks for links between diet and cardiovascular health, he's intrigued by that reduced risk. Because the traditional Inuit diet is "so restricted," he says, it's easier to study than the famously heart-healthy Mediterranean diet, with its cornucopia of vegetables, fruits, grains, herbs, spices, olive oil, and red wine.

A key difference in the typical Nunavik Inuit's diet is that more than 50 percent of the calories in Inuit native foods come from fats. Much more important, the fats come from wild animals.

Wild-animal fats are different from both farm-animal fats and processed fats, says Dewailly. Farm animals, cooped up and stuffed with agricultural grains (carbohydrates) typically have lots of solid, highly saturated fat. Much of our processed food is also riddled with solid fats, or so-called trans fats, such as the reengineered vegetable oils and shortenings cached in baked goods and snacks. "A lot of the packaged food on supermarket shelves contains them. So do commercial french fries," Dewailly adds.

Trans fats are polyunsaturated vegetable oils tricked up to make them more solid at room temperature. Manufacturers do this by hydrogenating the oils—adding extra hydrogen atoms to their molecular structures—which "twists" their shapes. Dewailly makes twisting sound less like a chemical transformation than a perversion, an act of public-health sabotage: "These man-made fats are dangerous, even worse for the heart than saturated fats." They not only lower high-density lipoprotein cholesterol (HDL, the "good" cholesterol) but they also raise low-density lipoprotein cholesterol (LDL, the "bad" cholesterol) and triglycerides, he says. In the process, trans fats set the stage for heart attacks because they lead to the increase of fatty buildup in artery walls.

Wild animals that range freely and eat what nature intended, says Dewailly, have fat that is far more healthful. Less of their fat is saturated, and more of it is in the monounsaturated form (like olive oil). What's more, cold-water fishes and sea mammals are particularly rich in polyunsaturated fats called n-3 fatty acids or omega-3 fatty acids. These fats appear to benefit the heart and vascular system. But the polyunsaturated fats in most Americans' diets are the omega-6 fatty acids supplied by vegetable oils. By contrast, whale blubber consists of 70 percent monounsaturated fat and close to 30 percent omega-3s, says Dewailly.

Dieting is the price we pay for too little exercise and too much mass-produced food.

Omega-3s evidently help raise HDL cholesterol, lower triglycerides, and are known for anticlotting effects. (Ethnographers have remarked on an Eskimo propensity for nosebleeds.) These fatty acids are believed to protect the heart from life-threatening arrhythmias that can lead to sudden cardiac death. And like a "natural aspirin," adds Dewailly, omega-3 polyunsaturated fats help put a damper on runaway inflammatory processes, which play a part in atherosclerosis, arthritis, diabetes, and other so-called diseases of civilization.

You can be sure, however, that Atkins devotees aren't routinely eating seal and whale blubber. Besides the acquired taste problem, their commerce is extremely restricted in the United States by the Marine Mammal Protection Act, says Bruce Holub, a nutritional biochemist in the department of human biology and nutritional sciences at the University of Guelph in Ontario.

"In heartland America it's probable they're not eating in an Eskimo-like way," says Gary Foster, clinical director of the Weight and Eating Disorders Program at the Pennsylvania School of Medicine. Foster, who describes himself as open-minded about Atkins, says he'd nonetheless worry if people saw the diet as a green light to eat all the butter and bacon—saturated fats—they want. Just before rumors surfaced that Robert Atkins had heart and weight problems when he died, Atkins officials themselves were stressing saturated fat should account for no more than 20 percent of dieters' calories. This seems to be a clear retreat from the diet's original don't-count-the-calories approach to bacon and butter and its happy exhortations to "plow into those prime ribs." Furthermore, 20 percent of calories from saturated fats is *double* what most nutritionists advise. Before plowing into those prime ribs, readers of a recent edition of the *Dr. Atkins' New Diet Revolution* are urged to take omega-3 pills to help protect their hearts. "If you watch carefully," says Holub wryly, "you'll see many popular U.S. diets have quietly added omega-3 pills, in the form of fish oil or flaxseed capsules, as supplements."

Needless to say, the subsistence diets of the Far North are not "dieting." Dieting is the price we pay for too little exercise and too much mass-produced food. Northern diets were a way of life in places too cold for agriculture, where food, whether hunted, fished, or foraged, could not be taken for granted. They were about keeping weight on.

This is not to say that people in the Far North were fat: Subsistence living requires exercise—hard physical work. Indeed, among the good reasons for native people to maintain their old way of eating, as far as it's possible today, is that it provides a hedge against obesity, type 2 diabetes, and heart disease. Unfortunately, no place on Earth is immune to the spreading taint of growth and development. The very well-being of the northern food chain is coming under threat from global warming, land development, and industrial pollutants in the marine environment. "I'm a pragmatist," says Cochran, whose organization is involved in pollution monitoring and disseminating food-safety information to native villages. "Global warming we don't have control over. But we can, for example, do cleanups of military sites in Alaska or of communication cables leaching lead into fish-spawning areas. We can help communities make informed food choices. A young woman of childbearing age may choose not to eat certain organ meats that concentrate contaminants. As individuals, we do have options. And eating our salmon and our seal is still a heck of a better option than pulling something processed that's full of additives off a store shelf."

Not often in our industrial society do we hear someone speak so familiarly about "our" food animals. We don't talk of "our pig" and "our beef." We've lost that creature feeling, that sense of kinship with food sources. "You're taught to think in boxes," says Cochran. "In our culture the connectivity between humans, animals, plants, the land they live on, and the air they share is ingrained in us from birth.

"You truthfully can't separate the way we get our food from the way we live," she says. "How we get our food is intrinsic to our culture. It's how we pass on our values and knowledge to the young. When you go out with your aunts and uncles to hunt or to gather, you learn to smell the air, watch the wind, understand the way the ice moves, know the land. You get to know where to pick which plant and what animal to take."

"It's part, too, of your development as a person. You share food with your community. You show respect to your elders by offering them the first catch. You give thanks to the animal that gave up its life for your sustenance. So you get all the physical activity of harvesting your own food, all the social activity of sharing and preparing it, and all the spiritual aspects as well," says Cochran. "You certainly don't get all that, do you, when you buy prepackaged food from a store?"

"That's why some of us here in Anchorage are working to protect what's ours, so that others can continue to live back home in the villages," she adds. "Because if we don't take care of our food, it won't be there for us in the future. And if we lose our foods, we lose who we are." The word Inupiat means "the real people." "That's who we are," says Cochran.

Critical Thinking

1. What kinds of diseases are on the increase among the Inuit and why?

2. Discuss the traditional high-protein, high-fat diet. How does this compare with the "balanced diet" most of us grew up with? What does this mean, according to Harold Draper?

3. Discuss the contrasting sources of vitamins A, D, and C between our diet and the diet of the Inuit. What is the advantage of eating meat and fish raw?

4. What is a "protein ceiling" and why? How did hunter-gatherers cope with the problem?

5. Where do the more healthful fats (monounsaturated and omega-3 fatty acids) come from? What are their benefits?

6. Why is it that Atkins-dieters are not really eating in an "Eskimo-like way"?

7. What are the differences between the subsistence diets of the Far North and "dieting"?

8. Were people of the Far North fat? Why not? In what ways did the old way of eating protect them?

9. How is the northern food chain threatened?

10. In what sense is there a kinship with food sources in the Far North that our industrial societies does not have and why? Why is it also a part of one's development as a person?

Create Central

www.mhhe.com/createcentral

Internet References

The Paleolithic Diet Page
www.paleodiet.com

The Institute for Intercultural Studies
www.interculturalstudies.org/main.html

Article   Prepared by: Elvio Angeloni, *Pasadena City College*

Cell Phones, Sharing, and Social Status in an African Society

Daniel Jordan Smith

Learning Outcomes

After reading this article, you will be able to:

- Discuss the economics, the politics, and the sociality of cell phone use in Nigeria.

- Discuss the ways in which cell phones are perceived as status symbols in Nigeria.

Contemporary processes of globalization have stimulated many anthropologists to begin asking new research questions. One important area of innovative research pertains to the global spread of technology and its influence on local people, practices, values, and behaviors. Globalization involves the worldwide transfer of technology, capital, industry, people, and cultural ideas. It has made the world a smaller place, but it has also increased social inequalities across the "digital divide."

In the twentieth century, radio and television played powerful roles in creating linkages between previously disconnected areas of the world. Without a doubt, new mass media brought the signs, symbols, images, and cultural values of the industrialized "First World" to people and communities in poorer "Third World" regions. The globalization of technology is not a top-down, unidirectional process. New technologies create new ways in which small groups of people can shape the ideas, values, political opinions, and even the actions of large groups of people within a particular town, district, country, or world region.

Recent technological developments are influencing people and communities in new ways, raising new research questions for anthropologists. One such development is the Internet, although on a global scale fewer people have access to that technology than the topic of this selection: cell phones. Like radio and television before them, cell phones create new and unprecedented opportunities for communication across distances. As this selection vividly demonstrates, the ways in which people use cell phones are powerfully influenced by local ideas, values, customs, and practices. In other words, global processes always take place within local contexts. Both the symbolic meaning and the social rules for using cell phones change in different cultural contexts.

Introduction

On July 19, 2004, the popular BBC Africa Service morning news program, *Network Africa,* carried a curious story from its Nigeria correspondent. He described a recent epidemic of rumors circulating in the country, purporting that anyone who answered calls on their cellular telephones originating from several specific numbers risked madness, and even death. I had heard a similar story in the previous few days from dozens of friends and acquaintances in and around the towns of Owerri and Umuahia in southeastern Nigeria, where I was conducting research. Ironically, cell phone usage around the country surged in the wake of the rumors, as people phoned and sent text messages to friends and relatives, warning them of the "killer numbers."

Once the popular rumors circulated widely, Nigerian newspapers carried stories printing some of the suspected numbers and incorporating quotations from citizens who allegedly witnessed the effects of these sinister calls (Akinsuyi 2004). But the newspapers also published statements from spokespersons for the country's major mobile telephone service providers, denying that such killer numbers existed (Ikhemuemhe 2004). Further, they published interviews with government authorities and university scientists disputing the technological feasibility of transmitting witchcraft through cell phones. Radio call-in programs and television talk shows buzzed with debate about the story, mesmerizing the nation for the better part of two weeks. Eventually, popular attention faded, as it had with regard to a previous rumor suggesting that men who carried cell phones in their pockets or strapped them to their belts risked becoming infertile.

The rumors that mobile phones might be implicated in infertility, madness, and murder are a testament to how dramatically this new technology has affected Nigeria. A few elite Nigerians had access to older cellular telephone technologies beginning in the 1990s, but the number of such phones was minuscule. The introduction of the Global System for Mobile Communications (GSM) technology to Nigeria in 2001 and the liberalization of Nigeria's previously government-controlled telecommunications industry transformed cell phones from an extreme rarity into an everyday technology to which literally millions of ordinary citizens have access. When GSM technology was first introduced in Nigeria, the country had only approximately 500,000 landlines for over 100 million people (Obadare 2004), a number which had not increased significantly in many years. By the end of 2004, less than four years after the first GSM cellular phones and services went on sale to the Nigerian public, the country had over 7 million subscribers (Mobile Africa 2005), with some recent estimates putting the number of mobile phones users in Nigeria at over 11 million (PANA 2005).

In addition, millions more people without their own phones were provided easy access to cell phone service, as individual cell phone owners became small-scale entrepreneurs, converting their personal phones into informal businesses. By the time the BBC story was broadcast, thousands of call centers, most with just one or two phones and a single attendant, dotted Nigeria's landscape. Every major city and many small towns are now connected, and countless rural and urban communities that have no running water and little or no electricity service are integrated into the country's vast and expanding mobile telephone network.

Cell phones have produced dramatic changes in communication in Nigeria, with many positive effects. Mobile phones have been integrated into long-standing patterns of social relationship, enabling Nigerians separated by great distances to continue to interact based on expectations of sharing and reciprocity. But just as important, they have become symbols of social status. Nigerians assert and express modern identities by purchasing, using, and publicly displaying the latest consumer commodities. Mastery of the new phone technology is a marker of being middle class, educated, and urban. Yet the reality is that cell phones represent a level of economic achievement that is out of reach to most Nigerians. The majority of new cell phone consumers experience the costs of usage as exorbitant, reinforcing the sense that middle-class status remains elusive. Thus, while the burgeoning popularity of cell phones in Nigeria, and throughout sub-Saharan Africa, represents the aspirations of ordinary people for better lives, this new technology exposes the pronounced and enduring nature of social inequality.

Cell Phone Economics

Owning and using a cell phone in Nigeria requires three primary investments: (1) buying a phone; (2) accessing service from one of the country's four major providers through the purchase of a SIM (Subscriber Identity Module) card that is installed in the back of the phone to connect it to the service network; and (3) procuring "recharge cards," through which call time is paid for by loading a unique pin number each time one wants to add credit to an individual account. While the phone and the SIM card are one-time acquisitions, access to service depends on the regular purchase of the recharge cards to load call time as previously purchased amounts are exhausted.

In 2005, new phones are available in Nigeria for as little as 6,000 naira (approximately 45 U.S. dollars), and as much as 60,000 naira (over U.S. $450), depending on the brand, the model, and the complexity of features offered on the phone.

The price of SIM cards declined dramatically in the past several years, to about five to ten dollars, with companies sometimes offering free SIM cards as part of periodic marketing campaigns. The vast majority of customers use the "pay as you go" recharge card system.

Most crucial from the perspective of ordinary Nigerians is the cost of calls themselves. As with every other feature of cell phone service, the cost of calls has declined significantly over the four years since GSM service was introduced. But the price of calls per minute and per second (a choice between these rates is now available to most consumers) is still expensive, relative to both Nigerians' purchasing power and the cost of cell phone service in other countries (Obadare 2004). Importantly, although incoming calls are free, every outgoing call is charged—there are no free minutes per month or at night and on weekends, though lower rates apply in off-peak hours. Further, recharge cards expire. Credit not utilized within a specified period of time is forever lost. For example, ten dollars of credit would typically need to be used within about two weeks.

Initially, when GSM cell phone service was first introduced, domestic calls cost approximately 50 naira (37 U.S. cents) per minute. Recently, the cost has declined to about 25 naira (19 cents) per minute, with the precise amount depending upon the volume of calls per month, whether the call is in or out of network, the time of day, and so on. Each of the country's four main service providers (Glomobile, Mtel, MTN, and Vmobile) offers a diverse range of service packages and special deals, but most consumers cannot afford to make enough calls to qualify for the plans that offer the cheapest calling rates. Indeed, an entire discourse of complaint about the high cost of cell phone calls has emerged in Nigeria (Obadare 2004). Popular reaction to the economics of personal cell phone use has generated a new lexicon and a growing repertoire of behaviors designed to mitigate the financial burdens of cell phone ownership.

"The Fire That Consumes Money"

In southeastern Nigeria, where I work, and where the predominant language is Igbo, the vernacular name for a cell phone is *oku na iri ego,* which translates literally as "the fire that consumes money." This popular local name reflects ordinary citizens' frustrations with the perceived exorbitant costs of cell phone calls. New linguistic turns of phrase and innovative social practices that have evolved with the proliferation of cell phone technology build on people's aggravation over the strain of cell phone ownership, but they also indicate the degree to which cell phone culture has taken root in everyday life.

Nigerians have adapted their cell phone usage to suit their economic circumstances, and some aspects of the service plans offered by the country's main providers are clearly designed to attract and keep customers who cannot afford to make a high volume of phone calls. For example, the Short Messaging Systems (SMS), through which customers can send "text messages," is extremely popular in Nigeria and typically costs only 15 naira (about 10 U.S. cents) per message. Text messages must be limited in size, usually no more than 160 characters. Text messaging is particularly popular with younger customers and it has generated its own lexicon of abbreviations, an economy of language that has also become part of Nigeria's youth culture, as it has in other settings (for literature on text messaging generally see Fox 2001; Dooring 2002; and Sylvia and Hady 2004).

Text messaging has become a common way for Nigerians who cannot afford regular phone calls to communicate using the new technology. But for older people, and even among young folks, using text messages too frequently without also calling can be interpreted as sign of unwillingness to spend money on a particular relationship—reflecting either stinginess or a lack of deep concern about the relationship or both. As a consequence, although text messaging is extremely popular, people are careful not to rely on it too exclusively, lest they become objects of criticism. In times of economic hardship, the willingness to spend money on a phone call is evidence of interest or commitment to a relationship, whether it is a friendship, a family tie, a business partnership, or a romance. The consequences of the microeconomics of cell phone use reflect the importance and the complexity of how issues of wealth, inequality, and status are negotiated in human relationships.

"Flash Me, I Flash You"

Other common practices besides text messaging illustrate the economics and micropolitics of cell phone behavior, and the importance of these behaviors in navigating issues of inequality in social relationships. For example, a major consequence of the fact that many cell phone owners cannot afford to maintain credit on a regular basis is the innovation of what Nigerians call "flashing." To "flash" someone means to call the recipient's line and allow the phone to ring just once, so that the incoming number is displayed to the recipient, but the caller hangs up before the recipient answers. This way, the recipient knows the number of the person trying to reach him or her, and hopefully has enough credit to call back. Flashing is possible because one can make a call without paying for it as long as no one picks up. Under the prevailing plans in Nigeria, it is possible to receive incoming calls even when one does not have any credit.

From my experience observing scores of friends and acquaintances receiving flashes, whether or not the recipient of the flash could identify the caller from the incoming number was not necessarily a good predictor of a callback. Sometimes knowledge of the identity of the incoming caller created the incentive to call back immediately, perhaps out of obligation, affection, or some prior awareness about the reason for the call. Conversely, on other occasions, knowledge of the identity of the caller had the opposite effect, the attitude being that anyone who had something important to communicate would find a way to pay for a call, even if only for a minute or two. People often refused to call back after a flash out of suspicion that the caller wanted the recipient to bear the cost of the conversation. Nevertheless, unidentified flashes often sparked curiosity, and people frequently responded to them.

Given that countless Nigerians who own cell phones are often in a position where credit is exhausted or very low, and therefore very precious, flashing can sometimes become a comical exchange in which no one wants to bear the costs of a call. In the Pidgin English that is often the lingua franca in Nigeria,

people expressed the phenomenon of reciprocal flashing, in which no one was willing to pay for a call, with the phrase "flash me, I flash you." Mostly in good humor, friends frequently suspected each other of trying to transfer and defray the costs of communication through flashing. As a consequence, people sometimes tried to answer their phones before the end of the first ring, engaging the call before the flasher could hang up. This practice was particularly common when someone flashed more than once, giving the recipient time to prepare for a quick answer. Over the past couple of years I witnessed numerous comic scenes where people plotted to "catch" flashers before they could hang up, making them pay for the connection.

Sharing Credit: Inequality and Sociality

Of course most people who communicate by telephone eventually see each other in person, and past episodes of flashing are often topics of discussion. A typical face-to-face conversation about flashing might include a query by the flasher as to why the recipient did not call back, followed by an admission (or assertion) by the recipient that he or she did not have any credit. The recipient, in turn, may accuse the flasher of having credit and being unwilling to use it. These mostly good-natured conversations reproduce some of the complexity of how people in Nigeria navigate the social representation of wealth more generally. On the one hand, using and sharing one's cell phone liberally are clear signals of wealth, and, like many kinds of conspicuous consumption in Nigeria, seemingly carefree cell phone usage can be rewarded with recognition and prestige. On the other hand, in Nigeria's current economic climate, in which most people are struggling to make ends meet, a strong ethos prevails in which even the relatively affluent portray themselves as just getting by, particularly among people who are otherwise their peers.

These contradictory dimensions of people's public representations of wealth play out constantly in the arena of cell phone socioeconomics. For those who really are struggling, claiming one has no credit can be a strategy for protecting a precious and dwindling resource. Conversely, using one's cell phone generously even when one cannot actually afford it can be a way of portraying or maintaining social status that is threatened by economic hardship. For those who are better off, claiming not to have credit can be a form of humility, representing oneself as just as much of a victim of Nigeria's unjust political economy as one's peers. But the balance can be precarious. Humility can easily be interpreted as stinginess if a wealthy person persists too long in feigning hardship. However, acting too carefree can be seen as ostentatious or arrogant. Ultimately, affluent people are meant to demonstrate and share their prosperity, but in ways that do not humiliate their peers. The proliferation of cell phones has created a very prominent sphere in which the micropolitics of social inequality in Nigeria are enacted (for other examples see Barber 1995; Cornwall 2002; and Smith 2004).

Although Nigerians' cell phone-related social behaviors illustrate the importance of economics in how people manage their phone usage, including strategizing about the social representation of one's wealth, it would be a mistake to emphasize only the economic dimensions of Nigeria's emerging cell phone culture and its associated behavior. A good deal of cell phone-related behavior requires a social rather than an economic interpretation.

Perhaps the most striking example is the way that Nigerians conceptualize cell phone credit. Clearly, everyone who uses cell phones knows how much phone calls cost, and people are aware of the exact amounts in which recharge cards are sold. Further, as the discussion above regarding the phenomenon of flashing suggests, there is a considerable degree of conscious jockeying with regard to sharing and spending one's credit. However, to a remarkable extent, Nigerians seem to think of cell phone credit in much different terms than they think of money. Once money is transformed into cell phone credit through the purchase and loading of recharge cards, cell phone credit becomes much more like food or drink than money, in the sense that people feel more entitled to share in it without the strict incursion of a debt that would be the case if one asked to borrow money. As with food or drink, there is a strong social expectation that cell phone credit should be shared if one has it.

My awareness of the difference between Nigerian and Western (or at least American) sensibilities in this matter was driven home to me by the experience of an American student who worked as my summer research assistant. She lived with a Nigerian family and found them amazingly hospitable and generous, to the point where they refused to allow her to pay rent or contribute to the household budget for food. She felt guilty about this, knowing the family's limited means, and we devised ways that she could contribute without offending her hosts. But when it came to the student's cell phone, the situation was quite the opposite. She had acquired a cell phone mainly so that her parents could call her at any time from the United States. Over the course of the summer, she found that people in the household had no compunctions about asking if she had credit, and, if she did, they had no hesitation in asking to use her phone to make calls. One young woman in the household asked to use her phone so often that the student finally became exasperated and reported it to me. She could not understand how the same family that was so generous and so unwilling to accept her money could expect to use her cell phone in ways that, from her perspective, seemed so insensitive.

Conceived of as a consumable commodity, cell phone credit was easily incorporated into long-standing traditions of sharing, gift giving, and reciprocity, in which people are expected and often genuinely desire to share without incurring the equivalent of a monetary debt. Of course money too is highly implicated in social relationships, and it can be gifted and shared as well as borrowed, lent, or spent, but it was clear from my student's experience, and from numerous similar interactions that I have since participated in and observed, that cell phone credit is transformed into a medium of social exchange that is much different from money once it is loaded into a phone. Nigerians routinely ask their friends and family, and even acquaintances of less intimacy, whether or not they have credit, in ways they would rarely, if ever, ask so openly about money.

The politics of sharing cell phone credit is nonetheless complicated, both because forms of nonmonetary sharing and reciprocity have their own moral economy, with numerous unspoken rules and expectations, and because cell phone credit is, in fact, in some ways more like money than are consumable commodities like food or drink. Even in the sharing of food and drink, in which Nigerians, like people in many societies, are extremely generous and social, there are expectations of generalized reciprocity (Bearman 1997). Although one does not incur a quantifiable debt by sharing someone's food, if, over time, one only takes and never gives, this will be recognized and admonished in some way. Similarly, with the sharing of cell phone credit, someone asking to make calls on another's phone cannot expect indefinite cooperation if favors are not eventually reciprocated.

However, cell phone credit is still more like money than is a beer or a plate of cooked meat. Although ordinary Nigerians have obviously participated in the conversion of cell phone credit from money into a commodity that carries a more social definition, this transformation is not complete. People routinely lied to their friends about their credit, and I observed countless instances in which people were "caught" misrepresenting their credit. At a club in Nigeria where I play tennis, men would commonly pick up a person's phone while he was on the court to check how much credit was available. Someone caught underreporting his credit would almost certainly have to relent and share his phone. Through such actions people contribute to the demonetization of cell phone credit. But this demonetization did not occur without ambivalence. Indeed, the social expectation that one must share phone credit contributed further to the notion that cell phones are a "fire that consumes money."

As these anecdotes suggest, sociality is at least as important a dynamic in Nigerian social life as inequality, and not just in terms of sharing, but also with regard to the importance of regularly greeting and communicating with people in one's social network. The preeminent value of sociality has greatly influenced cell phone usage, in ways that have significant economic implications, even if economic calculations are not always foremost in the minds of cell phone users. Although much of what I have described above demonstrates that Nigerians are highly conscious of the economics of cell phone use and deeply aware of the social implications of cell phone behavior, it is also true that people's penchant for regular communication for purely social purposes means that people make many calls just to say hello and to be in touch. To have a phone and not use it to reach out to family and friends is similar to the idea of living alone or preferring solitude and privacy to social interaction. For most Nigerians it is not only unconscionable, it is unthinkable (Uchendu 1965). As a consequence, although many Nigerians rightly extol the virtues of the country's new cell phone services for promoting business and facilitating a more effective and productive commercial sector, my observations suggest that the vast majority of ordinary customers use a good deal of their credit making calls that are the cellular telephone version of a friendly visit. All this suggests that while cell phone technology has sparked some changes in social life, in many ways the new technology has also adapted to and been incorporated into longer-standing behavioral customs.

"Glo with Pride:" Cell Phones as Status Symbols

As I sat down in the parlor of my friend's house in the south-eastern town of Owerri, her twenty-three-year-old son, Uzoma, inquired whether I owned a cell phone. I said I did, and he asked to see it. After a quick inspection of my very simple and obviously low-end Motorola phone, Uzoma declared dismissively: "This phone doesn't fit you." He meant that a person of my status should have a fancier and more expensive phone, preferably the type currently most popular in Nigeria, where the face flips open, the phone has numerous elaborate technical features, and the screen looks like a computer LCD. I defended my simple phone, but I was not surprised at Uzoma's evaluation. I had encountered this reaction to my phone many times before in a society where cell phones have become important markers of social status.[1]

The relatively educated, mostly urban, and at least marginally economically successful Nigerians who own the majority of the country's more than ten million cell phones are acutely aware of the status distinctions conferred by different models. People are constantly noting the quality of their peers' phones, openly conveying approval or disapproval in ways that consciously connect cell phones to social status. Even where people cannot afford to upgrade their phones, the quality of one's cell phone cover and the type and number of accessories owned can be the subject of more fine-grained attempts to assert both status and fashion. Indeed, as status symbols, the cell phones operate at the cusp between economics and fashion, marking both financial position and sense of style. Uzoma assumed I could afford a more expensive phone, so he concluded that I was either too cheap to own a phone fit for a man of my means or too fashion-challenged to know that my phone was a disgrace.

In a huge country like Nigeria, where many people migrate from their villages of origin to cities and towns in search of education, employment, and economic advancement (Geschiere and Gugler 1998; Gugler 2002), the advent of cell phones in a context where landlines served less than 1 percent of the population has revolutionized communication between family and friends separated by long distances. It is little wonder that so many people want cell phones, or that people who can barely afford some of the basic necessities of everyday life make extraordinary efforts to acquire one. But aside from the practical advantages of cell phone ownership, there is no doubt that cell phones have become an important form of symbolic capital, and that the social status conferred by owning a cell phone is a major motivation for many people (Bourdieu 1984). The cell phone companies cultivate and exploit the symbolic dimensions of cell phone ownership in their advertising, and the pressure of seeing peers enjoy the benefits and social recognition of cell phone ownership induces ever larger numbers of consumers to take the leap.

Whereas just ten years ago, before the advent of GSM technology in Nigeria, cell phones were the exclusive province of the superelite, by 2004 many Nigerians who were not wealthy enough to own their own houses and could not afford to buy a used car were able to acquire the latest marker of modernity.

The transition from an elite exoticism to an almost essential accessory for an aspiring middle class happened remarkably fast. Just two years ago, Umuahia, a small city of less than 200,000 that is the capital of Abia State, had not yet been linked to the network of any of the four main service providers. However, for those who really wanted cell phone service, a regional company called Baudex provided a mostly effective but very expensive service.

At the social club where I frequently played tennis, a playground for the town's elite, approximately fifteen to twenty men owned these Baudex phones in the summer of 2003. To call further attention to the status they displayed by owning and sporting these expensive phones, the owners formed a club within the club. They called themselves "*Ofo* United." "*Ofo*" refers to a mystical staff that is the emblem of traditional authority in Igbo society, a symbol that implies supernatural backing. "United" presumably refers to the name of famous football teams, most notably the world-famous Manchester United, but also to teams in Nigeria that use "United" in their names. The members of *Ofo* United sometimes further separated themselves from other members of the larger club, sharing a roasted goat and several cartons of beer, greeting each other saying "*Ofo* United," and brandishing their phones like some sort of secret society symbol. Just a year later, all this changed dramatically, as both MTN and Glomobile had established full service in Umuahia. By the time I left Nigeria in December of 2004, literally every member of the tennis club had a phone, as did the club's receptionists, one of the bar girls, and some of the kitchen staff. *Ofo* United was no more.

As cell phones have come within the reach of more ordinary citizens, their availability has only intensified the status competition associated with the new technology. Just as the poorest Nigerians have for many years worn watches that do not keep time in order to appear better off than they are, one now sees many young people carrying cell phones that are just shells—though being exposed in such a deception is worse than having no phone at all. Because so many people can aspire to having a cell phone, the distinctions noticed with regard to brands, models, and accessories have become even more fine-grained. Many wealthier people now own multiple phones, with one line for each provider, and they carry them wherever they go. Having a cell phone is no longer so distinctive, but having two or three is still notable. Similarly, making calls to friends or relatives in London or New York, seemingly without a care about the higher cost, can still impress one's peers. In late 2004, camera phones were just hitting the Nigerian market, and I have no doubt they will be all the rage in a very short time.

Conclusion

Although it is impossible to pinpoint the origin of the "killer numbers" rumors described at the start of this article, I suggest that their currency and appeal were related to popular discontents about the role of cell phones in highlighting and sometimes aggravating social inequality. Some speculated that the rumors were the work of one provider trying to undermine the business of another (the killer numbers were first associated with the phone numbers of one company, though, in time, it spread to them all). Others argued that the rumors were a form of consumer revenge, with the allegations meant to damage the reputation and profits of companies toward which customers felt increasing anger. Still others suggested that the rumors were started by some among the vast majority of Nigerians who still cannot afford to own cell phones, in order to strike fear into those who were intimidating their economic inferiors with their ostentatious use of this flashy new technology. More important than these theories about origin is the speed with which the rumors spread and the extent to which they captured popular imagination. The fascination they generated reflects the fact that, as happy as most Nigerians are for their newfound access to a modern communications technology, ordinary citizens remain extremely discontented over the extent of inequality in their society. The new technology is being interpreted, to a large extent, in relation to these discontents.

Note

1. In 2000, *The New York Times* published an article suggesting the importance of cell phones not only for displaying social status generally, but for the attraction of mates. The newspaper account drew on an article in the journal *Human Nature,* entitled "Mobile Phones as Lekking Devices among Human Males" (Lycett and Dunbar 2000). Regardless of whether one finds a sociobiological argument convincing, the association of cell phones with social status seems to strike a chord across many societies.

References

Akinsuyi, Yemi. 2004. Anxiety Over 'Satanic' GSM Phone Numbers. *This Day* (Nigeria), July 23.

Barber, Karin. 1995. Money, Self-Realization, and the Person Yoruba Texts. In *Money Matters: Instability, Values and Social Payments in the Modern History of West African Communities,* ed. J. Guyer, 205–224. Portsmouth, NH: Heinemann.

Bearman, Peter. 1997. Generalized Exchange. *American Journal of Sociology* 102(5): 1383–1415.

Bourdieu, Pierre. 1984. *Distinction: A Social Critique of the Judgement of Taste.* Translated by Richard Nice. Cambridge: Harvard University Press.

Cornwall, Andrea. 2002. Spending Power: Love, Money, and the Reconfiguration of Gender Relations in Ado-Odo, Southwestern Nigeria. *American Ethnologist* 29(4): 963–980.

Dooring, Nicolas. 2002. 'Kurzm-wird-gesendet'—Abbreviations and Acronyms in SMS Communication (Short-Message-Service). *Muttersparche.*

Fox, Barry. 2001. No 2MORO for Text Messaging Lingo. *New Scientist* 171(2298): 24.

Geschiere, Peter, and Josef Gugler. 1998. The Urban-Rural Connection: Changing Issues of Belonging and Identification. *Africa* 68(3): 309–319.

Gugler, Josef. 2002. The Son of a Hawk Does Not Remain Abroad: The Urban-Rural Connection in Africa. *African Studies Review* 45(1): 21–41.

Ikhemuemhe, Godfrey. 2004. The Killer Phone Rumour—Operators Cry Foul. *Vanguard* (Nigeria), July 26, 2004.

Lycett, John, and Robin Dunbar. 2000. Mobile Phones as Lekking Devices among Human Males. *Human Nature* 11(1): 93–104.

Mobile Africa. 2005. Cellular/Mobile Phone Networks in Africa, www.mobileafrica.net/mobile-phone-networks-in-africa.php. (Accessed June 7, 2005).

Obadare, Ebenezer. 2004. "The Great GSM (cell phone) Boycott: Civil Society, Big Business and the State in Nigeria." Dark Roast Occasional Paper Series, No. 18. Cape Town: South Africa: Isandla Institute.

PANA (Pan African News Agency). 2005. Nigeria's Phone Subscriber Base Hits 12 Million. *PanAfrican News Agency Daily Newswire,* May 4.

Smith, Daniel Jordan. 2004. Burials and Belonging in Nigeria: Rural-Urban Relations and Social Inequality in a Contemporary African Ritual. *American Anthropologist* 106(3): 569–579.

Sylvia, K. N., and S. W. Hady. 2004. Communication Pattern with SMS: Short Message Service and MMS: Multimedia Message Service as a Trend of Conduct of Modern Teenagers. *International Journal of Psychology* 39(5–6): 289.

Uchendu, Victor. 1965. *The Igbo of Southeast Nigeria.* Fort Worth, TX: Holt, Reinhart, Winston.

Critical Thinking

1. How and why does cell phone use touch upon wealth, inequality, and status in Nigeria? How are these issues reflected in the vernacular name, "the fire that eats money" and in the use of text messaging? In "flashing"?

2. Describe the economic dimensions of cell phone use and sharing.

3. How do Nigerians think about cell phone credit in different terms than they think of money?

4. In what sense is cell phone use a reflection of sociality?

5. In what respects can cell phones be seen as status symbols in Nigeria?

Create Central

www.mhhe.com/createcentral

Internet References

Smithsonian Institution
  www.si.edu

The Royal Anthropological Institute of Great Britain and Ireland (RAI)
  www.therai.org.uk

DANIEL JORDAN SMITH, "Cell Phones, Sharing, and Social Status in African Society." Reprinted with permission of the author.

Unit 4

UNIT

Prepared by: Elvio Angeloni, *Pasadena City College*

Other Families, Other Ways

Because most people in small-scale societies of the past spent their whole lives within a local area, it is understandable that their primary interactions—economic, religious, and otherwise—were with their relatives. It also makes sense that, through marriage customs, they strengthened those kinship relationships that clearly defined their mutual rights and obligations. More recently, the family structure has had to be surprisingly flexible and adaptive.

For these reasons, anthropologists have looked upon family and kinship as the key mechanisms for transmitting culture from one generation to the next. Social changes may have been slow to take place throughout the world, but as social horizons have widened, family relationships and community alliances are increasingly based upon new principles. Even when birth rates have increased, kinship networks have diminished in size and strength. As people have increasingly become involved with others as coworkers in a market economy, our associations depend more and more upon factors such as personal aptitudes, educational backgrounds, and job opportunities. Yet the family still exists. Except for some rather unusual exceptions, the family is small, but still functions in its age-old nurturing and protective role, even under conditions where there is little affection or under conditions of extreme poverty and a high infant mortality rate. Beyond the immediate family, the situation is in a state of flux. Certain ethnic groups, especially those in poverty, still have a need for the broader network and in some ways seem to be reformulating those ties.

We do not know where these changes will lead us and which ones will ultimately prevail. One thing is certain: Anthropologists will be there to document the trends, because the discipline of anthropology has had to change as well. Indeed, anthropologists exhibit a growing interest in the study of complex societies where old theoretical perspectives are inadequate. The current trends, however, do not necessarily depict the decline of the kinship unit. The large family network is still the best guarantee of individual survival and well-being in an urban setting.

Article   Prepared by: Elvio Angeloni, *Pasadena City College*

The Invention of Marriage

STEPHANIE COONTZ

Learning Outcomes

After reading this article, you will be able to:

- Explain why marriage was an early and vitally important human invention.

- Discuss the various social strategies people have used to create ties between groups and to defuse tensions among hunter-gatherers.

Marriage is a social invention, unique to humans. Of the hundreds of theories, stories, and fables explaining its origins, my favorite is a Blackfoot Indian tale recorded in 1911. I love this story not because I think it's any "truer" than the others but because it makes such a wonderful change from the equally fanciful theories most of us were taught in high school and college during the 1950s and 1960s. Before marriage was invented, according to the Piegan, or Blackfoot Indians:

> The men and women of the ancient Piegans did not live about together in the beginning. The women . . . made buffalo corrals. Their lodges were fine. . . . They tanned the buffalo-hides, those were their robes. They would cut the meat in slices. In summer they picked berries. They used those in winter. Their lodges all were fine inside. And their things were just as fine. . . . Now, the men were . . . very poor. . . . They had no lodges. They wore raw-hides. . . . They did not know, how they should make lodges. They did not know, how they should tan the buffalo-hides. They did not know, too, how they should cut dried meat, how they should sew their clothes.[1]

In the Blackfoot legend, it was the men, not the women, who needed marriage. Hungry and cold, the men followed the women and found out where they lived. Then they gathered on a nearby hill and waited patiently until the women decided to choose husbands and allow them into their lodges. The female chief selected her mate first, and the rest of the women followed suit.

This is only a folktale, of course, but it is no further off the mark than the story that some anthropologists and sociobiologists have told for years. Before marriage was invented, according to an Anglo-American anthropological theory,

The men hunted wild animals and feasted on their meat. Their brains became very large because they had to cooperate with each other in the hunt. They stood upright, made tools, built fires, and invented language. Their cave art was very fine. . . . But the women were very poor. They were tied down by childbearing, and they did not know how to get food for themselves or their babies. They did not know how to protect themselves from predators. They did not know, too, how to make tools, produce art, and build lodges or campfires to keep themselves warm.

In this story, as in the Blackfoot tale, the invention of marriage supplies the happy ending for the hapless sex. Here, however, women were the weaker gender. They initiated marriage by offering to trade sex for protection and food. Instead of the men waiting patiently on the hill for the women to pick their mates, the men got to pick the women, and the strongest, most powerful males got first choice. Then the men set their women up by the hearth to protect them from predators and from rival males.

The story that marriage was invented for the protection of women is still the most widespread myth about the origins of marriage. According to the protective or provider theory of marriage, women and infants in early human societies could not survive without men to bring them the meat of woolly mammoths and protect them from marauding saber-toothed tigers and from other men seeking to abduct them. But males were willing to protect and provide only for their "own" females and offspring they had good reason to believe were theirs, so a woman needed to find and hold on to a strong, aggressive mate.

One way a woman could hold a mate was to offer him exclusive and frequent sex in return for food and protection. According to the theory, that is why women lost the estrus cycle that is common to other mammals, in which females come into heat only at periodic intervals. Human females became sexually available year-round, so they were able to draw men into long-term relationships. In anthropologist Robin Fox's telling of this story, "The females could easily trade on the male's tendency to want to monopolize (or at least think he was monopolizing) the females for mating purposes, and say, in effect 'okay, you get the monopoly . . . and we get the meat.'"[2]

The male willingness to trade meat for sex (with the females throwing in whatever nuts and berries they'd gathered to sweeten the deal) was, according to Fox, "the root of truly human society." Proponents of this protective theory of marriage claim that the nuclear family, based on a sexual division of labor between the male hunter and the female hearth keeper, was the most important unit of survival and protection in the Stone Age.

People in the mid-twentieth century found this story persuasive because it closely resembled the male breadwinner/female homemaker family to which they were accustomed. The male breadwinner model of marriage, as we shall see later, was a late and relatively short-lived way of organizing gender roles and dividing work in human history. But in the 1950s, 1960s, and 1970s most people believed it was the natural and "traditional" family form.

In 1975, sociobiologist E. O. Wilson drew a direct line from the male hunter marriages that he imagined had prevailed on the African savanna at the dawn of human history to the marriages he observed in the jungle of Wall Street: "During the day the women and children remain in the residential area while the men forage for game or its symbolic equivalent in the form of money."[3] The protective theory is still periodically recycled to explain why women are supposedly attracted to powerful, dominant men, while men seek younger women who will be good breeders and hearth keepers.

But since the 1970s other researchers have poked holes in the protective theory of marriage. Some denied that male dominance and female dependence came to us from our primate ancestors. Among baboons, they pointed out, a female who pairs up with a male does not get more access to food than females outside such a relationship. Among chimpanzees, most food sharing occurs between mothers and their offspring, not between male and female sexual partners. Adult female chimps give food to other females (even unrelated ones) just as often as males give food to females, and female chimps are often more protective of other females than males are. A female chimp who wants food from a male may make sexual overtures, or a male chimp who has meat to spare may use it as a bargaining chip. But males cannot control the sexual behavior of the estrus females. And when members of the group, male or female, want food from a female, they hold or play with her infant, in effect offering babysitting for handouts.[4]

Studies of actual human hunting and gathering societies also threw doubt on the male provider theory. In such societies, women's foraging, not men's hunting, usually contributes the bulk of the group's food. The only exceptions to this rule are Eskimo and other herding or hunting peoples in areas where extremely hostile climates make foraging for plants difficult.[5]

Nor are women in foraging societies tied down by child rearing. One anthropologist, working with an African hunter-gatherer society during the 1960s, calculated that an adult woman typically walked about twelve miles a day gathering food, and brought home anywhere from fifteen to thirty-three pounds. A woman with a child under two covered the same amount of ground and brought back the same amount of food while she carried her child in a sling, allowing the child to nurse as the woman did her foraging. In many societies women also participate in hunting, whether as members of communal hunting parties, as individual hunters, or even in all-female hunting groups.

Today most paleontologists reject the notion that early human societies were organized around dominant male hunters providing for their nuclear families. For one thing, in the early phases of hominid and human evolution, hunting big game was less important for group survival than were gathering plants, bird eggs, edible insects, and shellfish, trapping the occasional small animal, and scavenging the meat of large animals that had died of natural causes.

When early humans began to hunt large animals, they did so by driving animals over cliffs or into swamps. These activities involved the whole group, women as well as men. That is what happens in the surrounds conducted by modern-day foragers, where the entire band encircles the game and gradually herds it into a trap.[6]

We cannot know for sure how the earliest hominids and humans organized their reproduction and family lives. But there are three general schools of thought on the subject. Some researchers believe that early humans lived in female-centered groups made up of mothers, sisters, and their young, accompanied by temporary male companions. Younger males, they suggest, left the group when they reached mating age. Other scholars argue that the needs of defense would have encouraged the formation of groups based on male kin, in which fathers, brothers, and sons, along with their female mates, stayed together. In this view, the female offspring rather than males left the group at puberty. A third group of researchers theorizes that hominid groups were organized around one male mating with several females and traveling with them and their offspring. [7]

But none of these three theories, not even the male with his harem, suggests that an individual male provided for "his" females and children or that the male–female pair was the fundamental unit of economic survival and cooperation. No one could have survived very long in the Paleolithic world if individual nuclear families had had to take primary responsibility for all food production, defense, child rearing, and elder care.[8]

A division of labor between males and females certainly developed fairly early and was reinforced when groups developed weapons effective enough to kill moving animals from a distance. Such weapons made it possible for small groups to hunt solitary, fast-moving animals. Hunting with projectile weapons became the domain of men, partly because it was hard for women to chase swift game while they were nursing. So wherever humans organized small hunting parties that left the main camp, they were likely to be all or mostly male. However, this did not make women dependent upon their individual mates.

Women, keeping their children near, were more likely to specialize in gathering and processing plants and shellfish, manufacturing clothing, trapping small animals, and making digging or cooking implements. This gender specialization led to greater interdependence between males and females. As these productive techniques became more complicated, people had to invest more time in teaching them to children, providing an incentive for couples to stay together for longer stretches.

Having a flexible, gender-based division of labor within a mated pair was an important tool for human survival. One partner, typically the female, could concentrate on the surer thing, finding food through foraging or digging. The other partner could try for a windfall, hunting for food that would be plentiful and filling if it could be caught. Yet this division of labor did not make nuclear families self-sufficient. Collective hunting and gathering remained vital to survival.[9]

Couples in the Paleolithic world would never have fantasized about running off by themselves to their own little retreats in the forest. No Stone Age lovers would have imagined in their wildest dreams that they could or should be "everything" to each other. That way lay death.

Until about twelve thousand years ago, say archaeologists Colin Renfrew and Paul Bahn, nearly all human societies were comprised of bands of mobile hunter-gatherers who moved seasonally between different sleeping camps and work sites, depending on the weather and food supply. Humans lived in these band-level societies and small, semipermanent hamlets far longer than the few millennia they have lived in more complex villages, cities, states, and empires.[10]

Reconstructions by archaeologists suggest that bands were made up of anywhere from a handful to as many as a hundred people, but commonly numbered around two dozen. Bands lived off the land, using simple tools to process a wide range of animals and plants for food, medicines, clothing, and fuel. They typically moved back and forth over a home territory until resources were depleted or other environmental changes spurred them to move on. Periodically they might travel longer distances to find valued raw materials and take advantage of seasonal game or fish runs.[11]

Sometimes the band would break down into individual family groups that foraged alone. But the archaeological record shows that families regularly came back to a main camp, or hooked up with a new one, for protection and to cooperate in communal hunts. Regional networks of camps routinely came together at water holes or to collectively exploit fish runs or seasonally abundant plants. During those times, dances, festivals, and other rituals took place, building connections between families and bands that were dispersed for much of the year. On such occasions, people might seek mates—or change them—from within the larger groups.

No one suggests that prehistoric bands existed in utopian harmony. But social interactions were governed by the overwhelming need to pool and share resources. The band's mobility made it impractical for people to accumulate significant surpluses, which would have to be lugged from place to place. In the absence of money and nonperishable wealth, the main currency in nomadic foraging societies would have been favors given and owed. Sharing beyond the immediate family or local group was a rudimentary form of banking. It allowed people to accumulate personal credit or goodwill that could be drawn on later.[12]

Using computer simulations and mathematical calculations to compare the outcome of different ways of organizing the production and consumption of food, economic anthropologist Bruce Winterhalder has established the decisive importance of prehistoric sharing. His calculations show that because the results of hunting and gathering varied on a daily basis, the surest way for individuals to minimize the risk of not having enough to eat on a bad day was not to save what they gathered or killed on good days for later use by their "own" nuclear family, but to pool and divide the whole harvest among the entire group every day.[13]

With few exceptions, hunting and gathering societies throughout history have emphasized sharing and reciprocity. Band-level societies put extraordinary time and energy into establishing norms of sharing. People who share gain status, while individuals who refuse to share are shunned and ostracized. Ethnographer Lorna Marshall reports that for the Dobe !Kung Bushmen of the Kalahari Desert in Africa, "the idea of eating alone and not sharing is shocking. . . . It makes them shriek with uneasy laughter." They think that "lions could do that, not men." In seventeenth-century America, William Penn marveled that the Indians always redistributed the gifts or trade goods that European settlers brought, rather than keep them for their own families. "Wealth circulateth like the Blood," he wrote. "All parts partake."[14]

Many simple hunting and gathering societies place so much emphasis on sharing that a person who kills an animal gets no more of its meat than do his companions. A review of twenty-five hunting and gathering societies found that in only three did the hunter get the largest share of his kill. In most, the hunter was obliged to share the meat equally with other camp members, and in a few he got less than he distributed to others. Anthropologist Polly Wiessner observes that these customs create total interdependence among families: "[T]he hunter spends his life hunting for others, and others spend their lives hunting for him."[15]

The idea that in prehistoric times a man would spend his life hunting only for the benefit of his own wife and children, who were dependent solely upon his hunting prowess for survival, is simply projection of 1950s marital norms onto the past. The male/female pair was a good way to organize sexual companionship, share child rearing, and divide daily work. A man who was a skilled hunter might have been an attractive mate, as would have been a woman who was skilled at foraging or making cooking implements, but marrying a good hunter was not the main way that a woman and her children got access to food and protection.

Marriage was certainly an early and a vitally important human invention. One of its crucial functions in the Paleolithic era was its ability to forge networks of cooperation beyond the immediate family group or local band. Bands needed to establish friendly relations with others so they could travel more freely and safely in pursuit of game, fish, plants, and water holes or move as the seasons changed. Archaeologist Brian Hayden argues that hunter-gatherers of the past used a combination of five strategies to create such ties with other groups and to defuse tensions: frequent informal visits, interband sharing, gift giving, periodic large gatherings for ritual occasions, and the establishment of marriage and kinship ties.[16]

All these customs built goodwill and established social networks beyond a single camp or a group of families. But using marriage to create new ties of kinship was an especially powerful way of binding groups together because it produced children who had relatives in both camps. The Maori of New Zealand say that "a gift connection may be severed, but not so a human link."[17]

However, a kin group that sent its daughters or sons to other groups as marriage partners also needed to make sure that it received spouses in return. Moreover, to create lasting links among groups, the exchange of spouses had to be renewed in later generations.

Sometimes such marriage exchanges would be very direct and immediate, a sister from one group being exchanged for a sister from the other. The exchange need not occur simultaneously, as long as the obligation to pay back one person with another was acknowledged. In other cases, spouses were not exchanged directly. Instead several lineages or clans would be linked in a pattern in which the sisters always married in one direction around the circle while the brothers always married in the opposite one. Lineage A would send its sisters and daughters as wives to lineage B, which sent wives to C, which sent them to A. As practiced among one present-day hunter-gatherer group, the Murngin of Australia, the circle of wife exchange takes seven generations to complete.[18]

Some people believe that from the very beginning, marriage alliances led to strict controls over a young person's choice of mates, especially a woman's. Among the Aborigines of Australia, one of the few places where hunter-gatherer societies lived completely untouched by contact with other societies for thousands of years, marriages were traditionally arranged when girls were still in their childhood and were strictly controlled by elders. Because of the scarcity of food and water in that harsh environment and the need to travel over long distances to ensure survival, Aboriginal elders had to ensure that their community's children were distributed in ways that gave the community family connections to the land and resources wherever they traveled. No rebellion against this system was tolerated.[19]

But the Indians of northeastern North America, who also lived for thousands of years in a "pristine" setting similar to the environment in which many of our Stone Age ancestors operated, traditionally took a very different approach toward marriage, divorce, and sexual activity from that of the Australian Aborigines. Among the Chippewyan people of Canada, the main function of marriage was also to build far-flung personal networks that gave people access to hunting, natural resources, or water holes in other regions. But in this more forgiving environment, individuals tended to make their own marital choices, and no one interfered if a couple decided to part.[20]

Nevertheless, many people argue that marriage originated as a way of exchanging women. Marriage alliances, the eminent anthropologist Claude Lévi-Strauss declared, were "not established between men and women, but between men by means of women." Women were merely the vehicle for establishing this relationship.[21]

In the 1970s several feminist researchers built on this idea to turn the protective theory of marriage on its head. They suggested that marriage originated not to protect women but to oppress them. These researchers argued that because women

probably played a leading role in the invention of agriculture through their experimentation with plants and food preservation, and because women were certainly responsible for the physical reproduction of the group, the origins of marriage lay not in the efforts of women to attract protectors and providers but in the efforts of men to control the productive and reproductive powers of women for their own private benefit.[22]

According to this oppressive theory, men coerced women into marriage, often using abduction, gang rape, or wife beating to enforce their will. Brothers essentially traded their sisters for wives. Fathers gained power in the community by passing their daughters out to young men, who gave the fathers gifts and services in return. Rich men accumulated many wives, who worked for them and bore more daughters who could be exchanged to place other men in their debt.

Like the protective theory of marriage, the oppressive theory still has defenders. Philosopher Iris Marion Young maintains that the historical function of marriage was "to use women as a means of forging alliances among men and perpetuating their 'line.'" Even today, Young says, marriage is "the cornerstone of patriarchal power." Christine Delphy and Diana Leonard argue that marriage is one of the primary ways that "men benefit from, and exploit, the work of women."[23]

In today's political climate, in which men's power over their wives and daughters has greatly diminished, it is tempting to write off the oppressive theory of marriage as a product of 1970s feminist excesses. But there is strong historical evidence that in many societies marriage was indeed a way that men put women's labor to their private use. We can watch this process develop as recently as the eighteenth and nineteenth centuries among the Plains Indians.

In the Blackfoot legend about the origins of marriage, the men got dried meat and berries, warm robes, soft moccasins, and fine lodges only after the women chose to take them as husbands. In real life, men began to accumulate buffalo hides, large lodges, and other "fine" things, including, often, more than one wife, in a process that involved far less female choice.

Before the Europeans introduced the horse to the western United States, the Blackfoot and other Plains Indians hunted buffalo on foot, using surrounds. The entire group—men, women, and children—took part in driving the animals into traps or over cliffs. The men clubbed the buffalo to death, and the women dried the meat and tanned the hides. Although the men took on the more risky, up-close killing tasks, the work was evenly divided, and it was episodic; a good hunt could provide meat and clothes for a long time.[24]

But once Europeans introduced the horse, the gun, and the fur trade to North America, everything changed. Indian men were able to hunt buffalo individually. They had both the opportunity and incentive to kill more buffalo than they needed for their own subsistence because they could trade their surplus to whites for personal gain. This hugely increased the number of hides to be tanned and the amount of meat to be dried. The most successful hunters could now kill far more buffalo than one wife could process, and having more wives suddenly meant having more wealth. Richer men began to accumulate wives by offering horses to girls' fathers.

The expansion of the trade in buffalo hides brought a sharp increase in the number of wives per hunter. It also caused the age of marriage for women to drop to preadolescence, and it greatly multiplied social restrictions upon wives. According to nineteenth-century observers, the practice of keeping multiple wives was most common among groups that traded with the fur companies, and in these groups women's labor was much more intensive. These tribes too were more likely to practice forms of punishment such as cutting off a woman's nose for adultery.[25]

There are many other examples of societies in which men have exchanged women without consulting them and in which husbands have used the labor of their wives and children to produce surpluses that increased the men's prestige and power. It is also true that many more societies exchange women in marriage than exchange men, and there are some disadvantages to being the sex that moves after marriage. But in small-scale societies these disadvantages were not necessarily severe. Women could return home to their parents or call on their brothers for protection. Furthermore, in some societies men were the ones who moved at marriage. In these cases, one could just as easily argue that men were being exchanged by women.

In a current example, the Minangkabau of Indonesia, where marriage perpetuates the female line, refer to a husband as "the borrowed man." In traditional Hopi Indian marriages, a woman's kin made "a ceremonial presentation of cornmeal to the groom's household, conceptualized by the Hopi as 'paying for him.'" There is evidence that marriage systems in which men rather than women were circulated may have been more common in kinship societies of the distant past than in those observed over the past several hundred years.[26]

Even in cultures where women move at marriage, there has always been a huge variation in how much male dominance accompanies this arrangement. There are also enough exceptions to the practice of controlling women through marriage to call the oppressive theory into question. In the early eighteenth century a French baron, traveling among hunting and gathering peoples in what is now Canada, was scandalized to find that native parents believed "their Daughters have the command of their own Bodies and may dispose of their Persons as they think fit; they being at liberty to do what they please."[27]

In many hunting and gathering and simple horticultural societies, parents are likely to arrange a first marriage. They may even force a woman into a match. However, in most societies without extensive private property, marriages tend to be fragile, and women whose families have arranged their marriages frequently leave their husbands or run off with lovers without suffering any reprisals.[28]

I do not believe, then, that marriage was invented to oppress women any more than it was invented to protect them. In most cases, marriage probably originated as an informal way of organizing sexual companionship, child rearing, and the daily tasks of life. It became more formal and more permanent as groups began to exchange spouses over larger distances. There was nothing inherent in the institution of marriage that protected women and children from violence or produced the fair and loving relationships that many modern couples aspire to. But there was also nothing inherent in the institution of marriage, as there was, say, in slavery, that required one group to subordinate another. The effect of marriage on people's individual lives has always depended on its functions in economic and social life, functions that have changed immensely over time.

It is likely that our Stone Age ancestors varied in their behaviors just as do the hunting and gathering societies observed in more recent times. But in early human societies, marriage was primarily a way to extend cooperative relations and circulate people and resources beyond the local group. When people married into new groups, it turned strangers into relatives and enemies into allies.

That changed, however, as societies developed surpluses and became more sedentary, populous, and complex.[29] As kin groups began to assert permanent rights over territory and resources, some families amassed more goods and power than others. When that happened, the wealthier families lost interest in sharing resources, pooling labor, or developing alliances with poorer families. Gradually marriage exchanges became a way of consolidating resources rather than creating a circle of reciprocal obligations and connections.

With the growth of inequality in society, the definition of an acceptable marriage narrowed. Wealthy kin groups refused to marry with poorer ones and disavowed any children born to couples whose marriage they hadn't authorized. This shift constituted a revolution in marriage that was to shape people's lives for thousands of years. Whereas marriage had once been a way of expanding the number of cooperating groups, it now became a way for powerful kin groups to accumulate both people and property.

The Transformation of Marriage in Ancient Societies

Wherever this evolution from foraging bands to sedentary agriculturalists occurred, it was accompanied by a tendency to funnel cooperation and sharing exclusively through family ties and kinship obligations and to abandon more informal ways of pooling or sharing resources. In the American Southwest we can trace this transition through changes in architectural patterns. Originally surplus grains were stored in communal spaces in open, visible parts of the village. Later, storage rooms were enclosed within individual residences and could be entered only from the rooms where the family or household actually lived. Surpluses had become capital to be closely guarded, with access restricted to family members.[30]

As some kin groups became richer than others, they sought ways to enhance their own status and to differentiate themselves from "lesser" families. Excavations of ancient living sites throughout the world show growing disparities in the size and quality of dwellings, as well as in the richness of the objects buried with people.

Greater economic differentiation reshaped the rules of marriage. A kin group or lineage with greater social status and material resources could demand a higher "price" for handing over one of its children in marriage. Within the leading lineages, young men often had to borrow from their seniors in order to marry, increasing the control of elders over junior men as well as over women. A lineage that couldn't pay top prices for spouses had to drop out of the highest rungs of the marriage exchange system. Sometimes a poorer lineage would forgo the bridewealth a groom's family traditionally paid and give its daughters away as secondary wives or concubines to the leading lineages, in order to forge even a second-class connection with a leading family. But in other cases, lower-status kin groups were not allowed to intermarry with those of higher status under any circumstances.[31]

As dominant kin groups became more wealthy and powerful, they married in more restricted circles. Sometimes they even turned away from exogamy (the practice of marrying out of the group) and engaged in endogamy (marriage with close kin), in order to preserve and consolidate their property and kin members.[32] The more resources were at stake in marriage alliances, the more the relatives had an interest in whom their kin married, whether a marriage lasted, and whether a second marriage, which might produce new heirs to complicate the transmission of property, could be contracted if the first one ended.

In many ancient agricultural societies, if an heir was already in place and the birth of another child would complicate inheritance and succession, a woman might be forced to remain single and celibate after her husband's death. In a few cultures the ideal was for a widow to kill herself after her husband died.[33] More often, the surviving spouse was required to marry another member of the deceased's family in order to perpetuate the alliance between the two kin groups.

In India, early law codes provided that a widow with no son had to marry her husband's brother, in order to produce a male child to carry on his lineage. The Old Testament mentions several examples of the same custom. Indeed, it seems to have been preferred practice among the ancient Hebrews. A man who refused to marry his brother's widow had to go through a public ceremony of halizah, or "unshoeing." This passage from the Torah shows how intense the social pressure was against making such a choice: "Then shall his brother's wife come unto him in the presence of the elders, and loose his shoe from off his foot, and spit in his face, and shall answer and say, so shall it be done unto that man that will not build up his brother's house. And his name shall be called in Israel the house of him that hath his shoe loosed."[34]

As marriage became the primary vehicle for transmitting status and property, both men and women faced greater restrictions on their behavior. Men, like women, could be forced to marry women chosen by their parents. But because women could bear a child with an "impure" bloodline, introducing a "foreign interest" into a family, their sexual behavior tended to be more strictly supervised, and females were subject to severe penalties for adultery or premarital sex. The laws and moral codes of ancient states exhorted men to watch carefully over their wives "lest the seed of others be sown on your soil."[35]

Distinctions between legitimate and illegitimate children became sharper in all the early states. Children born into unauthorized liaisons could not inherit land, titles, or citizenship rights and so in many cases were effectively condemned to slavery or starvation.

The subordination of wives in the ancient world was exacerbated by the invention of the plow. Use of the plow diminished the value of women's agricultural labor, because plowing requires greater strength than women were believed to have and is less compatible with child care than gardening with a hoe. Husbands began to demand dowries instead of giving bridewealth for wives, and daughters were devalued to the point that families sometimes resorted to female infanticide. The spread of warfare that accompanied the emergence of early states also pushed women farther down in the hierarchy.[36]

As societies became more complex and differentiated, upper classes sometimes displayed their wealth by adopting standards of beauty or behavior that effectively hobbled women. Restrictive clothing, heavy jewelry, or exceedingly long fingernails, for example, made a public statement that the family had slaves to do the work once done by wives and daughters. By the second millennium B.C. the practice of secluding women in special quarters had become widespread in the Middle East. This was done not just to guard their chastity but to signify that a family had so much wealth that its women did not even have to leave the home.

Much later, in China, binding the feet of young girls became a symbol of prestige. Upper-class girls had their feet bound so tightly that the small bones broke and the feet were permanently bowed over, making it excruciatingly painful to walk.[37]

In many societies, elaborate ideologies of purity grew up around the women of the highest-ranking classes. A man who courted a high-ranking woman outside regular channels faced harsh sanctions or even death, while women who stepped out of their assigned places in the marriage market were severely punished.

Assyrian laws from the twelfth and eleventh centuries B.C. guarded women's premarital virginity and condemned to death married women who committed adultery. Married women were required to wear veils, but concubines were forbidden to do so. A man who wanted to raise the status of his concubine and make her his wife could have her veiled. But a woman who veiled herself without the authority of a propertied husband was to be flogged fifty times, have tar poured over her head, and have her ears cut off.[38]

Women's bodies came to be regarded as the properties of their fathers and husbands. Assyrian law declared: "A man may flog his wife, pluck her hair, strike her and mutilate her ears. There is no guilt." The Old Testament suggests that a bride whose virginity was not intact could be stoned to death.[39]

Centuries later in China, Confucius defined a wife as "someone who submits to another." A wife, according to Confucian philosophy, had to follow "the rule of the three obediences: while at home she obeys her father, after marriage she obeys her husband, after he dies she obeys her son."[40]

But men too faced new controls over their personal behavior. If a woman could no longer choose her mate, this also meant that a man could not court a wife on his own initiative but needed to win her father's permission. And in many states, the confinement of wives to household activities "freed" their husbands to be drafted into the army or dragooned into back-breaking labor on huge public works projects.[41]

By the time we have written records of the civilizations that arose in the ancient world, marriage had become the way most wealth and land changed hands. Marriage was also the main vehicle by which leading families expanded their social networks and political influence. It even sealed military alliances and peace treaties.

With so much at stake, it is hardly surprising that marriage became a hotbed of political intrigue. Families and individuals developed elaborate strategies to create unions that furthered their interests and to block marriages that might benefit their rivals. Elites jockeyed to acquire powerful in-laws. If, after they had agreed to seal a match, a better one presented itself, they maneuvered (and sometimes murdered) to get out of the old one.

Commoners could no longer hope to exchange marriage partners with the elites. At best they might hope to have one of their children marry up. Even this became more difficult as intricate distinctions were created between the rights of primary wives, secondary wives, and concubines. Formal rules detailed what kinds of marriage could and could not produce legitimate heirs. In some places authorities prohibited lower-class groups from marrying at all or made it illegal for individuals from different social classes to wed each other.

The right to decide who could marry whom had become an extremely valuable political and economic weapon and remained so for thousands of years. From the Middle Eastern kingdoms that arose three thousand years before the birth of Christ to the European ones fifteen hundred years later, factions of the ruling circles fought over who had the right to legitimize marriages or authorize divorces. These battles often changed the course of history.

For millennia, the maneuvering of families, governing authorities, and social elites prevailed over the individual desires of young people when it came to selecting or rejecting marriage partners. It was only two hundred years ago that men and women began to wrest control over the right to marry from the hands of parents, church, and state. And only in the last hundred years have women had the independence to make their marital choices without having to bow to economic need and social pressure.

Have we come full circle during the past two centuries, as the power of kin, community, and state to arrange, prohibit, and interfere in marriages has waned? Legal scholar Harry Wille-kins argues that in most modern industrial societies, marriages are contracted and dissolved in ways that have more in common with the habits of some egalitarian band-level societies than the elaborate rules that governed marriage in more complex societies over the past 5,000 years.[42] In many contemporary societies, there is growing acceptance of premarital sex, divorce, and remarriage, along with an erosion of sharp distinctions between cohabitation and marriage and between "legitimate" and out-of-wedlock births.

Some people note this resemblance between modern family relations and the informal sexual and marital norms of many band-level societies and worry that we are throwing away the advantages of civilization. They hope to reinstitutionalize marriage as the main mechanism that regulates sexuality, legitimizes children, organizes the division of labor between men and women, and redistributes resources to dependents. But the last century of social change makes this highly unlikely. Yet if it is unrealistic to believe we can reimpose older social controls over marriage, it is also naive to think we can effortlessly revive the fluid interpersonal relationships that characterized simpler cultures. In hunting and gathering bands and egalitarian horticultural communities, unstable marriages did not lead to the impoverishment of women or children as they often do today. Unmarried women participated in the work of the group and were entitled to a fair share, while children and other dependents were protected by strong customs that mandated sharing beyond the nuclear family.

This is not the case today, especially in societies such as the United States, where welfare provisions are less extensive than in Western Europe. Today's winner-take-all global economy may have its strong points, but the practice of pooling resources and sharing with the weak is not one of them. The question of how we organize our personal rights and obligations now that our older constraints are gone is another aspect of the contemporary marriage crisis.

Critical Thinking

1. Explain why the story that marriage was invented for the protection of women was such a persuasive theory in the mid-twentieth century. In what ways have researchers poked holes in this theory?

2. What have been the three general schools of thought on how the earliest hominids and humans organized their reproduction and family lives?

3. How does the author characterize early hunter-gatherer societies and their gender-based division of labor and why?

4. What were such societies like, according to reconstructions by archaeologists?

5. Discuss the importance of prehistoric sharing. How is this contrary to the 1950s marital norms?

6. Why was marriage "an early and a vitally important human invention"?

7. According to archaeologist Brian Hayden, what were the five strategies used to create ties with groups and to defuse tensions?

8. Be familiar with some of the means by which marriage became an especially powerful way of binding groups together.

9. Discuss the "oppressive theory" as to the origin of marriage and the evidence provided by the author to contradict it.

10. How did the development of surpluses and a more sedentary life-style change the function of marriage?

11. How did greater economic differentiation reshape the rules of marriage, inheritance, and sexual behavior?

12. How was the subordination of wives in the ancient world exacerbated by the invention of the plow?

13. How is it that, as societies became more complex and differentiated, upper classes sometimes displayed their wealth by adopting standards of beauty or behavior that effectively hobbled women? What kinds of controls did men face?

14. In what ways did marriage become a "hotbed of political intrigue"?

15. Now that women have achieved some degree of economic independence and there is a degree of resemblance in family relations between ourselves and band-level societies, have we come full circle? Explain.

Create Central

www.mhhe.com/createcentral

Internet References

Kinship and Social Organization
www.umanitoba.ca/anthropology

Sex and Marriage
http://anthro.palomar.edu/marriage/default.htm

Wedding Traditions and Customs
http://worldweddingtraditions.com

Article   Prepared by: Elvio Angeloni, *Pasadena City College*

When Brothers Share a Wife

Among Tibetans, the Good Life Relegates Many Women to Spinsterhood

MELVYN C. GOLDSTEIN

Learning Outcomes

After reading this article, you will be able to:

- Discuss why "fraternal polyandry" is socially acceptable in Tibet but not in our society.

- Explain the disappearance and subsequent revival of fraternal polyandry in Tibet.

Eager to reach home, Dorje drives his yaks hard over the 17,000-foot mountain pass, stopping only once to rest. He and his two older brothers, Pema and Sonam, are jointly marrying a woman from the next village in a few weeks, and he has to help with the preparations.

Dorje, Pema, and Sonam are Tibetans living in Limi, a 200-square-mile area in the northwest corner of Nepal, across the border from Tibet. The form of marriage they are about to enter—fraternal polyandry in anthropological parlance—is one of the world's rarest forms of marriage but is not uncommon in Tibetan society, where it has been practiced from time immemorial. For many Tibetan social strata, it traditionally represented the ideal form of marriage and family.

The mechanics of fraternal polyandry are simple. Two, three, four, or more brothers jointly take a wife, who leaves her home to come and live with them. Traditionally, marriage was arranged by parents, with children, particularly females, having little or no say. This is changing somewhat nowadays, but it is still unusual for children to marry without their parents' consent. Marriage ceremonies vary by income and region and range from all the brothers sitting together as grooms to only the eldest one formally doing so. The age of the brothers plays an important role in determining this: very young brothers almost never participate in actual marriage ceremonies, although they typically join the marriage when they reach their mid-teens.

The eldest brother is normally dominant in terms of authority, that is, in managing the household, but all the brothers share the work and participate as sexual partners. Tibetan males and females do not find the sexual aspect of sharing a spouse the least bit unusual, repulsive, or scandalous, and the norm is for the wife to treat all the brothers the same.

Offspring are treated similarly. There is no attempt to link children biologically to particular brothers, and a brother shows no favoritism toward his child even if he knows he is the real father because, for example, his other brothers were away at the time the wife became pregnant. The children, in turn, consider all of the brothers as their fathers and treat them equally, even if they also know who is their real father. In some regions children use the term "father" for the eldest brother and "father's brother" for the others, while in other areas they call all the brothers by one term, modifying this by the use of "elder" and "younger."

Unlike our own society, where monogamy is the only form of marriage permitted, Tibetan society allows a variety of marriage types, including monogamy, fraternal polyandry, and polygyny. Fraternal polyandry and monogamy are the most common forms of marriage, while polygyny typically occurs in cases where the first wife is barren. The widespread practice of fraternal polyandry, therefore, is not the outcome of a law requiring brothers to marry jointly. There is choice, and in fact, divorce traditionally was relatively simple in Tibetan society. If a brother in a polyandrous marriage became dissatisfied and wanted to separate, he simply left the main house and set up his own household. In such cases, all the children stayed in the main household with the remaining brother(s), even if the departing brother was known to be the real father of one or more of the children.

The Tibetans' own explanation for choosing fraternal polyandry is materialistic. For example, when I asked Dorje why he decided to marry with his two brothers rather than take his own wife, he thought for a moment, then said it prevented the division of his family's farm (and animals) and thus facilitated all of them achieving a higher standard of living. And when I later asked Dorje's bride whether it wasn't difficult for her to cope with three brothers as husbands, she laughed and echoed the rationale of avoiding fragmentation of the family and land, adding that she expected to be better off economically, since she would have three husbands working for her and her children.

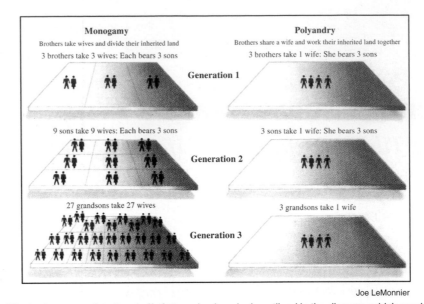

Monogamy		Polyandry
Brothers take wives and divide their inherited land		Brothers share a wife and work their inherited land together
3 brothers take 3 wives: Each bears 3 sons	**Generation 1**	3 brothers take 1 wife: She bears 3 sons
9 sons take 9 wives: Each bears 3 sons	**Generation 2**	3 sons take 1 wife: She bears 3 sons
27 grandsons take 27 wives	**Generation 3**	3 grandsons take 1 wife

Joe LeMonnier

Family Planning in Tibet An economic rationale for fraternal polyandry is outlined in the diagram, which emphasizes only the male offspring in each generation. If every wife is assumed to bear three sons, a family splitting up into monogamous households would rapidly multiply and fragment the family land. In this case, a rule of inheritance, such as primogeniture, could retain the family land intact, but only at the cost of creating many landless male offspring. In contrast, the family practicing fraternal polyandry maintains a steady ratio of persons to land.

Exotic as it may seem to Westerners, Tibetan fraternal polyandry is thus in many ways analogous to the way primogeniture functioned in nineteenth-century England. Primogeniture dictated that the eldest son inherited the family estate, while younger sons had to leave home and seek their own employment—for example, in the military or the clergy. Primogeniture maintained family estates intact over generations by permitting only one heir per generation. Fraternal polyandry also accomplishes this but does so by keeping all the brothers together with just one wife so that there is only one *set* of heirs per generation.

While Tibetans believe that in this way fraternal polyandry reduces the risk of family fission, monogamous marriages among brothers need not necessarily precipitate the division of the family estate: brothers could continue to live together, and the family land could continue to be worked jointly. When I asked Tibetans about this, however, they invariably responded that such joint families are unstable because each wife is primarily oriented to her own children and interested in their success and well-being over that of the children of the other wives. For example, if the youngest brother's wife had three sons while the eldest brother's wife had only one daughter, the wife of the youngest brother might begin to demand more resources for her children since, as males, they represent the future of the family. Thus, the children from different wives in the same generation are competing sets of heirs, and this makes such families inherently unstable. Tibetans perceive that conflict will spread from the wives to their husbands and consider this likely to cause family fission. Consequently, it is almost never done.

Although Tibetans see an economic advantage to fraternal polyandry, they do not value the sharing of a wife as an end in itself. On the contrary, they articulate a number of problems inherent in the practice. For example, because authority is customarily exercised by the eldest brother, his younger male siblings have to subordinate themselves with little hope of changing their status within the family. When these younger brothers are aggressive and individualistic, tensions and difficulties often occur despite there being only one set of heirs.

In addition, tension and conflict may arise in polyandrous families because of sexual favoritism. The bride normally sleeps with the eldest brother, and the two have the responsibility to see to it that the other males have opportunities for sexual access. Since the Tibetan subsistence economy requires males to travel a lot, the temporary absence of one or more brothers facilitates this, but there are also other rotation practices. The cultural ideal unambiguously calls for the wife to show equal affection and sexuality to each of the brothers (and vice versa), but deviations from this ideal occur, especially when there is a sizable difference in age between the partners in the marriage.

Dorje's family represents just such a potential situation. He is fifteen years old and his two older brothers are twenty-five and twenty-two years old. The new bride is twenty-three years old, eight years Dorje's senior. Sometimes such a bride finds the youngest husband immature and adolescent and does not treat him with equal affection; alternatively, she may find his youth attractive and lavish special attention on him. Apart from that consideration, when a younger male like Dorje grows up, he may consider his wife "ancient" and prefer the company of a woman his own age or younger. Consequently, although men and women do not find the idea of sharing a bride or bridegroom repulsive, individual likes and dislikes can cause familial discord.

Two reasons have commonly been offered for the perpetuation of fraternal polyandry in Tibet: that Tibetans practice female infanticide and therefore have to marry polyandrously, owing to a shortage of females; and that Tibet, lying at extremely high altitudes, is so barren and bleak that Tibetans would starve without resort to this mechanism. A Jesuit who lived in Tibet during the eighteenth century articulated this second view: "One reason for this most odious custom is the sterility of the soil, and the small amount of land that can be cultivated owing to the lack of water. The crops may suffice if the brothers all live together, but if they form separate families they would be reduced to beggary."

Both explanations are wrong, however. Not only has there never been institutionalized female infanticide in Tibet, but Tibetan society gives females considerable rights, including inheriting the family estate in the absence of brothers. In such cases, the woman takes a bridegroom who comes to live in her family and adopts her family's name and identity. Moreover, there is no demographic evidence of a shortage of females. In Limi, for example, there were (in 1974) sixty females and fifty-three males in the fifteen- to thirty-five-year age category, and many adult females were unmarried.

The second reason is also incorrect. The climate in Tibet is extremely harsh, and ecological factors do play a major role perpetuating polyandry, but polyandry is not a means of preventing starvation. It is characteristic, not of the poorest segments of the society, but rather of the peasant landowning families.

In the old society, the landless poor could not realistically aspire to prosperity, but they did not fear starvation. There was a persistent labor shortage throughout Tibet, and very poor families with little or no land and few animals could subsist through agricultural labor, tenant farming, craft occupations such as carpentry, or by working as servants. Although the per person family income could increase somewhat if brothers married polyandrously and pooled their wages, in the absence of inheritable land, the advantage of fraternal polyandry was not generally sufficient to prevent them from setting up their own households. A more skilled or energetic younger brother could do as well or better alone, since he would completely control his income and would not have to share it with his siblings. Consequently, while there was and is some polyandry among the poor, it is much less frequent and more prone to result in divorce and family fission.

An alternative reason for the persistence of fraternal polyandry is that it reduces population growth (and thereby reduces the pressure on resources) by relegating some females to lifetime spinsterhood. Fraternal polyandrous marriages in Limi (in 1974) averaged 2.35 men per woman, and not surprisingly, 31 percent of the females of child-bearing age (twenty to forty-nine) were unmarried. These spinsters either continued to live at home, set up their own households, or worked as servants for other families. They could also become Buddhist nuns. Being unmarried is not synonymous with exclusion from the reproductive pool. Discreet extramarital relationships are tolerated, and actually half of the adult unmarried women in Limi had one or more children. They raised these children as single mothers, working for wages or weaving cloth and blankets for

sale. As a group, however, the unmarried woman had far fewer offspring than the married women, averaging only 0.7 children per woman, compared with 3.3 for married women, whether polyandrous, monogamous, or polygynous. While polyandry helps regulate population, this function of polyandry is not consciously perceived by Tibetans and is not the reason they consistently choose it.

If neither a shortage of females nor the fear of starvation perpetuates fraternal polyandry, what motivates brothers, particularly younger brothers, to opt for this system of marriage? From the perspective of the younger brother in a land-holding family, the main incentive is the attainment or maintenance of the good life. With polyandry, he can expect a more secure and higher standard of living, with access not only to this family's land and animals but also to its inherited collection of clothes, jewelry, rugs, saddles, and horses. In addition, he will experience less work pressure and much greater security because all responsibility does not fall on one "father." For Tibetan brothers, the question is whether to trade off the greater personal freedom inherent in monogamy for the real or potential economic security, affluence, and social prestige associated with life in a larger, labor-rich polyandrous family.

A brother thinking of separating from his polyandrous marriage and taking his own wife would face various disadvantages. Although in the majority of Tibetan regions all brothers theoretically have rights to their family's estate, in reality Tibetans are reluctant to divide their land into small fragments. Generally, a younger brother who insists on leaving the family will receive only a small plot of land, if that. Because of its power and wealth, the rest of the family usually can block any attempt of the younger brother to increase his share of land through litigation. Moreover, a younger brother may not even get a house and cannot expect to receive much above the minimum in terms of movable possessions, such as furniture, pots, and pans. Thus, a brother contemplating going it on his own must plan on achieving economic security and the good life not through inheritance but through his own work.

The obvious solution for younger brothers—creating new fields from virgin land—is generally not a feasible option. Most Tibetan populations live at high altitudes (above 12,000 feet), where arable land is extremely scarce. For example, in Dorje's village, agriculture ranges only from about 12,900 feet, the lowest point in the area, to 13,300 feet. Above that altitude, early frost and snow destroy the staple barley crop. Furthermore, because of the low rainfall caused by the Himalayan rain shadow, many areas in Tibet and northern Nepal that are within the appropriate altitude range for agriculture have no reliable sources of irrigation. In the end, although there is plenty of unused land in such areas, most of it is either too high or too arid.

Even where unused land capable of being farmed exists, clearing the land and building the substantial terraces necessary for irrigation constitute a great undertaking. Each plot has to be completely dug out to a depth of two to two and half feet so that the large rocks and boulders can be removed. At best, a man might be able to bring a few new fields under cultivation in the first years after separating from his brothers, but he could not expect to acquire substantial amounts of arable land this way.

In addition, because of the limited farmland, the Tibetan subsistence economy characteristically includes a strong emphasis on animal husbandry. Tibetan farmers regularly maintain cattle, yaks, goats, and sheep, grazing them in the areas too high for agriculture. These herds produce wool, milk, cheese, butter, meat, and skins. To obtain these resources, however, shepherds must accompany the animals on a daily basis. When first setting up a monogamous household, a younger brother like Dorje would find it difficult to both farm and manage animals.

In traditional Tibetan society, there was an even more critical factor that operated to perpetuate fraternal polyandry—a form of hereditary servitude somewhat analogous to serfdom in Europe. Peasants were tied to large estates held by aristocrats, monasteries, and the Lhasa government. They were allowed the use of some farmland to produce their own subsistence but were required to provide taxes in kind and corvée (free labor) to their lords. The corvée was a substantial hardship, since a peasant household was in many cases required to furnish the lord with one laborer daily for most of the year and more on specific occasions such as the harvest. This enforced labor, along with the lack of new land and ecological pressure to pursue both agriculture and animal husbandry, made polyandrous families particularly beneficial. The polyandrous family allowed an internal division of adult labor, maximizing economic advantage. For example, while the wife worked the family fields, one brother could perform the lord's corvée, another could look after the animals, and a third could engage in trade.

Although social scientists often discount other people's explanations of why they do things, in the case of Tibetan fraternal polyandry, such explanations are very close to the truth. The custom, however, is very sensitive to changes in its political and economic milieu and, not surprisingly, is in decline in most Tibetan areas. Made less important by the elimination of the traditional serf-based economy, it is disparaged by the dominant non-Tibetan leaders of India, China, and Nepal. New opportunities for economic and social mobility in these countries, such as the tourist trade and government employment, are also eroding the rationale for polyandry, and so it may vanish within the next generation.

Author's Note

The Revival of Fraternal Polyandry in Tibet: Old Solutions for New Problems

In spite of my observation at the end of this article—that political and economic changes were eroding the rationality for fraternal polyandry—there has been a remarkable revival of polyandry in the Tibet Autonomous Region.

After the failed Tibetan Uprising in 1959, the Chinese government acted to end the traditional land-holding system and replace it with communes in which individual commune members worked under a set of managers. Fraternal polyandry ended, as families had no land to conserve and farm.

The rise to power of Deng Xiaoping in 1978 changed China radically. China now opened its doors to the West and adopted Western-style market economics complete with the reintroduction of the profit motive and individual wealth seeking. In rural Tibet, this resulted in communes closing in 1980–81, with each commune member receiving an equal share of the commune's land regardless of age or sex. Thus, if each person received 1 acre, a family of 6 received 6 acres, on which it now managed to maximize production and income. However, families actually held this land as a long-term lease from the government so land could not be bought or sold. Consequently, as children were born and the size of families grew, land per capita began to decrease. At the same time, as sons reached the age of marriage, it was obvious that if families with several sons allowed each to marry and set up nuclear families, the land the family received from the commune would decline dramatically, and with no way to buy more land, each of the family units would have difficulty growing enough grain for subsistence. Families, therefore, as in the old society, began to utilize traditional fraternal polyandry to keep their sons together at marriage to conserve the family's land intact across generations.

A second factor underlying the widespread revival of fraternal polyandry concerned its concentration of male labor in the family. However, in the new socioeconomic environment, this has not been used to fulfill corvée labor obligations to one's lord (as mentioned in the article), but rather to increase family income by sending surplus labor (one or more of the set of siblings) to "go for income," i.e., to go outside the village as migrant laborers to earn cash income working for part of the year in cities or on rural construction projects. By the time of my last stint of fieldwork in rural Tibet in 2009, this had become the largest source of rural family income.

Fraternal polyandry has therefore undergone an unexpected revival in Tibet because its traditional functions of conserving land intact across generations and concentrating male labor in the family has offered families in the new economic system old solutions to new problems. Rapidly changing socioeconomic conditions, therefore, do not necessarily erode traditional cultural practices. They can, as in this case, revive and sustain them as well.

Critical Thinking

1. What is "fraternal polyandry"? How is it arranged?

2. How do marriage ceremonies vary? When do younger brothers typically join the marriage?

3. How are authority, work, and sex dealt with?

4. Describe the relationship between fathers and children. How is family structure reflected in kinship terminology?

5. What types of marriage are allowed in Tibetan society? Which are the most common? When does polygyny typically occur? Is fraternal polyandry a matter of law or choice? What happens if a brother is dissatisfied? What about his children?

6. How do the Tibetans explain fraternal polyandry? How is this analogous to primogeniture in 19th-century England?

7. Why does it seem that monogamous marriages among brothers in the same household would not work?

8. What kinds of problems occur with fraternal polyandry that make it less than ideal?

9. What two reasons have been commonly offered for the perpetuation of fraternal polyandry in Tibet and how does the author refute these?

10. What percentage of women remain unmarried in Tibetan society? What happens to them? To what extent does polyandry thereby limit population growth? Are the Tibetans aware of this effect?

11. Why would a younger brother accept such a marriage form?

12. How is the polyandrous family more adaptive to the system of hereditary servitude in traditional Tibet?

13. Why is the custom of fraternal polyandry in decline?

14. Explain the disappearence and subsequent revival of fraternal polyandry in Tibet.

Create Central

www.mhhe.com/createcentral

Internet References

Sex and Marriage
http://anthro.palomar.edu/marriage/default.htm

Wedding Traditions and Customs
http://worldweddingtraditions.com

MELVYN C. GOLDSTEIN, now a professor of anthropology at Case Western Reserve University in Cleveland, has been interested in the Tibetan practice of fraternal polyandry (several brothers marrying one wife) since he was a graduate student in the 1960s.

Goldstein., Melvyn C. From *Natural History*, March 1987, pp. 39–48. Copyright © 1987 by Natural History Magazine. Reprinted by permission.

Article   Prepared by: Elvio Angeloni, *Pasadena City College*

No More Angel Babies on the Alto do Cruzeiro

A dispatch from brazil's revolution in child survival.

NANCY SCHEPER-HUGHES

Learning Outcomes

After reading this article, you will be able to:

- Describe and explain the "normalization" of infant death as it once occurred on the Alto do Cruzeiro in Brazil.

- Discuss the economic and political changes in Brazil that led to the decline in "angel babies."

It was almost 50 years ago that I first walked to the top of the Alto do Cruzeiro (the Hill of the Crucifix) in Timbaúba, a sugar-belt town in the state of Pernambuco, in Northeast Brazil. I was looking for the small mud hut, nestled in a cliff, where I was to live. It was December 1964, nine months after the coup that toppled the left-leaning president, João Goulart. Church bells were ringing, and I asked the woman who was to host me as a Peace Corps volunteer why they seemed to ring at all hours of the day. "Oh, it's nothing," she told me. "Just another little angel gone to heaven."

That day marked the beginning of my life's work. Since then, I've experienced something between an obsession, a trauma, and a romance with the shantytown. Residents of the newly occupied hillside were refugees from the military junta's violent attacks on the peasant league movement that had tried to enforce existing laws protecting the local sugarcane cutters. The settlers had thrown together huts made of straw, mud, and sticks or, lacking that, lean-tos made of tin, cardboard, and scrap materials. They had thrown together families in the same makeshift fashion, taking whatever was at hand and making do. In the absence of husbands, weekend play fathers did nicely as long as they brought home the current baby's powdered milk, if not the bacon. Households were temporary; in such poverty women were the only stable force, and babies and fathers were circulated among them. A man who could not provide support would be banished to take up residence with another, even more desperate woman; excess infants and babies were often rescued by older women, who took them in as informal foster children.

Premature death was an everyday occurrence in a shanty-town lacking water, electricity, and sanitation and beset with food scarcity, epidemics, and police violence. My assignment was to immunize children, educate midwives, attend births, treat infections, bind up festering wounds, and visit mothers and newborns at home to monitor their health and refer them as needed to the district health post or to the emergency room of the private hospital—owned by the mayor's brother—where charity cases were sometimes attended, depending on the state of local patron-client relations.

I spent several months making the rounds between the miserable huts on the Alto with a public-health medical kit strapped on my shoulder. Its contents were pathetic: a bar of soap, scissors, antiseptics, aspirin, bandages, a glass syringe, some ampules of vaccine, several needles, and a pumice stone to sharpen the needles, which were used over and over again for immunizations. Children ran away when they saw me coming, and well they might have.

But what haunted me then, in addition to my own incompetence, was something I did not have the skill or maturity to understand: Why didn't the women of the Alto grieve over the deaths of their babies? I tucked that question away. But as Winnicott, the British child psychoanalyst, liked to say, "Nothing is ever forgotten."

Sixteen years elapsed before I was able to return to the Alto do Cruzeiro, this time as a medical anthropologist. It was in 1982—during the period known as the abertura, or opening, the beginning of the end of the military dictatorship—that I made the first of the four trips that formed the basis for my 1992 book, *Death Without Weeping: The Violence of Everyday Life in Brazil.* My goal was to study women's lives, specifically mother love and child death under conditions so dire that the Uruguayan writer Eduardo Galeano once described the region as a concentration camp for 30 million people. It was not a gross exaggeration. Decades of nutritional studies of sugarcane cutters and their families in Pernambuco showed hard evidence of slow starvation and stunting. These nutritional dwarfs were surviving on a daily caloric intake similar to that of the inmates of the Buchenwald concentration camp. Life on the Alto resembled prison-camp culture, with a moral ethic based on triage and survival.

If mother love is the cultural expression of what many attachment theorists believe to be a bioevolutionary script, what could this script mean to women living in these conditions? In my sample of three generations of mothers in the sugar plantation zone of Pernambuco, the average woman had 9.5 pregnancies, 8 live births, and 3.5 infant deaths. Such high rates of births and deaths are typical of societies that have not undergone what population experts call the demographic transition, associated with economic development, in which first death rates and, later, birth rates drop as parents begin to trust that more of their infants will survive. On the contrary, the high expectation of loss and the normalization of infant death was a powerful conditioner of the degree of maternal attachments. Mothers and infants could also be rivals for scarce resources. Alto mothers renounced breastfeeding as impossible, as sapping far too much strength from their own "wrecked" bodies.

Scarcity made mother love a fragile emotion, postponed until the newborn displayed a will to live—a taste (gusto) and a knack (jeito) for life. A high expectancy of death prepared mothers to "let go" of and to hasten the death of babies that were failing to thrive, by reducing the already insufficient food, water, and care. The "angel babies" of the Alto were neither of this Earth nor yet fully spirits. In appearance they were ghostlike: pale and wispy-haired; their arms and legs stripped of flesh; their bellies grossly distended; their eyes blank and staring; and their faces wizened, a cross between startled primate and wise old sorcerer.

The experience of too much loss, too much death, led to a kind of patient resignation that some clinical psychologists might label "emotional numbing" or the symptoms of a "masked depression." But the mothers' resignation was neither pathological nor abnormal. Moreover, it was a moral code. Not only had a continual exposure to trauma obliterated rage and protest, it also minimized attachment so as to diminish sorrow.

Infant death was so commonplace that I recall a birthday party for a four-year-old in which the birthday cake, decorated with candles, was placed on the kitchen table next to the tiny blue cardboard coffin of the child's nine-month-old sibling, who had died during the night. Next to the coffin a single vigil candle was lit. Despite the tragedy, the child's mother wanted to go ahead with the party. "Parabens para pace," we sang, clapping our hands. "Congratulations to you!" the Brazilian birthday song goes. And on the Alto it had special resonance: "Congratulations, you survivor you—you lived to see another year!"

When Alto mothers cried, they cried for themselves, for those left behind to continue the struggle. But they cried the hardest for their children who had almost died, but who surprised everyone by surviving against the odds. Wiping a stray tear from her eye, an Alto mother would speak with deep emotion of the child who, given up for dead, suddenly beat death back, displaying a fierce desire for life. These tough and stubborn children were loved above all others.

Staying alive in the shantytown demanded a kind of egoism that often pits individuals against each other and rewards those who take advantage of those weaker than themselves. People admired toughness and strength; they took pride in babies or adults who were cunning and foxy. The toddler that was wild and fierce was preferred to the quiet and obedient child. Men and women with seductive charm, who could manipulate those around them, were better off than those who were kind. Poverty doesn't ennoble people, and I came to appreciate what it took to stay alive.

Theirs were moral choices that no person should be forced to make. But the result was that infants were viewed as limitless. There was a kind of magical replaceability about them, similar to what one might find on a battlefield. As one soldier falls, another takes his place. This kind of detached maternal thinking allowed the die-offs of shantytown babies—in some years, as many as 40 percent of all the infants born on the Alto died—to pass without shock or profound grief. A woman who had lost half her babies told me, "Who could bear it, Nanci, if we are mistaken in believing that God takes our infants to save us from pain? If that is not true, then God is a cannibal. And if our little angels are not in heaven flying around the throne of Our Lady, then where are they, and who is to blame for their deaths?"

If mothers allowed themselves to be attached to each newborn, how could they ever live through their babies' short lives and deaths and still have the stamina to get pregnant and give birth again and again? It wasn't that Alto mothers did not experience mother love at all. They did, and with great intensity. But mother love emerged as their children developed strength and vitality. The apex of mother love was not the image of Mary and her infant son, but a mature Mary, grieving the death of her young adult son. The Pieta, not the young mother at the crèche, was the symbol of motherhood and mother love on the Alto.

In *Death Without Weeping*, I first told of a clandestine extermination group that had begun to operate in Timbaúba in the 1980s. The rise of these vigilantes seemed paradoxical, insofar as it coincided with the end of the 20-year military dictatorship. What was the relationship between democracy and death squads? No one knew who was behind the extrajudicial limpeza ("street cleaning," as their supporters called it) that was targeting "dirty" street children and poor young Black men from the shantytowns. But by 2000 the public was well aware of the group and the identity of its leader, Abdoral Gonçalves Queiroz. Known as the "Guardian Angels," they were responsible for killing more than 100 victims. In 2001 I was invited, along with my husband, to return to Timbaúba to help a newly appointed and tough-minded judge and state prosecutor to identify those victims whose relatives had not come forward. In the interim, the death squad group had infiltrated the town council, the mayor's office, and the justice system. But 11 of them, including their semiliterate gangster-boss, Queiroz, had been arrested and were going on trial.

The death squad was a residue of the old military regime. For 20 years, the military police had kept the social classes segregated, with "dangerous" street youths and unemployed rural men confined to the hillside slums or in detention. When the old policing structures loosened following the democratic transition, the shantytowns ruptured and poor people, especially unemployed young men and street children, flooded downtown streets and public squares, once the preserve of gente fina (the cultivated people). Their new visibility betrayed the illusion of Brazilian modernity and evoked contradictory emotions of fear, aversion, pity, and anger.

Excluded and reviled, unemployed Black youths and loose street kids of Timbaúba were prime targets of Queiroz and his gang. Depending on one's social class and politics, the band could be seen as hired serial killers or as justiceiros (outlaw heroes) who were protecting the community. Prominent figures—well-known businessmen and local politicians—applauded the work of the death squad, whom they also called "Police 2," and some of these leading citizens were active in the extrajudicial "courts" that were deciding who in Timbaúba should be the next to die.

During the 2001 death-squad field research expedition, I played cat-and-mouse with Dona Amantina, the dour manager of the cartorio civil, the official registry office. I was trying to assemble a body count of suspicious homicides that could possibly be linked to the death squad, focusing on the violent deaths of street kids and young Black men. Since members of the death squad were still at large, I did not want to make public what I was doing. At first, I implied that I was back to count infant and child deaths, as I had so many years before. Finally,

I admitted that I was looking into youth homicides. The manager nodded her head. "Yes, it's sad. But," she asked with a shy smile, "haven't you noticed the changes in infant and child deaths?" Once I began to scan the record books, I was wearing a smile, too.

Brazil's national central statistics bureau, the Instituto Brasileiro de Geografia e Estatística (IBGE), began reporting data for the municipality of Timbaúba in the late 1970s. In 1977, for example, IBGE reported 761 live births in the municipality and 311 deaths of infants (up to one year of age) for that same year, yielding an infant mortality rate of 409 per 1,000. A year later, the IBGE data recorded 896 live births and 320 infant deaths, an infant mortality rate of 357 per 1,000. If reliable, those official data indicated that between 36 and 41 percent of all infants in Timbaúba died in the first 12 months of life.

During the 1980s, when I was doing the research for *Death Without Weeping*, the then mayor of Timbaúba, the late Jacques Ferreira Lima, disputed those figures. "Impossible!" he fumed "This municipio is growing, not declining." He sent me to the local private hospital built by, and named for, his father, Joío Ferreira Lima, to compare the IBGE statistics with the hospital's records on births and deaths. There, the head nurse gave me access to her records, but the official death certificates only concerned stillbirths and perinatal deaths. In the end, I found that the best source of data was the ledger books of the cartorio civil, where births and infant and child deaths were recorded by hand. Many births were not recorded until after a child had died, in order to register a death and receive a free coffin from the mayor's office. The statistics were as grim as those of the IBGE.

In 2001, a single afternoon going over infant and toddler death certificates in the same office was enough to document that something radical had since taken place—a revolution in child survival that had begun in the 1990s. The records now showed a completed birth rate of 3.2 children per woman and a mortality rate of 35 per 1,000 births. Subsequent field trips in 2006 and 2007 showed even further reductions. The 2009 data from the IBGE recorded a rate of 25.2 child deaths per 1,000 births for Timbaúba.

Though working on other topics in my Brazilian field trips in 2001, 2006, and 2007, I took the time to interview several young women attending a pregnancy class at a newly constructed, government-run clinic. The women I spoke with—some first-time mothers, others expecting a second or third child—were confident in their ability to give birth to a healthy baby. No one I spoke to expected to have, except by accident, more than two children. A pair—that was the goal. Today, young women of the Alto can expect to give birth to three or fewer infants and to see all of them live at least into adolescence. The old stance of maternal watchful waiting accompanied by deselection of infants viewed as having no "talent" for life had been replaced by a maternal ethos of "holding on" to every infant, each seen as likely to survive. As I had noted in the past as well, there was a preference for girl babies. Boys, women feared, could disappoint their mothers—they could kill or be killed as adolescents and young men. The Alto was still a dangerous place, and gangs, drug dealers, and the death squads were still in operation. But women in the state-run clinic spoke of having control over their reproductive lives in ways that I could not have imagined.

By 2001 Timbaúba had experienced the demographic transition. Both infant deaths and births had declined so precipitously that it looked like a reproductive workers' strike. The numbers—though incomplete—were startling. Rather than the more than 200 annual infant and child mortalities of the early 1980s, by the late 1990s there were fewer than 50 childhood deaths recorded per year. And the causes of death were specific. In the past, the causes had been stated in vague terms: "undetermined," "heart stopped, respiration stopped," "malnutrition," or the mythopoetic diagnosis of "acute infantile suffering."

On my latest return, just this June, the reproductive revolution was complete. The little two-room huts jumbled together on the back roads of the Alto were still poor, but as I visited the homes of dozens of Alto residents, sometimes accompanied by a local community health agent, sometimes dropping in for a chat unannounced, or summoned by the adult child of a former key informant of mine, I saw infants and toddlers who were plump and jolly, and mothers who were relaxed and breastfeeding toddlers as old as three years. Their babies assumed a high status in the family hierarchy, as precious little beings whose beauty and health brought honor and substance—as well as subsistence—to the household.

Manufactured cribs with pristine sheets and fluffy blankets, disposal diapers, and plastic rattles were much in evidence. Powdered milk, the number one baby killer in the past, was almost a banned substance. In contrast, no one, literally, breastfed during my early years of research on the Alto. It was breast milk that was banned, banned by the owners of the sugar plantations and by the bourgeois patrons (mistresses of the house) for whom the women of the Alto washed clothes and cleaned and cooked and served meals. Today, those jobs no longer exist. The sugar mills and sugar estates have closed down, and the landowning class has long since moved, leaving behind a population of working-class poor, a thin middle class (with washing machines rather than maids), and a displaced rural labor force that is largely sustained by the largesse of New Deal–style federal assistance.

Direct cash transfers are made to poor and unemployed families, and grants (bolsas, or "purses") are given to women, mothers, babies, schoolchildren, and youth. The grants come with conditions. The balsa familiar (family grant), a small cash payment to each mother and up to five of her young children, requires the mother to immunize her babies, attend to their medical needs, follow medical directions, keep the children in school, monitor their homework, help them prepare for exams, and purchase school books, pens and pencils, and school clothes. Of the 30 Alto women between the ages of 17 and 40 my research associate, Jennifer S. Hughes, and I interviewed in June, the women averaged 3.3 pregnancies—higher than the national average, but the real comparison here is with their own mothers, who (based on the 13 of the 30 who could describe their mothers' reproductive histories) averaged 13.6 pregnancies and among them counted 61 infant deaths. Jennifer is my daughter and a professor of colonial and postcolonial Latin American history at the University of California, Riverside. I like to think that her awesome archival skills were honed more than 20 years ago when I enlisted her, then a teenager, to help me count the deaths of Alto babies in the civil registry office. She agreed to help me on this most recent field trip, and it was our first professional collaboration.

Jennifer, for example, looked up Luciene, the first-born daughter of Antonieta, one of my earliest key informants and my neighbor when I lived on the Alto do Cruzeiro. Now in her 40s, Luciene had only one pregnancy and one living child. Her mother had given birth to 15 babies, 10 of whom survived. Daughter and mother now live next door to each other, and they spoke openly and emotionally about the "old days," "the hungry times," "the violent years," in comparison to the present. "Today we are rich," Antonieta declared, "really rich," by which she meant her modernized home on the Alto Terezinha, their new color television set, washing machine, and all the food and delicacies they could want.

Four of the 30 women we interviewed had lost an infant, and one had lost a two year old who drowned playing with a large basin of water. Those deaths were seen as tragic and painful memories. The mothers did not describe the deaths in a monotone or dismiss them as inevitable or an act of mercy that relieved their suffering. Rather, they recalled with deep sadness the date, the time, and the cause of their babies' deaths, and remembered them by name, saying that Gloria would be 10 today or that Marcos would be eight years old today, had she or he lived.

What has happened in Timbaúba over the past decades is part of a national trend in Brazil. Over the past decade alone, Brazil's fertility rate has decreased from 2.36 to 1.9 children per family—a number that is below the replacement rate and lower than that of the United States. Unlike in China or India, this reproductive revolution occurred without state coercion. It was a voluntary transition and a rapid one.

A footnote in *Death Without Weeping* records the most common requests that people made of me in the 1960s and again in the 1980s: Could I possibly help them obtain false teeth?

[A] pair of eyeglasses? [A] better antibiotic for a sick older child? But most often I was asked—begged—by women to arrange a clandestine sterilization. In Northeast Brazil, sterilization was always preferable to oral contraceptives, IUDs, and condoms. Reproductive freedom meant having the children you wanted and then "closing down the factory." "A fábrica é fechada!" a woman would boastfully explain, patting her abdomen. Until recently, this was the privilege of the upper middle classes and the wealthy. Today, tubal ligations are openly discussed and arranged. One woman I interviewed, a devout Catholic, gushed that God was good, so good that he had given her a third son, her treasure trove, and at the same time had allowed her the liberty and freedom of a tubal ligation. "Praise to God!" she said. "Amen," I said.

In Brazil, the reproductive revolution is linked to democracy and the coming into political power of President Fernando Henrique Cardoso (1995–2002), aided by his formidable wife, the anthropologist and women's advocate Ruth Cardoso. It was continued by Luiz Inacio Lula da Silva, universally called "Lula," and, since 2011, by his successor, Dilma Rousseff. President Lula's Zero Hunger campaign, though much criticized in the popular media as a kind of political publicity stunt, in fact has supplied basic foodstuffs to the most vulnerable households.

Today food is abundant on the Alto. Schoolchildren are fed nutritious lunches, fortified with a protein mixture that is prepared as tasty milk shakes. There are food pantries and state and municipal milk distribution programs that are run by women with an extra room in their home. The monthly stipends to poor and single mothers to reward them for keeping their children in school has turned elementary school pupils into valuable household "workers," and literacy has increased for both the children and their mothers, who study at home alongside their children.

When I first went to the Alto in 1964 as a Peace Corps volunteer, it was in the role of a visitadora, a public-health community worker. The military dictatorship was suspicious of the program, which mixed health education and immunizations with advocating for water, street lights, and pit latrines as universal entitlements—owed even to those who had "occupied public land" (like the people of the Alto, who had been dispossessed by modernizing sugar plantations and mills). The visitadora program, Brazil's version of Chinese "barefoot doctors," was targeted by the military government as subversive, and the program ended by 1966 in Pernambuco. Many years later President Cardoso fortified the national health care system with a similar program of local "community health agents," who live and work in their micro-communities, visiting at-risk households, identifying crises, diagnosing common symptoms, and intervening to rescue vulnerable infants and toddlers from premature death. In Timbaúba, there are some 120 community health agents, male and female, working in poor micro-communities throughout the municipality, including dispersed rural communities. On the Alto do Cruzeiro 12 health agents each live and work in a defined area, each responsible for the health and well-being of some 150 families comprising 500 to 600 individuals. The basic requirement for a health worker is to have completed ensino fundamental, the equivalent of primary and middle school. Then, he or she must prepare for a public concurso, a competition based on a rigorous exam.

The community health agent's wage is small, a little more than the Brazilian minimum wage, but still less than US $700 a month for a 40-hour work week, most of it on foot up and down the hillside "slum" responding to a plethora of medical needs, from diaper rash to an emergency home birth. The agent records all births, deaths, illnesses, and other health problems in the micro-community; refers the sick to health posts, emergency rooms, and hospitals; monitors pregnancies and the health of newborns, the disabled, and the elderly. He or she identifies and reports communicable diseases and acts as a public-health and environmental educator. The agent participates in public meetings to shape health policies. Above all, the community health agent is the primary intermediary between poor people and the national health care system.

I am convinced that the incredible decline in premature deaths and useless suffering that I witnessed on the Alto is primarily the result of these largely unheralded medical heroes, who rescue mothers and their children in a large town with few doctors and no resident surgeons, pediatricians, and worst of all, obstetricians. A pregnant woman of the Alto suffers today from one of the worst dilemmas and anxieties a person in her condition can face: no certain location to give birth. The only solution at present is to refer women in labor to distant obstetric and maternity wards in public hospitals in Recife, the state capital, a 67-mile drive away. The result can be fatal: at least one woman in the past year was prevented (by holding her legs together) from delivering her baby in an ambulance, and both mother and child died following their arrival at the designated hospital in Recife. For this reason, Alto women and their health agents often choose prearranged cesarian sections well in advance of due dates, even though they know that C-sections are generally not in the best interest of mothers or infants.

Then, beyond the human factor, environmental factors figure in the decline in infant mortality in the shantytowns of Timbaúba and other municipalities in Northeast Brazil. The most significant of these is the result of a simple, basic municipal public-health program: the installation of water pipes that today reach nearly all homes with sufficient clean water. It is amazing to observe the transformative potential of material conditions: water = life!

Finally, what about the role of the Catholic Church? The anomaly is that, in a nation where the Catholic Church predominates in the public sphere and abortion is still illegal except in the case of rape or to save a mother's life, family size has dropped so sharply over the last two decades. What is going on? For one thing, Brazilian Catholics are independent, much like Catholics in the United States, going their own way when it comes to women's health and reproductive culture. Others have simply left Catholicism and joined evangelical churches, some of which proclaim their openness to the reproductive rights of women and men. Today only 60 percent of Brazilians identify as Roman Catholic. In our small sample of 30 women of the Alto, religion—whether Catholic, Protestant, Spiritist, or Afro-Brazilian—did not figure large in their reproductive lives.

The Brazilian Catholic Church is deeply divided. In 2009, the Archbishop of Recife announced the Vatican's excommunication of the doctors and family of a nine-year-old girl who had an abortion. She had been raped by her stepfather (thus the abortion was legal), and she was carrying twins—her tiny stature and narrow hips putting her life in jeopardy. After comparing abortion to the Holocaust, Archbishop José Cardoso Sobrinho told the media that the Vatican rejects believers who pick and choose their moral issues. The result was an immediate decline in church attendance throughout the diocese.

While the Brazilian Catholic hierarchy is decidedly conservative, the rural populace, their local clerics, and liberation theologians such as the activist ex-priest Leonardo Boff are open in their interpretations of Catholic spirituality and corporeality. The Jesus that my Catholic friends on the Alto embrace is a sensitive and sentient Son of God, a man of sorrows, to be sure, and also a man of compassion, keenly attuned to simple human needs. The teachings of liberation theology, while condemned by Pope John Paul II, helped to dislodge a baroque folk Catholicism in rural Northeast Brazil that envisioned God and the saints as authorizing and blessing the deaths of angel babies.

Padre Orlando, a young priest when I first met him in 1987, distanced himself from the quaint custom of blessing the bodies of dead infants as they were carried to the municipal graveyard in processions led by children. He also invited me and my Brazilian research assistant to give an orientation on family planning to poor Catholic women in the parish hall. When I asked what form of contraception I could teach, he replied, "I'm a celibate priest, how should I know? Teach it all, everything you know." When I reminded him that only the very unpredictable rhythm method was approved by the Vatican, he replied, "Just teach it all, everything you know, and then say, but the Pope only approves the not-so-safe rhythm method."

The people of the Alto do Cruzeiro still face many problems. Drugs, gangs, and death squads have left their ugly mark. Homicides have returned with a vengeance, but they are diffuse

and chaotic, the impulsive murders one comes to expect among poor young men—the unemployed, petty thieves, and small-time drug dealers—and between rival gangs. One sees adolescents and young men of the shantytowns, who survived that dangerous first year of life, cut down by bullets and knives at the age of 15 or 17 by local gangs, strongmen, bandidos, and local police in almost equal measure. The old diseases also raise their heads from time to time: schistosomiasis, Chagas disease, tuberculosis, and even cholera.

But the bottom line is that women on the Alto today do not lose their infants. Children go to school rather than to the cane fields, and social cooperatives have taken the place of shadow economies. When mothers are sick or pregnant or a child is ill, they can go to the well-appointed health clinic supported by both state and national funds. There is a safety net, and it is wide, deep, and strong.

Just as we were leaving in mid-June, angry, insurgent crowds were forming in Recife, fed up with political corruption, cronyism, and the extravagant public expenditures in preparation for the 2014 World Cup in Brazil—when the need was for public housing and hospitals. Those taking to the streets were mostly young, urban, working-class, and new middle-class Brazilians. The rural poor were generally not among them. The people of the Alto do Cruzeiro (and I imagine in many other communities like it) are strong supporters of the government led by the PT (Partido dos Trabalhadores, or Workers' Party). Under the PT, the government has ended hunger in Pernambuco and has opened family clinics and municipal schools that treat them and their children with respect for the first time in their lives.

The protesters in the streets are among the 40 million Brazilians who were added to the middle class between 2004 and 2010, under the government of President Lula, and whose rising expectations are combustible. When the healthy, literate children of the Alto do Cruzeiro grow up, they may yet join future protests demanding more accountability from their elected officials.

Critical Thinking

1. Discuss the conditions on the Alto do Cruzeiro that help to explain the "normalization" of infant death.

2. Describe the demographic transition and the effect it has on a mother's trust that her infant will survive.

3. When and why do Alto mothers cry?

4. Describe and explain the egoism that is admired and demanded in the shantytown.

5. Explain "magical replaceability" regarding children.

6. Discuss the "detached maternal thinking" and the emergence of mother love in the context of religious beliefs.

7. Explain the appearance of the death squads.

8. Describe the demographic transition in terms of what has brought it about and the resulting attitudes toward having children.

9. Describe the deep divisions within the Brazilian Catholic Church with respect to family planning.

Create Central

www.mhhe.com/createcentral

Internet References

American Anthropological Association Children and Childhood Interest Group

http://aaacig.usu.edu/

Journal of Medical Ethics

http://jme.bmj.com/

Latin American Studies

www.library.arizona.edu/search/subjects

NANCY SCHEPER-HUGHES'S renowned book *Death Without Weeping* was preceded by her *Natural History* article of the same title in October 1989. More recently, Scheper-Hughes contributed "Truth and Rumor on the Organ Trail" (October 1998). Scheper Hughes's most recent books are *Commodifying Bodies,* co-edited with Loic Waquant (Sage Publications Ltd, 2002), and *Violence in War and Peace: An Anthology,* co-edited with Philippe Bourgois (Basil Blackwell Ltd, 2003). An updated and abridged paperback edition of *Death Without Weeping* will be published by the University of California Press in the summer of 2014. Scheper-Hughes is Chancellor's Professor of Anthropology at the University of California, Berkeley, and the cofounder and director of Organs Watch, a medical human-rights project.

Article — Prepared by: Elvio Angeloni, *Pasadena City College*

Arranging a Marriage in India

SERENA NANDA

Learning Outcomes

After reading this article, you will be able to:

- List the pros and cons of arranged marriages versus love marriages.

- Discuss the factors that must be taken into account in arranging a marriage in India.

> Sister and doctor brother-in-law invite correspondence from North Indian professionals only, for a beautiful, talented, sophisticated, intelligent sister, 5'3", slim, M.A. in textile design, father a senior civil officer. Would prefer immigrant doctors, between 26–29 years. Reply with full details and returnable photo.
>
> A well-settled uncle invites matrimonial correspondence from slim, fair, educated South Indian girl, for his nephew, 25 years, smart, M.B.A., green card holder, 5'6". Full particulars with returnable photo appreciated.
>
> —*Matrimonial Advertisements,*
> India Abroad

In India, almost all marriages are arranged. Even among the educated middle classes in modern, urban India, marriage is as much a concern of the families as it is of the individuals. So customary is the practice of arranged marriage that there is a special name for a marriage which is not arranged: It is called a "love match."

On my first field trip to India, I met many young men and women whose parents were in the process of "getting them married." In many cases, the bride and groom would not meet each other before the marriage. At most they might meet for a brief conversation, and this meeting would take place only after their parents had decided that the match was suitable. Parents do not compel their children to marry a person who either marriage partner finds objectionable. But only after one match is refused will another be sought.

As a young American woman in India for the first time, I found this custom of arranged marriage oppressive. How could any intelligent young person agree to such a marriage without great reluctance? It was contrary to everything I believed about the importance of romantic love as the only basis of a happy marriage. It also clashed with my strongly held notions that the choice of such an intimate and permanent relationship could be made only by the individuals involved. Had anyone tried to arrange my marriage, I would have been defiant and rebellious!

At the first opportunity, I began, with more curiosity than tact, to question the young people I met on how they felt about this practice. Sita, one of my young informants, was a college graduate with a degree in political science. She had been waiting for over a year while her parents were arranging a match for her. I found it difficult to accept the docile manner in which this well-educated young woman awaited the outcome of a process that would result in her spending the rest of her life with a man she hardly knew, a virtual stranger, picked out by her parents.

"How can you go along with this?" I asked her, in frustration and distress. "Don't you care who you marry?"

"Of course I care," she answered. "This is why I must let my parents choose a boy for me. My marriage is too important to be arranged by such an inexperienced person as myself. In such matters, it is better to have my parents' guidance."

I had learned that young men and women in India do not date and have very little social life involving members of the opposite sex. Although I could not disagree with Sita's reasoning, I continued to pursue the subject.

Young men and women do not date and have very little social life involving members of the opposite sex.

"But how can you marry the first man you have ever met? Not only have you missed the fun of meeting a lot of different people, but you have not given yourself the chance to know who is the right man for you."

"Meeting with a lot of different people doesn't sound like any fun at all," Sita answered. "One hears that in America the girls are spending all their time worrying about whether they will meet a man and get married. Here we have the chance to enjoy our life and let our parents do this work and worrying for us."

She had me there. The high anxiety of the competition to "be popular" with the opposite sex certainly was the most prominent feature of life as an American teenager in the late fifties. The endless worrying about the rules that governed our behavior and about our popularity ratings sapped both our self-esteem and our enjoyment of adolescence. I reflected that absence of this competition in India most certainly may have contributed to the self-confidence and natural charm of so many of the young women I met.

And yet, the idea of marrying a perfect stranger, whom one did not know and did not "love," so offended my American ideas of individualism and romanticism, that I persisted with my objections.

"I still can't imagine it," I said. "How can you agree to marry a man you hardly know?"

"But of course he will be known. My parents would never arrange a marriage for me without knowing all about the boy's family background. Naturally we will not rely only on what the family tells us. We will check the particulars out ourselves. No one will want their daughter to marry into a family that is not good. All these things we will know beforehand."

Impatiently, I responded, "Sita, I don't mean know the family, I mean, know the man. How can you marry someone you don't know personally and don't love? How can you think of spending your life with someone you may not even like?"

"If he is a good man, why should I not like him?" she said. "With you people, you know the boy so well before you marry, where will be the fun to get married? There will be no mystery and no romance. Here we have the whole of our married life to get to know and love our husband. This way is better, is it not?"

Her response made further sense, and I began to have second thoughts on the matter. Indeed, during months of meeting many intelligent young Indian people, both male and female, who had the same ideas as Sita, I saw arranged marriages in a different light. I also saw the importance of the family in Indian life and realized that a couple who took their marriage into their own hands was taking a big risk, particularly if their families were irreconcilably opposed to the match. In a country where every important resource in life—a job, a house, a social circle—is gained through family connections, it seemed foolhardy to cut oneself off from a supportive social network and depend solely on one person for happiness and success.

Six years later I returned to India to again do fieldwork, this time among the middle class in Bombay, a modern, sophisticated city. From the experience of my earlier visit, I decided to include a study of arranged marriages in my project. By this time I had met many Indian couples whose marriages had been arranged and who seemed very happy. Particularly in contrast to the fate of many of my married friends in the United States who were already in the process of divorce, the positive aspects of arranged marriages appeared to me to outweigh the negatives. In fact, I thought I might even participate in arranging a marriage myself. I had been fairly successful in the United States in "fixing up" many of my friends, and I was

confident that my matchmaking skills could be easily applied to this new situation, once I learned the basic rules. "After all," I thought, "how complicated can it be? People want pretty much the same things in a marriage whether it is in India or America."

An opportunity presented itself almost immediately. A friend from my previous Indian trip was in the process of arranging for the marriage of her eldest son. In India there is a perceived shortage of "good boys," and since my friend's family was eminently respectable and the boy himself personable, well educated, and nice looking, I was sure that by the end of my year's fieldwork, we would have found a match.

The basic rule seems to be that a family's reputation is most important. It is understood that matches would be arranged only within the same caste and general social class, although some crossing of subcastes is permissible if the class positions of the bride's and groom's families are similar. Although dowry is now prohibited by law in India, extensive gift exchanges took place with every marriage. Even when the boy's family do not "make demands," every girl's family nevertheless feels the obligation to give the traditional gifts, to the girl, to the boy, and to the boy's family. Particularly when the couple would be living in the joint family—that is, with the boy's parents and his married brothers and their families, as well as with unmarried siblings—which is still very common even among the urban, upper-middle class in India, the girls' parents are anxious to establish smooth relations between their family and that of the boy. Offering the proper gifts, even when not called "dowry," is often an important factor in influencing the relationship between the bride's and groom's families and perhaps, also, the treatment of the bride in her new home.

In a society where divorce is still a scandal and where, in fact, the divorce rate is exceedingly low, an arranged marriage is the beginning of a lifetime relationship not just between the bride and groom but between their families as well.

In a society where divorce is still a scandal and where, in fact, the divorce rate is exceedingly low, an arranged marriage is the beginning of a lifetime relationship not just between the bride and groom but between their families as well. Thus, while a girl's looks are important, her character is even more so, for she is being judged as a prospective daughter-in-law as much as a prospective bride. Where she would be living in a joint family, as was the case with my friend, the girls's ability to get along harmoniously in a family is perhaps the single most important quality in assessing her suitability.

My friend is a highly esteemed wife, mother, and daughter-in-law. She is religious, soft-spoken, modest, and deferential. She rarely gossips and never quarrels, two qualities highly desirable in a woman. A family that has the reputation for gossip and conflict among its womenfolk will not find it easy to get

Even today, almost all marriages in India are arranged. It is believed that parents are much more effective at deciding whom their daughters should marry.

good wives for their sons. Parents will not want to send their daughter to a house in which there is conflict.

My friend's family were originally from North India. They had lived in Bombay, where her husband owned a business, for forty years. The family had delayed in seeking a match for their eldest son because he had been an Air Force pilot for several years, stationed in such remote places that it had seemed fruitless to try to find a girl who would be willing to accompany him. In their social class, a military career, despite its economic security, has little prestige and is considered a drawback in finding a suitable bride. Many families would not allow their daughters to marry a man in an occupation so potentially dangerous and which requires so much moving around.

The son had recently left the military and joined his father's business. Since he was a college graduate, modern, and well traveled, from such a good family, and, I thought, quite handsome, it seemed to me that he, or rather his family, was in a position to pick and choose. I said as much to my friend.

While she agreed that there were many advantages on their side, she also said, "We must keep in mind that my son is both short and dark; these are drawbacks in finding the right match." While the boy's height had not escaped my notice, "dark" seemed to me inaccurate; I would have called him "wheat" colored perhaps, and in any case, I did not realize that color would be a consideration. I discovered, however, that while a boy's skin color is a less important consideration than a girl's, it is still a factor.

An important source of contacts in trying to arrange her son's marriage was my friend's social club in Bombay. Many of the women had daughters of the right age, and some had already expressed an interest in my friend's son. I was most enthusiastic about the possibilities of one particular family who had five daughters, all of whom were pretty, demure, and well educated. Their mother had told my friend, "You can have your pick for your son, whichever one of my daughters appeals to you most."

I saw a match in sight. "Surely," I said to my friend, "we will find one there. Let's go visit and make our choice." But my friend held back; she did not seem to share my enthusiasm, for reasons I could not then fathom.

When I kept pressing for an explanation of her reluctance, she admitted, "See, Serena, here is the problem. The family has so many daughters, how will they be able to provide nicely for any of them? We are not making any demands, but still, with so many daughters to marry off, one wonders whether she will even be able to make a proper wedding. Since this is our eldest son, it's best if we marry him to a girl who is the only daughter, then the wedding will truly be a gala affair." I argued that surely the quality of the girls themselves made up for any deficiency in the elaborateness of the wedding. My friend admitted this point but still seemed reluctant to proceed.

"Is there something else," I asked her, "some factor I have missed?" "Well," she finally said, "there is one other thing. They have one daughter already married and living in Bombay. The mother is always complaining to me that the girl's in-laws don't let her visit her own family often enough. So it makes me wonder, will she be that kind of mother who always wants her daughter at her own home? This will prevent the girl from adjusting to our house. It is not a good thing." And so, this family of five daughters was dropped as a possibility.

Somewhat disappointed, I nevertheless respected my friend's reasoning and geared up for the next prospect. This was also the daughter of a woman in my friend's social club. There was clear interest in this family and I could see why. The family's reputation was excellent; in fact, they came from a subcaste slightly higher than my friend's own. The girl, who was an only daughter, was pretty and well educated and had a brother studying in the United States. Yet, after expressing an interest to me in this family, all talk of them suddenly died down and the search began elsewhere.

"What happened to that girl as a prospect?" I asked one day. "You never mention her any more. She is so pretty and so educated, what did you find wrong?"

"She is too educated. We've decided against it. My husband's father saw the girl on the bus the other day and thought her forward. A girl who 'roams about' the city by herself is not the girl for our family." My disappointment this time was even greater, as I thought the son would have liked the girl very much. But then I thought, my friend is right, a girl who is going to live in a joint family cannot be too independent or she will make life miserable for everyone. I also learned that if the family of the girl has even a slightly higher social status than the family of the boy, the bride may think herself too good for them, and this too will cause problems. Later my friend admitted to me that this had been an important factor in her decision not to pursue the match.

The next candidate was the daughter of a client of my friend's husband. When the client learned that the family was looking for a match for their son, he said, "Look no further, we have a daughter." This man then invited my friends to dinner to see the girl. He had already seen their son at the office and decided that "he liked the boy." We all went together for tea, rather than dinner—it was less of a commitment—and while we were there, the girl's mother showed us around the house. The girl was studying for her exams and was briefly introduced to us.

After we left, I was anxious to hear my friend's opinion. While her husband liked the family very much and was impressed with his client's business accomplishments and reputation, the wife didn't like the girl's looks. "She is short, no doubt, which is an important plus point, but she is also fat and wears glasses." My friend obviously thought she could do better for her son and asked her husband to make his excuses to his client by saying that they had decided to postpone the boy's marriage indefinitely.

By this time almost six months had passed and I was becoming impatient. What I had thought would be an easy matter

to arrange was turning out to be quite complicated. I began to believe that between my friend's desire for a girl who was modest enough to fit into her joint family, yet attractive and educated enough to be an acceptable partner for her son, she would not find anyone suitable. My friend laughed at my impatience: "Don't be so much in a hurry," she said. "You Americans want everything done so quickly. You get married quickly and then just as quickly get divorced. Here we take marriage more seriously. We must take all the factors into account. It is not enough for us to learn by our mistakes. This is too serious a business. If a mistake is made we have not only ruined the life of our son or daughter, but we have spoiled the reputation of our family as well. And that will make it much harder for their brothers and sisters to get married. So we must be very careful."

If a mistake is made we have not only ruined the life of our son or daughter, but we have spoiled the reputation of our family as well.

What she said was true and I promised myself to be more patient, though it was not easy. I had really hoped and expected that the match would be made before my year in India was up. But it was not to be. When I left India my friend seemed no further along in finding a suitable match for her son than when I had arrived.

Two years later, I returned to India and still my friend had not found a girl for her son. By this time, he was close to thirty, and I think she was a little worried. Since she knew I had friends all over India, and I was going to be there for a year, she asked me to "help her in this work" and keep an eye out for someone suitable. I was flattered that my judgment was respected, but knowing now how complicated the process was, I had lost my earlier confidence as a matchmaker. Nevertheless, I promised that I would try.

It was almost at the end of my year's stay in India that I met a family with a marriageable daughter whom I felt might be a good possibility for my friend's son. The girl's father was related to a good friend of mine and by coincidence came from the same village as my friend's husband. This new family had a successful business in a medium-sized city in central India and were from the same subcaste as my friend. The daughter was pretty and chic; in fact, she had studied fashion design in college. Her parents would not allow her to go off by herself to any of the major cities in India where she could make a career, but they had compromised with her wish to work by allowing her to run a small dress-making boutique from their home. In spite of her desire to have a career, the daughter was both modest and home-loving and had had a traditional, sheltered upbringing. She had only one other sister, already married, and a brother who was in his father's business.

I mentioned the possibility of a match with my friend's son. The girl's parents were most interested. Although their daughter was not eager to marry just yet, the idea of living in

Appendix
Further Reflections on Arranged Marriage . . .

This essay was written from the point of view of a family seeking a daughter-in-law. Arranged marriage looks somewhat different from the point of view of the bride and her family. Arranged marriage continues to be preferred, even among the more educated, Westernized sections of the Indian population. Many young women from these families still go along, more or less willingly, with the practice, and also with the specific choices of their families. Young women do get excited about the prospects of their marriage, but there is also ambivalence and increasing uncertainty, as the bride contemplates leaving the comfort and familiarity of her own home, where as a "temporary guest" she had often been indulged, to live among strangers. Even in the best situation she will now come under the close scrutiny of her husband's family. How she dresses, how she behaves, how she gets along with others, where she goes, how she spends her time, her domestic abilities—all of this and much more—will be observed and commented on by a whole new set of relations. Her interaction with her family of birth will be monitored and curtailed considerably. Not only will she leave their home, but with increasing geographic mobility, she may also live very far from them, perhaps even on another continent. Too much expression of her fondness for her own family, or her desire to visit them, may be interpreted as an inability to adjust to her new family, and may become a source of conflict. In an arranged marriage the burden of adjustment is clearly heavier for a woman than for a man. And that is in the best of situations.

In less happy circumstances, the bride may be a target of resentment and hostility from her husband's family, particularly her mother-in-law or her husband's unmarried sisters, for whom she is now a source of competition for the affection, loyalty, and economic resources of their son or brother. If she is psychologically, or even physically abused, her options are limited, as returning to her parents' home, or divorce, are still very stigmatized. For most Indians, marriage and motherhood are still considered the only suitable roles for a woman, even for those who have careers, and few women can comfortably contemplate remaining unmarried. Most families still consider "marrying off" their daughters as a compelling religious duty and social necessity. This increases a bride's sense of obligation to make the marriage a success, at whatever cost to her own personal happiness.

The vulnerability of a new bride may also be intensified by the issue of dowry, which although illegal, has become a more pressing issue in the consumer conscious society of contemporary urban India. In many cases, where a groom's family is not satisfied with the amount of dowry a bride brings to her marriage, the young bride will be constantly harassed to get her parents to give more. In extreme cases, the bride may even be murdered, and the murder disguised as an accident or suicide. This also offers the husband's family an opportunity to arrange another match for him, thus bringing in another dowry. This phenomena, called dowry death, calls attention not just to the "evils of dowry" but also to larger issues of the powerlessness of women as well.

Serena Nanda
March 1998

Bombay—a sophisticated, extremely fashion-conscious city where she could continue her education in clothing design—was a great inducement. I gave the girl's father my friend's address and suggested that when they went to Bombay on some business or whatever, they look up the boy's family.

Returning to Bombay on my way to New York, I told my friend of this newly discovered possibility. She seemed to feel there was potential but, in spite of my urging, would not make any moves herself. She rather preferred to wait for the girl's family to call upon them. I hoped something would come of this introduction, though by now I had learned to rein in my optimism.

A year later I received a letter from my friend. The family had indeed come to visit Bombay, and their daughter and my friend's daughter, who were near in age, had become very good friends. During that year, the two girls had frequently visited each other. I thought things looked promising.

Last week I received an invitation to a wedding: My friend's son and the girl were getting married. Since I had found the match, my presence was particularly requested at the wedding. I was thrilled. Success at last! As I prepared to leave for India, I began thinking, "Now, my friend's younger son, who do I know who has a nice girl for him . . . ?"

Critical Thinking

1. To what extent are marriages arranged in India? How do middle class families in modern urban India feel about marriage? What is a "love match"?

2. How does the author describe the process of the parents' "getting them married" (with regard to young men and women)? Why did the author find this "oppressive"?

3. Describe the arguments and counter-arguments regarding arranged marriages as revealed in the verbal exchanges between the author and Sita.

4. In what sense did the author see arranged marriage as successful in contrast to marriage in the United States?

5. Why was the author so sure that a match could be made quickly for her friend's son?

6. What factors must be taken into account in arranging a marriage?

7. Why was the friend's son originally not considered a good match? What happened that would change his prospects? What drawbacks remained?

8. Describe the "problems" that arose with regard to the various "prospects" as well as the positive factors involved in the final match.

Create Central

www.mhhe.com/createcentral

Internet References

Kinship and Social Organization
www.umanitoba.ca/anthropology

Sex and Marriage
http://anthro.palomar.edu/marriage/default.htm

Wedding Traditions and Customs
http://worldweddingtraditions.com

Edited by Philip R. DeVita.

Nanda, Serena. From *Stumbling Toward Truth: Anthropologists at Work,* Waveland Press, 2000, pp. 196–204. Copyright © 2000 by Serena Nanda. Reprinted by permission of the author. The author has also written *The Gift of a Bride: A Tale of Anthropology, Matrimony, and Murder* (with Joan Gregg). New York: Altamira/Rowman 2009.

Who Needs Love! In Japan, Many Couples Don't by Nicholas D. Kristof

109

Article

Prepared by: Elvio Angeloni, *Pasadena City College*

Who Needs Love!
In Japan, Many Couples Don't

NICHOLAS D. KRISTOF

Learning Outcomes

After reading this article, you will be able to:

- Determine whether the stability of Japanese marriages implies compatibility and contentment.

- Discuss the ingredients that lead to a strong marriage in Japan.

Yuri Uemura sat on the straw tatami mat of her living room and chatted cheerfully about her 40-year marriage to a man whom, she mused, she never particularly liked.

"There was never any love between me and my husband," she said blithely, recalling how he used to beat her. "But, well, we survived."

A 72-year-old midwife, her face as weathered as an old baseball and etched with a thousand seams, Mrs. Uemura said that her husband had never told her that he liked her, never complimented her on a meal, never told her "thank you," never held her hand, never given her a present, never shown her affection in any way. He never calls her by her name, but summons her with the equivalent of a grunt or a "Hey, you."

"Even with animals, the males cooperate to bring the females some food," Mrs. Uemura said sadly, noting the contrast to her own marriage. "When I see that, it brings tears to my eyes."

In short, the Uemuras have a marriage that is as durable as it is unhappy, one couple's tribute to the Japanese sanctity of family.

The divorce rate in Japan is at a record high but still less than half that of the United States, and Japan arguably has one of the strongest family structures in the industrialized world. As the United States and Europe fret about the disintegration of the traditional family, most Japanese families remain as solid as the small red table on which Mrs. Uemura rested her tea.

It does not seem that Japanese families survive because husbands and wives love each other more than American couples, but rather because they perhaps love each other less.

A study published last year by the Population Council, an international nonprofit group based in New York, suggested that the traditional two-parent household is on the wane not only in America but throughout most of the world. There was one prominent exception: Japan.

In Japan, for example, only 1.1 percent of births are to unwed mothers—virtually unchanged from 25 years ago. In the United States, the figure is 30.1 percent and rising rapidly.

Yet if one comes to a little Japanese town like Omiya to learn the secrets of the Japanese family, the people are not as happy as the statistics.

"I haven't lived for myself," Mrs. Uemura said, with a touch of melancholy, "but for my kids, and for my family, and for society."

Mrs. Uemura's marriage does not seem exceptional in Japan, whether in the big cities or here in Omiya. The people of Omiya, a community of 5,700 nestled in the rain-drenched hills of the Kii Peninsula in Mie Prefecture, nearly 200 miles southwest of Tokyo, have spoken periodically to a reporter about various aspects of their daily lives. On this visit they talked about their families.

Survival Secrets, Often the Couples Expect Little

Osamums Torida furrowed his brow and looked perplexed when he was asked if he loved his wife of 33 years.

"Yeah, so-so, I guess," said Mr. Torida, a cattle farmer. "She's like air or water. You couldn't live without it, but most of the time, you're not conscious of its existence."

The secret to the survival of the marriage, Mr. Torida acknowledged, was not mutual passion.

"Sure, we had fights about our work," he explained as he stood beside his barn. "But we were preoccupied by work and our debts, so we had no time to fool around."

That is a common theme in Omiya. It does not seem that Japanese families survive because husbands and wives love each other more than American couples, but rather because they perhaps love each other less.

"I think love marriages are more fragile than arranged marriages," said Tomika Kusukawa, 49, who married her high-school sweetheart and now runs a car repair shop with him. "In love marriages, when something happens or if the couple falls out of love, they split up."

GETTING ALONG

Matchmaker, Matchmaker

How countries compare on an index of compatibility of spouses, based on answers to questions about politics, sex, social issues, religion and ethics, from a survey by the Dentsu Research Institute and Leisure Development Center in Japan. A score of 500 would indicate perfect compatibility.

If there is a secret to the strength of the Japanese family it consists of three ingredients: low expectations, patience, and shame.

The advantage of marriages based on low expectations is that they have built in shock absorbers. If the couple discover that they have nothing in common, that they do not even like each other, then that is not so much a reason for divorce as it is par for the course.

Even the discovery that one's spouse is having an affair is often not as traumatic in a Japanese marriage as it is in the West. A little sexual infidelity on the part of a man (though not on the part of his wife) was traditionally tolerated, so long as he did not become so besotted as to pay his mistress more than he could afford.

Tsuzuya Fukuyama, who runs a convenience store and will mark her 50th wedding anniversary this year, toasted her hands on an electric heater in the front of the store and declared that a woman would be wrong to get angry if her husband had an affair.

The durability of the Japanese family is particularly wondrous because couples are, by international standards, exceptionally incompatible.

"It's never just one side that's at fault," Mrs. Fukuyama said sternly. "Maybe the husband had an affair because his wife wasn't so hot herself. So she should look at her own faults."

Mrs. Fukuyama's daughter came to her a few years ago, suspecting that her husband was having an affair and asking what to do.

"I told her, 'Once you left this house, you can only come back if you divorce; if you're not prepared to get a divorce, then you'd better be patient,'" Mrs. Fukuyama recalled. "And so she was patient. And then she got pregnant and had a kid, and now they're close again."

The word that Mrs. Fukuyama used for patience is "gaman," a term that comes up whenever marriage is discussed in Japan. It means toughing it out, enduring hardship, and many Japanese regard gaman with pride as a national trait.

Many people complain that younger folks divorce because they do not have enough gaman, and the frequency with which the term is used suggests a rather bleak understanding of marriage.

"I didn't know my husband very well when we married, and afterward we used to get into bitter fights," said Yoshiko Hirowaki, 56, a store owner. "But then we had children, and I got very busy with the kids and with this shop. Time passed."

Now Mrs. Hirowaki has been married 34 years, and she complains about young people who do not stick to their vows.

"In the old days, wives had more gaman," she said. "Now kids just don't have enough gaman."

The durability of the Japanese family is particularly wondrous because couples are, by international standards, exceptionally incompatible.

One survey asked married men and their wives in 37 countries how they felt about politics, sex, religion, ethics, and social issues. Japanese couples ranked dead last in compatibility of views, by a huge margin. Indeed, another survey found that if they were doing it over again, only about one-third of Japanese would marry the same person.

A national survey found that 30 percent of fathers spend less than 15 minutes a day on weekends talking with or playing with their children.

Incompatibility might not matter so much, however, because Japanese husbands and wives spend very little time talking to each other.

"I kind of feel there's nothing new to say to her," said Masayuki Ogita, an egg farmer, explaining his reticence.

In a small town like Omiya, couples usually have dinner together, but in Japanese cities there are many "7-11 husbands," so called because they leave at 7 A.M. and return after 11 P.M.

Masahiko Kondo now lives in Omiya, working in the chamber of commerce, but he used to be a salesman in several big cities. He would leave for work each morning at 7, and about four nights a week would go out for after-work drinking or mah-jongg sessions with buddies.

"I only saw my baby on Saturdays or Sundays," said Mr. Kondo, a lanky good-natured man of 37. "But in fact, I

Who Needs Love! In Japan, Many Couples Don't by Nicholas D. Kristof

111

really enjoyed that life. It didn't bother me that I never spent time with my kid on weekdays."

Mr. Kondo's wife, Keiko, had her own life, spent with her child and the wives of other workaholic husbands.

"We had birthday parties, but they were with the kids and the mothers," she remembers. "No fathers ever came."

A national survey found that 30 percent of fathers spend less than 15 minutes a day on weekdays talking with or playing with their children. Among eighth graders, 51 percent reported that they never spoke with their fathers on weekdays.

Traditionally, many companies were reluctant to promote employees who had divorced or who had major problems at home.

As a result, the figures in Japan for single-parent households can be deceptive. The father is often more a theoretical presence than a homework-helping reality.

Still, younger people sometimes want to see the spouses in daylight, and a result is a gradual change in focus of lives from work to family. Two decades ago, nearly half of young people said in surveys that they wanted their fathers to put priority on work rather than family. Now only one-quarter say that.

Social Pressures
Shame Is Keeping Bonds in Place

For those who find themselves desperately unhappy, one source of pressure to keep plugging is shame.

"If you divorce, you lose face in society," said Tatsumi Kinoshita, a tea farmer. "People say, 'His wife escaped.' So folks remain married because they hate to be gossiped about."

Shame is a powerful social sanction in Japan, and it is not just a matter of gossip. Traditionally, many companies were reluctant to promote employees who had divorced or who had major problems at home.

"If you divorce, it weakens your position at work," said Akihiko Kanda, 27, who works in a local government office. "Your bosses won't give you such good ratings, and it'll always be a negative factor."

The idea, Mr. Kanda noted, is that if an employee cannot manage his own life properly, he should not be entrusted with important corporate matters.

Financial sanctions are also a major disincentive for divorce. The mother gets the children in three-quarters of divorces, but most mothers in Japan do not have careers and have few financial resources. Fathers pay child support in only 15 percent of all divorces with children, partly because women often hesitate to go to court to demand payments and partly because men often fail to pay even when the court orders it.

"The main reason for lack of divorce is that women can't support themselves," said Mizuko Kanda, a 51-year-old housewife. "My friends complain about their husbands and say that they'd divorce if they could, but they can't afford to."

The result of these social and economic pressures is clear.

Even in Japan, there are about 24 divorces for every 100 marriages, but that compares with 32 in France, and 42 in England, and 55 in the United States.

The Outlook
Change Creeps in, Imperiling Family

But society is changing in Japan, and it is an open question whether these changes will undermine the traditional family as they have elsewhere around the globe.

The nuclear family has already largely replaced the extended family in Japan, and shame is eroding as a sanction. Haruko Okumura, for example, runs a kindergarten and speaks openly about her divorce.

"My Mom was uneasy about it, but I never had an inferiority complex about being divorced," said Mrs. Okumura, as dozens of children played in the next room. "And people accepted me easily."

Mrs. Okumura sees evidence of the changes in family patterns every day: fathers are playing more of a role in the kindergarten. At Christmas parties and sports contests, fathers have started to show up along with mothers. And Mrs. Okumura believes that divorce is on the upswing.

"If there's a weakening of the economic and social pressures to stay married," she said, "surely divorce rates will soar."

Already divorce rates are rising, approximately doubling over the last 25 years. But couples are very reluctant to divorce when they have children, and so single-parent households account for exactly the same proportion today as in 1965.

Shinsuke Kawaguchi, a young tea farmer, is one of the men for whom life is changing. Americans are not likely to be impressed by Mr. Kawaguchi's open-mindedness, but he is.

"I take good care of my wife," he said. "I may not say 'I love you,' but I do hold her hand. And I might say, after she makes dinner, 'This tastes good.'"

"Of course," Mr. Kawaguchi quickly added, "I wouldn't say that unless I'd just done something really bad."

Even Mrs. Uemura, the elderly woman whose husband used to beat her, said that her husband was treating her better.

"The other day, he tried to pour me a cup of tea," Mrs. Uemura recalled excitedly. "It was a big change. I told all my friends."

Critical Thinking

1. How does the author describe the marriage of Yuri Uemura?
2. How does the current Japanese divorce rate compare with the past and with that of the United States?
3. What are the statistics regarding unwed mothers?
4. In what sense are love marriages more fragile than arranged marriages?
5. What three ingredients add to the strength of Japanese marriages?
6. How do low expectations strengthen Japanese marriages?
7. Why is an affair "not as traumatic"?
8. What is "gaman" and how important is it to the Japanese?

9. To what extent are Japanese couples incompatible? What is the measure of this? Why does it not seem to matter much?

10. How much time do Japanese fathers spend with their children? What trend does the author see in this regard?

11. What are the social pressures working against divorce?

12. What changes does the author see with regard to the nuclear family versus the extended family and with regard to shame as a social sanction?

13. What changes are occurring with regard to the role of the father?

14. Are divorce rates rising? Under what specific circumstances?

Create Central

www.mhhe.com/createcentral

Internet References

Women Watch
www.un.org/womenwatch/about

Sex and Marriage
http://anthro.palomar.edu/marriage/default.htm

Unit 5

UNIT

Prepared by: Elvio Angeloni, *Pasadena City College*

Gender and Status

The feminist movement in the United States has had a significant impact upon the development of anthropology. Feminists have rightly charged that anthropologists have tended to gloss over the lives of women in studies of society and culture. In part this is because, until recent times, most anthropologists have been men. The result has been an undue emphasis on male activities as well as male perspectives in descriptions of particular societies.

These charges, however, have proven to be a firm corrective. In the last few decades, anthropologists have studied women and, more particularly, the division of labor based on gender and its relation to biology, as well as to social and political status. In addition, these changes in emphasis have been accompanied by an increase in the number of women in the field.

Feminist anthropologists have critically attacked many of the established anthropological beliefs. They have shown, for example, that field studies of nonhuman primates, which were often used to demonstrate the evolutionary basis of male dominance, distorted the actual evolutionary record by focusing primarily on baboons. While male baboons, for instance, have been shown to be especially dominant and aggressive, other, less-quoted primate studies show how dominance and aggression are highly situational phenomena, sensitive to ecological variation. Feminist anthropologists have also shown that the subsistence contribution of women was likewise ignored by anthropologists. A classic case is that of the !Kung, a hunting and gathering group in southern Africa, where women provide the bulk of the foodstuffs, including most of the available protein, and who, not coincidentally, enjoy a more egalitarian relationship than usual with men. Thus, since political control is a matter of cultural variation, male authority is not biologically predetermined. In fact, there are many cultures in which some men may play a more feminine or, at least, asexual role, showing that gender relationships are deeply embedded in social experience and that the gender categories employed in any given culture may be inadequate to the task of doing justice to the actual diversity that exists.

Lest we think that gender issues are primarily academic, we should keep in mind that gender equality in this world is still a distant dream.

Article   Prepared by: Elvio Angeloni, *Pasadena City College*

The Berdache Tradition

Walter L. Williams

Learning Outcomes

After reading this article, you will be able to:

- Define berdache and explain how it highlights the ways in which different societies accommodate atypical individuals.

- Discuss Native American beliefs regarding the berdache.

B ecause it is such a powerful force in the world today, the Western Judeo-Christian tradition is often accepted as the arbiter of "natural" behavior of humans. If Europeans and their descendant nations of North America accept something as normal, then anything different is seen as abnormal. Such a view ignores the great diversity of human existence.

This is the case of the study of gender. How many genders are there? To a modern Anglo-American, nothing might seem more definite than the answer that there are two: men and women. But not all societies around the world agree with Western culture's view that all humans are either women or men. The commonly accepted notion of "the opposite sex," based on anatomy, is itself an artifact of our society's rigid sex roles.

Among many cultures, there have existed different alternatives to "man" or "woman." An alternative role in many American Indian societies is referred to by anthropologists as *berdache*. . . . The role varied from one Native American culture to another, which is a reflection of the vast diversity of aboriginal New World societies. Small bands of hunter-gatherers existed in some areas, with advanced civilizations of farming peoples in other areas. With hundreds of different languages, economies, religions, and social patterns existing in North America alone, every generalization about a cultural tradition must acknowledge many exceptions.

This diversity is true for the berdache tradition as well, and must be kept in mind. My statements should be read as being specific to a particular culture, with generalizations being treated as loose patterns that might not apply to peoples even in nearby areas.

Briefly, a berdache can be defined as a morphological male who does not fill a society's standard man's role, who has a non-masculine character. This type of person is often stereotyped as effeminate, but a more accurate characterization is androgyny. Such a person has a clearly recognized and accepted social status, often based on a secure place in the tribal mythology.

Berdaches have special ceremonial roles in many Native American religions, and important economic roles in their families. They will do at least some women's work, and mix together much of the behavior, dress, and social roles of women and men. Berdaches gain social prestige by their spiritual, intellectual, or craftwork/artistic contributions, and by their reputation for hard work and generosity. They serve a mediating function between women and men, precisely because their character is seen as distinct from either sex. They are not seen as men, yet they are not seen as women either. They occupy an alternative gender role that is a mixture of diverse elements.

In their erotic behavior berdaches also generally (but not always) take a nonmasculine role, either being asexual or becoming the passive partner in sex with men. In some cultures the berdache might become a wife to a man. This male-male sexual behavior became the focus of an attack on berdaches as "sodomites" by the Europeans who, early on, came into contact with them. From the first Spanish conquistadors to the Western frontiersmen and the Christian missionaries and government officials, Western culture has had a considerable impact on the berdache tradition. In the last two decades, the most recent impact on the tradition is the adaptation of a modern Western gay identity.

To Western eyes berdachism is a complex and puzzling phenomenon, mixing and redefining the very concepts of what is considered male and female. In a culture with only two recognized genders, such individuals are gender nonconformist, abnormal, deviant. But to American Indians, the institution of another gender role means that berdaches are not deviant—indeed, they do conform to the requirements of a custom in which their culture tells them they fit. Berdachism is a way for society to recognize and assimilate some atypical individuals without imposing a change on them or stigmatizing them as deviant. This cultural institution confirms their legitimacy for what they are.

Societies often bestow power upon that which does not neatly fit into the usual. Since no cultural system can explain everything, a common way that many cultures deal with these inconsistencies is to imbue them with negative power, as taboo, pollution, witchcraft, or sin. That which is not understood is seen as a threat. But an alternative method of dealing with such things, or people, is to take them out of the realm of threat and to sanctify them.[1] The berdaches' role as mediator is thus not just between women and men, but also between the physical and the spiritual. American Indian cultures have taken what Western culture calls negative, and made it a positive; they have successfully utilized the different skills and insights of a class of people that Western culture has stigmatized and whose spiritual powers have been wasted.

Many Native Americans also understood that gender roles have to do with more than just biological sex. The standard Western view that one's sex is always a certainty, and that one's gender identity and sex role always conform to one's morphological sex is a view that dies hard. Western thought is typified by such dichotomies of groups perceived to be mutually exclusive: male and female, black and white, right and wrong, good and evil. Clearly, the world is not so simple; such clear divisions are not always realistic. Most American Indian worldviews generally are much more accepting of the ambiguities of life. Acceptance of gender variation in the berdache tradition is typical of many native cultures' approach to life in general.

Overall, these are generalizations based on those Native American societies that had an accepted role for berdaches. Not all cultures recognized such a respected status. Berdachism in aboriginal North America was most established among tribes in four areas: first, the Prairie and western Great Lakes, the northern and central Great Plains, and the lower Mississippi Valley; second, Florida and the Caribbean; third, the Southwest, the Great Basin, and California; and fourth, scattered areas of the Northwest, western Canada, and Alaska. For some reason it is not noticeable in eastern North America, with the exception of its southern rim. . . .

American Indian Religions

Native American religions offered an explanation for human diversity by their creation stories. In some tribal religions, the Great Spiritual Being is conceived as neither male nor female but as a combination of both. Among the Kamia of the Southwest, for example, the bearer of plant seeds and the introducer of Kamia culture was a man-woman spirit named Warharmi.[2] A key episode of the Zuni creation story involves a battle between the kachina spirits of the agricultural Zunis and the enemy hunter spirits. Every four years an elaborate ceremony commemorates this myth. In the story a kachina spirit called *ko'lhamana* was captured by the enemy spirits and transformed in the process. This transformed spirit became a mediator between the two sides, using his peacemaking skills to merge the differing lifestyles of hunters and farmers. In the ceremony, a dramatic reenactment of the myth, the part of the transformed *ko'lhamana* spirit, is performed by a berdache.[3] The Zuni word for berdache is *lhamana,* denoting its closeness to the spiritual mediator who brought hunting and farming together.[4] The moral of this story is that the berdache was created by the deities for a special purpose, and that this creation led to the improvement of society. The continual reenactment of this story provides a justification for the Zuni berdache in each generation.

In contrast to this, the lack of spiritual justification in a creation myth could denote a lack of tolerance for gender variation. The Pimas, unlike most of their Southwestern neighbors, did not respect a berdache status. *Wi-kovat,* their derogatory word, means "like a girl," but it does not signify a recognized social role. Pima mythology reflects this lack of acceptance in a folk tale that explains male androgyny as due to Papago witchcraft. Knowing that the Papagos respected berdaches, the Pimas blamed such an occurrence on an alien influence.[5] While the Pimas' condemnatory attitude is unusual, it does point out the importance of spiritual explanations for the acceptance of gender variance in a culture.

Other Native American creation stories stand in sharp contrast to the Pima explanation. A good example is the account of the Navajos, which presents women and men as equals. The Navajo origin tale is told as a story of five worlds. The first people were First Man and First Woman, who were created equally and at the same time. The first two worlds that they lived in were bleak and unhappy, so they escaped to the third world. In the third world lived two twins, Turquoise Boy and White Shell Girl, who were the first berdaches. In the Navajo language the world for berdache is *nadle,* which means "changing one" or "one who is transformed." It is applied to hermaphrodites—those who are born with the genitals of both male and female—and also to "those who pretend to be *nadle,*" who take on a social role that is distinct from either men or women.[6]

In the third world, First Man and First Woman began farming, with the help of the changing twins. One of the twins noticed some clay and, holding it in the palm of his/her hand, shaped it into the first pottery bowl. Then he/she formed a plate, a water dipper, and a pipe. The second twin observed some reeds and began to weave them, making the first basket. Together they shaped axes and grinding stones from rocks, and hoes from bone. All these new inventions made the people very happy.[7]

The message of this story is that humans are dependent for many good things on the inventiveness of *nadle.* Such individuals were present from the earliest eras of human existence, and their presence was never questioned. They were part of the natural order of the universe, with a special contribution to make.

Later on in the Navajo creation story, White Shell Girl entered the moon and became the Moon Bearer. Turquoise Boy, however, remained with the people. When First Man realized that Turquoise Boy could do all manner of women's work as well as women, all the men left the women and crossed a big river. The men hunted and planted crops. Turquoise Boy ground the corn, cooked the food, and weaved cloth for the men. Four years passed with the women and men separated, and the men were happy with the *nadle.* Later, however the women wanted to learn how to grind corn from the *nadle,* and both the men and women had decided that it was not good to continue living separately. So the women crossed the river and the people were reunited.[8]

They continued living happily in the third world, until one day a great flood began. The people ran to the highest mountaintop, but the water kept rising and they all feared they would be drowned. But just in time, the ever-inventive Turquoise Boy found a large reed. They climbed upward inside the tall hollow reed, and came out at the top into the fourth world. From there, White Shell Girl brought another reed, and they climbed again to the fifth world, which is the present world of the Navajos.[9]

These stories suggest that the very survival of humanity is dependent on the inventiveness of berdaches. With such a mythological belief system, it is no wonder that the Navajos held *nadle* in high regard. The concept of the *nadle* is well formulated in the creation story. As children were educated by these stories, and all Navajos believed in them, the high status accorded to gender variation was passed down from generation to generation. Such stories also provided instruction for *nadle* themselves to live by. A spiritual explanation guaranteed a special place for a person who was considered different but not deviant.

For American Indians, the important explanations of the world are spiritual ones. In their view, there is a deeper reality than the here-and-now. The real essence or wisdom occurs when one finally gives up trying to explain events in terms of "logic" and "reality." Many confusing aspects of existence can better be explained by actions of a multiplicity of spirits. Instead of a concept of a single god, there is an awareness of "that which we do not understand." In Lakota religion, for example, the term *Wakan Tanka* is often translated as "god." But a more proper translation, according to the medicine people who taught me, is "The Great Mystery."[10]

While rationality can explain much, there are limits to human capabilities of understanding. The English language is structured to account for cause and effect. For example, English speakers say, "It is raining," with the implication that there is a cause "it" that leads to rain. Many Indian languages, on the other hand, merely note what is most accurately translated as "raining" as an observable fact. Such an approach brings a freedom to stop worrying about causes of things, and merely to relax and accept that our human insights can go only so far. By not taking ourselves too seriously, or overinflating human importance, we can get beyond the logical world.

The emphasis of American Indian religions, then, is on the spiritual nature of all things. To understand the physical world, one must appreciate the underlying spiritual essence. Then one can begin to see that the physical is only a faint shadow, a partial reflection, of a supernatural and extrarational world. By the Indian view, everything that exists is spiritual. Every object—plants, rocks, water, air, the moon, animals, humans, the earth itself—has a spirit. The spirit of one thing (including a human) is not superior to the spirit of any other. Such a view promotes a sophisticated ecological awareness of the place that humans have in the larger environment. The function of religion is not to try to condemn or to change what exists, but to accept the realities of the world and to appreciate their contributions to life. Everything that exists has a purpose.[11]

One of the basic tenets of American Indian religion is the notion that everything in the universe is related. Nevertheless, things that exist are often seen as having a counterpart: sky and earth, plant and animal, water and fire. In all of these polarities, there exist mediators. The role of the mediator is to hold the polarities together, to keep the world from disintegrating. Polarities exist within human society also. The most important category within Indian society is gender. The notions of Woman and Man underlie much of social interaction and are comparable to the other major polarities. Women, with their nurtural qualities, are associated with the earth, while men are associated with the sky. Women gatherers and farmers deal with plants (of the earth), while men hunters deal with animals.

The mediator between the polarities of woman and man, in the American Indian religious explanation, is a being that combines the elements of both genders. This might be a combination in a physical sense, as in the case of hermaphrodites. Many Native American religions accept this phenomenon in the same way that they accept other variations from the norm. But more important is their acceptance of the idea that gender can be combined in ways other than physical hermaphroditism. The physical aspects of a thing or a person, after all, are not nearly as important as its spirit. American Indians use the concept of a person's *spirit* in the way that other Americans use the concept of a person's *character*. Consequently, physical hermaphroditism is not necessary for the idea of gender mixing. A person's character, their spiritual essence, is the crucial thing.

The Berdache's Spirit

Individuals who are physically normal might have the spirit of the other sex, might range somewhere between the two sexes, or might have a spirit that is distinct from either women or men. Whatever category they fall into, they are seen as being different from men. They are accepted spiritually as "Not Man." Whichever option is chosen, Indian religions offer spiritual explanations. Among the Arapahos of the Plains, berdaches are called *haxu'xan* and are seen to be that way as a result of a supernatural gift from birds or animals. Arapaho mythology recounts the story of Nih'a'ca, the first *haxu'xan*. He pretended to be a woman and married the mountain lion, a symbol for masculinity. The myth, as recorded by ethnographer Alfred Kroeber about 1900, recounted that "These people had the natural desire to become women, and as they grew up gradually became women. They gave up the desires of men. They were married to men. They had miraculous power and could do supernatural things. For instance, it was one of them that first made an intoxicant from rainwater."[12] Besides the theme of inventiveness, similar to the Navajo creation story, the berdache role is seen as a product of a "natural desire." Berdaches "gradually became women," which underscores the notion of woman as a social category rather than as a fixed biological entity. Physical biological sex is less important in gender classification than a person's desire—one's spirit.

They myths contain no prescriptions for trying to change berdaches who are acting out their desires of the heart. Like many other cultures' myths, the Zuni origin myths simply sanction the idea that gender can be transformed independently of biological sex.[13] Indeed, myths warn of dire consequences when interference with such a transformation is attempted. Prince Alexander Maximilian of the German state of Wied, traveling in the northern Plains in the 1830s, heard a myth about a warrior who once tried to force a berdache to avoid women's clothing. The berdache resisted, and the warrior shot him with an arrow. Immediately the berdache disappeared, and the warrior saw only a pile of stones with his arrow in them. Since then, the story concluded, no intelligent person would try to coerce a berdache.[14] Making the point even more directly, a Mandan myth told of an Indian who tried to force *mihdake* (berdaches) to give up their distinctive dress and status, which led the spirits to punish many people with death. After that, no Mandans interfered with berdaches.[15]

With this kind of attitude, reinforced by myth and history, the aboriginal view accepts human diversity. The creation story of the Mohave of the Colorado River Valley speaks of a time when people were not sexually differentiated. From this perspective, it is easy to accept that certain individuals might combine elements of masculinity and femininity.[16] A respected Mohave elder, speaking in the 1930s, stated this viewpoint simply: "From the very beginning of the world it was meant that there should be [berdaches], just as it was instituted that there should be shamans. They were intended for that purpose."[17]

This elder also explained that a child's tendencies to become a berdache are apparent early, by about age nine to twelve, before the child reaches puberty: "That is the time when young persons become initiated into the functions of their sex. . . . None but young people will become berdaches as a rule."[18] Many tribes have a public ceremony that acknowledges the acceptance of berdache status. A Mohave shaman related the ceremony for his tribe: "When the child was about ten years old his relatives would begin discussing his strange ways. Some of them disliked it, but the more intelligent began envisaging an initiation ceremony." The relatives prepare for the ceremony without letting the boy know of it. It is meant to take him by surprise, to be both an initiation and a test of his true inclinations. People from various settlements are invited to attend. The family wants the community to see it and become accustomed to accepting the boy as an *alyha.*

On the day of the ceremony, the shaman explained, the boy is led into a circle: "If the boy showed a willingness to remain standing in the circle, exposed to the public eye, it was almost certain that he would go through with the ceremony. The singer, hidden behind the crowd, began singing the songs. As soon as the sound reached the boy he began to dance as women do." If the boy is unwilling to assume *alyha* status, he would refuse to dance. But if his character—his spirit—is *alyha,* "the song goes right to his heart and he will dance with much intensity. He cannot help it. After the fourth song he is proclaimed." After the ceremony, the boy is carefully bathed and receives a woman's skirt. He is then led back to the dance ground, dressed as an *alyha,* and announces his new feminine name to the crowd. After that he would resent being called by his old male name.[19]

Among the Yuman tribes of the Southwest, the transformation is marked by a social gathering, in which the berdache prepares a meal for the friends of the family.[20] Ethnographer Ruth Underhill, doing fieldwork among the Papago Indians in the early 1930s, wrote that berdaches were common among the Papago Indians, and were usually publicly acknowledged in childhood. She recounted that a boy's parents would test him if they noticed that he preferred female pursuits. The regular pattern, mentioned by many of Underhill's Papago informants, was to build a small brush enclosure. Inside the enclosure they placed a man's bow and arrows, and also a woman's basket. At the appointed time the boy was brought to the enclosure as the adults watched from outside. The boy was told to go inside the circle of brush. Once he was inside, the adults "set fire to the enclosure. They watched what he took with him as he ran

out and if it was the basketry materials, they reconciled themselves to his being a berdache."[21]

What is important to recognize in all of these practices is that the assumption of a berdache role was not forced on the boy by others. While adults might have their suspicions, it was only when the child made the proper move that he was considered a berdache. By doing woman's dancing, preparing a meal, or taking the woman's basket he was making an important symbolic gesture. Indian children were not stupid, and they knew the implications of these ceremonies beforehand. A boy in the enclosure could have left without taking anything, or could have taken both the man's and the woman's tools. With the community standing by watching, he was well aware that his choice would mark his assumption of berdache status. Rather than being seen as an involuntary test of his reflexes, this ceremony may be interpreted as a definite statement by the child to take on the berdache role.

Indians do not see the assumption of berdache status, however, as a free will choice on the part of the boy. People felt that the boy was acting out his basic character. The Lakota shaman Lame Deer explained:

> They were not like other men, but the Great Spirit made them *winktes* and we accepted them as such. . . . We think that if a woman has two little ones growing inside her, if she is going to have twins, sometimes instead of giving birth to two babies they have formed up in her womb into just one, into a half-man/half-woman kind of being. . . . To us a man is what nature, or his dreams, make him. We accept him for what he wants to be. That's up to him.[22]

While most of the sources indicate that once a person becomes a berdache it is a lifelong status, directions from the spirits determine everything. In at least one documented case, concerning a nineteenth-century Klamath berdache named Lele'ks, he later had a supernatural experience that led him to leave the berdache role. At that time Lele'ks began dressing and acting like a man, then married women, and eventually became one of the most famous Klamath chiefs.[23] What is important is that both in assuming berdache status and in leaving it, supernatural dictate is the determining factor.

Dreams and Visions

Many tribes see the berdache role as signifying an individual's proclivities as a dreamer and a visionary. . . .

Among the northern Plains and related Great Lakes tribes, the idea of supernatural dictate through dreaming—the vision quest—had its highest development. The goal of the vision quest is to try to get beyond the rational world by sensory deprivation and fasting. By depriving one's body of nourishment, the brain could escape from logical thought and connect with the higher reality of the supernatural. The person doing the quest simply sits and waits for a vision. But a vision might not come easily; the person might have to wait for days.

The best way that I can describe the process is to refer to my own vision quest, which I experienced when I was living on a Lakota reservation in 1982. After a long series of prayers and blessings, the shaman who had prepared me for the ceremony took me out to an isolated area where a sweat lodge had been set up for my quest. As I walked to the spot, I worried that I might not be able to stand it. Would I be overcome by hunger? Could I tolerate the thirst? What would I do if I had to go to the toilet? The shaman told me not to worry, that a whole group of holy people would be praying and singing for me while I was on my quest.

He had me remove my clothes, symbolizing my disconnection from the material would, and crawl into the sweat lodge. Before he left me I asked him, "What do I think about?" He said, "Do not think. Just pray for spiritual guidance." After a prayer he closed the flap tightly and I was left in total darkness. I still do not understand what happened to me during my vision quest, but during the day and a half that I was out there, I never once felt hungry or thirsty or the need to go to the toilet. What happened was an intensely personal experience that I cannot and do not wish to explain, a process of being that cannot be described in rational terms.

When the shaman came to get me at the end of my time, I actually resented having to end it. He did not need to ask if my vision quest was successful. He knew that it was even before seeing me, he explained, because he saw an eagle circling over me while I underwent the quest. He helped interpret the signs I had seen, then after more prayers and singing he led me back to the others. I felt relieved, cleansed, joyful, and serene. I had been through an experience that will be a part of my memories always.

If a vision quest could have such an effect on a person not even raised in Indian society, imagine its impact on a boy who from his earliest years had been waiting for the day when he could seek his vision. Gaining his spiritual power from his first vision, it would tell him what role to take in adult life. The vision might instruct him that he is going to be a great hunter, a craftsman, a warrior, or a shaman. Or it might tell him that he will be a berdache. Among the Lakotas, or Sioux, there are several symbols for various types of visions. A person becomes *wakan* (a sacred person) if she or he dreams of a bear, a wolf, thunder, a buffalo, a white buffalo calf, or Double Woman. Each dream results in a different gift, whether it is the power to cure illness or wounds, a promise of good hunting, or the cxalted role of a *heyoka* (doing things backward).

A white buffalo calf is believed to be a berdache. If a person has a dream of the sacred Double Woman, this means that she or he will have the power to seduce men. Males who have a vision of Double Woman are presented with female tools. Taking such tools means that the male will become a berdache. The Lakota word *winkte* is composed of *win,* "woman," and *kte,* "would become."[24] A contemporary Lakota berdache explains, "To become a *winkte,* you have a medicine man put you up on the hill, to search for your vision. "You can become a *winkte* if you truly are by nature. You see a vision of the White Buffalo Calf Pipe. Sometimes it varies. A vision is like a scene in a movie."[25] Another way to become a *winkte* is to have a vision given by a *winkte* from the past.[26]. . .

By interpreting the result of the vision as being the work of a spirit, the vision quest frees the person from feeling responsible for his transformation. The person might even claim that the change was done against his will and without his control.

Such a claim does not suggest a negative attitude about berdache status, because it is common for people to claim reluctance to fulfill their spiritual duty no matter what vision appears to them. Becoming any kind of sacred person involves taking on various social responsibilities and burdens.[27]. . .

A story was told among the Lakotas in the 1880s of a boy who tried to resist following his vision from Double Woman. But according to Lakota informants "few men succeed in this effort after having taken the strap in the dream." Having rebelled against the instructions given him by the Moon Being, he committed suicide.[28] The moral of that story is that one should not resist spiritual guidance, because it will lead only to grief. In another case, an Omaha young man told of being addressed by a spirit as "daughter," whereupon he discovered that he was unconsciously using feminine styles of speech. He tried to use male speech patterns, but could not. As a result of this vision, when he returned to his people he resolved himself to dress as a woman.[29] Such stories function to justify personal peculiarities as due to a fate over which the individual has no control.

Despite the usual pattern in Indian societies of using ridicule to enforce conformity, receiving instructions from a vision inhibits others from trying to change the berdache. Ritual explanation provides a way out. It also excuses the community from worrying about the cause of that person's difference, or the feeling that it is society's duty to try to change him.[30] Native American religions, above all else, encourage a basic respect for nature. If nature makes a person different, many Indians conclude, a mere human should not undertake to counter this spiritual dictate. Someone who is "unusual" can be accommodated without being stigmatized as "abnormal." Berdachism is thus not alien or threatening; it is a reflection of spirituality.

Notes

1. Mary Douglas, *Purity and Danger* (Baltimore: Penguin, 1966), p. 52. I am grateful to Theda Perdue for convincing me that Douglas's ideas apply to berdachism. For an application of Douglas's thesis to berdaches, see James Thayer, "The Berdache of the Northern Plains: A Socioreligious Perspective," *Journal of Anthropological Research 36* (1980): 292–93.

2. E. W. Gifford, "The Kamia of Imperial Valley," *Bureau of American Ethnology Bulletin 97* (1931): 12.

3. By using present tense verbs in this text, I am not implying that such activities are necessarily continuing today. I sometimes use the present tense in the "ethnographic present," unless I use the past tense when I am referring to something that has not continued. Past tense implies that all such practices have disappeared. In the absence of fieldwork to prove such disappearance, I am not prepared to make that assumption, on the historic changes in the berdache tradition.

4. Elsie Clews Parsons, "The Zuni La' Mana," *American Anthropologist 18* (1916): 521; Matilda Coxe Stevenson, "Zuni Indians," *Bureau of American Ethnology Annual Report 23* (1903): 37; Franklin Cushing, "Zuni Creation Myths," *Bureau of American Ethnology Annual Report 13* (1894): 401–3. Will Roscoe clarified this origin story for me.

5. W. W. Hill, "Note on the Pima Berdache," *American Anthropologist 40* (1938): 339.

6. Aileen O'Bryan, "The Dine': Origin Myths of the Navaho Indians," *Bureau of American Ethnology Bulletin 163* (1956): 5; W. W. Hill, "The Status of the Hermaphrodite and Transvestite in Navaho Culture," *American Anthropologist 37* (1935): 273.

7. Martha S. Link, *The Pollen Path: A Collection of Navajo Myths* (Stanford: Stanford University Press, 1956).

8. O'Bryan, "Dine'," pp. 5, 7, 9–10.

9. Ibid.

10. Lakota informants, July 1982. See also William Powers, *Oglala Religion* (Lincoln: University of Nebraska Press, 1977).

11. For this admittedly generalized overview of American Indian religious values, I am indebted to traditionalist informants of many tribes, but especially those of the Lakotas. For a discussion of native religions see Dennis Tedlock, *Finding the Center* (New York: Dial Press, 1972); Ruth Underhill, *Red Man's Religion* (Chicago: University of Chicago Press, 1965); and Elsi Clews Parsons, *Pueblo Indian Religion* (Chicago: University of Chicago Press, 1939).

12. Alfred Kroeber, "The Arapaho," *Bulletin of the American Museum of Natural History 18* (1902–7): 19.

13. Parsons, "Zuni La' Mana," p. 525.

14. Alexander Maximilian, *Travels in the interior of North America, 1832–1834,* vol. 22 of *Early Western Travels,* ed. Reuben Gold Thwaites, 32 vols. (Cleveland: A. H. Clark, 1906), pp. 283–84, 354. Maximilian was quoted in German in the early homosexual rights book by Ferdinand Karsch-Haack, *Das Gleichgeschlechtliche Leben der Naturvölker* (The same-sex life of nature peoples) (Munich: Verlag von Ernst Reinhardt, 1911; reprinted New York: Arno Press, 1975), pp. 314, 564.

15. Oscar Koch, *Der Indianishe Eros* (Berlin: Verlag Continent, 1925), p. 61.

16. George Devereux, "Institutionalized Homosexuality of the Mohave Indians," *Human Biology 9* (1937): 509.

17. Ibid., p. 501

18. Ibid.

19. Ibid., pp. 508–9.

20. C. Daryll Forde, "Ethnography of the Yuma Indians," *University of California Publications in American Archaeology and Ethnology 28* (1931): 157.

21. Ruth Underhill, *Social Organization of the Papago Indians* (New York: Columbia University Press, 1938), p. 186. This story is also mentioned in Ruth Underhill, ed., *The Autobiography of a Papago Woman* (Menasha, Wisc.: American Anthropological Association, 1936), p. 39.

22. John Fire and Richard Erdoes, *Lame Deer, Seeker of Visions* (New York: Simon and Schuster, 1972), pp. 117, 149.

23. Theodore Stern, *The Klamath Tribe: A People and Their Reservation* (Seattle: University of Washington Press, 1965), pp. 20, 24; Theodore Stern, "Some Sources of Variability in Klamath Mythology," *Journal of American Folklore 69* (1956): 242ff; Leshe Spier, *Klamath Ethnography* (Berkeley: University of California Press, 1930), p. 52.

24. Clark Wissler, "Societies and Ceremonial Associations in the Oglala Division of the Teton Dakota," *Anthropological Papers of the American Museum of Natural History 11,* pt. 1 (1916): 92; Powers, *Oglala Religion,* pp. 57–59.

25. Ronnie Loud Hawk, Lakota informant 4, July 1982.

26. Terry Calling Eagle, Lakota informant 5, July 1982.

27. James S. Thayer, "The Berdache of the Northern Plains: A Socioreligious Perspective," *Journal of Anthropological Research 36* (1980): 289.

28. Fletcher, "Elk Mystery," p. 281.

29. Alice Fletcher and Francis La Flesche, "The Omaha Tribe," *Bureau of American Ethnology Annual Report 27* (1905–6): 132.

30. Harriet Whitehead offers a valuable discussion of this element of the vision quest in "The Bow and the Burden Strap: A New Look at Institutionalized Homosexuality in Native North America," in *Sexual Meanings,* ed. Sherry Ortner and Harriet Whitehead (Cambridge: Cambridge University Press, 1981), pp. 99–102. See also Erikson, "Childhood," p. 329.

Critical Thinking

1. What is a berdache? What special roles have berdaches played in Native American societies?

2. What kinds of erotic behavior have they exhibited?

3. How have Europeans and American Indians differed in their treatment of the berdaches? How does the author explain these two different approaches?

4. How does the author contrast Western thought with Native American views regarding gender?

5. Why do Native Americans explain things in spiritual terms rather than "logic" and "reality"?

6. What is the emphasis of American Indian religions? What is the function of such religion?

7. What is one of the most basic tenets of American Indian religion? What kinds of polarities exist? Why are mediators necessary?

8. What is the most important category within Indian society? How do men and women differ?

9. Describe some of the Native American beliefs regarding the berdache.

Create Central

www.mhhe.com/createcentral

Internet References

Sexualities
http://sexualities.sagepub.com

Sexuality Studies
https://sxs.sfsu.edu

Sexuality Studies.net
http://sexualitystudies.net/programs

The Kinsey Institute
www.kinseyinstitute.org/about

Gender & History
www.blackwellpublishing.com/journal.asp?ref=0953-5233&site=1

Article

Prepared by: Elvio Angeloni, *Pasadena City College*

The Hijras: An Alternative Gender in India

SERENA NANDA

Learning Outcomes

After reading this article, you will be able to:

- Describe the transgender hijra of India in terms of their traditional social and religious roles.

- Discuss the ways in which the hijra of India challenge the binary sex/gender notions of the West.

My first encounter with the hijras was in 1971. While walking on Churchgate in Bombay with an Indian friend one day, we were confronted by two persons in female clothing, who stood before us, blocking our passage. They clapped their hands in a peculiar manner and then put out their upturned palms in the traditional Indian gesture of a request for alms. My friend hurriedly dropped a few rupees into the outstretched palms in front of us, and pulled me along at a quick pace, almost shoving me in front of her. Startled at her abrupt reaction, I took another look at the two people who had intercepted us. It was only then that I realized that they were not females at all, but men, dressed in women's clothing. Now curious, I asked my friend who these people were and why she had reacted so strongly to their presence, but she just shook her head and would not answer me. Sensing her discomfort, I let the subject drop but raised it with other friends at a later time. In this way I found out a little about the hijras, and became determined to learn more.

For the next 10 years my professional interests as an anthropologist centered on culture and gender roles. As part of my interest in sexual variation I read what little I could find on the hijras, asking my Indian friends and relatives about them, and extending this interest through several field trips over the next twenty years. I learned that the hijras, described as neither men nor women, performed on auspicious occasions such as births and marriages, where they are believed to have the power to confer blessings of fertility; from some male acquaintances I discovered that hijras may also be prostitutes. Hijras were called eunuchs, but also said to be born intersexed, a contradiction I could not untangle. I realized that without talking with hijras themselves, I could not distinguish fact from fiction, myth from reality.

In 1981 I lived in India for a year with my family and decided to learn more about the hijras. During this time I met and interviewed many hijras in several of the major cities in North and South India. I spent days with them in their homes, attended their performances, met their husbands and customers, and also members of their families, and formed some good friendships among them. As a result of one of these friendships, I was made a ritual younger sister to a hijra guru. I also visited the temple of Bahuchara Mataji, the special deity of the hijras, located close to Ahmadabad. In addition, I spoke at length with doctors and social scientists in India who had personal knowledge of individual hijras or had written about them. All of these investigators were males, however, and I think being a woman gave me a great advantage in getting to know individual hijras in a more personal, and therefore, deeper way.

While hijras are regarded as deviant, and even bizarre, perhaps, in Indian society, in my hundreds of conversations with them, I was most forcibly struck by them as individuals who share in our common humanity. Like human beings everywhere, hijras are both shaped by their culture and the role they play in society, but are also individuals who vary in their emotions, behavior, and outlook on life. Some hijras were outgoing, flirtatious, and jolly, and loved to dress up, perform, and have their photos taken. They met the difficulties of their lives with a good sense of humor, which they often turned on themselves. Kamladevi was one of these: she was a favorite friend of mine because she was so amusing and she spoke fluent English, having graduated from a convent high school. She was a great gossip and imitated her hijra friends and elders in funny and very insightful ways. In telling a story of how she and several other hijra prostitutes were picked up by the police one evening, she captured to perfection the intimidating attitude of the police, the arrogance of the magistrate, and the combination of innocence and boldness she had used in telling them off. Like many hijra prostitutes, Kamladevi worked very hard under the watchful and demanding eye of the hijra "madam" who swallowed most of her earnings. Although she made a fair living as a prostitute, Kamladevi always spent more than she had as she could not resist buying saris and jewelry. But in spite of her poverty, and ill health as well, she always had an eye for the humorous side of things.

Other hijras I knew were very serious and even shy. They saw their life as a fate "written on their forehead," and accepted with resignation whatever insults or abuses were meted out to them. They worked all day, every day, at whatever they did to earn a living, whether begging alms from shops, or serving in bathhouses, or at various domestic chores within their households, which included cooking, cleaning, or small tasks such as grinding spices, which they did for outsiders to earn a few extra rupees. These hijras had few interests or social contacts, some even relatively isolated within the hijra community itself. Hijras who earned a living performing at marriages and childbirths were the elite of their community. Although they also worked very hard, they were better rewarded financially and gained status within the hijra community for earning a living in this traditional manner, rather than practicing prostitution or eking out a living begging for alms. Kavita, for example, one of the hijra performers I knew well, was determined to sing and dance whenever she got the opportunity. She not only performed at marriages and childbirths, but also in more contemporary settings, such as "stag parties" and college functions. Her energy in dancing for hours at a time, as well as her ability to "keep her cool" in the face of the teasing and rowdiness of large crowds of men was a well deserved source of pride to her.

While younger hijras are often playful and sometimes even outrageously bold in public, hijra elders, or gurus, as they are called, most often maintain a great degree of dignity. They, like other middle aged and elderly Indian women, tend to wear simple clothing and little jewelry, though what they wear is often real gold. They are modest in their manner, and also, like many middle class housewives, do not "roam about" but stay close to home, supervising the households of which they are in charge. Hijra gurus are also the ones who are most familiar with their place in India, which is rooted both in Hindu mythology, which incorporates many transgender figures, and in Islam, with its tradition of eunuchs who served at the courts of kings (Nanda 1999). Most gurus I met were happy to share this information with me, as it is the basis of their power and respect in Indian society.

But whatever their personality, their age, or social status within the hijra community, I almost always found a very courteous, and even hospitable reception among the hijras I visited. Occasionally hijras in the largest cities were hostile or even aggressive, an attitude undoubtedly fostered by the abuse or prurient curiosity they sometimes receive from the larger society, including foreigners. Given the many reasons hijras have to resent outsiders, I was overcome by the welcome I received, and the several close relationships that I formed. But even when courteous and hospitable, not all the hijras I met were interested in being interviewed. Some hijras would reveal nothing about their lives before they joined the community, while others were more forthcoming.

My interviews convince me, however, that the common belief in India that all hijras are born intersexed (hermaphrodites) and are taken away from their parents and brought into the hijra community as infants, is not correct. Most hijras are physically normal men, whose effeminacy, sometimes accompanied by an interest in homosexual activity, led them to seek out the hijra community in their late childhood or adolescence. Their childhood effeminacy, expressed in a wish to wear girl's clothing and imitate girl's behavior was the source of ridicule or abuse by their peers and family and the only solution appeared to be that of leaving their families and joining up with the hijras. While many hijras subsequently lose all contact with their families, others maintain a connection; they may occasionally visit their parents or siblings or these family members may visit them.

Rukhmini was a hijra whose break with her family was permanent and complete. She came from a middle class family and her father was a high ranking police officer. In spite of the many attempts of her father and brothers to prevent her, she persisted in acting and dressing as a girl. When it became known to her father that Rukhmini had had sexual relations with the gardener's son, he almost killed her by holding her head down in a barrel of water and beating her with his cross belt. "My mother cried tears of blood," she said. After this incident, Rukhmini ran away from her home and never returned.

In Sushila's case, she lived at home until her late teens, in relative peace with her family, until one night an elder brother falsely accused her of stealing some money from him. In his anger he told her to "use your own money that you get from selling your anus." She was more outraged at the false accusation of theft than the insult about her homosexuality and then and there left her home to join a hijra commune in a nearby city. Sushila keeps in touch with her family, and sends them gifts on the occasion of her brothers' and sisters' marriage. Meera, a hijra guru, joined the hijra community from a different and less typical route. She had grown up with the desires to be like a female, but followed the conventions of society by having her family arrange her marriage. She was married for over twenty years, and the father of several children, before she "upped one day and joined the hijras." She, too, keeps track of her family and occasionally sends them money when they need it.

As physically normal men, Kavita, Kamladevi, Rukhmini, Sushila, Rekha, and Meera were required to undergo an "operation" which removed their male genitals and transformed them into hijras. This operation, called "nirvana" or rebirth, is a religious ritual for hijras which positions them as ascetics, whose creative powers derive from their rejecting and thus transcending normal sexuality. This role connects them to Shiva, the great Hindu deity, who through his asceticism was given powers to create by Lord Brahma. The operation also identifies hijras with their special goddess and gives them the power to confer blessings of fertility, and equally, curse those who resist their demand for alms. For the small percentage of hijras who are born intersexed, no such operation is necessary. Salima, for example, a hijra from Bombay, told me that from a very early age she had "an organ that was very small." Her mother thought it would grow as she grew older, but when this did not happen her mother took her to many doctors, all to no avail. When Salima was about ten years old, a doctor told her mother, "nothing can be done, your child is neither a man nor a woman," and so Salima's mother gave her to a household of hijras who lived nearby. Salima lived with this group very happily and reported that they treated her with great kindness when she was a child.

But whatever their former lives had been, whether they had joined the hijras voluntarily, or been given to the community in despair by their parents, once an individual joins the community, they become subject to its rules and must adapt to its restrictions. This is not easy. In return for the emotional and economic security provided by the hijra community, an individual must give up some freedom, although probably not more than a young woman gives up when she becomes a bride living in a joint family. Unlike similar persons in the United States, who primarily live and work on their own, the hijras, shaped as they are by Indian culture in spite of their deviance, seem to prefer, like most Indians, to live in groups.

The Hijra Community

The hijra community in India has the qualities of both a religious cult and a caste and takes its customs, social organization and history from both Hinduism and Islam (Nanda 1999; Reddy 2005). Hijras find great pride in citing their identification with many of the great male figures of Hindu mythology who take on female forms in various situations. Familiar to all Hindus is Arjun's disguise as a eunuch in the Mahabharata and Shiva's form as Ardhanarisvara, half man/half woman, just two examples of powerful males in Hindu culture who act or dress as women or who partake of feminine qualities.

Many Hindu festivals include male transgenderism, like the one in south India that attracts thousands of hijras from all over India. This festival is based on a story of a king, who, in order to avert defeat in a war, promised to sacrifice his eldest son to the Gods, asking only that he first be allowed to arrange his son's marriage. Because no woman could be found who would marry a man about to be sacrificed, Lord Krishna came to earth as a woman to marry the King's son and the king won the battle, as the gods had promised. For the festival, men dress as women and go through a marriage ceremony with the deity. The priest performs the marriage, tying on the traditional wedding necklace. The next day the deity is carried to a burial ground and all of those who have "married" him remove their wedding necklaces, cry and beat their breasts, break their bangles, and remove the flowers from their hair, as a widow does in mourning. Hijra participation in this ritual affirms their identification with Krishna, one of the most important Indian deities.

The identification of males with female deities, expressed by the hijras through their cross dressing and emasculation, is a traditional part of Hinduism. This identification reinforces the legitimacy of the hijras as devotees of the Mother Goddess and vehicles of her power, which they use to confer blessings of fertility and prosperity at the births and weddings where they perform. The importance of the mother goddess in India is thus critical to understanding the role of the hijras. Hijra devotion to the goddess, Bahucharaji, a version of the Mother Goddess, closely identified with Durga, is central to their community. Bahucharaji's temple, near Ahmedabad, always has several hijra attendants present who bless visitors and tell them the stories of the powers of the goddess, which has specific references to transgenderism. It is in the name of the goddess that the hijras undergo their emasculation operation, which to them is a ritual of rebirth, transforming them from men to hijras.

Hindu, Muslim, and even Christian hijras revere the goddess, while at the same time embracing elements of Islamic culture. The Indian tradition among both Hindus and Muslims of seeking blessings from saint-like figures whose personal power and charisma supersedes their ascribed religion permits the hijras to find some respect in both these religious communities. In pre-independence India, for example, Muslim rulers gave land grants and special rights to hijras in their kingdoms. And while the hijra role is definitely rooted in early Hinduism, the use of eunuchs in the Mughal courts also strengthened its emergence as a distinct sub-culture. The incorporation of both Hinduism and Islam in the hijras' identity and community is characteristic of the power of Indian culture to incorporate seeming contradictions and paradoxes, into itself, including gender ambiguity, variation, and contradictions (O'Flaherty 1980).

As a caste (jati), or community (quam), hijras have a highly structured social organization whose dominant feature is a hierarchical relationship between the elders, or gurus, and the juniors, or chelas (the guru/chela relationship models itself on the teacher/disciple relationships which are an important feature of Hinduism). Each hijra joins the community under the sponsorship of a guru, and the guru/chela relationship ideally lasts a lifetime. Chelas of the same guru consider themselves "sisters" and adopt fictive kinship relations, such as "aunty" and "grandmother" with hijra elders. As chelas get older, they may become gurus by recruiting chelas for themselves. This process both offers scope for social mobility within the hijra community and also helps maintain the community over time. Hijra social organization, particularly in the guru/chela relationship, thus attempts to substitute for the family life which hijras have abandoned: the guru offers protection, care, and security to the chela and receives in return obedience, loyalty, and a portion of their earnings. Another important advantage of belonging to the hijra community is that it provides a haven when a hijra becomes aged or ill, and can no longer work. A hijra guru with many chelas will be well taken care of, but even a hijra with no chelas will be taken care of by the members of her community.

The typical effective working group of hijras is a communal household, consisting of 5–15 people, headed by a guru. The household members contribute part or all of their earnings to the household and share household chores. In return they get a roof over their heads, food, protection from the police for those who engage in prostitution, and a place from which to carry on their business. Most importantly, as all of the work hijras do, whether begging, entertaining, or prostitution, is strictly divided up among all the hijra households in a city, joining a hijra commune is practically the only way a hijra can get work. The hijra household is thus both an economic and a residential unit, as well as a family-like group which provides emotional satisfaction and a network of social relationships.

Living in a hijra household puts many restrictions on behavior. Just as an Indian bride must make adjustments to her in-laws when she moves into a joint family, so a new hijra must make many accommodations to her new "family" in a hijra commune. Kumari, an independent sort of person, who, with her guru's permission, eventually moved out to her own place, told me that "living with the hijras was very difficult. There were so many jobs to do . . . like cooking and housework. After coming home from a whole day of dancing, I then had to cook and do other chores. If I did the household chores during the day, I wouldn't have time to go out and the whole day would be lost. Gurus are very strict. If you don't keep your hair covered with your sari, if you don't cook properly, if the house is not spotlessly clean, for all these things they give you trouble. You can't just throw your dirty clothes down anywhere, you have to hang them up. If you don't serve food on the proper dishes, they will shout, 'What, are you a man that you cannot do these things properly!' I got tired of all that and so asked my guru permission to live on my own."

But even for hijras like Kumari, who prefer to live on their own, the idea of living as a hijra without the support of a guru is unthinkable. "You can never be without a guru," says Kumari, "anymore than you people (non-hijras) can be without a mother. Just as a daughter is known by her mother, so we are known by our guru. To belong to the hijra community, to live in a sari like this, you must have a guru; otherwise you will have no respect in society."

An individual can only join the hijra community under the sponsorship of a guru, and as a member of her guru's "house" (gharana). The "houses" into which the hijra community is divided are similar to symbolic descent groups, like clans or lineages. Although there are few meaningful distinctions between these "houses," each has its own founder and history. Hijras say the "houses" are like several brothers from the same mother, or two countries, like England and America, which have a common origin. A hijra remains in the "house" of her guru even if she moves her residence to some other household or even some other city. When a hijra dies, it is the elders of her "house," rather than her household, who arrange for her funeral; and a guru will pass her property to chelas belonging to her "house" when she dies.

Each "house" has a naik, or chief and it is the naiks who get together locally, and also nationally, to decide on major policy issues for the hijra community, or to celebrate some event within the community, such as the death anniversary of a famous guru. At the local level, it is the naiks who get together in a jamaat (meeting of the elders) to resolve conflict among hijra individuals or households within a city or region.

One of the most important tasks of the jamaat is to make sure that hijras do not violate the rules of their community. Honesty is one of the unshakable hijra norms. Hijras frequently change their residence, both within and between cities, and a hijra who has been found guilty of stealing someone's property will not be accepted in any hijra household. Without a household, a hijra will find herself without friends, and more important, without access to work. In respectable hijra households, individuals are expected to behave with some propriety, and hijras who drink heavily, or who are quarrelsome, or cannot control their aggression, will find themselves out on the street. The punishment for misbehavior varies with the crime: in some cases fines are levied; in more serious cases a hijra's hair will be cut as a way of stigmatizing her within the community, as

hijras are obliged to wear their hair long, like women. For the most serious offenses, such as abusing or assaulting one's guru, a hijra may be cast out of the community altogether and have to pay a very heavy fine to re-enter.

This had happened to Rehka. Rehka had been in the hijra community for the last 15 years, earning her keep by playing the dholak (drum) which always accompanies hijra performances. Several years ago, provoked in an argument over men and money, Rehka insulted her guru and struck her. A meeting of the naiks determined that she should be cast out of the hijra community. From living very comfortably and with her future secure, Rehka now found herself, literally, on the street. Her sister chelas would no longer talk to her, not even, she said, "give me a drink of water." There was no place within walking distance she could work that was not already part of another hijra group's territory. If she tried to perform or even beg, she would be chased away by other hijras. With no money, and no work, Rehka took up residence on the street, earning a few rupees caring for some neighbor's children, or sometimes walking miles to a suburb to beg for alms. When it rained she slept under a bus. Living in the open, her clothes became tattered, her appearance and her health deteriorated and she was constantly insulted by neighborhood rowdies. It was a vicious cycle: Rekha was cast out of the community until she could raise the substantial fine of over 1,000 rupees that the naiks determined as the price of her re-entry into the community and apart from the community it was hopeless to even think of earning that sum, never mind saving it. Rehka's transformation was not lost on the hijras in her city. For all who knew her, it acted as a powerful incentive to maintain their own obedience and loyalty to their gurus.

The most important conflicts that naiks resolve are those that occur when the rigid territorial allotment of work within a city is violated. Naiks reach agreement about which hijra groups may work—whether begging alms from shop owners or in traditional performances—in particular areas of a city. When a hijra group finds others encroaching on their assigned territory, there may be arguments or even fist fights, and the naiks must negotiate new allotments of territory or maintain traditional boundaries. Because hijras can hardly go to the police or courts to settle their disputes—nor would they wish to give up such power to outsiders—disputes are settled within the community.

The hijras today are an example of a highly successful cultural adaptation. Their structured social organization, which imitates both a family and a caste, the use of the guru/chela relationship as a recruitment strategy, their willingness to move into new economic niches, and the effective control over economic rights exercised within the community, provide hijras with both the flexibility and control needed to succeed in today's complex and highly competitive society. In the face of dwindling opportunities for their traditional performances, prostitution, always a lucrative profession, has expanded. Hijras now bless girl infants as well as boys; they have become tax collectors, and have successfully run for political office. In politics, hijras have largely succeeded by emphasizing that their ascetic role as neither man nor woman, with no families to support, which they contrast to the widespread nepotism and corruption engaged in by so many Indian politicians (Reddy 2003).

Hijras have also successfully weathered the attempts of the Indian government to outlaw their emasculation operation, which serves as the definitive symbol of their identity. Indeed, they have become politically organized and have petitioned various state governments to grant them, as members of the "sexually marginalized," rights to jobs, marriage, legal recognition as a third gender and to consider sending a hijra into space as part of India's space program (Reddy 2010:140).

Gender Variation in Other Cultures

The assumption by a man of a woman's character, sex/gender role and identity in a spiritual or religious context, and even as a means of salvation, which has long been part of the Hindu tradition, is found in many other cultural traditions as well (Herdt 1996), particularly in Southeast Asia (Peletz 2009). In many great agricultural civilizations of the ancient world, arising around 10,000 years ago, Mother Goddess cults were prominent. Some of these goddesses were attended by a priesthood that included men who acted and dressed as women, either specifically during religious rituals, or permanently, while other cults involved male priests who castrated themselves while in ecstasy, in a gesture of renunciation and identification with her, very similar to the hijra nirvana ritual. The numerous images of Hermaphroditus (from which the English term hermaphrodite derives) found in Greek mythology and statuary, make it clear that androgyny and sex-change also had special meaning for the ancient Greeks.

By the end of the 4th century, B.C.E., however, cultural diffusion, through the spread of Christianity and later, in the 8th century C.E. through the spread of Islam, led to the dominance of male deities. By the 8th century C.E., mother goddess worship had virtually disappeared (India is one of the few places where it remained culturally central), and with it, of course, the sexually ambiguous priesthoods. Still later, European colonialism began to have its effect in repressing sexual and gender diversity in the New World as well as the old. The British, for example, outlawed the land grants to hijras in India, which had been awarded in various princely states, and repressed the many transgender roles in Southeast Asia (Peletz 2009), while the 19th century American occupation of Hawai'i, led to the decline of the indigenous role of the mahu (Matzner 2001).

In the mid-20th century, the European medical model, which pathologized gender diversity and homosexuality, spread throughout Asia, and had a particularly negative impact in Thailand. The kathoey, a third gender, mentioned in ancient Buddhist scriptures and tolerated by society, as well as homosexuality, came to be viewed as "social problems," and were subject to both attempted "treatment" and repression (Jackson 1999; Costa and Matzner 2007). The contemporary global spread of fundamental Islam has also affected Islamic states such as Malaysia and Indonesia, whose previous casual toleration of indigenous transgender roles and male same-sex relationships, is now replaced by increasing public surveillance; in Indonesia a ban on the transsexual operation is being proposed.

At the same time, in recent decades, there has been a countercurrent to the decline of gender diversity, as the effects of ethnography, international human rights, the internet, and global media have sent information and images all over the world. Transgender beauty contests, long practiced in the Philippines—and based on American images of beauty rooted in the American occupation of the turn of the 20th century—have proliferated throughout Asia and the Pacific (Johnson 1997; Besnier 2011). In Indonesia, the waria, an indigenous transgender role, has become a symbol of nationalism and warias dominate beauty salons which prepare brides for traditional Indonesian weddings (Boellstorff 2005). The diffusion of a global gay identity, which is now associated with many different transgender roles throughout Asia, is spread by the media and by internet-based solidarity, even as it is transformed in local cultures in a variety of ways. Similarly, many international NGOs have set up HIV/AIDS clinics throughout Asia and Africa, which form a nexus of homosexual and transgender relationships, although in fact, AIDS in Asia and Africa is spread more by heterosexual than by same-sex relationships. Global migration, too, has been an important source of cultural diffusion, bringing for example, large numbers of transgendered Filipinos to Israel, where they dominate in the care of the aged (Heymann 2006). These globalizing dimensions of sex/gender diversity, have also affected the United States.

Sex/Gender Diversity and Change in the United States

One of the most important roles of anthropology is to increase our awareness of our own culture by reflecting on the cultures of others; as the famous anthropologist, Claude Levi-Strauss said, ethnography makes an important contribution to an ongoing critique of Western culture. The descriptions of sex/gender diversity in other cultures provokes us to re-examine the nature and assumptions of our own sex/gender system; the cultural basis of its categories; the relations between sex, sexuality, gender, and other aspects of culture; and the ways in which this impacts on individuals with alternative sex/gender identities who engage in diverse sexual practices (Nanda 2000).

Until the late 20th century, the binary Western concept of sex and gender—male and female—as well as condemnation of homosexuality, described in the book of Genesis, left no room for alternative sex/gender identities or varied sexual practices. The emergence of medical technology which enabled sex reassignment surgery both reflected and intensified this dichotomy. For an individual whose gender identity or sexual relationships were in conflict with his or her biological sex, the sex change operation provided one way out of the dilemma. Transsexuals in American culture were defined as "biologically normal persons of one sex convinced that they were members of the *opposite* sex" (Stoller, cited in Kessler and McKenna, 1978:115). The aim of sex reassignment surgery and the psychological and medical treatments (such as hormone therapy) that were required to accompany it, was the transformation of an individual from their natal sex into the sex with which they identified. An important aspect of the treatment required the individual to demonstrate to psychological and medical professionals that the individual was committed to, and was able to, make this transition.

This construction of the transsexual was consistent with the binary American sex/gender system and was supported in the larger culture by permitting various legal changes as part of a revised life story (Bolin 1988). Unlike alternative sex/gender figures in other cultures, however, transsexuals were viewed as a source of cultural anxiety, pathology, and a social problem; at best, as figures of scorn or pity. While the gay liberation movement in the United States helped our society become more humane and egalitarian in its response to sex and gender variations, our culture has not yet been able to incorporate the wide tolerance or spiritual roles for gender difference and ambiguity that traditionally existed in India and in other societies.

Even with emerging cultural and indeed legal supports of the construct of the transsexual as someone who crosses over completely to the "opposite" sex, this concept was not—and is not today—wholly accepted in our society. In a 2002 legal case in which a transsexual claimed the estate of her deceased spouse, the Kansas Supreme Court stated that both science and the courts are divided on whether transsexuals are more appropriately defined in terms of their birth sex status or their post-operative sex/gender status [*In re Marshall G. Gardiner, deceased.* (2002), in Norgren and Nanda 2006]. The Court held that, while "through surgery and hormones, a transsexual can be made to look like a woman . . . the sex assignment surgery does not create the sexual organs of a woman." The Court further held that while the plaintiff (a male to female transsexual) "wants and believes herself to be a woman [and] . . . has made every conceivable effort to make herself a female . . . her female anatomy, however, is still all man-made. The body [the plaintiff] inhabits is a male body in all aspects other than what the physicians have supplied . . . From that the Court has to conclude, that . . . as a matter of law [the plaintiff] is a male."

In spite of American resistance to changing concepts of sex and gender, illustrated by the legal decision cited above, the increasing awareness of the sex/gender systems of other cultures has led to a change in our own society. Within the last three decades America's rigid binary cultural boundaries—nature/culture, male/female, homosexual/heterosexual—have become blurred. Transgenderism is now a recognized cultural category, one that transcends the historical American "incorrigible proposition" that tells us that sex and gender are ascribed and permanent.

Transgenderism today incorporates a variety of subjective experiences, identities, and sexual practices that range widely over a sex/gender continuum, from androgynous to transsexual (Valentine 2007). Increasingly, persons defining themselves as transpeople see transgenderism as a way "out of the constraints imposed by a dichotomous sex/gender system [with the aim] . . . not to mandate anything, but to . . . be able to play with the categories, . . . to challenge the reductionism and essentialism that has accompanied these [binary] categories for so many millennia" (Ducat 2006: 48). In spite of the many differences among individuals experiencing transgender identities, one repeated theme of the transgender movement is that gender and sex categories are improperly imposed by society and its "sexual identity gatekeepers," referring here to the gender identity professionals who accepted and furthered the binary system of

American sex/gender roles (Bolin 1996: 447). The transgendered are challenging and stretching the boundaries of the American system of sex/gender binary oppositions, and renouncing the American definition of gender as dependent on a consistency of genitals, body type, identity, role behaviors, sexual orientation, and sexual practice. Contemporary transgender communities include a continuum of people, from those who wish to undergo sex reassignment surgery, to those who wish to live their lives androgynously (Winter 2006). The previous split between transsexuals who viewed surgery as the only authentic expression of a feminine nature, as opposed to "part time" gender crossers who did not wish to have sex reassignment surgery, has to some extent been reconciled by the emergence of a transgender community which attempts to validate a whole range of gender roles and identities. As one transperson expressed it, " . . . you no longer have to fit into a box . . . it is okay to be transgendered. You can now lay anywhere on the spectrum from non-gendered to full transsexual" (Bolin 1996: 475). Transpeople are trying not so much to do away with maleness and femaleness as to denaturalize them, that is, take away their privileged status in relation to all other possible combinations of behaviors, roles, and identities. The point for some transpeople is that gender categories should be something that individuals can construct for themselves, through self-reflection and observation (Cromwell 1997).

The dynamism of the contemporary transgender movement, which includes both transgender activists and mental health professionals, was recently acknowledged in a proposal by the New York City Board of Health to allow people to alter the sex on their birth certificate even if they have not had sex-change surgery (Cave 2006: A1). While this proposal, which emphasized the importance of separating anatomy from gender identity, ultimately failed, New York City has adopted other measures aimed at blurring the lines of gender identification. It has, for example, allowed beds in homeless shelters to be distributed according to appearance, applying equally to postoperative transsexuals, cross-dressers, and persons perceived to be androgynous. A Metropolitan Transit Authority policy also allows people to define their own gender when deciding whether to use men's or women's bathrooms. These new, even radical, policies are just one of the many aspects of the current transgender movement. Other aims of this movement are the redefining of gender diversity as a naturally occurring phenomenon rather than a psychological disorder; dismantling gender stereotypes, and reducing harassment and discrimination against those who do not wish to conform to current sex/gender norms (Brown 2006: A1). As Sam Winter, director of the Transgender Asia website suggests, although treating gender disorders as a mental illness, as in the United States, is useful for Western transsexuals in obtaining medical services, it extracts too high a price in substantially contributing to transphobia. For contemporary transpeople he says, "transgender is one aspect of human diversity. . . . It is a difference, not a disorder. . . . If we can speak to any gender identity disorder at all, it is in the inability of many societies to accept the particular gender identity difference we call transgender" (Winter, accessed 2006).

A core American cultural pattern which places a high value on the "authentic self"—on integrating the inner person with external actions—is central to the current transgender movement, as well as to contemporary gay activism. This core American cultural value is not universal, which makes it easier for sex/gender diversity to exist in other societies. In Thailand, for example, little value is attached to acknowledging or displaying one's private sexual orientation in public. In Thailand, how one acts is more important than how one feels. Leading a "double life" is a generally accepted feature of Thai culture, not necessarily equated with duplicity or deception as in the United States. Thus, "coming out" as a homosexual in Thailand brings shame or "loss of face" both to the individual and to the family without the compensation of expressing one's "true self" so valued in the United States. Similar values also hold in Indonesia (Wieringa 2008). In Malaysia, too, the Islamic emphasis on marriage and family takes precedence over asserting one's individuality and agency, as required in the process of "coming out" (Peletz 2009). Martin Manalansan, in his ethnography of transgendered Philippine migrants in New York, makes a similar point, quoting a "bakla" informant: "The Americans are different, darling. Coming out is their drama. When I studied at [a New England college] the queens had nothing better to talk about than coming out . . . the whites, my God, shedding tears, leaving the families. The stories are always so sad" (2003).

This contrast between cultural values, as they affect homosexuals and transgender people in Thailand, Malaysia and the Philippines, and those in the United States, casts a revealing perspective on the demand for repeal of "Don't Ask, Don't Tell," the shortsighted, politically motivated policy that banned openly gay men and women from the American military. That policy, which burdened the individual with the necessity of hiding his or her "true self" is quite simply incompatible with American culture and is now in the process of being repealed.

Unlike transsexualism, which reinforces the binary American sex/gender system, transgenderism is culturally subversive: it calls into question the rightness of binary sex/gender categories. It also provides a wider range of individual possibilities for those who experience distress by trying to conform to exclusively binary sex/gender categories, including sexual practices. The American transgender movement has been empowered by knowledge about alternative sex/gender systems throughout the world. Some of these sex/gender systems have offered American transpeople a source of meaning, and especially spiritual meaning, that they do not find in the binary, transphobic culture that is still dominant within the United States. As the West becomes more aware of alternatives and variations in gender roles in other cultures, both past and present, it can also perhaps become more accommodating of those individuals who do not fit into their traditionally prescribed—and limited—sex/gender categories.

References

Besnier, N. 2011. *On the edge of the global: Modern anxieties in a Pacific Island nation.* Stanford, CA: Stanford University Press.

Boelstorff, T. 2005. *The gay archipelago: Sexuality and nation in Indonesia.* Princeton, NJ: Princeton University Press.

Bolin, A. 1988. *In search of Eve: Transsexual rites of passage.* South Hadley, MA: Bergin and Garvey.

Bolin A. 1996. "Transcending and transgendering: Male-to-female transsexuals, dichotomy and diversity." In G. Herdt (Ed.), *Third sex third gender: Beyond sexual dimorphism in culture and history* (pp. 447–485). New York: Zone Books.

Brown, P.L. 2006. "Supporting boys or girls when the line isn't clear." *The New York Times,* December 2, p. A1.

Cave, D. 2006. "New York plans to make gender personal choice." *The New York Times,* November 7, p. A1.

Costa, L. and Andrew Matzner, A. 2007. *Male bodies, women's souls: Personal narratives of Thailand's transgendered youth.* Binghamton, NY: Haworth Press.

Cromwell, J. 1977. "Traditions of gender diversity and sexualities: A female-to-male transgendered perspective." In S. Jacobs, W. Thomas, and S. Lang (Eds.). *Two spirit people: Native American gender identity, sexuality, and spirituality.* Urbana, IL: University of Illinois Press.

Ducat, S. 2006. "Slipping into something more comfortable: Towards a liberated continuum of gender." *LiP,* Summer, pp. 46–61.

Herdt, G. 1996. *Third sex third gender: Beyond sexual dimorphism in culture and history.* New York: Zone Books.

Heymann, T. 2006. *Paper Dolls.* (film). Strand Releasing.

Jackson, P. 1999. *Lady boys, tom boys, rentboys: Male and female homosexualities in contemporary Thailand.* Binghamton, NY: Haworth Press.

Johnson, M. 1997. *Beauty and power: Transgendering and cultural transformation in the Southern Philippines.* New York: Berg.

Kessler, S.J., and W. McKenna. 1978. *Gender: An ethnomethodological approach.* New York: Wiley.

Manalansan, M. 2003. *Global divas: Filipino gay men in the diaspora.* Durham, NC: Duke University Press.

Matzner, A. 2001. *'O au no keia: Voices from Hawai'i's Mahu and transgender community.'* Philadelphia: XLibris.

Nanda, S. 1999. *Neither man nor woman: the hijras of India.* 2nd Ed. Belmont, CA: Wadsworth.

Nanda, S. 2000. *Gender diversity: crosscultural variations.* Prospect Heights, IL: Waveland.

Norgren, J. and S. Nanda. 2006. *American cultural pluralism and law.* Westport, CN: Praeger.

O'Flaherty, W.D. 1980. *Women, androgynies, and other mythical beasts.* Chicago: University of Chicago Press.

Peletz, M. 2009. *Gender pluralism: southeast asia since early modern times.* NY: Routledge.

Reddy, G. 2003. "'Men' who would be kings: celibacy, emasculation and reproduction of hijras in contemporary Indian politics. *Social Research,* 70, no. 1:163–198.

Reddy, G. 2005. *With respect to sex: negotiating hijra identity in South India.* Chicago: University of Chicago Press.

Reddy, G. 2010. "Crossing 'Lines' of difference: Transnational Movements and Sexual Subjectivities In Hyderabad, India." In Diane P. Mines and Sarah Lamb (Eds.), *Everyday life in south Asia,* 2nd Ed. Bloomington, IN: University of Indiana Press.

Valentine, D. 2007. *Imagining transgender: An ethnography of a category.* Durham, NC: Duke University Press.

Wieringa, S. 2008. "If there is no feeling . . . The Dilemma between Silence and Coming Out in a Working Class Butch/Femme Community in Jakarta." In Mark B. Padilla, Jennifer S. Hirsch, Miguel Munoz-Laboy, Robert E. Sember, and Richard G. Parker (Eds.), *Love and globalization: Transformations of intimacy in the contemporary world.* Nashville, TN: University of Vanderbilt Press, pp. 70–90.

Winter, S. 2006. "Transphobia: A price worth paying for gender identity disorder? Retrieved from http://web.hku.hk/~sjwinter/TransgenderASIA/index.htm.

Critical Thinking

1. Be aware of the various social roles played by the hijra and how individuals become part of a hijra community.

2. What is the significance of the operation known as "nirvana"?

3. Be familiar with the hijra community in terms of its religious and caste qualities.

4. Be familiar with the hijra household in terms of its structure and rules.

5. What kinds of tasks are carried out by the "naiks" and the "jamaat"?

6. In what respects are the hijras an example of a highly successful cultural adaptation?

7. What evidence is there of gender variation throughout history? How did cultural diffusion and colonialism suppress it? How and why have there been countercurrents to such suppression?

8. What is meant by the American notion of a "binary sex and gender"? How has this been reinforced by medical technology?

9. What kinds of changes did the "transgender movement" bring about?

10. How and why is "coming out" treated differently in the United States and Thailand?

11. Why is "transgenderism" more subversive than "transsexualism"?

Create Central

www.mhhe.com/createcentral

Internet References

Indian Journal of Gender Studies
http://ijg.sagepub.com

Intersections: Gender, History and Culture in the Asian Context
http://intersections.anu.edu.au

Gay, Lesbian, Bisexual, Transgender and Queer Studies, Canadian Online Journal for Queer Studies in Education
http://jqstudies.library.utoronto.ca/index.php/jqstudies

International Journal of Transgenderism
www.haworthpress.com/store/product.asp?sid=PX1MHCJ72GN18MGK
KNXMG90SQVEV15K4&sku=J485&AuthType=4

SERENA NANDA is Professor Emeritus, Anthropology, at John Jay College, City University of New York. Many thanks to Joan Gregg, Mary Winslow, Cory Harris, and Barry Kass for their encouragement and suggestions.

Article   Prepared by: Elvio Angeloni, *Pasadena City College*

Where Fat Is a Mark of Beauty

In a rite of passage, some Nigerian girls spend months gaining weight and learning customs in a special room. "To be called a 'slim princess' is an abuse," says a defender of the practice.

ANN M. SIMMONS

Learning Outcomes

After reading this article, you will be able to:

- Explain how and why perceptions of feminine beauty vary from culture to culture.

- Discuss the traditional role of the fattening room in Nigeria.

Margaret Bassey Ene currently has one mission in life: gaining weight.

The Nigerian teenager has spent every day since early June in a "fattening room" specially set aside in her father's mud-and-thatch house. Most of her waking hours are spent eating bowl after bowl of rice, yams, plantains, beans and *gari,* a porridge-like mixture of dried cassava and water.

After three more months of starchy diet and forced inactivity, Margaret will be ready to reenter society bearing the traditional mark of female beauty among her Efik people: fat.

In contrast to many Western cultures where thin is in, many culture-conscious people in the Efik and other communities in Nigeria's southeastern Cross River state hail a woman's rotundity as a sign of good health, prosperity and allure.

The fattening room is at the center of a centuries-old rite of passage from maidenhood to womanhood. The months spent in pursuit of poundage are supplemented by daily visits from elderly matrons who impart tips on how to be a successful wife and mother. Nowadays, though, girls who are not yet marriage-bound do a tour in the rooms purely as a coming-of-age ceremony. And sometimes, nursing mothers return to the rooms to put on more weight.

"The fattening room is like a kind of school where the girl is taught about motherhood," said Sylvester Odey, director of the Cultural Center Board in Calabar, capital of Cross River state. "Your daily routine is to sleep, eat and grow fat."

Like many traditional African customs, the fattening room is facing relentless pressure from Western influences. Health campaigns linking excess fat to heart disease and other illnesses are changing the eating habits of many Nigerians, and urban dwellers are opting out of the time-consuming process.

Effiong Okon Etim, an Efik village chief in the district of Akpabuyo, said some families cannot afford to constantly feed a daughter for more than a few months. That compares with a stay of up to two years, as was common earlier this century, he said.

But the practice continues partly because "people might laugh at you because you didn't have money to allow your child to pass through the rite of passage," Etim said. What's more, many believe an unfattened girl will be sickly or unable to bear children.

Etim, 65, put his two daughters in a fattening room together when they were 12 and 15 years old, but some girls undergo the process as early as age 7, after undergoing the controversial practice of genital excision.

Bigger Is Better, According to Custom

As for how fat is fat enough, there is no set standard. But the unwritten rule is the bigger the better, said Mkoyo Edet, Etim's sister.

"Beauty is in the weight," said Edet, a woman in her 50s who spent three months in a fattening room when she was 7. "To be called a 'slim princess' is an abuse. The girl is fed constantly whether she likes it or not."

In Margaret's family, there was never any question that she would enter the fattening room.

"We inherited it from our forefathers; it is one of the heritages we must continue," said Edet Essien Okon, 25, Margaret's stepfather and a language and linguistics graduate of the University of Calabar. "It's a good thing to do; it's an initiation rite."

His wife, Nkoyo Effiong, 27, agreed: "As a woman, I feel it is proper for me to put my daughter in there, so she can be educated."

Effiong, a mother of five, spent four months in a fattening room at the age of 10.

Margaret, an attractive girl with a cheerful smile and hair plaited in fluffy bumps, needs only six months in the fattening room because she was already naturally plump, her stepfather said.

During the process, she is treated as a goddess, but the days are monotonous. To amuse herself, Margaret has only an instrument made out of a soda bottle with a hole in it, which she taps on her hand to play traditional tunes.

Still, the 16-year-old says she is enjoying the highly ritualized fattening practice.

"I'm very happy about this," she said, her belly already distended over the waist of her loincloth. "I enjoy the food, except for *gari*."

Day in, day out, Margaret must sit cross-legged on a special stool inside the secluded fattening room. When it is time to eat, she sits on the floor on a large, dried plantain leaf, which also serves as her bed. She washes down the mounds of food with huge pots of water and takes traditional medicine made from leaves and herbs to ensure proper digestion.

As part of the rite, Margaret's face is decorated with a white, claylike chalk.

"You have to prepare the child so that if a man sees her, she will be attractive," Chief Etim said.

Tufts of palm leaf fiber, braided and dyed red, are hung around Margaret's neck and tied like bangles around her wrists and ankles. They are adjusted as she grows.

Typically, Margaret would receive body massages using the white chalk powder mixed with heavy red palm oil. But the teen said her parents believe the skin-softening, blood-stimulating massages might cause her to expand further than necessary.

Margaret is barred from doing her usual chores or any other strenuous physical activities. And she is forbidden to receive visitors, save for the half a dozen matrons who school Margaret in the etiquette of the Efik clan.

They teach her such basics as how to sit, walk and talk in front of her husband. And they impart wisdom about cleaning, sewing, child care and cooking—Efik women are known throughout Nigeria for their chicken pepper soup, pounded yams and other culinary creations.

"They advise me to keep calm and quiet, to eat the *gari,* and not to have many boyfriends so that I avoid unwanted pregnancy," Margaret said of her matron teachers. "They say that unless you have passed through this, you will not be a full-grown woman."

What little exercise Margaret gets comes in dance lessons. The matrons teach her the traditional *ekombi,* which she will be expected to perform before an audience on the day she emerges from seclusion—usually on the girl's wedding day, Etim said.

But Okon said his aim is to prepare his stepdaughter for the future, not to marry her off immediately. Efik girls receive more education than girls in most parts of Nigeria, and Okon hopes Margaret will return to school and embark on a career as a seamstress before getting married.

Weddings Also Steeped in Tradition

Once she does wed, Margaret will probably honor southeastern Nigeria's rich marriage tradition. It begins with a letter from the family of the groom to the family of the bride, explaining that "our son has seen a flower, a jewel, or something beautiful in your family, that we are interested in," said Josephine Effah-Chukwuma, program officer for women and children at the Constitutional Rights Project, a law-oriented nongovernmental organization based in the Nigerian commercial capital of Lagos.

If the girl and her family consent, a meeting is arranged. The groom and his relatives arrive with alcoholic beverages, soft drinks and native brews, and the bride's parents provide the food. The would-be bride's name is never uttered, and the couple are not allowed to speak, but if all goes well, a date is set for handing over the dowry. On that occasion, the bride's parents receive about $30 as a token of appreciation for their care of the young woman. "If you make the groom pay too much, it is like selling your daughter," Effah-Chukwuma said. Then, more drinks are served, and the engagement is official.

On the day of the wedding, the bride sits on a specially built wooden throne, covered by an extravagantly decorated canopy. Maidens surround her as relatives bestow gifts such as pots, pans, brooms, plates, glasses, table covers—everything she will need to start her new home. During the festivities, the bride changes clothes three times.

The high point is the performance of the *ekombi,* in which the bride twists and twirls, shielded by maidens and resisting the advances of her husband. It is his task to break through the ring and claim his bride.

Traditionalists are glad that some wedding customs are thriving despite the onslaught of modernity.

Traditional weddings are much more prevalent in southeastern Nigeria than so-called white weddings, introduced by colonialists and conducted in a church or registry office.

"In order to be considered married, you have to be married in the traditional way," said Maureen Okon, a woman of the Qua ethnic group who wed seven years ago but skipped the fattening room because she did not want to sacrifice the time. "Tradition identifies a people. It is important to keep up a culture. There is quite a bit of beauty in Efik and Qua marriages."

Critical Thinking

1. How do the Efik contrast with many Western cultures with respect to a woman's "rotundity"?
2. What was the traditional role of the fattening room? What purpose does it serve today?
3. What kind of pressure does the fattening room face today? Why does the practice continue today?
4. What is the unwritten rule about "how fat"?
5. How does the author describe the fattening room experience? What exercise does Margaret get and why?

Create Central

www.mhhe.com/createcentral

Internet References

JENdA: A Journal of Culture and African Women Studies
www.jendajournal.com/index.htm

Journal of International Women's Studies
www.bridgew.edu/soas/jiws/

Kinship and Social Organization
www.umanitoba.ca/anthropology

Article Prepared by: Elvio Angeloni, *Pasadena City College*

Kidnapping Women: Discourses of Emotion and Social Change in the Kyrgyz Republic

NOOR O'NEILL BORBIEVA

Learning Outcomes

After reading this article, you will be able to:

- Discuss the pros and cons of kidnapping women as brides as it occurs among the Kyrgyz.

- Discuss whether kidnapping brides represents "gender inequality."

Abstract

In 1974, Anthropological Quarterly *published a special issue on bride theft. Since then, considerable work has been published on the practice. Drawing on my fieldwork in the Kyrgyz Republic, I assess current understandings of the practice. I argue that although functionalist and symbolic approaches to kidnapping are still relevant, it is necessary to consider kidnapping in the context of intensifying discursive competition over marriage, gender roles, and authority. In my account, kidnapping is a practice that both supports and undermines existing systems of oppression. As such, it has become a powerful engine of social change.*

An institution—say, a marriage system—is at once a system of social relations, economic arrangements, political processes, cultural categories, norms, values, ideals, emotional patterns, and so on and on (Ortner 1984:148). Although prohibited by law, the traditional practice of kidnapping women and girls for forced marriage continued in rural areas [of Kyrgyzstan]. Cultural traditions discouraged victims from going to the authorities (US Department of State 2010).

In a segment of *Bride Kidnapping in the Kyrgyz Republic,* a 2004 documentary produced by political scientist Petr Lom, a young woman is carried, struggling, into a rustic dwelling. She stands in the corner of a dimly-lit room, surrounded by elder women in bright dresses and sweater-vests. Wielding a white scarf, they tell her she must marry the young man who has brought her there, against her will. At times she resists, crying and arguing with the women. At times she sits passively, even laughing at their jokes. She finally puts on the scarf, and the last time we see her, she and her new husband stand next to each other, smiling and proclaiming their happiness.

Conventional wisdom among the Kyrgyz asserts that bride kidnapping (*alyp kachuu*[1]) is a unique Kyrgyz practice.[2] Actually, bride kidnapping, which is also known as bride "theft," "capture," or "abduction," has been documented all over the world and throughout recorded history (e.g., Århem 1981, Ayres 1974, Barnes 1999, Bates et al. 1974, Evans-Grubb 1989, McLaren 2001). In most societies where it has been observed, bride kidnapping is a rule-governed practice, an alternative to more acceptable forms of marriage, such as arrangement (Bates et al. 1974). Barbara Ayres (1974:238) defines bride kidnapping as "the forceable abduction of a woman for the purpose of marriage, without her foreknowledge or consent and without the knowledge or consent of her parents or guardians" then qualifies that kidnapping can be "genuine" (forced abduction) or "mock" (elopement). The extent to which a young woman is involved in the planning of the abduction can vary in different societies and contexts (Kudat 1974, Werner 2004), but many societies (including the Kyrgyz) do not formally distinguish between kidnappings that are forced and those that are elopements.

Bride kidnapping is particularly well-documented in the former Soviet Union where early Soviet ethnographers detailed its popularity among a number of ethnic groups (Kleinbach and Salimjanova 2007). Fannina Halle, a European ethnographer who traveled through Central Asia and the Caucasus in the 1930s, described Soviet efforts to outlaw the practice as part of a project to raise the status of the Union's southern women (Halle 1938:129, see also Keinbach and Salimjanova 2007:226). Soviet reformers viewed kidnapping as an index of the wildness of outlying lands and the need for socialism's civilizing mission, says Bruce Grant (2005:49), and considered it "the ur-example of gender inequality in Caucasian societies." Kidnapping was illegal under socialism, as it is today, but laws against it have always been difficult to enforce (Kleinbach and Salimjanova 2007).

Since the dissolution of the USSR, a number of scholars have noted that the practice seems to be on the rise in Central Asia (Amsler and Kleinbach 1999, Bauer et al. 1997, Human Rights Watch 2006, Kleinbach 2003, Kleinbach et al. 2005, Werner 2004). This scholarship has been accompanied by front page articles in *The New York Times* (Smith 2005) and *The Chicago Tribune* (Rodriguez 2005), as well as articles in *The Independent* (Lloyd-Roberts 1999a), *The Economist* (1996), and numerous webzines.[3] The release of Petr Lom's film in 2004, perhaps more than any other depiction, has made bride kidnapping part of the American imagination. The documentary, which was broadcast on PBS and shown at film festivals all over the world, includes footage of three actual kidnappings as well as interviews with the participants. Although the film provides no commentary and has been charged with violating ethical standards of filmmaking, it is a valuable ethnographic document.

Barnes (1999:69) writes in his survey of the 19th century scholarship, "We may be led astray by the tendency to see marriage by capture as a unitary institution . . . and therefore to expect for the 'problem of marriage capture' a single answer." Earlier scholarship interpreted bride kidnapping using functional or symbolic analysis, or presented kidnapping as a means by which patriarchal systems of oppression are reinforced. Although these accounts provide useful insight, they do not ultimately explain kidnapping, at least as it is practiced in Kyrgyz society. Drawing on four years spent in Kyrgyzstan (including two years of ethnographic research) as well as ethnographic accounts collected by other scholars, I argue that kidnapping in Kyrgyz society is used in a variety of ways by individuals who are struggling to respond to changing conceptions of love, marriage, and authority. By mediating competing ideals, kidnapping ultimately serves as a potent force for social change.

Encountering Kidnapping

The formerly Soviet nations of Central Asia include five republics: Kazakhstan, Kyrgyzstan,[4] Tajikistan, Turkmenistan, and Uzbekistan. These republics became independent (mostly against the will of local populations) in 1991, when the Soviet Union dissolved. The Kyrgyz Republic, where I did fieldwork, lies on the eastern edge of the region, sharing a border with China. Kyrgyzstan is a diverse nation of 5.6 million people,[5] comprising numerous ethnic groups, languages, and religions. According to 1999 figures, 65 percent of the population is ethnically Kyrgyz. There are sizable minority populations of Uzbeks and Russians and smaller populations of many other ethnicities. Seventy-five percent of the population identifies as Muslim.

I first arrived in Kyrgyzstan in 1997 as a prospective Peace Corps volunteer. Like most westerners who visit Kyrgyzstan, I heard about bride kidnapping almost immediately. During our three-month Peace Corps training, stories were passed among the women in my group about two of our language teachers—young, attractive Kyrgyz women—who had been "kidnapped" and were now divorced. Confused, we collected and shared information, ultimately coming to understand bride kidnapping as a tradition by which a young man abducts a woman he likes, sometimes a woman he has never talked to, and forces her to marry him. If the marriage does not work out, he will be able to find someone new. She, however, will probably remain alone, like our language teachers. Female virginity is highly prized among Kyrgyz, so the marital choices of a divorced woman are limited.

That fall I moved to my field site, a small town in the south. The two eldest daughters in my host family were close to marrying age, and the topic of kidnapping came up often. Nurjana[6] and Gülayim enjoyed shocking me with stories of relatives and friends who had been kidnapped back in their parents' mountain village of Ak Tash.

Within a month of my arrival, one of the girls' cousins was kidnapped. "Our *eje*[7] is really crying now," Nurjana said to me one day in September. Elmira was 24. Her parents were wealthy and prominent in Ak Tash, and she was studying at a university in Bishkek, the capital city. She had been spending the summer at home when Meder, a former boyfriend, invited her to accompany him to meet some mutual friends. Instead of taking her to meet them, however, he brought her to his home. Nurjana told me that Elmira did not want to marry Meder. She had another boyfriend in Bishkek whom she loved. If Elmira's parents had supported her she could have left, Nurjana explained, but they told her she had to marry Meder. I told Nurjana I did not understand why Elmira's parents would force her to marry someone she did not love. Nurjana explained that Kyrgyz people believe a young woman cannot leave the home of a suitor when she is brought to his house as a bride. Once she has entered, her happiness lies in that house. Nurjana went on, "If she leaves, she will be known as a girl who has 'crossed the threshold [*bosogodon ötüü*].' We believe she will never be happy in her life." Shortly thereafter, we traveled to Ak Tash to attend Elmira and Meder's lavish *nike toi* (wedding celebration[8]).

About a year and a half later, a family living near my host family kidnapped a bride. Several months before the kidnapping, I was visiting them for tea when the young man in the family, Dastan (22), mentioned he had started visiting Zura, a young woman who lived in his father's village. He said he hoped to marry her soon. Their parents knew each other (the families were distantly related) and approved of the match. She was 16 and still in school, however, and the families agreed the couple should wait to get married until after she graduated a few months later. When I next visited, Dastan announced that he was planning to kidnap her. She would not agree to marry him before her graduation parties. Kyrgyz society is patrilocal; at marriage, the bride leaves her family to live with her husband and begin a new life in his community. According to Dastan, Zura wanted to finish school and celebrate with her childhood friends, but he knew that graduation parties are notorious for kidnappings and was afraid he would lose her to another admirer.

A few months later, Dastan did kidnap Zura. The day after the kidnapping, I accompanied a few neighborhood women to pay respects to the new bride. We brought white scarves and baskets of bread and sweets. At the house, the mood was festive. Relatives bustled around the courtyard and everywhere cooking pots and samovars steamed. We entered the large receiving room where a curtain had been strung across a corner to hide the bride. In many regions of Kyrgyzstan, it is customary for a bride to be secluded in this way for up to three days after she is married. She does not have to do any housework during these three days, and must cover when she goes outside. Guests may meet the bride, but they must bring a gift of money or food *(köründük)* in exchange for the privilege of seeing her.

When I went behind the curtain, Zura stood up and bowed several times. Dastan stood proudly next to her. I had been instructed to drape a scarf (*jooluk*) on Zura's head, kiss her, and wish her happiness, which I did. She had a sweet, young face. I searched her eyes for the despair and resentment I expected in a girl who had just been through a traumatic abduction, but she seemed calm, even happy.

Afterwards, drinking tea in the next room with the women from the neighborhood, I heard the full story. Dastan had told several of Zura's relatives that he was going to kidnap her, and they agreed. On the fateful night, he went to her house and invited her out for a walk, as he often did. Rather than walking around the neighborhood with her, however, he led her to a waiting car and took her to his family's home. At the house, she cried and fought, and even tried to climb over the garden wall. Those shocking words ringing in my ears, I told Dastan as he walked us out that I was disappointed in him. I was puzzled when he protested, "No, no, she wanted to come [*özü kaalagan*]!"

Analyzing Kidnapping
Defining Kidnapping

Although individual kidnappings vary considerably, Kyrgyz described kidnapping to me as follows[9]: a man abducts a woman and brings her to his house. He turns her over to his female relatives who sequester her in a room and try to convince her to put on a white jooluk. By putting on the jooluk, she signals her acceptance of the marriage. The women are not supposed to force her to put it on, nor should they put it on her themselves. Rather, with words—both sweet and harsh—they try to get her to agree to the marriage. This will not be easy, however. Even if the kidnapping was an elopement instigated by the bride, she must perform resistance (as Zura did). At the groom's house, she must weep, fight, and try to escape. This performance is one way she asserts her honor; local convention holds that a woman should not publicly show eagerness to marry.[10]

While the women of the household are with the kidnapped woman, news of the abduction is sent to her family. The parents of the kidnapped woman often have final say in the outcome of a kidnapping. If it is clear their daughter does not want to be there, and if they have concerns about the reputation or socio-economic status of the kidnapping family, they may give her permission to leave. More often, however, they will tell her to stay. Often, a woman who does not want to marry her kidnapper will stay to marry her kidnapper if her parents so wish.[11]

After all the parties have expressed agreement, an *imam* (cleric) will be summoned to perform the Islamic marriage ceremony, and the couple will begin living together as husband and wife.

Among Kyrgyz, kidnapping is one of several ways a marriage can begin. Although kidnapping appears to be on the rise (Kleinbach et al. 2005), arrangement is preferred. In Kyrgyz culture, as elsewhere, arranged marriage often allows the potential spouses some say in the proceedings (De Munck 1996, Hart 2007, Tekçe 2004, Werner 2009:321, Zaidi and Shuraydi 2002:496). Arranged marriages are often initiated when a young man tells his parents about a young woman he fancies. In fact, many Kyrgyz families expect a son to do this (it is an expectation some Kyrgyz young people described to me as a "burden"). He may identify a woman he barely knows or a woman he knows well and who may reciprocate his affections. His parents visit her parents, and, in the course of discussion, both families decide if the match is suitable. If the match is deemed suitable, negotiations begin for the various exchanges that lead to marriage. These may cover the payment of a bride price (*kalym*[12]), the size of the toi, and the contents of the dowry (*sep*). At the least, arranged marriage is a relatively transparent negotiation that maximizes the benefit to all and initiates an alliance between two families that will last several generations. Kidnapping, in contrast, may be instigated by any one individual or combination of the interested parties, and asserts the interests of the aggressing party/ies over those of the others. There are no negotiations. The couple begins to cohabit, and the exchanges and parties occur at the families' convenience (if they happen at all).

Function, Symbol, and Power in Kidnapping Scholarship

In the 19th century, "marriage by capture" figured prominently in anthropological studies of kinship and was associated with early stages of cultural evolution (e.g., McLennan 1970:20ff, Tylor 1889:260). In tribal society, McLennan (1970:40ff) argues, families insisted on exogamous marriage but did not have good relationships with other tribes, making marriage by capture a necessity. Later writers also linked kidnapping to a desire to extend alliances as far as possible (Barnes 1999:64, Bates 1974:283, Bates el al. 1974:236).

Recent scholarship, including a collection of articles in a special issue of *Anthropological Quarterly* (1974), recognized bride kidnapping's utilitarian function. Kidnapping is a "rational strategy" allowing those with few resources to meet their needs or maximize the benefit of available resources, wrote Barbara Ayres (1974:241, see also McLaren 2001:978). In some societies, the scholarship shows, kidnapping helps young people, especially young men, circumvent obstacles to marriage (Ahearn 2001:106, Stross 1974). In societies where premarital contact between the sexes is discouraged and it is difficult to identify potential spouses, kidnapping is a quick way to secure a wife (Kiefer 1974:123).[13] Indeed, most commentators agree it plays a role in the Kyrgyz context, where female chastity is highly valued. In many Kyrgyz communities (especially outside urban areas), unmarried young women are kept at home and young people have few opportunities to meet, much less get to know, potential spouses. Long courtships can lead to damaging gossip. A Kyrgyz female activist quoted in

The *Chicago Tribune* comments, "People say, 'Our young people do not have opportunities to meet or date each other. If you say [kidnapping] is such a bad tradition, suggest something new'" (Rodriguez 2005, see also Kleinbach et al. 2005:197).[14]

A number of scholars have noted that the monetary cost of marriage, which is often highest for the groom's family, is another obstacle to marriage mitigated by kidnapping. The ethnographic record shows that by preempting the negotiations of an arranged marriage, kidnapping can lower the expected financial contribution of a groom's family (Ahearn 2001:105, Conant 1974:324, Kiefer 1974:123, Kudat 1974:289, Lockwood 1974:262, McLaren 2001:957, Stross 1974:342, Werner 1997, 2009:326). Aryes, however, finds no correlation between bride price and kidnapping in her survey (1974:242), and in many societies bride kidnapping does not reduce the cost of marriage but raises it. Barnes notes that in some Indonesian societies, bride price after a kidnapping is many times higher than before and a kidnapping family's status will be lowered (1999:59). In many societies, kidnapping can lead to a blood feud or criminal prosecution (Bates 1974:275, Lockwood 1974:254, Stross 1974:344).

In the pre-Soviet era, bride kidnappings in Central Asia may have resulted in high indemnity payments (Kleinbach and Salimjanova 2007:222). Today, however, kidnapping appears to lower the cost of marriage for the groom's family in both Kyrgyz and Kazakh communities (Kuehnast 1997:299, Werner 2004:71). Among Kyrgyz, the groom's family pays a bride price, sponsors the toi, and provides the new couple with a place to live. The bride's family gives the household property. In the second segment of Lom's (2004) film, a kidnapper's father describes the unreasonable demands of families they have approached. "They say, 'give money, bring it to the toi. Show us everything beforehand.'"[15] After kidnapping, he says, his family will be able to keep the marriage payments on their own terms.[16] Lom also links bride kidnapping's popularity to the economic crisis:

> Kyrgyzstan has suffered a lot during the transition from communism. Unemployment, particularly rural unemployment, is very high—estimates put it as high as 40 percent. And there are similar estimates about the numbers of people living below the poverty line, around 40 percent. Because Kyrgyz marriages are traditionally very expensive . . . bride kidnapping has become a much more attractive option. If you kidnap a girl, you usually still have to pay a dowry, but the bride price is usually around a third lower. (Sadiq 2004)

In all of the societies mentioned in this scholarship, marriage marks a change of status, when young men and women become adults and full members of a community, therefore gaining access to new material and social resources. Men (and women) who do not marry may be considered "social deviants" (Stross 1974:344).[17] By allowing a greater number of young people to marry in an otherwise highly regulated and inflexible system of marriage, this scholarship suggests kidnapping functions as a "safety valve" (Stross 1974:344) that reduces social frustrations and tensions. This frequently appears to be true among the Kyrgyz. Because marriage offers so many benefits, few Kyrgyz men and women remain single, and those that do, experience intense pressure from their parents and from society in general to marry.

Acknowledging kidnapping's function in these societies, however, does not exhaust its ethnographic interest. Functional accounts leave kidnapping's distinctive ritual form unexplained. The symbolic power of the kidnapping act is acknowledged even in the earliest scholarship. According to Barnes (1999:67–69), early theorists understood marriage by capture as a signification of a bride's sorrow over leaving her family or of her subjection to her parents, or as a rite of passage. As elopement, it could invoke a society's collective memory of a more violent past, when marriages occured by legitimate capture (Barnes 1999:60). Ayres (1974) and Kiefer (1974) understand kidnapping as a way for suitors to challenge the emotional bond between parents and children. Among the Tausug of the Philippines for example, kidnapping is "the symbolic taking of the mother (wife) from the father (wife's father) who controls her" (Kiefer 1974:123). Ayres (1974:248) views kidnapping as a "delayed and displaced acting out of the Oedipal conflict." Michael Herzfeld (1985:42) shows that kidnapping in a Greek village, as disguised elopement, was a way for a prospective groom to demonstrate his resourcefulness and masculinity to his future affines, thereby winning their acceptance. In the Kyrgyz context, Lori Handrahan (2004) argues that kidnapping is an assertion of ethnic identity and male power.

Even though the ethnographic record reveals kidnapping to be almost exclusively a practice in which a *woman* is taken by a *man,* kidnapping's implications for our understanding of gender relations in these societies is neglected in the earlier scholarship. In the *AQ* collection, only Kudat (1974:302) explicitly acknowledges that kidnapping can be linked to the more general oppression of women. Barbara Ayres (1974) finds that bride abduction has been documented mostly in societies in which both fathers and mothers are involved in childrearing—not exactly the classic image of patriarchy.

The recent literature, most of it on Central Asia, in contrast, interprets kidnapping as a form of violence that reinforces systems of gender inequality. In this scholarship, Central Asian culture is described as patriarchal[18] and kidnapping as "a product, producer, and reproducer of gender stratification and inequality" (Amsler and Kleinbach 1999:195). Kleinbach and varying co-authors have conducted survey research in Kyrgyz communities to measure the popularity of kidnapping and document changing rates of kidnappings[19] (Amsler and Kleinbach 1999, Kleinbach 2003, Kleinbach et al. 2005). Their findings that the rate of kidnapping is increasing, they argue, "points to an increase in male dominance" (Kleinbach et al. 2005:198–199). Cynthia Werner views kidnapping (among Kazakhs) as a form of gender-based violence that "serves as a mechanism for men to assert and maintain power over women" (2009:328). Recognizing that a kidnapped woman can agree not to stay, Werner proposes that women usually stay because of the increasing salience of a "discourse of shame," which tells women they will disgrace themselves, their families, and the kidnapping families if they refuse to marry their kidnappers. She argues that the increasing power of this discourse has become a means by which "men assert further control over female mobility and female sexuality" and marks "a shift towards greater patriarchy" (2009:315).

Response

These three theoretical approaches to kidnapping provide useful insights, but the third requires special comment because of increased scholarly interest in the extent to which women are oppressed by the complex of beliefs and practices theorists refer to as "culture" or "tradition" (e.g., Merry 2006, Narayan 1997). I do not contest that Central Asian culture is patriarchal. Men tend to have more economic and political power in Kyrgyzstan, and rely on what Paula Johnson (1976) has called "direct" (rather than "indirect") power and "concrete" (rather than "personal") resources.[20] I question, however, the assumption that patriarchy and kidnapping are uniquely linked, or that kidnapping's popularity is an indicator—the canary in the coal mine—that Kyrgyz women's greatest concern at this historical moment is oppression suffered at the hands of Kyrgyz men. Leaving aside the literature's neglect of global systems of inequality which arguably have a much more devastating impact on Kyrgyzstani citizens of all sexes, these arguments are problematic for several reasons. First of all, it has long been a truism in feminist anthropology that female subordination is "one of the true universals, a pan-cultural fact" (Ortner 1974:67). Assuming this to be true, describing a society as male-dominant just restates the obvious, and says little about the unique way inequality manifests practically. In other words, if we accept that kidnapping is linked to male dominance, the burden is still on us to explain why male dominance has manifested in this particular form.

Second, the understanding of kidnapping as a practice by which young men wield power over young women is based on a simplistic, "binary" theorization of power which assumes discrete agents (in this case, young men) wield power against discrete victims (young women). This assertion neglects the contributions of Foucault and his followers, who have shown that power operates in more subtle and diffuse ways than through straightforward processes of domination (Foucault 1990:92, Mohanty 1991:71).[21]

Finally, the gender inequality argument is problematic because it does not satisfactorily address the widespread complicity of Kyrgyz (and Kazakh) men *and* women, young and old. Responding to the recent glut of western scholarship and activist projects against kidnapping in Kyrgyzstan, a Kyrgyzstani reporter comments, "It so happens that our people's attitude to forced marriages (*ala kachuu* in Kyrgyz) is rather tolerant" (Karimova 2004). Widespread acceptance of the practice is evident in the Lom (2004) documentary, in which at least two mothers encourage their sons to kidnap, groups of married women aggressively urge a kidnapped woman to stay (some of them acknowledging that they were kidnapped themselves), and female relatives of a spurned kidnapper express their disappointment that the girl has left, recalling how they cursed her as she went. In one segment, the film crew approaches a shy girl of ten or eleven, a member of a poor, rural household that has kidnapped a possible bride. They ask how she feels about the kidnapping. She is glad, she says, because a new woman around the house will mean less work for everyone else. In another segment, family members, young and old, male and female, sit around a table, encouraging the young man of the family to kidnap a bride, even advising him about possible candidates.

Contemporary authors acknowledge the widespread acceptance of kidnapping among Kyrgyz and Kazakhs, but their theoretical models cannot satisfactorily account for it. Werner invokes Deniz Kandiyoti's (1988) idea of the "patriarchal bargain" to argue Kazakh women's participation in kidnapping does not undermine the gender inequality argument. Kandiyoti argues elder women in patriarchal societies acquire limited benefits and status by colluding with patriarchal institutions' oppression of younger women. In Werner's telling, elder Kazakh women's complicity in kidnapping is a paradigmatic example of this patriarchal bargain. They encourage sons to kidnap, even if it is harmful to young women, because they anticipate the arrival of a bride will give them more power in the household. The problem with Kandiyoti's (and Werner's) argument is its oversimplification of women's motivations. Kyrgyz women I knew did gain authority and status as they aged, but they wielded this authority in ways that showed they were driven by a variety of motivations. Although some may have been motivated (in part) by a desire to inflict upon others abuse they had suffered, I believe most of the women I knew were motivated (at least in part) by a desire to work for the good of their families and communities. Even if an elder woman's participation in a kidnapping may look, from the outside, like an attempt to increase her own power, she may also be acting in accord with dominant discourses that tell her that her actions serve the best interests of all (or most) of the individuals involved.

Kleinbach and Salimjanova (2007) offer an alternative explanation, implying that widespread complicity is a symptom of Kyrgyz traditionalism. They mention that in the course of their research, they have often heard the refrain, "kidnapping is 'our tradition,'" from both women and men (2007:218–219). This was a discourse I, too, often heard. After Zura's kidnapping, when I was drinking tea with the women of the neighborhood, they talked cheerfully about Zura's struggles, seeming to take heartless pleasure in what sounded like a traumatic experience for a defenseless young woman. "How can you approve of this when she obviously did not want to come?" I finally interrupted. "Oh, it is just our tradition," one woman said, dismissively. Kleinbach and Salimjanova (2007) seem to understand this discourse as evidence that Kyrgyz people do not question ideas that are part of society's conventional wisdom.[22] They were motivated by this discourse to do extensive historical research which they then used to argue that kidnapping, at least as practiced today, is not a tradition with a long historical record (Kleinbach and Salimjanova 2007). Although the research their study produced is useful in its own right, the scholars seem to miss the point of the contemporary "tradition" discourse, which I interpret as an evasive response. For a people overwhelmed by development discourses imposed upon it by aggressive foreign organizations, the "tradition" discourse is a way Kyrgyz politely but firmly deflect criticism of their culture and traditions by outsiders who they might consider to be unreasonably critical or merely uninformed.[23]

Kidnapping and Cultural Change

In order to understand why kidnapping is both widely practiced and widely tolerated in Kyrgyz society, it is necessary to consider not just the functional, symbolic, and gendered implications of the practice, but also its role at a unique historical moment. Kyrgyzstani citizens today are living through an era of disorienting social change and economic instability. Changing material realities and the influx of foreign ideologies force Kyrgyz people to question the dominant discourses of their society, especially the dominant discourses regarding love and marriage. In the following sections, I argue that kidnapping is compelling and popular today because it mediates the tensions caused by different understandings of love and marriage that can arise between young people and elders and within families. As a practice that subsumes qualitatively different acts into one ritual form, kidnapping helps people with widely varying convictions about love and marriage inaugurate and/or maintain productive social relationships. In other words, it is something that those who support conservative discourses of love and marriage as well as those who would like to subvert them can agree on; kidnapping allows both groups to participate in social life but, at the same time, leaves open a space of debate.

Dominant Discourses

Before considering how kidnapping challenges the dominant discourses of love and marriage, it is useful to give a brief overview. In the dominant Kyrgyz discourse of marriage, it is an institution that serves a number of important functions. Marriage builds alliances between families, thereby extending social networks, increasing influence and professional opportunity, and reinforcing the solidarity of the community (e.g., Kuchumkulova 2007:122). Marriage is a rite of passage, bestowing adult status on the marrying couple and raising the status of the parents, who by marrying their children publicly fulfill one of the most sacred responsibilities of a Kyrgyz adult. Finally, marriage supports the physical and emotional wellbeing of the couple involved. Parents want to see their children marry as reassurance that their children will be taken care of in sickness and/or old age.[24]

This focus on marriage as an institution reflects a de-emphasis on romantic love. Although I heard many Kyrgyz boast that Kyrgyz young people marry "for love" (in contrast to young people of other Central Asian ethnic groups[25]), this must be contextualized because understandings of love vary from culture to culture. The type of love familiar to members of democratic, capitalistic societies is what Anthony Giddens (1992:2–3) has called the "pure relationship": a relationship of constant emotional intimacy and equality between two people. Abu-Rabia-Quedar writes of this ideal, "The individual expresses his/her uniqueness and falls in love with another individual's uniqueness; and through love the individual realizes his/her absolute

right to choose a spouse" (2007:318). In capitalist societies, this ideal is upheld by the convention of long courtships which allow a couple to get to know each other intimately in the course of an extended series of meetings. For many Kyrgyz young people I knew, "marrying for love" implied a very different ideal. Like the liberal discourse, it implied some element of choice, but the courtships young people described to me sounded extremely short by my western standards. In other words, the pressure to marry quickly prevents many young people from establishing the level of intimacy, romantic attachment, and recognition of each other's "uniqueness" before marriage that is inherent to Giddens' "pure relationship."

Many Kyrgyz families encourage their young people to keep courtships short, partly to avoid damaging gossip (premarital sexual activity—although common—is not socially acceptable) but also because Kyrgyz do not believe a lengthy courtship is useful for revealing whether a couple will successfully weather the trials and challenges of marriage. Furthermore, young people are encouraged to marry early for a variety of reasons, and long courtships only delay this.[26] Perhaps the most important reason is that marriage marks the transition to full adult status. To be full-grown and unmarried in this society is to be "matter out of place" and can attract unwanted attention and scorn (Douglas 1966:40). Unmarried men and women I knew—even those who were wealthy and successful—found themselves with little respect in their communities.[27] The parents of young women have unique reasons to press their daughters to marry young. In Kyrgyz culture, partly because childbearing is so important, women in their late 20s are already viewed as less desirable.[28] Also, the aging parents of young men have unique reasons to press their sons to marry early—they are eager to welcome a new bride to the household, as she will help with housework and care for the family's elders.[29]

Finally, it is important to consider how marriages are judged by society. According to the dominant discourse of marriage, the success of a marriage should be judged less by the existence or persistence of the "pure relationship," than on the mutual respect that emerges over time and creates a situation of friendliness (*yntymak*), prosperity (*bereke*), and fecundity. Kyrgyz expect spouses to fulfill culturally defined roles in the family (men having the responsibility to provide for the family and women having the responsibility to give birth to children and take care of the physical needs of family members in the home). If the individuals fulfill these roles successfully, many Kyrgyz told me, the marriage is likely to be peaceful and prosperous.

In this context, the importance of fecundity cannot be overemphasized. Kyrgyz people told me children, not spouses or even professional accomplishments, are the most reliable and enduring sources of happiness and satisfaction for a human being.[30] Women, particularly, are believed to find happiness through children. Salamat-eje, my former host mother, used to tell me, "Don't wait for the perfect man. There is no such person. It is more important to find someone who will do, so that you can get married and have children, because every woman has to have children. That is her destiny. That is the one thing that will truly make her happy." A woman interviewed for Lom's (2004) film tells the film crew that she had been kidnapped. Asked if she and her husband love each other, she answers, "Of course. After having five children together, how can you not?" Many Kyrgyz people cannot understand why a couple would stay together if they could not have children. My friend Burul, 26, told me she was happy for a classmate of hers who had recently remarried. The young man had been married unhappily—his first wife was not able to have children. He divorced, married a different woman, and soon after, had a baby. "He's really happy," she said. "I'm so glad for him." I told her I thought a married couple would stay together because of romantic love, even if they could not have children. She said, "But you have to understand that in Kyrgyz culture, children are the most important thing. That's the reason for marriage."

The continued preference for arranged marriage conforms to these dominant discourses of love and marriage, but kidnapping can also serve these discourses. Several of the kidnappings documented in the Lom film occurred in response to encouragement or pressure from elders. Elmira's kidnapping, which I described earlier, is another example. Elmira was 24 and nearing an age when she would no longer be a desirable bride. Her kidnapping came at an opportune moment for her parents, who were clearly eager for her to settle down. Another example is the marriage of Farhat, a policeman, to Ainura. Farhat is the youngest son in his family and was the last child to marry. At the time of his marriage, his parents were elderly and anxious to fulfill their responsibility to marry him.[31] They also desired a daughter-in-law who would care for them and help around the house.[32] Farhat had a sweetheart in Bishkek, but his parents did not approve of her because she was a city girl and they worried she would not adapt well to life in their village. Ainura, who lived in Farhat's village, was suggested as a possible candidate. The two met, and discovered that the only thing they had in common was they each loved someone else. Without telling Farhat, his family organized a kidnapping of Ainura with the help of Farhat's friend, Aziz. The kidnapping was an unpleasant surprise for both Ainura and Farhat, but they both agreed to the marriage and today have two children. In all of these cases, kidnapping was used in a way that conformed to conservative discourses of marriage: it ensured young people married young, without long courtships, and/or to individuals approved of by their elders. Most notably, it affirmed marriage as a social institution whose main function is to strengthen social solidarity and ensure social welfare.

Cultural Change

In a recent study of a Nepali village, Laura Ahearn (2001) considers how changing attitudes about marriage and love are connected to other forms of social change. Drawing on Raymond Williams's notion of "structures of feeling," which she defines as the "qualitative changes in the way people experience and interpret events" (Ahearn 2001:52–53), she argues that social shifts occur when new social and/or economic contexts make old discourses problematic. In Ahearn's fieldwork community, emergent changes in structures of feeling include increased appreciation for the value of individual agency (as opposed to fate), romantic love, free choice in marriage, and gender equity. She links these changes to new economic opportunity and the rise of the development sector.

Similarly, in Kyrgyzstan today, ideas about love, marriage, gender, and agency are changing in the context of drastic social and economic shifts. Since independence, the Kyrgyz Republic has experienced profound economic, political, and social change. Movements critical of corruption and oppressive policies ousted two presidents. The Republic's withdrawal from the Soviet Union and the neoliberal reforms imposed by world financial institutions have resulted in a drastic reduction in the availability and quality of social services, as well as growing poverty, high unemployment, and corruption. In addition to these economic and political shifts (and partly because of them), numerous foreign ideologies have entered the country since independence and are changing the way people think about self, community, and authority. These ideologies include liberal discourses such as capitalism and democracy, along with global religious movements such as evangelical Christianity and scripturalist Islam. By emphasizing individualism and critical thinking, these ideologies empower Kyrgyzstani citizens (especially members of the younger generations) to question traditional mores—such as the authority of elders or the pursuit of professional advancement—even if this means putting off marriage.

The increasing popularity of foreign faiths requires special comment, as young people involved in these groups may find themselves forced to follow nontraditional paths to marriage, either because families reject members who have converted to new faiths or because converts fear their parents will force them into marriages with people they view, for religious reasons, to be unsuitable. In these cases, religious communities often take on responsibilities that were traditionally shouldered by parents and relatives, including helping young people find suitable mates, serving as a support community for a new couple, and even helping pay wedding expenses. The case of Nurjana (introduced above) serves as an example of these dynamics. While in high school, Nurjana became involved with a Turkish Muslim organization, and grew critical of her parents' lax attitudes toward religion. Once she was in her early 20s, she turned to her religious community to help her find a potential mate. When her Turkish friends introduced her to a young Kyrgyz man who was part of the network, she agreed to marry him and only later informed her parents. One of several wedding celebrations held in their honor was subsidized by the Turkish community.

Another important source of changing ideas about love and marriage is global popular media. Since the era of *glasnost*[33], young people in the region have had access to world media (Fierman 1988). Today, movies from Hollywood and Bollywood, translations of western romance novels, and soap operas from the Americas influence ideas about love and marriage as well as deeper conceptions of identity, gender ideals, and life goals (Kuehnast 1998, McBrien 2007). Many young people I knew mentioned wanting to experience the kind of romantic love they saw in popular media, love that more closely approximates Giddens' ideal of the pure relationship, even if that meant delaying marriage until they found partners who met drastically raised expectations.

For couples who have been influenced by these changing discourses, kidnapping is an attractive option. Like elopement, kidnapping allows young people to marry when their elders disapprove of a sweetheart for financial or social reasons, to speed up a marriage they feel could be undermined by parental hesitation, or to avoid an arranged marriage that is being forced upon them. Just as kidnapping can be used to serve conservative interests, it can be used as a way for young people to assert their marital desires. In the next section, I explore how one practice can serve such diverse purposes.

Consent

Some scholars who study kidnapping in contemporary Central Asia suggest that studying elopement and forced abduction together is "misleading" (e.g., Amsler and Kleinbach 1999:187). These scholars argue that in order to construct a theoretical understanding of kidnapping, researchers must "distinguish between the qualitatively different acts referred to by this name" (Amsler and Kleinbach 1999:187), and they do so by focusing on the level of the prospective bride's consent.[34] Although I agree that Kyrgyz kidnappings are of many types, I do not believe creating a classification system based on the bride's consent contributes to a theoretical understanding of the practice.[35] I argue, instead, that kidnapping is compelling to Kyrgyz *because of its ability to subsume qualitatively different acts in a unified ritual form.* Kidnapping makes it impossible to know who consented to what. This ambiguity allows kidnapping to be a force both for conservative values and for their subversion.

Three ethnographic examples illustrate the difficulty of assigning consent to a kidnapping event and demonstrate how kidnapping is both conservative and subversive. Consider the example of Zura and Dastan (mentioned above). This kidnapping is difficult to categorize as consensual or nonconsensual. One complication I did not mention above is that Dastan's family had suffered a tragedy in the winter preceding the kidnapping, making it inappropriate to hold a toi. This meant kidnapping was inevitable if the couple was to marry soon. All parties to the marriage probably understood this, including Zura. Since the community knew they were sweethearts, the community would assume a kidnapping was consensual. This could be awkward for Zura, however, because a Kyrgyz woman is not supposed to show eagerness to marry (see above, page xx, and endnote 10). Dastan and his relatives found a better solution. Long before the kidnapping, Dastan started telling people in the neighborhood that Zura did not want to marry him before graduation, and then boasting he would kidnap her. After the kidnapping, the family emphasized Zura's surprise and her aggressive resistance. Whether or not the kidnapping was the "forced" kidnapping of the family's version, their assertion of force confirms the point I made above, that forced kidnappings are not merely tolerated but widely accepted as a respectable form of marriage among Kyrgyz. If this were not the case, Dastan's family would have de-emphasized Zura's resistance so as not to attract community censure. By pointing out that Dastan's family actively portrayed the event as a forced kidnapping, however, I am not asserting that their version was necessarily a distortion and the kidnapping was consensual. Certainly, ample evidence exists to suggest that it was

not. (e.g., Did Zura hesitate to allow time for another sweetheart to act?) Whatever the reality—which is impossible to know—by emphasizing Zura's surprise and resistance, Dastan and his family upheld her honor in the eyes of the community, and by extension, their own.

The second example concerns Qilich and Aigerim. In his last year at the local university, Qilich met and started dating Aigerim, also a student at the university, but several years younger. They wanted to marry, but Aigerim's parents refused, saying they wanted her to finish her studies first (see endnote 26). Qilich was concerned that if they waited, he would graduate and move elsewhere, and they would never see each other again. He proposed kidnapping, and she agreed. Although the kidnapping was described to me, many years later, as an elopement, at the time it was presented to the community as a "forced" kidnapping. By staging a "forced" kidnapping, Qilich and Aigerim were able to marry for love. More importantly, Aigerim was able to marry against the wishes of her parents without compromising her good relationship with them.

One more ethnographic example is the story of Bakyt and Kunduz, students at a high school in my community, who married by kidnapping soon after graduation. According to rumor, Kunduz was pregnant and forced Bakyt to kidnap her by going to his house and refusing to leave. Whether this was true or malicious gossip is hard to know, but despite the rumors, the marriage was respectable in the eyes of the community because it was presented, publicly, as a kidnapping, which implied Bakyt had forced the marriage. In a society whose dominant discourses of marriage condemn premarital sex (and punish women disproportionately for the impropriety), the illusion of forced kidnapping can be particularly useful to women in such compromising circumstances, allowing them to secure a quick marriage and avoid public shame.

In all three cases, the ability of kidnapping, as a ritual form, to obscure desire and render it difficult for an outsider to know who wanted what, made possible marriages that went against conservative expectations and/or family desires. In the case of Dastan and Zura's marriage, the families wanted the young people to marry, even though it was unseemly so soon after a death in the family. Kidnapping allowed Qilich and Aigerim, a young couple, to flout their elders' attempts to postpone (or perhaps prevent) a marriage. For Bakyt and Kunduz, kidnapping may have allowed a young couple to transgress conservative community mores without suffering repercussions. These kidnappings are not unusual in the way they make it difficult to locate consent. Instead, this ambiguity is what makes kidnapping useful and popular among Kyrgyz today.

The Pace of Change

As Ahearn discovered in her community, changes in "structures of feeling" do not emerge quickly and linearly, but gradually and "dialogically . . . through the social and linguistic interactions of individuals" (2001:52). In Kyrgyz society, new discourses about love and marriage have not replaced existing ideas but instead intensified disagreement and anxiety. If most elders caution that young people who put off marriage to build careers or find one's "true love" will find happiness and security more elusive, young people are unsure. They are attracted to new, romantic visions, but often find the more conservative ideals, such as the belief that the most reliable source of happiness is not romantic love or career but family—raising children, watching them grow up, marrying them off, and seeing the cycle begin again—confirmed by their experiences.

By the time a young Kyrgyz woman has reached adulthood, she has seen many friends and relatives married by kidnapping. Many Kyrgyz women I talked to admitted that even though they did not want to be kidnapped, they believed the success of a marriage has little to do with how it begins. Nurjana, Gülaiym, and I explored this question in countless conversations about married females we knew, in which we compared what we knew about their lives and their marriages. In these conversations, we discovered that freedom of choice did not always correspond with marital happiness. Many women we knew who married for love were unhappy because their husbands were abusive or unfaithful, or could not support them financially. In contrast, one of the women who seemed happiest was an aunt who had been kidnapped against her will. According to the aunt's own telling, she was miserable when she was kidnapped, because she was in love with someone else. Many years later, she learned that her sweetheart died young. Now she says she is glad she was kidnapped, because if she had married her sweetheart, she would not have a husband and would be unhappy. Gülaiym and Nurjana thought this aunt and her husband were happy, noting the way their aunt was eager to make herself attractive for her husband and the way he worked hard to support her and their three children. Saying this is not to dismiss or trivialize her initial distress, but to point out that Kyrgyz young women are attentive both to the distress a kidnapped woman may feel, as well as to the later trajectory of the marriage.[36]

A particularly poignant example of how a young woman struggled to reconcile competing discourses about love and marriage is the story of Cholpon, a college graduate and former beauty queen. In college, she had many suitors, but rejected them all. In her early 20s when I knew her, she was increasingly anxious about finding a husband. In our conversations, Cholpon told me about a boy she fancied, who resisted her advances. She also told me about Timur, a respectable young man much older than she and highly regarded by her parents, who had made known his desire to marry her. She confided to me that she was not in love with him, and expressed the hope that another candidate—a "true love"—would materialize. One afternoon shortly before her 24th birthday, she was kidnapped from her office by a young man from her village. He and several of his friends took her by car to his house, where she was received as a bride. Cholpon refused to agree to the marriage, insisting her parents would not make her stay. Indeed, they soon came to take her home. Shortly after the kidnapping, however, Cholpon was wearing a new pair of gold earrings. They were an engagement gift from Timur's family. Although Cholpon had said she wanted to wait for her "true love," the kidnapping seemed to add to her increasing sense of vulnerability vis-à–vis the unforgiving Kyrgyz marriage market, forcing her to give up her earlier dreams of love. In the remaining weeks before the wedding, she spoke differently of Timur. She expressed her respect and love for him, and seemed to look forward eagerly to beginning a family with him. Although leaving a kidnapping is to flout conservative discourses and could be viewed as a relatively subversive act (on the part of both Cholpon and her family), the refusal only sent Cholpon back into a social milieu governed by the same conservative discourses. Her story reveals that the challenges facing young Kyrgyz women are less about any one practice, than the coercion inherent in a social system that imposes a uniform vision of the "good life" on all individuals.

Conclusions

Many Kyrgyz kidnappings are disguised elopements. In these cases, kidnapping is employed by young people to assert their romantic desires in contradiction to dominant discourses, such as the importance of marriage as an alliance between families, elders' control over marriage, and the de-emphasis on romantic love. If kidnapping were merely used to challenge the dominant discourses of marriage, however, it would not be so widely tolerated by men and women of all ages and backgrounds. Kidnapping is widely tolerated because it can be used to affirm the desires of young people and new discourses about romantic love and free choice, just as easily as it can be used to enforce the dominant discourses. In fact, even when it is used by young people to challenge the authority of their elders, it may still uphold other ideals of marriage with which the elders would agree, including the importance of keeping courtships short and marrying early in life.

In this paper, I have explored how common explanations of kidnapping are incomplete. Kidnapping not only serves important economic and social functions, it also is a compelling ritual and a manifestation of male dominance. In order to account for the varied functions of kidnapping, it is important to attend to the historical context. Kidnapping's popularity is a response to tension over changing structures of feeling that have emerged in an era of rapid social and economic change. The ambiguity inherent to the kidnapping act mediates the tension that might otherwise result within families and communities over different beliefs about marriage. Kidnapping allows an act of desire to be disguised as an act of coercion and gives an act of coercion (and by extension an act of desire) a veneer of respectability and promise. Marriage is risky; it is a liminal moment when new social relations are formed and young people take on unfamiliar roles. Kidnapping helps preserve good feelings during an otherwise dangerous transition.

Acknowledgments—Thanks to Zamir Borbiev, Steven Caton, Michael Herzfeld, Engseng Ho, Zahra Jamal, Russell Kleinbach, Linda Racioppi, Fatima Sartbaeva, John Schoeberlein, Cynthia Werner, two anonymous reviewers, and my many Kyrgyz friends and informants. Special thanks to Zamir and Fatima for helping with Kyrgyz spellings and translations. Any errors that remain are my own. Drafts of this paper were presented at the Harvard Anthropology Department's Middle East Workshop (fall 2006), in John Schoeberlein's "Culture Wars in Central Asia" (fall 2007), at the Michigan State University's

Asia Studies Center (fall 2009), and at the Indiana University–Purdue University Fort Wayne's Anthropology Club (spring 2010). Thank you to everyone who participated in these fora. Funding for research and writing was provided by (in chronological order) the IIE Fulbright Program, the Social Sciences Research Council, the Harvard University Department of Anthropology, the Harvard University Graduate Council, the Kellogg Institute at the University of Notre Dame, and an IPFW Summer Faculty Grant.

Notes

1. Also spelled *ala kachuu*.

2. Pusurmankulova (2004) quotes a Kyrgyz official who says, "No other nation upholds this tradition. We should feel ashamed."

3. Handrahan 2000a, 2000b; Lloyd-Roberts 1999b; Pratova 2006; Sadiq 2004.

4. Officially, the Kyrgyz Republic.

5. All figures taken from CIA World Factbook 2011, but reflect 1999 census figures.

6. In the ethnographic sections, the names of most people and places are pseudonymous.

7. Eje literally means "older sister," but is required when addressing or referring to females older than the speaker.

8. Toi is used to refer to large feasts held to mark a number of occasions, including marriage, the birth of a child, a circumcision, or the purchase of a home. Nike is the Islamic marriage ceremony and distinguishes the feast as linked to a marriage.

9. The kidnappings filmed by Petr Lom (2004) follow this ideal quite closely. See Werner (2009:316) for a similar ideal among Kazakhs.

10. Even in non-kidnapping weddings, a bride must demonstrate her reluctance to leave her family. She performs a weepy, often hysterical farewell when the groom arrives to take her from her home, and sits glumly at the wedding feast.

11. See the Lom (2004) film for an exception. In the opening segment, the kidnapping family tells the girl her family has agreed to the marriage, but she still leaves.

12. Also spelled *kalyng*.

13. In a quantitative analysis of the Human Relations Area Files probability sample, Ayres (1974:244), could not demonstrate a correlation between kidnapping and restrictions to pre-marital contact. She finds, instead, that kidnapping is common in societies where childrearing is shared between men and women. Interestingly, men do play a larger role in childrearing among Kyrgyz (who accept bride kidnapping) than among Uzbeks (who do not) (see, e.g., Kuchumkulova 2007:105).

14. Kuehnast's informant tells her kidnapping is "the result of the helplessness of a man who thinks that there is no other way to marry a woman" (1997:298). An official interviewed by Human Rights Watch comments, "Many women are very shy. . . . We advise women not to associate with men. Our girls don't know how to deal with men. When they grow up, they don't know what to do. Some women are grateful (to be kidnapped), otherwise they say they would never have gotten married" (2006:88, parentheses in original).

15. English translations of the film dialogue are my own.

16. According to *The New York Times*, "Kyrgyz men say they snatch women because it is easier than courtship and cheaper than paying the standard 'bride price' " (Smith 2005).

17. Human Rights Watch (2006:93) comments, "Fear of being stigmatized as an unsuccessful man can influence a man's decision to 'get' a bride through kidnapping."

18. Petr Lom states that, "Kyrgyzstan is still a very patriarchal, male-dominated society" (Sadiq 2004). Human Rights Watch also describes Kyrgyzstan as "highly patriarchal, with women's roles in public and private life circumscribed" (2006:6). Lori Handrahan writes, "Of all the violations committed against women in the current nation-building process, bride kidnapping is the primary assault" (2000b:21). *The Chicago Tribune* comments, "The abduction of [Kyrgyz] women to coerce them into marriage has become . . . ingrained in the country's male-dominated society" (Rodriguez 2005). Kleinbach et al. write "Non-consensual kidnapping of a bride is obviously an act of male dominance" (2005:196).

19. These authors acknowledge that their research is part of an activist project to stop kidnapping (e.g., Kleinbach et al. 2005:200, Kleinbach et al. 2008–2009).

20. According to Johnson (1976:100–101), direct power is rendered openly, such as by giving an order. Indirect power is wielded unobtrusively, such as through manipulation, and with the hope that the individual will achieve a desired outcome without others realizing that influence is being asserted. Concrete resources include material resources, knowledge, and physical strength. Personal resources include relationships and popularity.

21. "By power," Foucault writes, ". . . I do not have in mind a general system of domination exerted by one group over another, a system whose effects, through successive derivations, pervade the entire social body" (1990:92).

22. This discourse, that Kyrgyz (and Central Asians in general) lack the "critical thinking" skills to question inherited traditions, was commonplace among members of the ex-pat community when I was working there.

23. Kleinbach and Salimjanova (2007) do not acknowledge the influential volume edited by Hobsbawm and Ranger (1983), in which a number of scholars argue that the importance of a "tradition" is not found in its history but in the way it is constructed and reconstructed by actors in support of immediate interests.

24. Kanybek, 31 and divorced, described the pressure from his mother to remarry: "She says to me, 'Please, we will worry about you. We are old. We will die soon. Get married and we won't worry.' " Kanykei, 26, heard similar things from her parents, who told her to marry because they were concerned about her. "They say, 'We will worry about you until you get married.' I know it's because they love me and don't want me to be alone' " She tells them she is happy, "but my mother and father are elderly, and I can understand them. I know they will never be at peace until I marry."

25. One discursive construction of ethnic difference I heard while doing fieldwork among Uzbeks and Kyrgyz in the Ferghana Valley was that Uzbek marriages are always arranged by elders, with the young people meeting only briefly (if at all) prior to marriage, while Kyrgyz young people get to choose who they marry. Although this construction is somewhat idealized, it is interesting to note that kidnapping is almost unheard of among Uzbeks. When I first lived in Kyrgyzstan, it seemed ironic

to me that Kyrgyz, who give young people more freedom in marriage, tolerate a practice like kidnapping, while Uzbeks do not. I have come to believe that it is exactly this tension between freedom and control that creates the need for a mediating factor like kidnapping.

26. There is considerable variety among Kyrgyz regarding the ideal age of marriage. In villages, and/or among families that do not send their young people to university, this can be as early as the late teens. Among educated classes and urban Kyrgyz, however, many parents hope young people will finish a university degree before marriage (c.f. the story of Qilich and Aigerim, page 160). After the degree is finished, however, parents will be anxious to see a child marry.

27. Aizat, a successful professional woman in her early 30s, told me that the questions regarding why she remained unmarried had become so unpleasant that she barely leaves her parents' house when she visits her native village.

28. One of the kidnapped women in Petr Lom's film, Norkuz, had a boyfriend at the time she was kidnapped, but was happy with the marriage. Lom remarks, "Why? Well, first, she was 25 and not married, and this is very old to be single in Kyrgyzstan" (Sadiq 2004).

29. A mitigating factor, however, is that the groom's family is responsible for most of the marital expenses and may need to delay marriage until sufficient funds have been collected. In such cases, kidnapping can be an attractive alternative.

30. In many of the kidnapping narratives reported by Kleinbach and co-authors, Kyrgyz informants end a harrowing story of a forced abduction with an account of how many children the couple has. The implication, possibly lost on the western reader, is that the couple has found happiness, whatever the initial context of their marriage. When people learned I was childless, they often quoted the following Kyrgyz *makal* (saying), "*Balasy barüi bazar, balasy joküimazar*" (A house with children is a bazaar, a house without children is a graveyard). It is also important to note that children are particularly important today because of the economic crisis and the dismantling of the socialist welfare system. In the absence of state structures to support the elderly, family networks are the only reliable source of support and care in old age.

31. This is also true of at least two kidnappings portrayed in the film (Lom 2004). In the film, a number of elders speak of their eagerness to see the young men in question kidnap their brides because they want the men to marry.

32. Many Kyrgyz observe the tradition that all the children move away from home except the youngest son, whose family cares for his parents until their death and then inherits their property.

33. Glasnost' refers to the period in the USSR when Gorbachev eased government control of the press and other media.

34. They propose categories to distinguish types of kidnapping based on the level of consent of the woman involved. In the work of Kleinbach and co-authors, a kidnapping can be "consensual" or "non-consensual." "Non-consensual" kidnapping is defined as kidnapping. "By deception or force, not in love and woman not wanting to be kidnapped" (2005:197). More usefully, Cynthia Werner divides kidnappings into three categories: high consent, medium consent, and low consent (2004:82–84).

35. In her discussion of a small village in Nepal, Ahearn (2001) points out that the notion of consent is itself inherently problematic. In the language of her field community (as,

indeed, in our own), consent implies passivity. In her community, even though village sentiment has, to some degree, turned against capture marriage because it implies a lack of consent from the woman, the consent that is expected in examples of elopement still reaffirms a patriarchal system in which a man is expected to be an active agent who persuades a woman to marry him (2001:249–250). In other words, the existence of consent does not imply the absence of coercion. In the case of Kyrgyz kidnapping, the contemporary scholars who want to distinguish kidnappings based on consent forget that kidnapping is not itself marriage, and that any kidnapping that ends in marriage implies the existence of consent in some form.

36. In contrast, Nurjana and Gülaiym believe Elmira, also kidnapped against her will, did not end up happily married.

References

Abu-Rabia-Queder, Sarab. 2007. "Coping With 'Forbidden Love' and Loveless Marriage: Educated Bedouin Women from the Negev." *Ethnography* 8(3):297–323.

Ahearn, Laura. 2001. *Invitations to Love: Literacy, Love Letters, and Social Change in Nepal.* Ann Arbor: University of Michigan Press.

Amsler, Sarah and Russell L. Kleinbach. 1999. "Bride Kidnapping in the Kyrgyz Republic." *International Journal of Central Asian Studies* 4(4):185–216.

Århem, Kaj. 1981. "Bride Capture, Sister Exchange and Gift Marriage among the Makuna: A Model of Marriage Exchange." *Ethnos* 46(1–2):47–63.

Asad, Talal. 1993. "Introduction." *Genealogies of Religion: Discipline and Reasons of Power in Christianity and Islam,* 1–24. Baltimore: Johns Hopkins University Press.

Ayres, Barbara. 1974. "Bride Theft and Raiding for Wives in Cross-Cultural Perspective." *Anthropological Quarterly* 47(3):238–252.

Barnes, R. H. 1999. "Marriage by Capture." *Journal of the Royal Anthropological Institute* 5(1):57–73.

Bates, Daniel G. 1974. "Normative and Alternative Systems of Marriage among the Yörük of Southeastern Turkey." *Anthropological Quarterly* 47(3):270–287.

Bates, Daniel G., Francis Conant, and Ayse Kudat. 1974. "Introduction: Kidnapping and Elopement as Alternative Systems of Marriage." *Anthropological Quarterly* 47(3):233–237.

Bauer, Armin, David Green, and Kathleen Kuehnast. 1997. *Women and Gender Relations: The Kyrgyz Republic in Transition.* Manila: Asian Development Bank.

CIA World Factbook. 2011. Kyrgystan. Central Asia. Accessed from https:www.cia.gov/library/publications/the-world-factbook/geos/kg.html on Dec 8, 2011.

Conant, Francis P. 1974. "Frustration, Marriage Alternatives and Subsistence Risks among the Pokot of East Africa: Impressions of Co-Variance." *Anthropological Quarterly* 47(3):314–327.

de Munck, Victor C. 1996. "Love and Marriage in a Sri Lankan Muslim Community: Toward a Reevaluation of Dravidian Marriage Practices." *American Ethnologist* 23(4):698–716.

Douglas, Mary. 1990. "Forward: No Free Gifts." In Marcel Mauss, *The Gift: The Form and Reason for Exchange in Archaic Societies,* vii–xviii. New York: Norton.

_____. 1996. *Purity and Danger: An Analysis of the Concepts of Pollution and Taboo.* London: Ark.

The Economist. 1996. "The Stolen Brides of Kyrgyzstan." November 23, p. 40.

Evans-Grubbs, Judith. 1989. "Abduction Marriage in Antiquity: A Law of Constantine (CTh IX. 24. I) and Its Social Context." *The Journal of Roman Studies* 79:59–83.

Fierman, William. 1988. "Western Pop Culture and Soviet Youth." *Central Asian Survey* 7(1):7–36.

Foucault, Michel. 1990 [1978]. *The History of Sexuality Volume 1: An Introduction.* Robert Hurley, trans. New York: Vintage.

Giddens, Anthony. 1992. *The Transformation of Intimacy: Sexuality, Love and Eroticism in Modern Societies.* Stanford: Stanford University Press.

Grant, Bruce. 2005. "The Good Russian Prisoner: Naturalizing Violence in the Caucasus Mountains." *Cultural Anthropology* 20(1):39–67.

Halle, Fannina W. 1938. *Women in the Soviet East.* Margaret M. Green, trans. New York: Dutton.

Handrahan, Lori. 2000a. "International Human Rights Law and Bride Kidnapping in Kyrgyzstan." EurasiaNet.org. Part 1, January 28. Accessed from http://www.eurasianet.org/departments/insight/articles/eav012400.shtml on December 8, 2011. Part 2, February 2. Accessed from http://www.eurasianet.org/departments/insight/articles/eav020100.shtml on Dec 8, 2011.

_____. 2000b. "Kidnapping Brides in Kyrgyzstan: Prescriptive Human Rights Measures. *Human Rights Tribune* 7(1), March, pp. 21–22. Accessed from http://www.hri.ca/pdfs/HRT%20March%20 2000,%20Volume%207,%20No.%201.pdf on Dec 8, 2011.

_____. 2004. "Hunting for Women: Bride-Kidnapping in Kyrgyzstan." *International Feminist Journal of Politics* 6(2):207–233.

Hart, Kimberly. 2007. "Love by Arrangement: The Ambiguity Of 'Spousal Choice' In a Turkish Village." *Journal of the Royal Anthropological Institute* 13:345–362.

Herzfeld, Michael. 1985. "Gender Pragmatics: Agency, Speech, and Bride-Theft in a Cretan Mountain Village." *Anthropology* 9(1–2):25–44.

Hobsbawm, Eric J. and Terence O. Ranger, eds. 1983. *The Invention of Tradition.* London: Cambridge University Press.

Human Rights Watch. 2006. *Reconciled to Violence: State Failure to Stop Domestic Abuse and Abduction of Women in Kyrgyzstan.* September, Volume 18(9d). Accessed from http://hrw.org/reports/2006/kyrgyzstan0906 on Dec 8, 2011.

Johnson, Paula. 1976. "Women and Power: Toward a Theory of Effectiveness." *Journal of Social Issues* 32(3):99–110.

Kandiyoti, Deniz. 1988. "Bargaining with Patriarchy." *Gender and Society* 2(3):274–290.

Karimova, Gulchekhra. 2004. "Ala-Kachuu. The Kyrgyz Prisoner." *Vecherniy Bishkek,* April 16.

Kiefer, Thomas M. 1974. "Bride Theft and the Abduction of Women among the Tausug of Jolo: Some Cultural and Psychological Factors." *Philippine Quarterly of Culture and Society* 2(3):123–132.

Kleinbach, Russell L. 2003. "Frequency of Non-Consensual Bride Kidnapping in the Kyrgyz Republic." *International Journal of Central Asian Studies* 8(8):108–128.

Kleinbach, Russell L., Mehrigiul Ablezova, and Medina Aitieva. 2005. "Kidnapping for Marriage (*Ala Kachuu*) in a Kyrgyz Village." *Central Asian Survey* 24(2):191–202.

Kleinbach, Russell L., Gazbubu Babiarova, and Nuraiym Orozobekova. 2008–2009. "Reducing Non-Consensual Bride Kidnapping in Kyrgyzstan." Russell Kleinbach; Kyz-Korgon Institute; 2008–2009 Reduction. Accessed from http://faculty.philau.edu/kleinbachr/new_page_14.htm on Dec 11, 2011.

Kleinbach, Russell L. and Lilly Salimjanova. 2007. "*Kyz Ala Kachuu* and *Adat:* Non-Consensual Bride Kidnapping and Tradition in Kyrgyzstan." *Central Asian Survey* 26(2):217–233.

Kuchumkulova, Elmira M. 2007. "Kyrgyz Nomadic Customs and the Impact of Re-Islamization after Independence." Ph.D. Dissertation, Department of Near and Middle Eastern Studies, University of Washington.

Kudat, Ayse. 1974. "Institutional Rigidity and Individual Initiative in Marriages of Turkish Peasants." *Anthropological Quarterly* 47(3):288–303.

Kuehnast, Kathleen Rae. 1997. "Let the Stone Lie Where It Has Fallen: Dilemmas of Gender and Generation in Post-Soviet Kyrgyzstan." Ph.D. Dissertation, Graduate School, University of Minnesota.

_____. 1998. "From Pioneers to Entrepreneurs: Young Women, Consumerism, and The 'World Picture' In Kyrgyzstan." *Central Asian Survey* 17(4):639–654.

Lloyd-Roberts, Sue. 1999a. "Stolen Brides at Last Learn to Fight Back." *The Independent,* March 6, Foreign News, p. 18.

_____. 1999b. "Kyrgyz Bride Theft Goes Awry." *BBC World,* March 22. Accessed from http://news.bbc.co.uk/2/hi/programmes/from_our_own_correspondent/299512.stm on Dec 8, 2011.

Lockwood, William G. 1974. "Bride Theft and Social Maneuverability in Western Bosnia." *Anthropological Quarterly* 47(3):253–269.

Lom, Petr. 2004. *Bride Kidnapping in Kyrgyzstan.* First Run/Icarus Films.

McBrien, Julie. 2007. "Brazilian TV and Muslimness in Kyrgyzstan." *ISIM Review* 19:16–17.

McLaren, Anne E. 2001. "Marriage by Abduction in Twentieth Century China." *Modern Asian Studies* 35(4):953–984.

McLennan, John F. 1970 [1865]. *Primitive Marriage: An Inquiry into the Origin of the Form of Capture in Marriage Ceremonies.* Chicago: University of Chicago Press.

Merry, Sally Engle. 2006. *Human Rights and Gender Violence: Translating International Law into Local Justice.* Chicago: University of Chicago Press.

Mohanty, Chandra Talpade. 1991. "Under Western Eyes: Feminist Scholarship and Colonial Discourses." In Chandra Talpade Mohanty, Ann Russo, and Lourdes Torres, eds. *Third World Women and the Politics of Feminism,* 51–80. Bloomington: Indiana University Press.

Narayan, Uma. 1997. "Restoring History and Politics To 'Third-World Traditions.' " In *Dislocating Cultures: Identities, Traditions, and Third World Feminisms,* 41–80. New York: Routledge.

Ortner, Sherry B. 1974. "Is Female to Male as Nature Is to Culture?" In Michelle Zimbalist Rosaldo and Louise Lamphere, eds. *Woman, Culture, and Society,* 67–87. Stanford: Stanford University Press.

_____. 1984. "Theory in Anthropology since the Sixties." *Comparative Studies in Society and History* 26:126–166.

Pratova, Zaripa. 2006. "Reports from Southern Kyrgyzstan Indicate That the Families That Followed the Ancient Tradition of Bride Abduction Mostly End in Divorces." Accessed from http://enews.ferghana.ru/article.php?id=1296www.ferghana.su on Dec 7, 2011.

Pusurmankulova, Burulai. 2004. "Bride Kidnapping. Benign Custom or Savage Tradition?" Russell Kleinbach; Kyz-Korgon Institute; Custom or Tradition. Accessed from http://faculty.philau.edu/KleinbachR/freedom.htm on Dec 7, 2011.

Rodriguez, Alex. 2005. "Kidnapped, Forced to Wed." *The Chicago Tribune,* July 24. Front page.

Sadiq, Sheraz. 2004. Interview with Petr Lom: Marriage by Abduction. Frontline World. March. Accessed from http://www.pbs.org/frontlineworld/stories/kyrgyzstan/lom.html on Dec 8, 2011.

Smith, Craig S. 2005. "Abduction, Often Violent, a Kyrgyz Wedding Rite." *The New York Times,* April 30, Front page. Accessed from http://www.nytimes.com/2005/04/30/international/asia/30brides.html?sq+kyrgyz%20abduction%20smith&st=cse&adxnnl=1&adxnnlx=1323357261-9TEeazhv46C1gw+ttQQ/TQ on Dec 8, 2011.

Stross, Brian. 1974. "Tzeltal Marriage by Capture." *Anthropological Quarterly* 47(3):328–346.

Tekçe, Belgin. 2004. "Paths of Marriage in Istanbul: Arranging Choices and Choice in Arrangements." *Ethnography* 5(2):173–201.

Tylor, Edward B. 1889. "On a Method of Investigating the Development of Institutions; Applied to Laws of Marriage and Descent." *Journal of the Anthropological Institute of Great Britain and Ireland* 18:245–272.

US Department of State. 2010. "Kyrgyz Republic." US Department of State; Under Secretary for Democracy and Global Affairs; Bureau of Democracy, Human Rights, and Labor; Releases; Human Rights Reports; 2010 Country Reports on Human Rights Practices; South and Central Asia. Accessed from http://www.state.gov/documents/organization/160059.pdf on Dec 12, 2011.

Wilson, Jon E. 2006. "Subjects and Agents in the History of Imperialism and Resistance." In David Scott and Charles Hirschkind, eds. *Powers of the Secular Modern: Talal Asad and His Interlocutors,* 180–205. Stanford: Stanford University.

Werner, Cynthia. 1997. "Marriage, Markets, and Merchants: Changes in Wedding Feasts and Household Consumption Patterns in Rural Kazakhstan." *Culture and Agriculture* 19(1/2):6–13.

_____. 2004. "Women, Marriage, and the Nation-State: The Rise of Nonconsensual Bride Kidnapping in Post-Soviet Kazakhstan." In Paula Jones Luong, ed. *The Transformation of Central Asia: States and Societies from Soviet Rule to Independence,* 59–89. Ithaca: Cornell University Press.

_____. 2009. "Bride Abduction in Post-Soviet Central Asia: Marking a Shift Towards Patriarchy through Local Discourses of Shame and Tradition." *Journal of the Royal Anthropological Institute* 15:314–331.

Zaidi, Arshia U. and Muhammad Shuraydi. 2002. "Perceptions of Arranged Marriages by Young Pakistani Muslim Women Living in a Western Society." *Journal of Comparative Family Studies* 33(4):495–514.

Critical Thinking

1. How does the author characterize the frequency and character of bride kidnapping?

2. How was bride kidnapping treated by the former Soviet Union? What has happened since the dissolution of the USSR?

3. How does the author describe the tradition of bride kidnapping? What if the marriage does not work out? Be familiar with the examples cited.

4. How do the Kyrgyz themselves describe the kidnapping?

5. How do the Kygyz describe arranged marriages and their benefits? How do they contrast with kidnapping?

6. How did 19th-century anthropologists explain "marriage by capture"? How has scholarship explained it as a "rational strategy"?

7. How might kidnapping be used to circumvent obstacles? What are the pros and cons regarding the idea that it avoids the high cost of marriage?

8. In what sense might kidnapping function as a "safety valve"?

9. How has kidnapping been variously seen as a symbolic act?

10. Discuss the pros and cons of the "gender inequality" argument.

11. How can both arranged marriages and kidnappings conform to conservative discourses of marriage and affirm marriage as a social institution?

12. How can kidnapping also be used by young people to assert their marital desires?

13. Why is it difficult to separate elopement from forced abduction on the basis of "consent"?

Create Central

www.mhhe.com/createcentral

Internet References

Ideal Bride
www.idealbride.sg

Journal of Middle East Women's Studies
http://inscribe.iupress.org/loi/mew

Population Council
www.popcouncil.org

Article   Prepared by: Elvio Angeloni, *Pasadena City College*

Rising Number of Dowry Deaths in India

AMANDA HITCHCOCK

Learning Outcomes

After reading this article, you will be able to:

- Explain why there is a rising number of dowry deaths in India.
- Discuss the traditional function of the dowry and how it has been recently transformed.

May 27: Young Housewife Burnt Alive for Dowry

Lucknow: For nineteen-year-old Rinki the dream of a happily married life was never to be. Barely a month after her marriage, she was allegedly tortured and then set ablaze by her in-laws for dowry in Indiranagar in the small hours of Saturday. Daughter of late Gyan Chand, a fish contractor who expired a year ago, Rinki was married to Anil on April 19. . . . However, soon after the marriage, Balakram [Anil's father] demanded a colour television instead of a black and white one and a motorcycle as well. When Rinki's mother failed to meet their demands, the teenage housewife was subjected to severe physical torture, allegedly by her husband and mother-in-law. . . . On Saturday morning she [her mother] was informed that Rinki was charred to death when a kerosene lamp accidentally fell on her and her clothes caught fire. However, prima-facie it appeared that the victim was first attacked as her teeth were found broken. Injuries were also apparent on her wrist and chest.

June 7: Woman Ends Life Due to Dowry Harassment

Haveri: Dowry harassment claimed yet another life here recently. Jyoti, daughter of Chandrashekhar Byadagi, married to Ajjappa Siddappa Kaginelle in Guttal village (Haveri taluk) had taken her life after being allegedly harassed by her husband Ajjappa, mother-in-law Kotravva, sister-in-law Nagavva and father-in-law Siddappa for more dowry, the police said. Police said that the harassment compelled her to consume poison. . . . The Guttal police have arrested her husband and father-in-law.

June 7: Body Found Floating

Haveri: The police said that a woman's body was found floating in a well at Tilawalli (Hanagal taluk) near here. . . . The deceased has been identified as Akhilabanu Yadawad (26). The police said that Akhilabanu was married to Abdul Razaksab Yadawad five years ago. In spite of dowry being given, her husband and his family tortured her to bring some more dowry. Her father, Abdulrope Pyati in his complaint, alleged that she was killed by them. Her husband and his two brothers have been arrested, the police added.

These three chilling reports from *The Times of India* are typical of the many accounts of dowry-related deaths that take place in the country every year. One cannot help but be struck by the offhand way in which a young woman's life and death is summed up, matter of factly, without any undue cause for alarm or probing of the causes. It is much as one would report a traffic accident or the death of a cancer patient—tragic certainly, but such things are to be expected.

The character of the articles points to the fact that the harassment, beating and in some cases murder of women over dowry is both common and commonly ignored or even tacitly condoned in official circles—by the police, the courts, politicians and media. These crimes are not isolated to particular groups, social strata, geographical regions or even religions. Moreover, they appear to be on the rise.

According to an article in *Time* magazine, deaths in India related to dowry demands have increase 15-fold since the mid-1980s from 400 a year to around 5,800 a year by the middle of the 1990s. Some commentators claim that the rising number simply indicates that more cases are being reported as a result of increased activity of women's organisations. Others, however, insist that the incidence of dowry-related deaths has increased.

An accurate picture is difficult to obtain, as statistics are varied and contradictory. In 1995, the National Crime Bureau of the Government of India reported about 6,000 dowry deaths every year. A more recent police report stated that dowry deaths had risen by 170 percent in the decade to 1997. All of these official figures are considered to be gross understatements of the real situation. Unofficial estimates cited in a 1999 article by Himendra Thakur "Are our sisters and daughters for sale?" put the number of deaths at 25,000 women a year, with many more left maimed and scarred as a result of attempts on their lives.

Some of the reasons for the under-reporting are obvious. As in other countries, women are reluctant to report threats and abuse to the police for fear of retaliation against themselves and their families. But in India there is an added disincentive. Any attempt to seek police involvement in disputes over dowry transactions may result in members of the woman's own family being subject to criminal proceedings and potentially imprisoned. Moreover, police action is unlikely to stop the demands for dowry payments.

The anti-dowry laws in India were enacted in 1961 but both parties to the dowry—the families of the husband and wife—are criminalised. The laws themselves have done nothing to halt dowry transactions and the violence that is often associated with them. Police and the courts are notorious for turning a blind eye to cases of violence against women and dowry associated deaths. It was not until 1983 that domestic violence became punishable by law.

Many of the victims are burnt to death—they are doused in kerosene and set light to. Routinely the in-laws claim that what happened was simply an accident. The kerosene stoves used in many poorer households are dangerous. When evidence of foul play is too obvious to ignore, the story changes to suicide—the wife, it is said, could not adjust to new family life and subsequently killed herself.

Research done in the late 1990s by Vimochana, a women's group in the southern city of Bangalore, revealed that many deaths are quickly written off by police. The police record of interview with the dying woman—often taken with her husband and relatives present—is often the sole consideration in determining whether an investigation should proceed or not. As Vimochana was able to demonstrate, what a victim will say in a state of shock and under threat from her husband's relatives will often change markedly in later interviews.

Of the 1,133 cases of "unnatural deaths" of women in Bangalore in 1997, only 157 were treated as murder while 546 were categorised as "suicides" and 430 as "accidents". But as Vimochana activist V. Gowramma explained: "We found that of 550 cases reported between January and September 1997, 71 percent were closed as 'kitchen/cooking accidents' and 'stove-bursts' after investigations under section 174 of the Code of Criminal Procedures." The fact that a large proportion of the victims were daughters-in-law was either ignored or treated as a coincidence by police.

Figures cited in *Frontline* indicate what can be expected in court, even in cases where murder charges are laid. In August 1998, there were 1,600 cases pending in the only special court in Bangalore dealing with allegations of violence against women. In the same year three new courts were set up to deal with the large backlog but cases were still expected to take six to seven years to complete. Prosecution rates are low. *Frontline* reported the results of one court: "Of the 730 cases pending in his court at the end of 1998, 58 resulted in acquittals and only 11 in convictions. At the end of June 1999, out of 381 cases pending, 51 resulted in acquittals and only eight in convictions."

Marriage as a Financial Transaction

Young married women are particularly vulnerable. By custom they go to live in the house of their husband's family following the wedding. The marriage is frequently arranged, often in response to advertisements in newspapers. Issues of status, caste and religion may come into the decision, but money is nevertheless central to the transactions between the families of the bride and groom.

The wife is often seen as a servant, or if she works, a source of income, but has no special relationship with the members of her new household and therefore no base of support. Some 40 percent of women are married before the legal age of 18. Illiteracy among women is high, in some rural areas up to 63 percent. As a result they are isolated and often in no position to assert themselves.

Demands for dowry can go on for years. Religious ceremonies and the birth of children often become the occasions for further requests for money or goods. The inability of the bride's family to comply with these demands often leads to the daughter-in-law being treated as a pariah and subject to abuse. In the worst cases, wives are simply killed to make way for a new financial transaction—that is, another marriage.

A recent survey of 10,000 Indian women conducted by India's Health Ministry found that more than half of those interviewed considered violence to be a normal part of married life—the most common cause being the failure to perform domestic duties up to the expectations of their husband's family.

The underlying causes for violence connected to dowry are undoubtedly complex. While the dowry has roots in traditional Indian society, the reasons for prevalence of dowry-associated deaths have comparatively recent origins.

Traditionally a dowry entitled a woman to be a full member of the husband's family and allowed her to enter the marital home with her own wealth. It was seen as a substitute for inheritance, offering some security to the wife. But under the pressures of cash economy introduced under British colonial rule, the dowry like many of the structures of pre-capitalist India was profoundly transformed.

Historian Veena Oldenburg in an essay entitled "Dowry Murders in India: A Preliminary Examination of the Historical Evidence" commented that the old customs of dowry had been perverted "from a strongly spun safety net twist into a deadly noose". Under the burden of heavy land taxes, peasant families were inevitably compelled to find cash where they could or lose their land. As a result the dowry increasingly came to be seen as a vital source of income for the husband's family.

Oldenburg explains: "The will to obtain large dowries from the family of daughters-in-law, to demand more in cash, gold and other liquid assets, becomes vivid after leafing through pages of official reports that dutifully record the effects of indebtedness, foreclosures, barren plots and cattle dying for lack of fodder. The voluntary aspects of dowry, its meaning as a mark of love for the daughter, gradually evaporates. Dowry becomes dreaded payments on demand that accompany and follow the marriage of a daughter."

What Oldenburg explains about the impact of money relations on dowry is underscored by the fact that dowry did not wither away in India in the 20th century but took on new forms. Dowry and dowry-related violence is not confined to rural areas or to the poor, or even just to adherents of the Hindu religion. Under the impact of capitalism, the old custom has been transformed into a vital source of income for families desperate to meet pressing social needs.

A number of studies have shown that the lower ranks of the middle class are particularly prone. According to the Institute of Development and Communication, "The quantum of dowry exchange may still be greater among the middle classes, but 85 percent of dowry death and 80 percent of dowry harassment occurs in the middle and lower stratas." Statistics produced by Vimochana in Bangalore show that 90 percent of the cases of dowry violence involve women from poorer families, who are unable to meet dowry demands.

There is a definite market in India for brides and grooms. Newspapers are filled with pages of women seeking husbands and men advertising their eligibility and social prowess, usually using their caste as a bargaining chip. A "good" marriage is often seen by the wife's family as a means to advance up the social ladder. But the catch is that there is a price to be paid in the form of a dowry. If for any reason that dowry arrangements cannot be met then it is the young woman who suffers.

One critic, Annuppa Caleekal, commented on the rising levels of dowry, particularly during the last decade. "The price of the Indian groom astronomically increased and was based on his qualifications, profession and income. Doctors, charted accountants and engineers even prior to graduation develop the divine right to expect a 'fat' dowry as they become the most sought after cream of the graduating and educated dowry league."

The other side of the dowry equation is that daughters are inevitably regarded as an unwelcome burden, compounding the already oppressed position of women in Indian society. There is a high incidence of gender-based abortions—almost two million female babies a year. One article noted the particularly crass billboard advertisements in Bombay encouraging pregnant women to spend 500 rupees on a gender test to "save" a potential 50,000 rupees on dowry in the future. According to the UN Population Fund report for the year 2000, female infanticide has also increased dramatically over the past decade and infant mortality rates are 40 percent higher for girl babies than boys.

Critics of the dowry system point to the fact that the situation has worsened in the 1990s. As the Indian economy has been opened up for international investment, the gulf between rich and poor widened and so did the economic uncertainty facing the majority of people including the relatively well-off. It was a recipe for sharp tensions that have led to the worsening of a number of social problems.

One commentator Zenia Wadhwani noted: "At a time when India is enjoying unprecedented economic advances and boasts the world's fastest growing middle class, the country is also experiencing a dramatic escalation in reported dowry deaths and bride burnings. Hindu tradition has been transformed as a means to escaping poverty, augmenting one's wealth or acquiring the modern conveniences that are now advertised daily on television."

Domestic violence against women is certainly not isolated to India. The official rate of domestic violence is significantly lower than in the US, for example, where, according to UN statistics, a woman is battered somewhere in the country on average once every 15 seconds. In all countries this violence is bound up with a mixture of cultural backwardness that relegates women to an inferior status combined with the tensions produced by the pressures of growing economic uncertainty and want.

In India, however, where capitalism has fashioned out of the traditions of dowry a particularly naked nexus between marriage and money, and where the stresses of everyday life are being heightened by widening social polarisation, the violence takes correspondingly brutal and grotesque forms.

Critical Thinking

1. What is implied by the character of the three articles cited, according to the author?

2. Why are the number of dowry deaths in India under-reported?

3. What are the typical explanations for why a woman might be burned to death?

4. Why are so many such deaths quickly written off by the police?

5. Why are young married women in such a vulnerable situation?

6. Why does the dowry system lead to their abuse?

7. How did the dowry function traditionally? How and why has it been transformed? In what segment of society are women most vulnerable?

8. What have been the consequences with respect to gender-based abortion and female infant mortality rates?

Create Central

www.mhhe.com/createcentral

Internet References

Women Watch
www.un.org/womenwatch/about

Population Council
www.popcouncil.org

Violence Against Women
http://vaw.sagepub.com

Unit 6

UNIT

Prepared by: Elvio Angeloni, *Pasadena City College*

Religion, Belief, and Ritual

The anthropological interest in religion, belief, and ritual is not concerned with the scientific validity of such phenomena but rather with the way in which people relate various concepts of the supernatural to their everyday lives. From this practical perspective, some anthropologists have found that some traditional spiritual healing is just as helpful in the treatment of illness as is modern medicine; that religious beliefs and practices may be a form of social control; and that mystical beliefs and rituals are not absent from the modern world. In other words, this unit shows religion, belief, and ritual in relationship to practical human affairs. The placing of belief systems in social context thus helps to not only counter popular stereotypes, but also serves to promote a greater understanding of and appreciation for other viewpoints.

Every society is composed of feeling, thinking, and acting human beings who, at one time or another, are either conforming to or altering the social order into which they were born. Religion is an ideological framework that gives special legitimacy and validity to human experience within any given sociocultural system. In this way, monogamy as a marriage form, or monarchy as a political form, ceases to be simply one of many alternative ways in which a society can be organized, but becomes, for the believer, the only legitimate way. Religion considers certain human values and activities as sacred and inviolable. It is this mythic function that helps explain the strong ideological attachments that some people have, regardless of the scientific merits of their points of view.

While, under some conditions, religion may in fact be "the opiate of the masses," under other conditions such a belief system may be a rallying point for social and economic protest. A contemporary example of the former might be the "Moonies" (members of the Unification Church founded by Sun Myung Moon), while a good example of the latter is the role of the Black Church in the American Civil Rights movement, along with the prominence of religious figures such as Martin Luther King Jr. and Jesse Jackson. A word of caution must be set forth concerning attempts to understand belief systems of other cultures. At times, the prevailing attitude seems to be, "What I believe in is religion, and what you believe in is superstition." While anthropologists generally do not subscribe to this view, some tend to explain such behavior as incomprehensible and impractical without considering its full meaning and function within its cultural context. The articles in this unit should serve as a strong warning concerning the pitfalls of that approach.

Article

Prepared by: Elvio Angeloni, *Pasadena City College*

The Adaptive Value of Religious Ritual

Rituals promote group cohesion by requiring members to engage in behavior that is too costly to fake.

RICHARD SOSIS

Learning Outcomes

After reading this article, you will be able to:

- Explain how beliefs about the supernatural contribute to a sense of personal security, individual responsibility, and social harmony.
- Discuss the relationship between the demands upon members of a religious group and the levels of devotion and commitment achieved.

I was 15 years old the first time I went to Jerusalem's Old City and visited the 2,000-year-old remains of the Second Temple, known as the Western Wall. It may have foreshadowed my future life as an anthropologist, but on my first glimpse of the ancient stones I was more taken by the people standing at the foot of the structure than by the wall itself. Women stood in the open sun, facing the Wall in solemn worship, wearing long-sleeved shirts, head coverings and heavy skirts that scraped the ground. Men in their thick beards, long black coats and fur hats also seemed oblivious to the summer heat as they swayed fervently and sang praises to God. I turned to a friend, "Why would anyone in their right mind dress for a New England winter only to spend the afternoon praying in the desert heat?" At the time I thought there was no rational explanation and decided that my fellow religious brethren might well be mad.

Of course, "strange" behavior is not unique to ultraorthodox Jews. Many religious acts appear peculiar to the outsider. Pious adherents the world over physically differentiate themselves from others: Moonies shave their heads, Jain monks of India wear contraptions on their heads and feet to avoid killing insects, and clergy almost everywhere dress in outfits that distinguish them from the rest of society. Many peoples also engage in some form of surgical alteration. Australian aborigines perform a ritual operation on adolescent boys in which a bone or a stone is inserted into the penis through an incision in the urethra. Jews and Muslims submit their sons to circumcision, and in some Muslim societies daughters are also subject to circumcision or other forms of genital mutilation. Groups

as diverse as the Nuer of Sudan and the Iatmul of New Guinea force their adolescents to undergo ritual scarification. Initiation ceremonies, otherwise known as rites of passage, are often brutal. Among Native Americans, Apache boys were forced to bathe in icy water, Luiseno initiates were required to lie motionless while being bitten by hordes of ants, and Tukuna girls had their hair plucked out.

How can we begin to understand such behavior? If human beings are rational creatures, then why do we spend so much time, energy and resources on acts that can be so painful or, at the very least, uncomfortable? Archaeologists tell us that our species has engaged in ritual behavior for at least 100,000 years, and every known culture practices some form of religion. It even survives covertly in those cultures where governments have attempted to eliminate spiritual practices. And, despite the unparalleled triumph of scientific rationalism in the 20th century, religion continued to flourish. In the United States a steady 40 percent of the population attended church regularly throughout the century. A belief in God (about 96 percent), the afterlife (about 72 percent), heaven (about 72 percent) and hell (about 58 percent) remained substantial and remarkably constant. Why do religious beliefs, practices and institutions continue to be an essential component of human social life?

Such questions have intrigued me for years. Initially my training in anthropology did not provide an answer. Indeed, my studies only increased my bewilderment. I received my training in a subfield known as human behavioral ecology, which studies the adaptive design of behavior with attention to its ecological setting. Behavioral ecologists assume that natural selection has shaped the human nervous system to respond successfully to varying ecological circumstances. All organisms must balance trade-offs: Time spent doing one thing prevents them from pursuing other activities that can enhance their survival or reproductive success. Animals that maximize the rate at which they acquire resources, such as food and mates, can maximize the number of descendants, which is exactly what the game of natural selection is all about.

Behavioral ecologists assume that natural selection has designed our decision-making mechanisms to optimize the rate at which human beings accrue resources under diverse ecological conditions—a basic prediction of *optimal foraging theory*. Optimality models offer predictions of the "perfectly adapted" behavioral response, given a set of environmental constraints. Of course, a perfect fit with the environment is almost never achieved because organisms rarely have perfect information and because environments are always changing. Nevertheless, this assumption has provided a powerful framework to analyze a variety of decisions, and most research (largely conducted among foraging populations) has shown that our species broadly conforms to these expectations.

If our species is designed to optimize the rate at which we extract energy from the environment, why would we engage in religious behavior that seems so counterproductive? Indeed, some religious practices, such as ritual sacrifices, are a conspicuous display of wasted resources. Anthropologists can explain why foragers regularly share their food with others in the group, but why would anyone share their food with a dead ancestor by burning it to ashes on an altar? A common response to this question is that people believe in the efficacy of the rituals and the tenets of the faith that give meaning to the ceremonies. But this response merely begs the question. We must really ask why natural selection has favored a psychology that believes in the supernatural and engages in the costly manifestations of those beliefs.

Ritual Sacrifice

Behavioral ecologists have only recently begun to consider the curiosities of religious activities, so at first I had to search other disciplines to understand these practices. The scholarly literature suggested that I wasn't the only one who believed that intense religious behavior was a sign of madness. Some of the greatest minds of the past two centuries, such as Marx and Freud, supported my thesis. And the early anthropological theorists also held that spiritual beliefs were indicative of a primitive and simple mind. In the 19th century, Edward B. Tylor, often noted as one of the founding fathers of anthropology, maintained that religion arose out of a misunderstanding among "primitives" that dreams are real. He argued that dreams about deceased ancestors might have led the primitives to believe that spirits can survive death.

Eventually the discipline of anthropology matured, and its practitioners moved beyond the equation that "primitive equals irrational." Instead, they began to seek functional explanations of religion. Most prominent among these early 20th-century theorists was the Polish-born anthropologist Bronislaw Malinowski. He argued that religion arose out of "the real tragedies of human life, out of the conflict between human plans and realities." Although religion may serve to allay our fears of death, and provide comfort from our incessant search for answers, Malinowski's thesis did not seem to explain the origin of rituals. Standing in the midday desert sun in several layers of black clothing seems more like a recipe for increasing anxiety than treating it. The classical anthropologists didn't have the right answers to my questions. I needed to look elsewhere.

Fortunately, a new generation of anthropologists has begun to provide some explanations. It turns out that the strangeness of

religious practices and their inherent costs are actually the critical features that contribute to the success of religion as a universal cultural strategy and why natural selection has favored such behavior in the human lineage. To understand this unexpected benefit we need to recognize the adaptive problem that ritual behavior solves. William Irons, a behavioral ecologist at Northwestern University, has suggested that the universal dilemma is the promotion of cooperation within a community. Irons argues that the primary adaptive benefit of religion is its ability to facilitate cooperation within a group—while hunting, sharing food, defending against attacks and waging war—all critical activities in our evolutionary history. But, as Irons points out, although everyone is better off if everybody cooperates, this ideal is often very difficult to coordinate and achieve. The problem is that an individual is even better off if everyone else does the cooperating, while he or she remains at home enjoying an afternoon siesta. Cooperation requires social mechanisms that prevent individuals from free riding on the efforts of others. Irons argues that religion is such a mechanism.

The key is that religious rituals are a form of communication, which anthropologists have long maintained. They borrowed this insight from ethologists who observed that many species engage in patterned behavior, which they referred to as "ritual." Ethologists recognized that ritualistic behaviors served as a form of communication between members of the same species, and often between members of different species. For example, the males of many avian species engage in courtship rituals—such as bowing, head wagging, wing waving and hopping (among many other gestures)—to signal their amorous intents before a prospective mate. And, of course, the vibration of a rattlesnake's tail is a powerful threat display to other species that enter its personal space.

Irons's insight is that religious activities signal commitment to other members of the group. By engaging in the ritual, the member effectively says, "I identify with the group and I believe in what the group stands for." Through its ability to signal commitment, religious behavior can overcome the problem of free riders and promote cooperation within the group. It does so because trust lies at the heart of the problem: A member must assure everyone that he or she will participate in acquiring food or in defending the group. Of course, hunters and warriors may make promises—"you have my word, I'll show up tomorrow"—but unless the trust is already established such statements are not believable.

It turns out that there is a robust way to secure trust. Israeli biologist Amotz Zahavi observes that it is often in the best interest of an animal to send a dishonest signal—perhaps to fake its size, speed, strength, health or beauty. The only signal that can be believed is one that is too costly to fake, which he referred to as a "handicap." Zahavi argues that natural selection has favored the evolution of handicaps. For example, when a springbok antelope spots a predator it often *stots*—it jumps up and down. This extraordinary behavior puzzled biologists for years: Why would an antelope waste precious energy that could be used to escape the predator? And why would the animal make itself more visible to something that wants to eat it? The reason is that the springbok is displaying its quality to

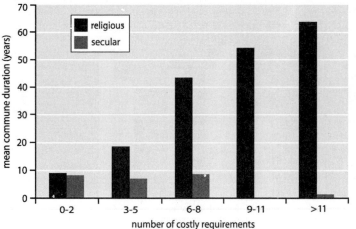

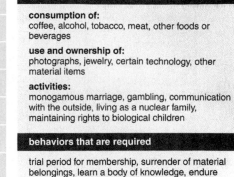

behaviors that are constrained

consumption of:
coffee, alcohol, tobacco, meat, other foods or
beverages

use and ownership of:
photographs, jewelry, certain technology, other
material items

activities:
monogamous marriage, gambling, communication
with the outside, living as a nuclear family,
maintaining rights to biological children

behaviors that are required

trial period for membership, surrender of material
belongings, learn a body of knowledge, endure
public sessions of criticism, certain clothing styles,
certain hairstyles, fasting

the predator—its ability to escape, effectively saying, "Don't bother chasing me. Look how strong my legs are, you won't be able to catch me." The only reason a predator believes the springbok is because the signal is too costly to fake. An antelope that is not quick enough to escape cannot imitate the signal because it is not strong enough to repeatedly jump to a certain height. Thus, a display can provide honest information if the signals are so costly to perform that lower quality organisms cannot benefit by imitating the signal.

In much the same way, religious behavior is also a costly signal. By donning several layers of clothing and standing out in the midday sun, ultraorthodox Jewish men are signaling to others: "Hey! Look, I'm a *haredi* Jew. If you are also a member of this group you can trust me because why else would I be dressed like this? No one would do this *unless* they believed in the teachings of ultraorthodox Judaism and were fully committed to its ideals and goals." The quality that these men are signaling is their level of commitment to a specific religious group.

Adherence to a set of religious beliefs entails a host of ritual obligations and expected behaviors. Although there may be physical or psychological benefits associated with some ritual practices, the significant time, energy and financial costs involved serve as effective deterrents for anyone who does not believe in the teachings of a particular religion. There is no incentive for nonbelievers to join or remain in a religious group, because the costs of maintaining membership—such as praying three times a day, eating only kosher food, donating a certain part of your income to charity and so on—are simply too high.

Those who engage in the suite of ritual requirements imposed by a religious group can be trusted to believe sincerely in the doctrines of their respective religious communities. As a result of increased levels of trust and commitment among group members, religious groups minimize costly monitoring mechanisms that are otherwise necessary to overcome free-rider problems that typically plague communal pursuits. Hence, the adaptive benefit of ritual behavior is its ability to promote and maintain cooperation, a challenge that our ancestors presumably faced throughout our evolutionary history.

Benefits of Membership

One prediction of the "costly signaling theory of ritual" is that groups that impose the greatest demands on their members will elicit the highest levels of devotion and commitment. Only committed members will be willing to dress and behave in ways that differ from the rest of society. Groups that maintain more-committed members can also offer more because it's easier for them to attain their collective goals than groups whose members are less committed. This may explain a paradox in the religious marketplace: Churches that require the most of their adherents are experiencing rapid rates of growth. For example, the Church of Jesus Christ of Latter-day Saints (Mormons), Seventh-day Adventists and Jehovah's Witnesses, who respectively abstain from caffeine, meat and blood transfusions (among other things), have been growing at exceptional rates. In contrast, liberal Protestant denominations such as the Episcopalians, Methodists and Presbyterians have been steadily losing members.

Economist Lawrence Iannaccone, of George Mason University, has also noted that the most demanding groups also have the greatest number of committed members. He found that the more distinct a religious group was—how much the group's lifestyle differed from mainstream America—the higher its attendance rates at services. Sociologists Roger Finke and Rodney Stark, of Penn State and the University of Washington, respectively, have argued that when the Second Vatican Council in 1962 repealed many of the Catholic Church's prohibitions and reduced the level of strictness in the church, it initiated a decline in church attendance among American Catholics and reduced the enrollments in seminaries. Indeed, in the late 1950s almost 75 percent of American Catholics were attending Mass weekly, but since the Vatican's actions there has been a steady decline to the current rate of about 45 percent.

The costly signaling theory of ritual also predicts that greater commitment will translate into greater cooperation within groups. My colleague Eric Bressler, a graduate student at McMaster University, and I addressed this question by looking at data from the records of 19th-century communes. All

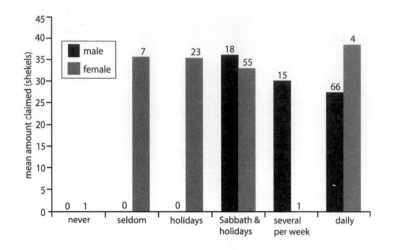

communes face an inherent problem of promoting and sustaining cooperation because individuals can free ride on the efforts of others. Because cooperation is key to a commune's survival, we employed commune longevity as a measure of cooperation. Compared to their secular counterparts, the religious communes did indeed demand more of their members, including such behavior as celibacy, the surrender of all material possessions and vegetarianism. Communes that demanded more of their members survived longer, overcoming the fundamental challenges of cooperation. By placing greater demands on their members, they were presumably able to elicit greater belief in and commitment toward the community's common ideology and goals.

I also wanted to evaluate the costly signaling theory of ritual within modern communal societies. The kibbutzim I had visited in Israel as a teenager provided an ideal opportunity to examine these hypotheses. For most of their 100-year history, these communal societies have lived by the dictum, "From each according to his abilities, to each according to his needs." The majority of the more than 270 kibbutzim are secular (and often ideologically antireligious); fewer than 20 are religiously oriented. Because of a massive economic failure—a collective debt of more than $4 billion—the kibbutzim are now moving in the direction of increased privatization and reduced communality. When news of the extraordinary debt surfaced in the late 1980s, it went largely unnoticed that the religious kibbutzim were financially stable. In the words of the Religious Kibbutz Movement Federation, "the economic position of the religious kibbutzim is sound, and they remain uninvolved in the economic crisis."

The success of the religious kibbutzim is especially remarkable given that many of their rituals inhibit economic productivity. For example, Jewish law does not permit Jews to milk cows on the Sabbath. Although rabbinic rulings now permit milking by kibbutz members to prevent the cows from suffering, in the early years none of this milk was used commercially. There are also significant constraints imposed by Jewish law on agricultural productivity. Fruits are not allowed to be eaten for the first few years of the tree's life, agricultural fields must lie fallow every seven years, and the corners of fields can never

be harvested—they must be left for society's poor. Although these constraints appear detrimental to productivity, the costly signaling theory of ritual suggests that they may actually be the key to the economic success of the religious kibbutzim.

I decided to study this issue with economist Bradley Ruffle of Israel's Ben Gurion University. We developed a game to determine whether there were differences in how the members of secular and religious kibbutzim cooperated with each other. The game involves two members from the same kibbutz who remain anonymous to each other. Each member is told there are 100 shekels in an envelope to which both members have access. Each participant decides how many shekels to withdraw and keep. If the sum of both requests exceeds 100 shekels, both members receive no money and the game is over. However, if the requests are less than or equal to 100 shekels, the money remaining in the envelope is increased by 50 percent and divided evenly among the participants. Each member also keeps the original amount he or she requested. The game is an example of a common-pool resource dilemma in which publicly accessible goods are no longer available once they are consumed. Since the goods are available to more than one person, the maintenance of the resources requires individual self-restraint; in other words, cooperation.

After we controlled for a number of variables, including the age and size of the kibbutz and the amount of privatization, we found not only that religious kibbutzniks were more cooperative with each other than secular kibbutzniks, but that male religious kibbutz members were also significantly more cooperative than female members. Among secular kibbutzniks we found no sex differences at all. This result is understandable if we appreciate the types of rituals and demands imposed on religious Jews. Although there are a variety of requirements that are imposed equally on males and females, such as keeping kosher and refraining from work on the Sabbath, male rituals are largely performed in public, whereas female rituals are generally pursued privately. Indeed, none of the three major requirements imposed exclusively on women—attending a ritual bath, separating a portion of dough when baking bread and lighting Shabbat and holiday candles—are publicly performed. They are not rituals that signal commitment to a wider group; instead they appear to signal commitment to the family. Men, however, engage in highly visible rituals, most notably public prayer, which they are expected to perform three times a day. Among male religious kibbutz members, synagogue attendance is positively correlated with cooperative behavior. There is no similar correlation among females. This is not surprising given that women are not required to attend services, and so their presence does not signal commitment to the group. Here the costly signaling theory of ritual provides a unique explanation of these findings. We expect that further work will provide even more insight into the ability of ritual to promote trust, commitment and cooperation.

We know that many other species engage in ritual behaviors that appear to enhance trust and cooperation. For example, anthropologists John Watanabe of Dartmouth University and Barbara Smuts at the University of Michigan have shown that greetings between male olive baboons serve to signal trust and commitment between former rivals. So why are human rituals often cloaked in mystery and the supernatural? Cognitive anthropologists Scott Atran of the University of Michigan and Pascal Boyer at Washington University in St. Louis have pointed out that the counterintuitive nature of supernatural concepts are more easily remembered than mundane ideas, which facilitates their cultural transmission. Belief in supernatural agents such as gods, spirits and ghosts also appears to be critical to religion's ability to promote long-term cooperation. In our study of 19th-century communes, Eric Bressler and I found that the strong positive relationship between the number of costly requirements imposed on members and commune longevity only held for religious communes, not secular ones. We were surprised by this result because secular groups such as militaries and fraternities appear to successfully employ costly rituals to maintain cooperation. Cultural ecologist Roy Rappaport explained, however, that although religious and secular rituals can both promote cooperation, religious rituals ironically generate greater belief and commitment because they sanctify unfalsifiable statements that are beyond the possibility of examination. Since statements containing supernatural elements, such as "Jesus is the son of God," cannot be proved or disproved, believers verify them "emotionally." In contrast to religious propositions, the kibbutz's guiding dictum, taken from Karl Marx, is not beyond question; it can be evaluated by living according to its directives by distributing labor and resources appropriately. Indeed, as the economic situation on the kibbutzim has worsened, this fundamental proposition of kibbutz life has been challenged and is now disregarded by many who are pushing their communities to accept differential pay scales. The ability of religious rituals to evoke emotional experiences that can be associated with enduring supernatural concepts and symbols differentiates them from both animal and secular rituals and lies at the heart of their efficiency in promoting and maintaining long-term group cooperation and commitment.

Evolutionary research on religious behavior is in its infancy, and many questions remain to be addressed. The costly signaling theory of ritual appears to provide some answers, and, of course, it has given me a better understanding of the questions I asked as a teenager. The real value of the costly signaling theory of ritual will be determined by its ability to explain religious phenomena across societies. Most of us, including ultraorthodox Jews, are not living in communes. Nevertheless, contemporary religious congregations that demand much of their members are able to achieve a close-knit social community—an impressive accomplishment in today's individualistic world.

Religion has probably always served to enhance the union of its practitioners; unfortunately, there is also a dark side to this unity. If the intragroup solidarity that religion promotes is one of its significant adaptive benefits, then from its beginning religion has probably always played a role in intergroup conflicts. In other words, one of the benefits for individuals of intragroup solidarity is the ability of unified groups to defend and compete against other groups. This seems to be as true today as it ever was, and is nowhere more apparent than in the region I visited as a 15-year-old boy—which is where I am as I write these words. As I conduct my fieldwork in the center of this war zone, I hope that by appreciating the depth of the religious need in the human psyche, and by understanding this powerful adaptation, we can learn how to promote cooperation rather than conflict.

References

Atran, S. 2002. *In Gods We Trust.* New York: Oxford University Press.

Iannaccone, L. 1992. Sacrifice and stigma: Reducing free-riding in cults, communes, and other collectives. *Journal of Political Economy* 100:271–291.

Iannaccone, L. 1994. Why strict churches are strong. *American Journal of Sociology* 99:1180–1211.

Irons, W. 2001. Religion as a hard-to-fake sign of commitment. In *Evolution and the Capacity for Commitment,* ed. R. Nesse, pp. 292–309. New York: Russell Sage Foundation.

Rappaport, R. 1999. *Ritual and Religion in the Making of Humanity.* Cambridge: Cambridge University Press.

Sosis, R. 2003. Why aren't we all Hutterites? Costly signaling theory and religious behavior. *Human Nature* 14:91–127.

Sosis, R., and C. Alcorta. 2003. Signaling, solidarity, and the sacred: The evolution of religious behavior. *Evolutionary Anthropology* 12:264–274.

Sosis, R., and E. Bressler. 2003. Cooperation and commune longevity: A test of the costly signaling theory of religion. *Cross-Cultural Research* 37:211–239.

Sosis, R., and B. Ruffle. 2003. Religious ritual and cooperation: Testing for a relationship on Israeli religious and secular kibbutzim. *Current Anthropology* 44:713–722.

Zahavi, A., and A. Zahavi. 1997. *The Handicap Principle.* New York: Oxford University Press.

Critical Thinking

1. What is the universal dilemma with regard to cooperation in a community, according to William Irons?

2. In what sense is religious ritual a form of communication?

3. What is the only kind of signal that can be believed? How does the example of the springbok antelope illustrate the point?

4. Why is there no incentive for nonbelievers to join or remain in a religious group? Are there costly monitoring mechanisms? Explain.

5. What is the relationship between demands upon members and levels of devotion and commitment? What paradox does this explain?

6. What groups have the most committed members?

7. What was observed among American Catholics once the Vatican Council reduced the level of strictness in the church?

8. Which 19th-century communes survived long and why?

9. Which kibbutzim survived better and why? What constraints existed among the religious kibbutzim and what effect did they have?

10. Describe the overall results of the game experiment with regard to religious versus secular kibbutzim and men versus women.

11. Why are religious rituals more successful at promoting belief than are secular rituals?

12. What is the "dark side" to the unity provided by religious intragroup solidarity?

Create Central

www.mhhe.com/createcentral

Internet References

Apologetics Index
www.apologeticsindex.org/site/index-c

Journal of Anthropology of Religion
www.mehtapress.com/social-science-a-humanities/
journal-of-anthropology-of-religion.html

RICHARD SOSIS is an assistant professor of anthropology at the University of Connecticut. His research interests include the evolution of cooperation, utopian societies and the behavioral ecology of religion. Address: Department of Anthropology, U-2176, University of Connecticut, Storrs, CT 06269–2176. Internet: richard.sosis@uconn.edu

Sosis, Richard. From *American Scientist*, March/April 2004, pp. 166–172. Copyright © 2004 by American Scientist, magazine of Sigma Xi, The Scientific Research Society. Reprinted by permission.

Article   Prepared by: Elvio Angeloni, *Pasadena City College*

Understanding Islam

KENNETH JOST

Learning Outcomes

After reading this article, you will be able to:

• Describe the basic tenets of Islam.

• Discuss whether Islam really clashes with Western values.

Is Islam Compatible with Western Values?

With more than 1 billion adherents, Islam is the world's second-largest religion after Christianity. Within its mainstream traditions, Islam teaches piety, virtue and tolerance. Ever since the Sept. 11, 2001, terrorist attacks in the United States, however, many Americans have associated Islam with the fundamentalist groups that preach violence against the West and regard "moderate" Muslims as heretics. Mainstream Muslims and religious scholars say Islam is wrongly blamed for the violence and intolerance of a few. But some critics say Muslims have not done enough to oppose terrorism and violence. They also contend that Islam's emphasis on a strong relationship between religion and the state is at odds with Western views of secularism and pluralism. Some Muslims are calling for a more progressive form of Islam. But radical Islamist views are attracting a growing number of young Muslims in the Islamic world and in Europe.

Overview

Aishah Azmi was dressed all in black, her face veiled by a *niqab* that revealed only her brown eyes through a narrow slit.

"Muslim women who wear the veil are not aliens," the 24-year-old suspended bilingual teaching assistant told reporters in Leeds, England, on Oct. 19. "Integration [of Muslims into British society] requires people like me to be in the workplace so that people can see that we are not to be feared or mistrusted."

But school officials defended their decision to suspend Azmi for refusing to remove her veil in class with a male teacher, saying it interfered with her ability to communicate with her students—most of them Muslims and, like Azmi, British Asians.

"The school and the local authority had to balance the rights of the children to receive the best quality education possible and Mrs. Azmi's desire to express her cultural beliefs," said local Education Minister Jim Dodds.

Although an employment tribunal rejected Azmi's discrimination and harassment claims, it said the school council had handled her complaint poorly and awarded her 1,100 British pounds—about $2,300.

Azmi's widely discussed case has become part of a wrenching debate in predominantly Christian England over relations with the country's growing Muslim population.

In September, a little more than a year after subway and bus bombings in London claimed 55 lives, a government minister called on Muslim parents to do more to steer their children away from violence and terrorism. Then, in October, a leaked report being prepared by the interfaith adviser of the Church of England complained that what he called the government's policy of "privileged attention" toward Muslims had backfired and was creating increased "disaffection and separation."

The simmering controversy grew even hotter after Jack Straw, leader of the House of Commons and former foreign secretary under Prime Minister Tony Blair, called full-face veils "a visible statement of separation and difference" that promotes separatism between Muslims and non-Muslims. Straw, whose constituency in northwestern England includes an estimated 25 percent Muslim population aired the comments in a local newspaper column.

Hamid Qureshi, chairman of the Lancashire Council of Mosques, called Straw's remarks "blatant Muslim-bashing."

"Muslims feel they are on center stage, and everybody is Muslim-bashing," says Anjum Anwar, the council's director of education. "They feel very sensitive."

Britain's estimated 1.5 million Muslims—comprising mostly Pakistani or Indian immigrants and their British-born children—are only a tiny fraction of Islam's estimated 1.2 billion adherents worldwide. But the tensions surfacing in the face-veil debate exemplify the increasingly strained relations between the predominantly Christian West and the Muslim world.

The world's two largest religions—Christianity has some 2 billion adherents—have had a difficult relationship at least since the time of the European Crusades against Muslim rulers, or caliphs, almost 1,000 years ago. Mutual suspicion and hostility have intensified since recent terrorist attacks around the world by militant Islamic groups and President George W. Bush proclaimed a worldwide "war on terror" in response to the Sept. 11, 2001, attacks in the United States.

Bush, who stumbled early on by referring to a "crusade" against terrorism, has tried many times since then to dispel perceptions of any official hostility toward Islam or Muslims generally. In Britain, Blair's government has carried on a 40-year-old policy of "multiculturalism" aimed at promoting cohesion among the country's various communities, Muslims in particular.

Despite those efforts, widespread distrust of Islam and Muslims prevails on both sides of the Atlantic. In a recent poll in the United States, 45 percent of those surveyed said they had an unfavorable view of Islam—a higher percentage than registered in a similar poll four years earlier.

British Muslim leaders also say they feel increasingly hostile anti-Muslim sentiments from the general public and government officials. "Muslims are very fearful, frustrated, upset, angry," says Asghar Bukhari, a spokesman for the Muslim Public Affairs Committee in London. "It's been almost like a mental assault on the Muslim psyche here."

As the face-veil debate illustrates, the distrust stems in part from an array of differences between today's Christianity and Islam as variously practiced in the so-called Muslim world, including the growing Muslim diaspora in Europe and North America.

In broad terms, Islam generally regards religion as a more pervasive presence in daily life and a more important source for civil law than contemporary Christianity, according to the British author Paul Grieve, who wrote a comprehensive guide to Islam after studying Islamic history and thought for more than three years. "Islam is a system of rules for all aspects of life," Grieve writes, while Western liberalism limits regulation of personal behavior. In contrast to the secular nation-states of the West, he explains, Islam views the ideal Muslim society as a universal community—such as the *ummah* established by the Prophet Muhammed in the seventh century.

Those theological and cultural differences are reflected, Grieve says, in Westerners' widespread view of Muslims as narrow-minded and extremist. Many Muslims correspondingly view Westerners as decadent and immoral.

The differences also can be seen in the debates over the role Islam plays in motivating terrorist violence by Islamic extremist groups such as al Qaeda and the objections raised by Muslims to what they consider unflattering and unfair descriptions of Islam in the West.

Muslim leaders generally deny responsibility for the violence committed by Islamic terrorists, including the 9/11 terrorist attacks in the United States and subsequent attacks in Indonesia, Spain and England. "Muslim organizations have done more than ever before in trying to advance community cohesion," Anwar says. They also deny any intention to deny freedom of expression, even though Muslims worldwide denounced a Danish cartoonist's satirical portrayal of Muhammad and Pope Benedict XVI's citation of a medieval Christian emperor's description of Islam as a violent religion.

For many Westerners, however, Islam is associated with radical Muslims—known as Islamists—who either advocate or appear to condone violence and who take to the streets to protest unfavorable depictions of Islam. "A lot of traditional or moderate Islam is inert," says Paul Marshall, a senior fellow at Freedom House's Center for Religious Freedom in Washington. "Many of the people who disagree with radicals don't have a developed position. They keep their heads down."

Meanwhile, many Muslims and non-Muslims alike despair at Islam's sometimes fratricidal intrafaith disputes. Islam split within the first decades of its founding in the seventh century into the Sunni and Shiite (Shia) branches. The Sunni-Shiite conflict helps drive the escalating insurgency in Iraq three years after the U.S.-led invasion ousted Saddam Hussein, a Sunni who pursued generally secularist policies. "A real geopolitical fracturing has taken place in the Muslim world since the end of the colonial era," says Reza Aslan, an Iranian-born Shiite Muslim now a U.S. citizen and author of the book *No god but God*.

The tensions between Islam and the West are on the rise as Islam is surging around the world, growing at an annual rate of about 7 percent. John Voll associate director of the Prince Alwaleed bin Talal Centre for Christian-Muslim Understanding at Georgetown University, notes that the growth is due largely to conversions, not the high birth rates that are driving Hinduism's faster growth.

Moreover, Voll says, Muslims are growing more assertive. "There has been an increase in intensity and an increase in strength in the way Muslims view their place in the world and their place in society," he says.

Teaching assistant Azmi's insistence on wearing the *niqab* exemplifies the new face of Islam in parts of the West. But her choice is not shared by all, or even, most of her fellow Muslim women. "I don't see why she needs to wear it," says Anwar. "She's teaching young children under 11." (Azmi says she wears it because she works with a male classroom teacher.)

Muslim experts generally agree the Koran does not require veils, only modest dress. Observant Muslim women generally comply with the admonition with a head scarf and loose-fitting attire. In particularly conservative cultures, such as Afghanistan under Taliban rule, women cover their entire bodies, including their eyes.

Still, despite the varying practices, many Muslim groups see a disconnect between the West's self-proclaimed tolerance and its pressure on Muslims to conform. "It's a Muslim woman's right to dress as she feels appropriate, given her religious views," says Ibrahim Hooper, director of communications for the Council on American-Islamic Relations in Washington. "But then when somebody actually makes a choice, they're asked not to do that."

Indeed, in Hamtramck, Mich., a judge recently came under fire for throwing out a small-claims case because the Muslim plaintiff refused to remove her full-face veil.

As the debates continue, here are some of the questions being considered:

Is Islam a Religion That Promotes Violence?

Within hours of the London subway and bus bombings on July 7, 2005, the head of the Muslim World League condemned the attacks as un-Islamic. "The heavenly religions, notably Islam, advocate peace and security," said Abdallah al-Turki, secretary-general of the Saudi-funded organization based in Mecca.

The league's statement echoed any number of similar denunciations of Islamist-motivated terrorist attacks issued since 9/11 by Muslims in the United States and around the world. Yet many non-Muslim public officials, commentators, experts and others say Muslims have not done enough to speak out against terrorism committed in the name of their religion.

"Mainstream Muslims have not stepped up to the plate, by and large," says Angel Rabasa, a senior fellow at the Rand Corp., a California think tank, and lead author of a U.S. Air Force-sponsored study, *The Muslim World after 9/11.*

Muslim organizations voice indignant frustration in disputing the accusation. "We can always do more," says Hooper. "The problem is that it never seems to be enough. But that doesn't keep us from trying."

Many Americans, in fact, believe Islam actually encourages violence among its adherents. A CBS poll in April 2006 found that 46 percent of those surveyed believe Islam encourages violence more than other religions. A comparable poll four years earlier registered a lower figure: 32 percent.

Those perceptions are sometimes inflamed by U.S. evangelical leaders. Harsh comments about Islam have come from religious leaders like Franklin Graham, Jerry Falwell, Pat Robertson and Jerry Vines, the former president of the Southern Baptist Convention. Graham called Islam "a very evil and wicked religion," and Vines called Muhammad, Islam's founder and prophet, a "demon-possessed pedophile." Falwell, on the CBS news magazine "60 Minutes" in October 2002, declared, "I think Muhammad was a terrorist."

Mainstream Muslims insist Islam is a peaceful religion and that terrorist organizations distort its tenets and teachings in justifying attacks against the West or other Muslims. But Islamic doctrine and history sometimes seem to justify the use of violence in propagating or defending the faith. The dispute revolves around the meaning of *jihad,* an Arabic word used in the Koran and derived from a root meaning "to strive" or "to make an effort for." Muslim scholars can point to verses in the Koran that depict *jihad* merely as a personal, spiritual struggle and to others that describe *jihad* as encompassing either self-defense or conquest against non-believers.

Georgetown historian Voll notes that, in contrast to Christianity, Islam achieved military success during Muhammad's life and expanded into a major world empire within decades afterward. That history "reinforces the idea that militancy and violence can, in fact, be part of the theologically legitimate plan of the Muslim believer," says Voll.

"Islam, like all religions, has its historical share of violence," acknowledges Stephen Schwartz, an adult convert to Islam and executive director of the Center for Islamic Pluralism in Washington. "But there's no reason to single out Islam."

Modern-day jihadists pack their public manifestos with Koranic citations and writings of Islamic theologians to portray themselves as warriors for Allah and defenders of true Islam. But Voll and others stress that the vast majority of Muslims do not subscribe to their views. "You have a highly visible minority that represents a theologically extreme position in the Muslim world," Voll says.

In particular, writes Seyyed Hossein Nasr, a professor of Islamic studies at George Washington University, Islamic law prohibits the use of force against women, children or civilians—even during war. "Inflicting injuries outside of this context," he writes, "is completely forbidden by Islamic law."

Rabasa says, however, that Muslims who disapprove of terrorism have not said enough or done enough to mobilize opposition to terrorist attacks. "Muslims see themselves as part of a community and are reluctant to criticize radical Muslims," he says.

In addition, many Muslims are simply intimidated from speaking out, he explains. "Radicals are not reluctant to use violence and the threat of violence," he says. Liberal and moderate Muslims are known to receive death threats on their cell phones, even in relatively peaceful Muslim countries such as Indonesia.

Voll also notes that Islamic radicals have simply outorganized the moderates. "There is no moderate organization that even begins to resemble some of the radical organizations that have developed," he says.

In Britain, Bukhari of the Muslim Public Affairs Committee criticizes Muslim leaders themselves for failing to channel young people opposed to Britain's pro-U.S. foreign policy into non-violent political action. "Children who could have been peaceful react to that foreign policy in a way that they themselves become criminals," he says.

The Council on American-Islamic Relations' Hooper details several anti-terrorism pronouncements and drives issued following the London bombings by various Muslim groups and leaders in Britain and in the United States, including *fatwas,* or legal opinions, rejecting terrorism and extremism.

For his part, Omid Safi, an associate professor of Islamic studies at the University of North Carolina in Chapel Hill, points out that virtually every Muslim organization in the United States issued condemnations of violence almost immediately after the 9/11 terrorist attacks.

"How long must we keep answering this question?" Safi asks in exasperation. But he concedes a few moments later that the issue is more than perception. "Muslims must come to terms with our demons," he says, "and one of those demons is violence."

Is Islam Compatible with Secular, Pluralistic Societies?

In 2003, Germany's famed Deutsche Oper staged an avant-garde remake of Mozart's opera "Idomeneo," which dramatizes the composer's criticism of organized religion, with a scene depicting the severed heads of Muhammad, Jesus, Buddha and Poseidon. That production was mounted without incident, but the company dropped plans to restage it in November 2006 after police warned of a possible violent backlash from Muslim fundamentalists.

The cancellation prompted protests from German officials and artistic-freedom advocates in Europe and in the United States, who saw the move as appeasement toward terrorists. Wolfgang Bornsen, a spokesman for conservative Chancellor Angela Merkel, said the cancellation was "a signal" to other artistic companies to avoid any works critical of Islam.

The debate continued even after plans were discussed to mount the production after all—with enhanced security and the blessing of German Muslim leaders. "We live in Europe, where democracy was based on criticizing religion," remarked Philippe Val, editor of the French satirical magazine *Charlie Hebdo.* "If we lose the right to criticize or attack religions in our free countries . . . we are doomed."

As with the issue of violence, Islam's doctrines and history can be viewed as pointing both ways on questions of pluralism and tolerance. "There are a great many passages [in the Koran] that support a pluralistic interpretation of Islam," says the Rand Corp.'s Rabasa. "But you also find a great many that would support an intolerant interpretation."

"Intellectual pluralism is traditional Islam," says Schwartz at the Center for Islamic Pluralism. An oft-quoted verse from the Koran specifically prohibits compulsion in religion, he says. Voll and other historians agree that Muslim countries generally tolerated Christians and Jews, though they were often subject to special taxes or other restrictions.

"Islam is the only major religious system that has built-in protections for minorities," says Hooper at the Council on American-Islamic Relations. "You don't see the kind of persecutions of minorities that we often saw in Europe for hundreds of years. Many members of the Jewish community fled to find safety within the Muslim world."

Even so, Islam's view of religion and politics as inseparable creates difficult issues. Outside the Arab world, most Muslims live in practicing democracies with fair to good human-rights records. But some Muslim countries—Arab and non-Arab—have either adopted or been urged to adopt provisions of Islamic law—*sharia*—that are antithetical to modern ideas of human rights, such as limiting women's rights and prescribing stoning or amputations as criminal penalties.

Muslims participating in a society as a minority population face different issues, according to author Grieve. "Islam is difficult to accommodate in a determinedly secular Western society where almost all views are equally respected, and none is seen as either right or wrong," he writes.

The tensions played out in a number of controversies in recent years were provoked by unflattering depictions of Islam in Europe. A Danish cartoonist's satirical view of Muhammad provoked worldwide protests from Muslim leaders and groups after they were publicized in early 2006. Scattered violence resulted in property damage and more than 30 deaths.

Somewhat similarly, Pope Benedict XVI drew sharp criticism after a Sept. 12, 2006, lecture quoting a medieval Christian emperor's description of Islam as "evil and inhuman." Along with verbal denunciations, protesters in Basra, Iraq, burned an effigy of the pope. Within a week, he disclaimed the remarks and apologized.

Freedom House's Marshall says such controversies, as well as the cancellation of the opera in Berlin, strengthens radical Muslim elements. "Bending to more radical demands marginalizes the voices of moderate Muslims and hands over leadership to the radicals," he says.

Many Muslims in European countries, however, view the controversies—including the current debate over the veil in

---

Basic Tenets of Islam

Islam is the youngest of the world's three major monotheistic religions. Like the other two, Judaism and Christianity, Islam (the word means both "peace" and "submission") holds there is but one God (Allah). Muslims believe God sent a number of prophets to teach mankind how to live according to His law. Muslims consider Jesus, Moses and Abraham as prophets of God and hold the Prophet Muhammad as his final and most sacred messenger. Many accounts found in Islam's sacred book, the Koran (Qur'an), are also found in sacred writings of Jews and Christians.

There are five basic pillars of Islam:

- Creed—Belief in God and Muhammad as his Prophet.
- Almsgiving—Giving money to charity is considered a sacred duty.
- Fasting—From dawn to dusk during the month of Ramadan.
- Prayer—Five daily prayers must be given facing Mecca, Islam's holiest city.
- Pilgrimage—All Muslims must make a baff to Mecca at least once during their lifetime, if they are physically able.

England—as evidence of pervasive hostility from the non-Muslim majorities. "There is a growing hatred of Muslims in Britain, and anybody who bashes Muslims can only get brownie points," says Bukhari of the Muslim Public Affairs Committee.

"These are not friendly times for Western Muslims," says Safi, at the University of North Carolina. "Whenever people find themselves under assault, opening their arms and opening their hearts is difficult."

Does Islam Need a "Reformation"?

If Pakistan's Punjab University expected a chorus of approval when it decided to launch a master's program in musicology in fall 2006, it was in for a surprise. At the Lahore campus, the conservative Islamic Assembly of Students, known as I.J.T., rose up in protest.

Handbills accused school authorities of forsaking Islamic ideological teachings in favor of "the so-called enlightened moderation" dictated by "foreign masters." Undeterred, administrators opened the program for enrollment in September. When fewer students applied than expected, they blamed the poor response in part on the I.J.T. campaign.

The episode reflects how Islam today is evolving differently in the West and in some parts of the Muslim world. Many Muslim writers and scholars in the United States and Europe are calling for Islam to adapt to modern times by, for example, embracing pluralism and gender equality. Introducing a collection of essays by "progressive" Muslims, the University of North Carolina's Safi says the movement seeks to "start swimming through the rising waters of Islam and modernity, to strive for justice in the midst of society."

In much of the Muslim world, however, Islam is growing—in numbers and intensity—on the strength of literal interpretations of the Koran and exclusivist attitudes toward the non-Muslim world. "In the Muslim world in general, more extreme or reactionary forms of Islam are getting stronger—in Africa, Asia and the Middle East," says Freedom House's Marshall, who has previously worked on issues pertaining to persecution of Christians around the world.

Islamist groups such as I.J.T. talk about "reforming" or "purifying" Islam and adopting Islamic law as the primary or exclusive source of civil law. In fact, one version of reformed Islam—Wahhabism[1] or the currently preferred term Salafism—espouses a literalistic reading of the Koran and a puritanical stance toward such modern practices as listening to music or watching television. It has been instituted in Saudi Arabia and has advanced worldwide because of financial backing from the oil-rich kingdom and its appeal to new generations of Muslims.

"The Salafi movement is a fringe," says the Rand Corp.'s Rabasa. "But it's growing because it's dynamic and revolutionary, whereas traditional Islam tends to be conservative. It has this appeal to young people looking for identity."

But the Center for Islamic Pluralism's Schwartz, an outspoken critic of Salafism, says many Muslims are rejecting it because of its tendency to view other branches of Islam as apostasy. "People are getting sick of this," he says. "They're tired of the social conflict and upheaval."

Voll at the Center for Christian-Muslim Understanding also says some Muslim legal scholars are disputing literalistic readings of *sharia* by contending that the Islamic law cited as divinely ordained is actually "a human construct subject to revision."

Some Western commentators refer to a "reformation" in calling for a more liberal form of Islam. Nicholas D. Kristof, a *New York Times* columnist who focuses on global human-rights issues, sees "hopeful rumblings . . . of steps toward a Muslim Reformation," especially on issues of gender equality. He notes that feminist Muslim scholars are reinterpreting passages in the Koran that other Muslims cite in justifying restrictions on women, such as the Saudi ban on women driving.

Safi says he avoids the term reformation because it has been adopted by Salafists and also because it suggests a need to break from traditional Islam. He says "progressive" Muslims return to the Prophet's vision of the common humanity of all human beings and seek "to hold Muslim societies accountable for justice and pluralism."

Rabasa also says reformation is historically inappropriate as a goal for liberal or progressive Muslims. "What is needed is not an Islamic reformation but an Islamic enlightenment," says Rabasa. The West's liberal tradition, he notes, was produced not by the Reformation but by the Enlightenment—the 18th-century movement that used reason to search for objective truth.

Whatever terms are used, the clash between different visions of Islam will be less susceptible to resolution than analogous disputes within most branches of Christianity because Islam lacks any recognized hierarchical structure. Islam has no pope or governing council. Instead, each believer is regarded as having a direct relationship with God, or Allah, with no ecclesiastical intermediary.

"In the face of contemporary Islam, there is absolutely the sense of an authority vacuum," says Safi. Islam's future, he adds, "is a question that can only be answered by Muslims."

Note

1. Wahhabism originated in the Arabian peninsula in the late 1700s from the teachings of Arabian theologian Muhammand ibn Abd al Wahhab (1703–1792).

Critical Thinking

1. What are the main points of contention regarding the strained relationship between the Christian West and Muslim world?
2. Does Islam encourage violence? Explain.
3. Is Islam compatible with secular, pluralistic societies? Explain.
4. Does Islam need a "Reformation"? Explain.

Create Central

www.mhhe.com/createcentral

Internet References

Journal of Anthropology of Religion
www.mehtapress.com/social-science-a-humanities/journal-of-anthropology-of-religion.html
Journal of Islamic Studies
http://jis.oxfordjournals.org

Jost, Kenneth. From *CQ Researcher*, November 3, 2005, pp. 915, 917–922. Copyright © 2005 by CQ Press, division of Congressional Quarterly, Inc. Reprinted by permission.

Article   Prepared by: Elvio Angeloni, *Pasadena City College*

Five Myths of Terrorism

MICHAEL SHERMER

Learning Outcomes

After reading this article, you will be able to:

- Discuss the actual motives of terrorists in contrast to what is commonly believed.

- Discuss the actual effectiveness of terrorism in contrast to its goals.

Because terrorism educes such strong emotions, it has led to at least five myths. The first began in September 2001, when President George W. Bush announced that "we will rid the world of the evildoers" and that they hate us for "our freedoms." This sentiment embodies what Florida State University psychologist Roy F. Baumeister calls "the myth of pure evil," which holds that perpetrators commit pointless violence for no rational reason.

This idea is busted through the scientific study of aggression, of which psychologists have identified four types that are employed toward a purposeful end (from the perpetrators' perspective): instrumental violence, such as plunder, conquest, and the elimination of rivals; revenge, such as vendettas against adversaries or self-help justice; dominance and recognition, such as competition for status and women, particularly among young males; and ideology, such as religious beliefs or Utopian creeds. Terrorists are motivated by a mixture of all four.

In a study of 52 cases of Islamist extremists who have targeted the U.S. for terrorism, for example, Ohio State University political scientist John Mueller concluded that their motives are often instrumental and revenge-oriented, a "boiling outrage at U.S. foreign policy—the wars in Iraq and Afghanistan, in particular, and the country's support for Israel in the Palestinian conflict." Ideology in the form of religion "was a part of the

consideration for most," Mueller suggests, "but not because they wished to spread Sharia law or to establish caliphates (few of the culprits would be able to spell either word). Rather they wanted to protect their coreligionists against what was commonly seen to be a concentrated war on them in the Middle East by the U.S. government."

As for dominance and recognition, University of Michigan anthropologist Scott Atran has demonstrated that suicide bombers (and their families) are showered with status and honor in this life and the promise of women in the next and that most "belong to loose, homegrown networks of family and friends who die not just for a cause but for each other." Most terrorists are in their late teens or early 20s and "are especially prone to movements that promise a meaningful cause, camaraderie, adventure, and glory," he adds.

Busting a second fallacy—that terrorists are part of a vast global network of top-down centrally controlled conspiracies against the West—Atran shows that it is "a decentralized, self-organizing and constantly evolving complex of social networks." A third flawed notion is that terrorists are diabolical geniuses, as when the 9/11 Commission report described them as "sophisticated, patient, disciplined, and lethal." But according to Johns Hopkins University political scientist Max Abrahms, after the decapitation of the leadership of the top extremist organizations, "terrorists targeting the American homeland have been neither sophisticated nor masterminds, but incompetent fools."

Examples abound: the 2001 airplane shoe bomber Richard Reid was unable to ignite the fuse because it was wet from rain; the 2009 underwear bomber Umar Farouk Abdulmutallab succeeded only in torching his junk; the 2010 Times Square bomber Faisal Shahzad managed merely to burn the inside of his Nissan Pathfinder; and the 2012 model airplane bomber Rezwan Ferdaus purchased faux C-4 explosives from FBI agents. Most recently, the 2013 Boston Marathon bombers appear to have been equipped with only one gun and had no exit strategy beyond hijacking a car low on gas that Dzhokhar Tsarnaev used to run over his brother, Tamerlan, followed by a failed suicide attempt inside a land-based boat.

A fourth fiction is that terrorism is deadly. Compared with the annual average of 13,700 homicides, however, deaths from terrorism are statistically invisible, with a total of 33 in the U.S. since 9/11.

Finally, a fifth figment about terrorism is that it works. In an analysis of 457 terrorist campaigns since 1968, George Mason University political scientist Audrey Cronin found that not one extremist group conquered a state and that a full 94 percent failed to gain even one of their strategic goals. Her 2009 book is entitled *How Terrorism Ends* (Princeton University Press). It ends swiftly (groups survive eight years on average) and badly (the death of its leaders).

We must be vigilant always, of course, but these myths point to the inexorable conclusion that terrorism is nothing like what its perpetrators wish it were.

Critical Thinking

1. Contrast the "myth of pure evil" with the actual motives for terrorist acts.
2. Discuss the notion that terrorists are part of a vast global network.
3. Discuss the evidence for the notion that terrorists are diabolical geniuses.
4. How deadly has terrorism actually been?
5. To what extent does terrorism achieve its goals?

Create Central

www.mhhe.com/createcentral

Internet References

Center for Terrorism and Security Studies
    http://www.uml.edu/Research/CTSS/default.aspx
Critical Studies on Terrorism
    www.tandfonline.com

Article Prepared by: Elvio Angeloni, *Pasadena City College*

The Secrets of Haiti's Living Dead

A Harvard botanist investigates mystic potions, voodoo rites, and the making of zombies.

GINO DEL GUERCIO

Learning Outcomes

After reading this article, you will be able to:

- Discuss voodoo as an important form of social control in rural Haiti.
- Discuss the "cultural answer" to the zombie mystery.

Five years ago, a man walked into l'Estère, a village in central Haiti, approached a peasant woman named Angelina Narcisse, and identified himself as her brother Clairvius. If he had not introduced himself using a boyhood nickname and mentioned facts only intimate family members knew, she would not have believed him. Because, eighteen years earlier, Angelina had stood in a small cemetery north of her village and watched as her brother Clairvius was buried.

The man told Angelina he remembered that night well. He knew when he was lowered into his grave, because he was fully conscious, although he could not speak or move. As the earth was thrown over his coffin, he felt as if he were floating over the grave. The scar on his right cheek, he said, was caused by a nail driven through his casket.

The night he was buried, he told Angelina, a voodoo priest raised him from the grave. He was beaten with a sisal whip and carried off to a sugar plantation in northern Haiti where, with other zombies, he was forced to work as a slave. Only with the death of the zombie master were they able to escape, and Narcisse eventually returned home.

Legend has it that zombies are the living dead, raised from their graves and animated by malevolent voodoo sorcerers, usually for some evil purpose. Most Haitians believe in zombies, and Narcisse's claim is not unique. At about the time he reappeared, in 1980, two women turned up in other villages saying they were zombies. In the same year, in northern Haiti, the local peasants claimed to have found a group of zombies wandering aimlessly in the fields.

But Narcisse's case was different in one crucial respect; it was documented. His death had been recorded by doctors at the American-directed Schweitzer Hospital in Deschapelles. On April 30, 1962, hospital records show, Narcisse walked into the hospital's emergency room spitting up blood. He was feverish and full of aches. His doctors could not diagnose his illness, and his symptoms grew steadily worse. Three days after he entered the hospital, according to the records, he died. The attending physicians, an American among them, signed his death certificate. His body was placed in cold storage for twenty hours, and then he was buried. He said he remembered hearing his doctors pronounce him dead while his sister wept at his bedside.

At the Centre de Psychiatrie et Neurologie in Port-au-Prince, Dr. Lamarque Douyon, a Haitian-born, Canadian-trained psychiatrist, has been systematically investigating all reports of zombies since 1961. Though convinced zombies were real, he had been unable to find a scientific explanation for the phenomenon. He did not believe zombies were people raised from the dead, but that did not make them any less interesting. He speculated that victims were only made to *look* dead, probably by means of a drug that dramatically slowed metabolism. The victim was buried, dug up within a few hours, and somehow reawakened.

The Narcisse case provided Douyon with evidence strong enough to warrant a request for assistance from colleagues in New York. Douyon wanted to find an ethnobotanist, a traditional-medicines expert, who could track down the zombie potion he was sure existed. Aware of the medical potential of a drug that could dramatically lower metabolism, a group organized by the late Dr. Nathan Kline—a New York psychiatrist and pioneer in the field of psychopharmacology—raised the funds necessary to send someone to investigate.

The search for that someone led to the Harvard Botanical Museum, one of the world's foremost institutes of ethnobiology. Its director, Richard Evans Schultes, Jeffrey professor of biology, had spent thirteen years in the tropics studying native medicines. Some of his best-known work is the investigation of curare, the substance used by the nomadic people of the Amazon to poison their darts. Refined into a powerful muscle relaxant called D-tubocurarine, it is now an essential component of the anesthesia used during almost all surgery.

Schultes would have been a natural for the Haitian investigation, but he was too busy. He recommended another Harvard ethnobotanist for the assignment, Wade Davis, a 28-year-old Canadian pursuing a doctorate in biology.

Davis grew up in the tall pine forests of British Columbia and entered Harvard in 1971, influenced by a *Life* magazine story on the student strike of 1969. Before Harvard, the only Americans he had known were draft dodgers, who seemed very exotic. "I used to fight forest fires with them," Davis says. "Like everybody else, I thought America was where it was at. And I wanted to go to Harvard because of that *Life* article. When I got there, I realized it wasn't quite what I had in mind."

Davis took a course from Schultes, and when he decided to go to South America to study plants, he approached his professor for guidance. "He was an extraordinary figure," Davis remembers. "He was a man who had done it all. He had lived alone for years in the Amazon." Schultes sent Davis to the rain forest with two letters of introduction and two pieces of advice: wear a pith helmet and try ayahuasca, a powerful hallucinogenic vine. During that expedition and others, Davis proved himself an "outstanding field man," says his mentor. Now, in early 1982, Schultes called him into his office and asked if he had plans for spring break.

"I always took to Schultes's assignments like a plant takes to water," says Davis, tall and blond, with inquisitive blue eyes. "Whatever Schultes told me to do, I did. His letters of introduction opened up a whole world." This time the world was Haiti.

Davis knew nothing about the Caribbean island—and nothing about African traditions, which serve as Haiti's cultural basis. He certainly did not believe in zombies. "I thought it was a lark," he says now.

Davis landed in Haiti a week after his conversation with Schultes, armed with a hypothesis about how the zombie drug—if it existed—might be made. Setting out to explore, he discovered a country materially impoverished, but rich in culture and mystery. He was impressed by the cohesion of Haitian society; he found none of the crime, social disorder, and rampant drug and alcohol abuse so common in many of the other Caribbean islands. The cultural wealth and cohesion, he believes, spring from the country's turbulent history.

During the French occupation of the late eighteenth century, 370,000 African-born slaves were imported to Haiti between 1780 and 1790. In 1791, the black population launched one of the few successful slave revolts in history, forming secret societies and overcoming first the French plantation owners and then a detachment of troops from Napoleon's army, sent to quell the revolt. For the next hundred years Haiti was the only independent black republic in the Caribbean, populated by people who did not forget their African heritage. "You can almost argue that Haiti is more African than Africa," Davis says. "When the west coast of Africa was being disrupted by colonialism and the slave trade, Haiti was essentially left alone. The amalgam of beliefs in Haiti is unique, but it's very, very African."

Davis discovered that the vast majority of Haitian peasants practice voodoo, a sophisticated religion with African roots. Says Davis, "It was immediately obvious that the stereotypes of voodoo weren't true. Going around the countryside, I found clues to a whole complex social world." Vodounists believe they communicate directly with, indeed are often possessed by, the many spirits who populate the everyday world. Vodoun society

is a system of education, law, and medicine; it embodies a code of ethics that regulates social behavior. In rural areas, secret vodoun societies, much like those found on the west coast of Africa, are as much or more in control of everyday life as the Haitian government.

Although most outsiders dismissed the zombie phenomenon as folklore, some early investigators, convinced of its reality, tried to find a scientific explanation. The few who sought a zombie drug failed. Nathan Kline, who helped finance Davis's expedition, had searched unsuccessfully, as had Lamarque Douyon, the Haitian psychiatrist. Zora Neale Hurston, an American black woman, may have come closest. An anthropological pioneer, she went to Haiti in the thirties, studied vodoun society, and wrote a book on the subject, *Tell My Horse,* first published in 1938. She knew about the secret societies and was convinced zombies were real, but if a power existed, she too failed to obtain it.

Davis obtained a sample in a few weeks.

He arrived in Haiti with the names of several contacts. A BBC reporter familiar with the Narcisse case had suggested he talk with Marcel Pierre. Pierre owned the Eagle Bar, a bordello in the city of Saint Marc. He was also a voodoo sorcerer and had supplied the BBC with a physiologically active powder of unknown ingredients. Davis found him willing to negotiate. He told Pierre he was a representative of "powerful but anonymous interests in New York," willing to pay generously for the priest's services, provided no questions were asked. Pierre agreed to be helpful for what Davis will only say was a "sizable sum." Davis spent a day watching Pierre gather the ingredients—including human bones—and grind them together with mortar and pestle. However, from his knowledge of poison, Davis knew immediately that nothing in the formula could produce the powerful effects of zombification.

Three weeks later, Davis went back to the Eagle Bar, where he found Pierre sitting with three associates. Davis challenged him. He called him a charlatan. Enraged, the priest gave him a second vial, claiming that this was the real poison. Davis pretended to pour the powder into his palm and rub it into his skin. "You're a dead man," Pierre told him, and he might have been, because this powder proved to be genuine. But, as the substance had not actually touched him, Davis was able to maintain his bravado, and Pierre was impressed. He agreed to make the poison and show Davis how it was done.

The powder, which Davis keeps in a small vial, looks like dry black dirt. It contains parts of toads, sea worms, lizards, tarantulas, and human bones. (To obtain the last ingredient, he and Pierre unearthed a child's grave on a nocturnal trip to the cemetery.) The poison is rubbed into the victim's skin. Within hours he begins to feel nauseated and has difficulty breathing. A pins-and-needles sensation afflicts his arms and legs, then progresses to the whole body. The subject becomes paralyzed; his lips turn blue for lack of oxygen. Quickly—sometimes within six hours—his metabolism is lowered to a level almost indistinguishable from death.

As Davis discovered, making the poison is an inexact science. Ingredients varied in the five samples he eventually acquired, although the active agents were always the same. And the poison came with no guarantee. Davis speculates that sometimes

Richard Schultes

His students continue his tradition of pursuing botanical research in the likeliest of unlikely places.

Richard Evans Schultes, Jeffrey professor of biology emeritus, has two homes, and they could not be more different. The first is Cambridge, where he served as director of the Harvard Botanical Museum from 1970 until last year, when he became director emeritus. During his tenure he interested generations of students in the exotic botany of the Amazon rain forest. His impact on the field through his own research is worldwide. The scholarly ethnobotanist with steel-rimmed glasses, bald head, and white lab coat is as much a part of the Botanical Museum as the thousands of plant specimens and botanical texts on the museum shelves.

In his austere office is a picture of a crew-cut, younger man stripped to the waist, his arms decorated with tribal paint. This is Schultes's other persona. Starting in 1941, he spent thirteen years in the rain forests of South America, living with the Indians and studying the plants they use for medicinal and spiritual purposes.

Schultes is concerned that many of the people he has studied are giving up traditional ways. "The people of so-called primitive societies are becoming civilized and losing all their forefathers' knowledge of plant lore," he says. "We'll be losing the tremendous amounts of knowledge they've gained over thousands of years. We're interested in the practical aspects with the hope that new medicines and other things can be developed for our own civilization."

Schultes's exploits are legendary in the biology department. Once, while gathering South American plant specimens hundreds of miles from civilization, he contracted beri-beri. For forty days he fought creeping paralysis and overwhelming fatigue as he paddled back to a doctor. "It was an extraordinary feat of endurance," says disciple Wade Davis. "He is really one of the last nineteenth-century naturalists."

Hallucinogenic plants are one of Schultes's primary interests. As a Harvard undergraduate in the thirties, he lived with Oklahoma's Kiowa Indians to observe their use of plants. He participated in their peyote ceremonies and wrote his thesis on the hallucinogenic cactus. He has also studied other hallucinogens, such as morning glory seeds, sacred mushrooms, and ayahuasca, a South American vision vine. Schultes's work has led to the development of anesthetics made from curare and alternative sources of natural rubber.

Schultes's main concern these days is the scientific potential of plants in the rapidly disappearing Amazon jungle. "If chemists are going to get material on 80,000 species and then analyze them, they'll never finish the job before the jungle is gone," he says. "The short cut is to find out what the [native] people have learned about the plant properties during many years of living in the very rich flora."

—G.D.G.

---

instead of merely paralyzing the victim, the compound kills him. Sometimes the victim suffocates in the coffin before he can be resurrected. But clearly the potion works well enough often enough to make zombies more than a figment of Haitian imagination.

Analysis of the powder produced another surprise. "When I went down to Haiti originally," says Davis, "my hypothesis was that the formula would contain *concombre zombi,* the 'zombie's cucumber,' which is a *Datura* plant. I thought somehow *Datura* was used in putting people down." *Datura* is a powerful psychoactive plant, found in West Africa as well as other tropical areas and used there in ritual as well as criminal activities. Davis had found *Datura* growing in Haiti. Its popular name suggested the plant was used in creating zombies.

But, says Davis, "there were a lot of problems with the *Datura* hypothesis. Partly it was a question of how the drug was administered. *Datura* would create a stupor in huge doses, but it just wouldn't produce the kind of immobility that was key. These people had to appear dead, and there aren't many drugs that will do that."

One of the ingredients Pierre included in the second formula was a dried fish, a species of puffer or blowfish, common to most parts of the world. It gets its name from its ability to fill itself with water and swell to several times its normal size when threatened by predators. Many of these fish contain a powerful poison known as tetrodotoxin. One of the most powerful nonprotein poisons known to man, tetrodotoxin turned up in every sample of zombie powder that Davis acquired.

Numerous well-documented accounts of puffer fish poisoning exist, but the most famous accounts come from the Orient, where *fugu* fish, a species of puffer, is considered a delicacy. In Japan, special chefs are licensed to prepare *fugu*. The chef removes enough poison to make the fish nonlethal, yet enough remains to create exhilarating physiological effects—tingles up and down the spine, mild prickling of the tongue and lips, euphoria. Several dozen Japanese die each year, having bitten off more than they should have.

"When I got hold of the formula and saw it was the *fugu* fish, that suddenly threw open the whole Japanese literature," says Davis. Case histories of *fugu* poisoning read like accounts of zombification. Victims remain conscious but unable to speak or move. A man who had "died" after eating *fugu* recovered seven days later in the morgue. Several summers ago, another Japanese poisoned by *fugu* revived after he was nailed into his coffin. "Almost all of Narcisse's symptoms correlated. Even strange things such as the fact that he said he was conscious and could hear himself pronounced dead. Stuff that I thought had to be magic, that seemed crazy. But, in fact, that is what people who get *fugu*-fish poisoning experience."

Davis was certain he had solved the mystery. But far from being the end of his investigation, identifying the poison was, in fact, its starting point. "The drug alone didn't make zombies," he explains. "Japanese victims of puffer-fish poisoning don't become zombies, they become poison victims. All the drug could do was set someone up for a whole series of psychological pressures that would be rooted in the culture. I wanted to know why zombification was going on," he says.

He sought a cultural answer, an explanation rooted in the structure and beliefs of Haitian society. Was zombification simply a random criminal activity? He thought not. He had discovered that Clairvius Narcisse and "Ti Femme," a second victim he interviewed, were village pariahs. Ti Femme was regarded as a thief. Narcisse had abandoned his children and deprived his brother of land that was rightfully his. Equally suggestive, Narcisse claimed that his aggrieved brother had sold him to a *bokor,* a voodoo priest who dealt in black magic; he made cryptic reference to having been tried and found guilty by the "masters of the land."

Gathering poisons from various parts of the country, Davis had come into direct contact with the vodoun secret societies. Returning to the anthropological literature on Haiti and pursuing his contacts with informants, Davis came to understand the social matrix within which zombies were created.

Davis's investigations uncovered the importance of the secret societies. These groups trace their origins to the bands of escaped slaves that organized the revolt against the French in the late eighteenth century. Open to both men and women, the societies control specific territories of the country. Their meetings take place at night, and in many rural parts of Haiti the drums and wild celebrations that characterize the gatherings can be heard for miles.

Davis believes the secret societies are responsible for policing their communities, and the threat of zombification is one way they maintain order. Says Davis, "Zombification has a material basis, but it also has a societal logic." To the uninitiated, the practice may appear a random criminal activity, but in rural vodoun society, it is exactly the opposite—a sanction imposed by recognized authorities, a form of capital punishment. For rural Haitians, zombification is an even more severe punishment than death, because it deprives the subject of his most valued possessions: his free will and independence.

The vodounists believe that when a person dies, his spirit splits into several different parts. If a priest is powerful enough, the spiritual aspect that controls a person's character and individuality, known as *ti bon ange,* the "good little angel," can be captured and the corporeal aspect, deprived of its will, held as a slave.

From studying the medical literature on tetrodotoxin poisoning, Davis discovered that if a victim survives the first few hours of the poisoning, he is likely to recover fully from the ordeal. The subject simply revives spontaneously. But zombies remain without will, in a trance-like state, a condition vodounists attribute to the power of the priest. Davis thinks it possible that the psychological trauma of zombification may be augmented by *Datura* or some other drug; he thinks zombies may be fed a *Datura* paste that accentuates their disorientation. Still, he puts the material basis of zombification in perspective: "Tetrodotoxin and *Datura* are only templates on which cultural forces and beliefs may be amplified a thousand times."

Davis has not been able to discover how prevalent zombification is in Haiti. "How many zombies there are is not the question," he says. He compares it to capital punishment in the United States: "It doesn't really matter how many people are electrocuted, as long as it's a possibility." As a sanction in Haiti, the fear is not of zombies, it's of becoming one.

Davis attributes his success in solving the zombie mystery to his approach. He went to Haiti with an open mind and immersed himself in the culture. "My intuition unhindered by biases served me well," he says. "I didn't make any judgments." He combined this attitude with what he had learned earlier from his experiences in the Amazon. "Schultes's lesson is to go and live with the Indians as an Indian." Davis was able to participate in the vodoun society to a surprising degree, eventually even penetrating one of the Bizango societies and dancing in their nocturnal rituals. His appreciation of Haitian culture is apparent. "Everybody asks me how did a white person get this information? To ask the question means you don't understand Haitians—they don't judge you by the color of your skin."

As a result of the exotic nature of his discoveries, Davis has gained a certain notoriety. He plans to complete his dissertation soon, but he has already finished writing a popular account of his adventures. To be published in January by Simon and Schuster, it is called *The Serpent and the Rainbow,* after the serpent that vodounists believe created the earth and the rainbow spirit it married. Film rights have already been optioned; in October Davis went back to Haiti with a screenwriter. But Davis takes the notoriety in stride. "All this attention is funny," he says. "For years, not just me, but all Schultes's students have had extraordinary adventures in the line of work. The adventure is not the end point, it's just along the way of getting the data. At the Botanical Museum, Schultes created a world unto itself. We didn't think we were doing anything above the ordinary. I still don't think we do. And you know," he adds, "the Haiti episode does not begin to compare to what others have accomplished—particularly Schultes himself."

Critical Thinking

1. What were the circumstances of Clairvius Narcisse's disappearance for eighteen years and what makes this case of "zombification" unique?

2. Describe and explain the cohesion of Haitian society.

3. Describe voodoo and its place in Haitian society.

4. How is the poison used and what are its effects on the victim? Why does it come with no guarantee?

5. What is the one ingredient which turns up in all of the formulas and where does it come from? How and why is this poison used in Japan? What effects have been observed there?

6. What is the "cultural answer" to the zombie mystery? Describe the secret societies and their importance in maintaining order.

7. Why is zombification seen as a punishment more severe than death?

8. How do the priests continue their control over the individual after the effects of tetrodotoxin have worn off, according to Davis?

9. Is it important that there be a lot of zombies in Haiti for social control to be achieved?

Create Central

www.mhhe.com/createcentral

Internet References

Journal of Anthropology of Religion
www.mehtapress.com/social-science-a-humanities/
journal-of-anthropology-of-religion.html

Magic and Religion
http://anthro.palomar.edu/religion/default.htm

Gino Del Guercio is a national science writer for United Press International.

Article   Prepared by: Elvio Angeloni, *Pasadena City College*

The Great New England Vampire Panic

Two hundred years after the Salem witch trials, farm communities became convinced that their dearly departed relatives were returning from the grave to feed on the living.

ABIGAIL TUCKER

Learning Outcomes

After reading this article, you will be able to:

- Describe the Great New England Vampire Panic of the 19th century.

- Explain the medical, communal, and social forces at work leading up to the Great New England Vampire Panic.

Children playing near a hillside gravel mine found the first graves. One ran home to tell his mother, who was skeptical at first—until the boy produced a skull.

Because this was Griswold, Connecticut, in 1990, police initially thought the burials might be the work of a local serial killer named Michael Ross, and they taped off the area as a crime scene. But the brown, decaying bones turned out to be more than a century old. The Connecticut state archaeologist, Nick Bellantoni, soon determined that the hillside contained a colonial-era farm cemetery. New England is full of such unmarked family plots, and the 29 burials were typical of the 1700s and early 1800s: The dead, many of them children, were laid to rest in thrifty Yankee style, in simple wood coffins, without jewelry or even much clothing, their arms resting by their sides or crossed over their chests.

Except, that is, for Burial Number 4. Bellantoni was interested in the grave even before the excavation began. It was one of only two stone crypts in the cemetery, and it was partially visible from the mine face.

Scraping away soil with flat-edged shovels, and then brushes and bamboo picks, the archaeologist and his team worked through several feet of earth before reaching the top of the crypt. When Bellantoni lifted the first of the large, flat rocks that formed the roof, he uncovered the remains of a red-painted coffin and a pair of skeletal feet. They lay, he remembers, "in perfect anatomical position." But when he raised the next stone, Bellantoni saw that the rest of the individual "had been completely . . . rearranged." The skeleton had been beheaded; skull and thighbones rested atop the ribs and vertebrae. "It looked like a skull-and-cross-bones motif, a Jolly Roger. I'd never seen anything like it," Bellantoni recalls.

Subsequent analysis showed that the beheading, along with other injuries, including rib fractures, occurred roughly five years after death. Somebody had also smashed the coffin.

The other skeletons in the gravel hillside were packaged for reburial, but not "J.B.," as the 50ish male skeleton from the 1830s came to be called, because of the initials spelled out in brass tacks on his coffin lid. He was shipped to the National Museum of Health and Medicine, in Washington, D.C., for further study. Meanwhile, Bellantoni started networking. He invited archaeologists and historians to tour the excavation, soliciting theories. Simple vandalism seemed unlikely, as did robbery, because of the lack of valuables at the site.

Finally, one colleague asked: "Ever heard of the Jewett City vampires?"

In 1854, in neighboring Jewett City, Connecticut, townspeople had exhumed several corpses suspected to be vampires that were rising from their graves to kill the living. A few newspaper accounts of these events survived. Had the Griswold grave been desecrated for the same reason?

In the course of his far-flung research, Bellantoni placed a serendipitous phone call to Michael Bell, a Rhode Island folklorist, who had devoted much of the previous decade to studying New England vampire exhumations. The Griswold case occurred at roughly the same time as the other incidents Bell had investigated. And the setting was right: Griswold was rural, agrarian and bordering southern Rhode Island, where multiple exhumations had occurred. Many of the other "vampires," like J.B., had been disinterred, grotesquely tampered with and reburied.

In light of the tales Bell told of violated corpses, even the posthumous rib fractures began to make sense. J.B.'s accusers had likely rummaged around in his chest cavity, hoping to remove, and perhaps to burn, his heart.

Headquartered in a charming old schoolhouse, the Middletown Historical Society typically promotes such fortifying topics as Rhode Island gristmill restoration and Stone Wall Appreciation Day. Two nights before Halloween, though, the atmosphere is full of dry ice vapors and high silliness. Fake cobwebs cover the exhibits, warty gourds crowd the shelves and a skeleton with keen red eyes cackles in the corner. "We'll turn him off when you start talking," the society's president assures Michael Bell, who is readying his slide show.

Bell smiles. Although he lectures across the country and has taught at colleges, including Brown University, he is used to people having fun with his scholarship. "Vampires have gone from a source of fear to a source of entertainment," he says, a bit rueful. "Maybe I shouldn't trivialize entertainment, but to me it's not anywhere as interesting as what really happened." Bell's daughter, 37-year-old Gillian, a member of the audience that night, has made futile attempts to tempt her father with the Twilight series, but "there's Buffy and Twilight, and then there's what my dad does," she says. "I try to get him interested in the pop culture stuff, but he wants to keep his mind pure." Indeed, Bell seems only mildly aware that the vampire—appearing everywhere from *True Blood* to *The Vampire Diaries*—has once again sunk its fangs into the cultural jugular. As far as he's concerned, the undead are always with us.

Bell wears his hair in a sleek silver bob and has a strong Roman nose, but his extremely lean physique is evidence of a long-distance running habit, not some otherworldly hunger. He favors black sweaters and leather jackets, an ensemble he can easily accentuate with dark sunglasses to fit in with the goth crowd, if research requires it. A consulting folklorist at the Rhode Island Historical Preservation & Heritage Commission for most of his career, Bell has been investigating local vampires for 30 years now—long enough to watch lettering on fragile slate gravestones fade before his eyes and prosperous subdivisions arise beside once-lonely graveyards.

He has documented about 80 exhumations, reaching as far back as the late 1700s and as far west as Minnesota. But most are concentrated in backwoods New England, in the 1800s—startlingly later than the obvious local analogue, the Salem, Massachusetts, witch hunts of the 1690s.

Hundreds more cases await discovery, he believes. "You read an article that describes an exhumation, and they'll describe a similar thing that happened at a nearby town," says Bell, whose book, *Food for the Dead: On the Trail of New England's Vampires,* is seen as the last word on the subject, though he has lately found so many new cases that there's a second book on the way. "The ones that get recorded, and I actually find them, are just the tip of the iceberg."

Almost two decades after J.B.'s grave was discovered, it remains the only intact archaeological clue to the fear that swept the region. Most of the graves are lost to time (and even in the cases where they aren't, unnecessary exhumations are frowned on by the locals). Bell mostly hunts for handwritten records in town hall basements, consults tombstones and old cemetery maps, traces obscure genealogies and interviews descendants. "As a folklorist, I'm interested in recurring patterns in communication and ritual, as well as the stories that accompany these rituals," he says. "I'm interested in how this stuff is learned and carried on and how its meaning changes from group to group, and over time." In part because the events were relatively recent, evidence of historic vampires isn't as scarce as one might imagine. Incredulous city newspaper

reporters dished about the "Horrible Superstition" on front pages. A traveling minister describes an exhumation in his daily log on September 3, 1810. (The "mouldy Specticle," he writes, was a "Solemn Site.") Even Henry David Thoreau mentions an exhumation in his journal on September 29, 1859.

Though scholars today still struggle to explain the vampire panics, a key detail unites them: The public hysteria almost invariably occurred in the midst of savage tuberculosis outbreaks. Indeed, the medical museum's tests ultimately revealed that J.B. had suffered from tuberculosis, or a lung disease very like it. Typically, a rural family contracted the wasting illness, and—even though they often received the standard medical diagnosis—the survivors blamed early victims as "vampires," responsible for preying upon family members who subsequently fell sick. Often an exhumation was called for, to stop the vampire's predations.

The particulars of the vampire exhumations, though, vary widely. In many cases, only family and neighbors participated. But sometimes town fathers voted on the matter, or medical doctors and clergymen gave their blessings or even pitched in. Some communities in Maine and Plymouth, Massachusetts, opted to simply flip the exhumed vampire facedown in the grave and leave it at that. In Connecticut, Rhode Island and Vermont, though, they frequently burned the dead person's heart, sometimes inhaling the smoke as a cure. (In Europe, too, exhumation protocol varied with region: Some beheaded suspected vampire corpses, while others bound their feet with thorns.)

Often these rituals were clandestine, lantern-lit affairs. But, particularly in Vermont, they could be quite public, even festive. One vampire heart was reportedly torched on the Woodstock, Vermont, town green in 1830. In Manchester, hundreds of people flocked to a 1793 heart-burning ceremony at a blacksmith's forge: "Timothy Mead officiated at the altar in the sacrifice to the Demon Vampire who it was believed was still sucking the blood of the then living wife of Captain Burton," an early town history says. "It was the month of February and good sleighing."

Bell attributes the openness of the Vermont exhumations to colonial settlement patterns. Rhode Island has about 260 cemeteries per 100 square miles, versus Vermont's mere 20 per 100 square miles. Rhode Island's cemeteries were small and scattered among private farms, whereas Vermont's tended to be much larger, often located in the center of town. In Vermont, it was much harder to keep a vampire hunt hush-hush.

As satisfying as such mini-theories are, Bell is consumed by larger questions. He wants to understand who the vampires and their accusers were, in death and life. During his Middletown lecture, he displays a picture of a man with salt-and-pepper sideburns and weary eyes: an artist's reconstruction of J.B.'s face, based on his skull. "I start with the assumption that people of past generations were just as intelligent as we are," Bell says. "I look for the logic: Why would they do this? Once you label something 'just a superstition' you lock off all inquiry into something that could have been reasonable. Reasonable is not always rational." He wrote his doctoral dissertation on African American voodoo practitioners in the South who cast love spells and curses; it's hard to imagine a population more different from the flinty, consumptive New Englanders he studies now, but Bell sees strong parallels in how they tried to manipulate the supernatural. "People find themselves in dire situations, where there's no recourse through regular channels," he explains. "The folk system offers an alternative, a choice." Sometimes, superstitions represent the only hope, he says.

The enduring sadness of the vampire stories lies in the fact that the accusers were usually direct kin of the deceased: parents, spouses and their children. "Think about what it would have taken to actually exhume the body of a relative," Bell says.

The tale he always returns to is in many ways the quintessential American vampire story, one of the last cases in New England and the first he investigated as a new PhD coming to Rhode Island in 1981 to direct a folk-life survey of Washington County funded by the National Endowment for the Humanities. History knows the 19-year-old, late-19th-century vampire as Mercy Brown. Her family, though, called her Lena.

Mercy Lena Brown lived in Exeter, Rhode Island— "Deserted Exeter," it was dubbed, or simply "one of the border towns." It was largely a subsistence farming community with barely fertile soil: "rocks, rocks and more rocks," says Sheila Reynolds-Boothroyd, president of the Exeter Historical Association. Farmers heaped stones into tumbledown walls, and rows of corn swerved around the biggest boulders.

In the late 19th century, Exeter, like much of agrarian New England, was even more sparsely populated than usual. Civil War casualties had taken their toll on the community, and the new railroads and the promise of richer land to the west lured young men away. By 1892, the year Lena died, Exeter's population had dipped to just 961, from a high of more than 2,500 in 1820. Farms were abandoned, many of them later to be seized and burned by the government. "Some sections looked like a ghost town," Reynolds-Boothroyd says.

And tuberculosis was harrying the remaining families. "Consumption," as it was called, had started to plague New England in the 1730s, a few decades before the first known vampire scares. By the 1800s, when the scares were at their height, the disease was the leading cause of mortality throughout the Northeast, responsible for almost a quarter of all deaths. It was a terrible end, often drawn out over years: a skyrocketing fever, a hacking, bloody cough and a visible wasting away of the body. "The emaciated figure strikes one with terror," reads one 18th-century description, "the forehead covered with drops of sweat; the cheeks painted with a livid crimson, the eyes sunk . . . the breath offensive, quick and laborious, and the cough so incessant as to scarce allow the wretched sufferer time to tell his complaints." Indeed, Bell says, symptoms "progressed in such a way that it seemed like something was draining the life and blood out of somebody."

People dreaded the disease without understanding it. Though Robert Koch had identified the tuberculosis bacterium in 1882, news of the discovery did not penetrate rural areas for some time, and even if it had, drug treatments wouldn't become available until the 1940s. The year Lena died, one physician blamed

tuberculosis on "drunkenness, and want among the poor." Nineteenth-century cures included drinking brown sugar dissolved in water and frequent horseback riding. "If they were being honest," Bell says, "the medical establishment would have said, 'There's nothing we can do, and it's in the hands of God.'"

The Brown family, living on the eastern edge of town, probably on a modest homestead of 30 or 40 stony acres, began to succumb to the disease in December 1882. Lena's mother, Mary Eliza, was the first. Lena's sister, Mary Olive, a 20-year-old dressmaker, died the next year. A tender obituary from a local newspaper hints at what she endured: "The last few hours she lived was of great suffering, yet her faith was firm and she was ready for the change." The whole town turned out for her funeral, and sang "One Sweetly Solemn Thought," a hymn that Mary Olive herself had selected.

Within a few years, Lena's brother Edwin—a store clerk whom one newspaper columnist described as "a big, husky young man"—sickened too, and left for Colorado Springs hoping that the climate would improve his health.

Lena, who was just a child when her mother and sister died, didn't fall ill until nearly a decade after they were buried. Her tuberculosis was the "galloping" kind, which meant that she might have been infected but remained asymptomatic for years, only to fade fast after showing the first signs of the disease. A doctor attended her in "her last illness," a newspaper said, and "informed her father that further medical aid was useless." Her January 1892 obituary was much terser than her sister's: "Miss Lena Brown, who has been suffering from consumption, died Sunday morning."

As Lena was on her deathbed, her brother was, after a brief remission, taking a turn for the worse. Edwin had returned to Exeter from the Colorado resorts "in a dying condition," according to one account. "If the good wishes and prayers of his many friends could be realized, friend Eddie would speedily be restored to perfect health," another newspaper wrote.

But some neighbors, likely fearful for their own health, weren't content with prayers. Several approached George Brown, the children's father, and offered an alternative take on the recent tragedies: Perhaps an unseen diabolical force was preying on his family. It could be that one of the three Brown women wasn't dead after all, instead secretly feasting "on the living tissue and blood of Edwin," as the *Providence Journal* later summarized. If the offending corpse—the Journal uses the term "vampire" in some stories but the locals seemed not to—was discovered and destroyed, then Edwin would recover. The neighbors asked to exhume the bodies, in order to check for fresh blood in their hearts.

George Brown gave permission. On the morning of March 17, 1892, a party of men dug up the bodies, as the family doctor and a Journal correspondent looked on. George was absent, for unstated but understandable reasons.

After nearly a decade, Lena's sister and mother were barely more than bones. Lena, though, had been dead only a few months, and it was wintertime. "The body was in a fairly well-preserved state," the correspondent later wrote. "The heart and liver were removed, and in cutting open the heart, clotted and decomposed blood was found." During this impromptu autopsy, the doctor again emphasized that Lena's lungs "showed diffuse tuberculous germs."

Undeterred, the villagers burned her heart and liver on a nearby rock, feeding Edwin the ashes. He died less than two months later.

So-called vampires do escape the grave in at least one real sense: through stories. Lena Brown's surviving relatives saved local newspaper clippings in family scrapbooks, alongside carefully copied recipes. They discussed the events on Decoration Day, when Exeter residents adorned the town's cemeteries.

But the tale traveled much farther than they knew.

Even at the time, New England's vampire panics struck onlookers as a baffling anachronism. The late 1800s were a period of social progress and scientific flowering. Indeed, many of the Rhode Island exhumations occurred within 20 miles of Newport, high society's summer nucleus, where the scions of the industrial revolution vacationed. At first, only people who'd lived in or had visited the vampire-ridden communities knew about the scandal: "We seem to have been transported back to the darkest age of unreasoning ignorance and blind superstition, instead of living in the 19th century, and in a State calling itself enlightened and Christian," one writer at a small-town Connecticut paper opined in the wake of an 1854 exhumation.

But Lena Brown's exhumation made news. First, a reporter from the *Providence Journal* witnessed her unearthing. Then a well-known anthropologist named George Stetson traveled to Rhode Island to probe "the barbaric superstition" in the surrounding area.

Published in the venerable *American Anthropologist* journal, Stetson's account of New England's vampires made waves throughout the world. Before long, even members of the foreign press were offering various explanations for the phenomenon: Perhaps the "neurotic" modern novel was driving the New England madness, or maybe shrewd local farmers had simply been pulling Stetson's leg. A writer for the *London Post* declared that whatever forces drove the "Yankee vampire," it was an American problem and most certainly not the product of a British folk tradition (even though many families in the area could trace their lineage directly back to England). In the *Boston Daily Globe,* a writer went so far as to suggest that "perhaps the frequent intermarriage of families in these back country districts may partially account for some of their characteristics."

One 1896 *New York World* clipping even found its way into the papers of a London stage manager and aspiring novelist named Bram Stoker, whose theater company was touring the United States that same year. His gothic masterpiece, *Dracula,* was published in 1897. Some scholars have said that there wasn't enough time for the news accounts to have influenced the Dracula manuscript. Yet others see Lena in the character of Lucy (her very name a tempting amalgam of "Lena" and "Mercy"), a consumptive-seeming teenage girl turned vampire, who is exhumed in one of the novel's most memorable scenes. Fascinatingly, a medical doctor presides over Lucy's disinterment, just as one oversaw Lena's.

Whether or not Lucy's roots are in Rhode Island, Lena's historic exhumation is referenced in H.P. Lovecraft's "The Shunned House," a short story about a man being haunted by dead relatives that includes a living character named Mercy.

And, through fiction and fact, Lena's narrative continues today.

Part of Bell's research involves going along on "legend trips," the modern graveside pilgrimages made by those who believe, or want to believe, that the undead stalk Rhode Island. On legend trips, Bell is largely an academic presence. He can even be a bit of a killjoy, declaring that the main reason that "no grass grows on a vampire's grave" is that vampire graves have so many visitors, who crush all the vegetation.

Two days before Halloween, Bell and I head through forests of swamp maple and swamp oak to Exeter. For almost a century after Lena died, the town, still sparsely settled, remained remarkably unchanged. Electric lights weren't installed in the western part of Exeter until the 1940s, and the town had two pound keepers, charged with safekeeping stray cattle and pigs, until 1957. In the 1970s, when I-95 was built, Exeter evolved into an affluent bedroom community of Providence. But visitors still occasionally turn a corner to discover the past: a dirt road cluttered with wild turkeys, or deer hopping over stone fences. Some elderly locals square-dance in barns on the weekends, and streets keep their old names: Sodom Trail, Nooseneck Hill. The white wooden Chestnut Hill Baptist Church in front of Lena's cemetery, built in 1838, has its original blown-glass windows.

An early nor'easter is brewing as we pull into the church parking lot. The heavy rain will soon turn to snow, and there's a bullying wind. Our umbrellas bloom inside out, like black flowers. Though it's a somber place, there's no immediate clue that an accused vampire was buried here. (Except, perhaps, for an unfortunately timed Red Cross blood drive sign in front of the farmer's grange next door.) Unlike Salem, Exeter doesn't promote its dark claim to fame, and remains in some respects an insular community. Old-timers don't like the hooded figures who turn up this time of year, or the cars idling with the lights off. They say the legend should be left alone, perhaps with good reason: Last summer a couple of teenagers were killed on a pilgrimage to Lena's grave when they lost control of their car on Purgatory Road.

Most vampire graves stand apart, in wooded spots outside modern cemetery fences, where snow melts slower and there's a thick understory of ferns. But the Chestnut Hill Cemetery is still in use. And here is Lena. She lies beside the brother who ate her heart, and the father who let it happen. Other markers are freckled with lichen, but not hers. The stone looks to have been recently cleaned. It has been stolen over the years, and now an iron strap anchors it to the earth. People have scratched their names into the granite. They leave offerings: plastic vampire teeth, cough drops. "Once there was a note that said, 'You go, girl,'" Bell says. Today, there's a bunch of trampled daisies, and dangling from the headstone's iron collar, a butterfly charm on a chain.

How did 19th-century Yankees, remembered as the most pious and practical of peoples, come to believe in vampires—especially when the last known vampire panics at the time hadn't occurred since 18th-century Europe? Some modern scholars have linked the legend to vampiric symptoms of diseases like rabies and porphyria (a rare genetic disorder that can cause extreme sensitivity to sunlight and turn teeth reddish-brown). Exeter residents at the time claimed that the exhumations were "a tradition of the Indians."

The legend originated in Slavic Europe, where the word "vampire" first appeared in the tenth century. Bell believes that Slavic and Germanic immigrants brought the vampire superstitions with them in the 1700s, perhaps when Palatine Germans colonized Pennsylvania, or Hessian mercenaries served in the Revolutionary War. "My sense is that it came more than one time through more than one source," he says.

The first known reference to an American vampire scare is a scolding letter to the editor of the *Connecticut Courant and Weekly Intelligencer,* published in June 1784. Councilman Moses Holmes, from the town of Willington, warned people to beware of "a certain Quack Doctor, a foreigner" who had urged families to dig up and burn dead relatives to stop consumption. Holmes had witnessed several children disinterred at the doctor's request and wanted no more of it: "And that the bodies of the dead may rest quiet in their graves without such interruption, I think the public ought to be aware of being led away by such an imposture."

But some modern scholars have argued that the vampire superstition made a certain degree of practical sense. In *Vampires, Burials and Death,* folklorist Paul Barber dissects the logic behind vampire myths, which he believes originally arose from unschooled but astute observations of decay. (Bloated dead bodies appear as if they have recently eaten; a staked corpse "screams" due to the escape of natural gases, etc.) The seemingly bizarre vampire beliefs, Barber argues, get at the essence of contagion: the insight that illness begets illness, and death, death.

Vampire believers "say that death comes to us from invisible agents," Barber says. "We say that death comes to us from invisible agents. The difference is that we can get out a microscope and look at the agents."

While New England's farmers may have been guided by something like reason, the spiritual climate of the day was also hospitable to vampire rumors. Contrary to their Puritanical reputation, rural New Englanders in the 1800s were a fairly heathen lot. Only about 10 percent belonged to a church. Rhode Island, originally founded as a haven for religious dissenters, was particularly lax: Christian missionaries were at various points dispatched there from more godly communities. "The missionaries come back and lament that there's no Bible in the home, no church-going whatsoever," says Linford Fisher, a Brown University colonial historian. "You have people out there essentially in cultural isolation." Mary Olive, Lena's sister, joined a church just two weeks before she died, her obituary said.

In place of organized worship, superstitions reigned: magical springs with healing powers, dead bodies that bled in the presence of their murderers. People buried shoes by fireplaces, to catch the Devil if he tried to come down the chimney. They nailed horseshoes above doors to ward off evil and carved daisy wheels, a kind of colonial hex sign, into the door frames.

If superstition likely fanned the vampire panics, perhaps the most powerful forces at play were communal and social. By 1893, there were just 17 people per square mile in Exeter. A fifth of the farms were fully abandoned, the fields turning slowly back into forest. In her monograph *The New England Vampire Belief: Image of the Decline,* gothic literature scholar Faye Ringel Hazel hints at a vampire metaphor behind the westward hemorrhage: The migration "seemed to drain rural New England of its most enterprising young citizens, leaving the old and unfit behind."

As Exeter teetered near collapse, maintaining social ties must have taken on new importance. An exhumation represented, first and foremost, a duty to one's own kin, dead or dying: the ritual "would alleviate the guilt someone might feel for not doing everything they could do to save a family, to leave no stone unturned," Bell says.

Even more significant, in small communities where disease could spread quickly, an exhumation was "an outward display that you are doing everything you can to fix the problem." Residents of the already beleaguered town were likely terrified. "They knew that if consumption wiped out the Brown family, it could take out the next family," Bell says. "George Brown was being entreated by the community." He had to make a gesture.

The strongest testament to the power of the vampire myth is that George Brown did not, in fact, believe in it, according to the *Providence Journal.* It was he who asked a doctor to perform an autopsy at the graveyard, and he who elected to be elsewhere during the ritual. He authorized his loved ones' exhumation, the Journal says, simply to "satisfy the neighbors," who were, according to another newspaper account, "worrying the life out of him"—a description with its own vampiric overtones.

Perhaps it was wise to let them have their way, since George Brown, apparently not prone to tuberculosis, had to coexist with his neighbors well into the next century. He died in 1922.

Relatives of the Browns still live in Exeter and are laid to rest on Chestnut Hill. Some, planning ahead, have erected their grave markers. It can be disconcerting to drive past somebody's tombstone on the way to his or her home for a vampire-oriented interview.

On a sunny Halloween morning, when Bell has left for a vampire folklore conference at the University of London, I return to the cemetery to meet several Brown descendants at the farmer's grange. They bring, swaddled in old sheets, a family treasure: a quilt that Lena sewed.

We spread it out on a scarred wooden table. The cotton bedspread is pink, blue and cream. What look from a distance like large patches of plain brown fabric are really fields of tiny daisies.

It's the work of a farm girl, without any wasteful appliqué; Lena clearly ran out of material in places and had to scrimp for more. Textile scholars at the University of Rhode Island have traced her snippets of florals, plaid and paisley to the 1870s and 1880s, when Lena was still a child; they wondered if she used her sister's and mother's old dresses for the project. Perhaps her mother's death, too, explains Lena's quilting abilities, which are considerable for a teenager: She might have had to learn household skills before other girls. The quilt is in immaculate condition and was likely being saved for something—Lena's hope chest, thinks her distant descendant Dorothy O'Neil, one of the quilt's recent custodians, and a knowledgeable quilter herself.

"I think the quilt is exquisite, especially in light of what she went through in her life," O'Neil says. "She ended up leaving something beautiful. She didn't know she'd have to leave it, but she did."

Lena hasn't left entirely. She is said to frequent a certain bridge, manifested as the smell of roses. She appears in children's books and paranormal television specials. She murmurs in the cemetery, say those who leave tape recorders there to capture her voice. She is rumored to visit the terminally ill, and to tell them that dying isn't so bad.

The quilt pattern that Lena used, very rare in Rhode Island, is sometimes called the Wandering Foot, and it carried a superstition of its own: Anybody who slept under it, the legend said, would be lost to her family, doomed to wander.

Critical Thinking

1. How has folklorist Michael Bell been able to accumulate evidence for vampire exhumations in New England?

2. How is vampire exhumation related to the incidence of tuberculosis? Be aware the details of exhumation varied.

3. Why were Vermont's exhumations more public as opposed to those of Rhode Island?

4. Why does Bell dismiss the notions that the vampire exhumers were not as as intelligent as we are and that they were simply "superstitious" and not reasonable?

5. What is the "enduring sadness" of the vampire stories? How does the case of Mercy Lena Brown and her family illustrate the point?

6. How did 19th-century Yankees come to believe in vampires?

7. In what respects did vampire beliefs make "a certain degree of practical sense"?

8. How was the spiritual climate of the day hospitable to vampire rumors? What were the communal and social forces at work?

Create Central

www.mhhe.com/createcentral

Internet References

Journal of Anthropology of Religion
www.mehtapress.com/social-science-a-humanities/journal-of-anthropolog-yof-religion.html

Yahoo: Society and Culture: Death
http://dir.yahoo.com/Society_and_Culture/Death_and_Dying

Article

Prepared by: Elvio Angeloni, *Pasadena City College*

Body Ritual among the Nacirema

Horace Miner

Learning Outcomes

After reading this article, you will be able to:

- Discuss the role of rituals and taboos in our modern industrial society.
- Discuss the ways in which this article serves as a cautionary note in interpreting other people's customs.

The anthropologist has become so familiar with the diversity of ways in which different peoples behave in similar situations that he is not apt to be surprised by even the most exotic customs. In fact, if all of the logically possible combinations of behavior have not been found somewhere in the world, he is apt to suspect that they must be present in some yet undescribed tribe. This point has, in fact, been expressed with respect to clan organization by Murdock (1949: 71). In this light, the magical beliefs and practices of the Nacirema present such unusual aspects that it seems desirable to describe them as an example of the extremes to which human behavior can go.

Professor Linton first brought the ritual of the Nacirema to the attention of anthropologists twenty years ago (1936: 326), but the culture of this people is still very poorly understood. They are a North American group living in the territory between the Canadian Cree, the Yaqui and Tarahumare of Mexico, and the Carib and Arawak of the Antilles. Little is known of their origin, though tradition states that they came from the east. According to Nacirema mythology, their nation was originated by a culture hero, Notgnishaw, who is otherwise known for two great feats of strength—the throwing of a piece of wampum across the river Pa-To-Mac and the chopping down of a cherry tree in which the Spirit of Truth resided.

Nacirema culture is characterized by a highly developed market economy which has evolved in a rich natural habitat. While much of the people's time is devoted to economic pursuits, a large part of the fruits of these labors and a considerable portion of the day are spent in ritual activity. The focus of this activity is the human body, the appearance and health of which loom as a dominant concern in the ethos of the people. While such a concern is certainly not unusual, its ceremonial aspects and associated philosophy are unique.

The fundamental belief underlying the whole system appears to be that the human body is ugly and that its natural tendency is to debility and disease. Incarcerated in such a body, man's only hope is to avert these characteristics through the use of the powerful influences of ritual and ceremony. Every household has one or more shrines devoted to this purpose. The more powerful individuals in the society have several shrines in their houses and, in fact, the opulence of a house is often referred to in terms of the number of such ritual centers it possesses. Most houses are of wattle and daub construction, but the shrine rooms of the more wealthy are walled with stone. Poorer families imitate the rich by applying pottery plaques to their shrine walls.

While each family has at least one such shrine, the rituals associated with it are not family ceremonies but are private and secret. The rites are normally only discussed with children, and then only during the period when they are being initiated into these mysteries. I was able, however, to establish sufficient rapport with the natives to examine these shrines and to have the rituals described to me.

The focal point of the shrine is a box or chest which is built into the wall. In this chest are kept the many charms and magical potions without which no native believes he could live. These preparations are secured from a variety of specialized practitioners. The most powerful of these are the medicine men, whose assistance must be rewarded with substantial gifts. However, the medicine men do not provide the curative potions for their clients, but decide what the ingredients should be and then write them down in an ancient and secret language. This writing is understood only by the medicine men and by the herbalists who, for another gift, provide the required charm.

The charm is not disposed of after it has served its purpose, but is placed in the charm-box of the household shrine. As these magical materials are specific for certain ills, and the real or imagined maladies of the people are many, the charm-box is usually full to overflowing. The magical packets are so numerous that people forget what their purposes were and fear to use them again. While the natives are very vague on this point, we can only assume that the idea in retaining all the old magical materials is that their presence in the charm-box, before which the body rituals are conducted, will in some way protect the worshipper.

Beneath the charm-box is a small font. Each day every member of the family, in succession, enters the shrine room, bows his head before the charm-box, mingles different sorts of holy water in the font, and proceeds with a brief rite of ablution. The holy waters are secured from the Water Temple of the community, where the priests conduct elaborate ceremonies to make the liquid ritually pure.

In the hierarchy of magical practitioners, and below the medicine men in prestige, are specialists whose designation is best translated "holy-mouth-men." The Nacirema have an almost pathological horror and fascination with the mouth, the condition of which is believed to have a supernatural influence on all social relationships. Were it not for the rituals of the mouth, they believe that their teeth would fall out, their gums bleed, their jaws shrink, their friends desert them, and their lovers reject them. (They also believe that a strong relationship exists between oral and moral characteristics. For example, there is a ritual ablution of the mouth for children which is supposed to improve their moral fiber.)

The daily body ritual performed by everyone includes a mouth-rite. Despite the fact that these people are so punctilious about care of the mouth, this rite involves a practice which strikes the uninitiated stranger as revolting. It was reported to me that the ritual consists of inserting a small bundle of hog hairs into the mouth, along with certain magical powders, and then moving the bundle in a highly formalized series of gestures.

In addition to the private mouth-rite, the people seek out a holy-mouth-man once or twice a year. These practitioners have an impressive set of paraphernalia, consisting of a variety of augers, awls, probes, and prods. The use of these objects in the exorcism of the evils of the mouth involves almost unbelievable ritual torture of the client. The holy-mouth-man opens the client's mouth and, using the above mentioned tools, enlarges any holes which decay may have created in the teeth. Magical materials are put into these holes. If there are no naturally occurring holes in the teeth, large sections of one or more teeth are gouged out so that the supernatural substance can be applied. In the client's view, the purpose of these ministrations is to arrest decay and to draw friends. The extremely sacred and traditional character of the rite is evident in the fact that the natives return to the holy-mouth-men year after year, despite the fact that their teeth continue to decay.

It is to be hoped that, when a thorough study of the Nacirema is made, there will be a careful inquiry into the personality structure of these people. One has but to watch the gleam in the eye of a holy-mouth-man, as he jabs an awl into an exposed nerve, to suspect that a certain amount of sadism is involved. If this can be established, a very interesting pattern emerges, for most of the population shows definite masochistic tendencies. It was to these that Professor Linton referred in discussing a distinctive part of the daily body ritual which is performed only by men. This part of the rite involves scraping and lacerating the surface of the face with a sharp instrument. Special women's rites are performed only four times during each lunar month, but what they lack in frequency is made up in barbarity. As part of this ceremony, women bake their heads in small ovens for about an hour. The theoretically interesting point is that what seems to be a preponderantly masochistic people have developed sadistic specialists.

The medicine men have an imposing temple, or *latipso*, in every community of any size. The more elaborate ceremonies required to treat very sick patients can only be performed at this temple. These ceremonies involve not only the thaumaturge but a permanent group of vestal maidens who move sedately about the temple chambers in distinctive costume and headdress.

The *latipso* ceremonies are so harsh that it is phenomenal that a fair proportion of the really sick natives who enter the temple ever recover. Small children whose indoctrination is still incomplete have been known to resist attempts to take them to the temple because "that is where you go to die." Despite this fact, sick adults are not only willing but eager to undergo the protracted ritual purification, if they can afford to do so. No matter how ill the supplicant or how grave the emergency, the guardians of many temples will not admit a client if he cannot give a rich gift to the custodian. Even after one has gained admission and survived the ceremonies, the guardians will not permit the neophyte to leave until he makes still another gift.

The supplicant entering the temple is first stripped of all his or her clothes. In every-day life the Nacirema avoids exposure of his body and its natural functions. Bathing and excretory acts are performed only in the secrecy of the household shrine, where they are ritualized as part of the body-rites. Psychological shock results from the fact that body secrecy is suddenly lost upon entry into the *latipso*. A man, whose own wife has never seen him in an excretory act, suddenly finds himself naked and assisted by a vestal maiden while he performs his natural functions into a sacred vessel. This sort of ceremonial treatment is necessitated by the fact that the excreta are used by a diviner to ascertain the course and nature of the client's sickness. Female clients, on the other hand, find their naked bodies are subjected to the scrutiny, manipulation, and prodding of the medicine men.

Few supplicants in the temple are well enough to do anything but lie on their hard beds. The daily ceremonies, like the rites of the holy-mouth-men, involve discomfort and torture. With ritual precision, the vestals awaken their miserable charges each dawn and roll them about on their beds of pain while performing ablutions, in the formal movements of which the maidens are highly trained. At other times they insert magic wands in the supplicant's mouth or force him to eat substances which are supposed to be healing. From time to time the medicine men come to their clients and jab magically treated needles into their flesh. The fact that these temple ceremonies may not cure, and may even kill the neophyte, in no way decreases the people's faith in the medicine men.

There remains one other kind of practitioner, known as a "listener." This witch-doctor has the power to exorcise the devils that lodge in the heads of people who have been bewitched. The Nacirema believe that parents bewitch their own children. Mothers are particularly suspected of putting a curse on children while teaching them the secret body rituals. The countermagic of the witch-doctor is unusual in its lack of ritual. The patient simply tells the "listener" all his troubles and fears, beginning with the earliest difficulties he can remember. The memory displayed by the Nacirema in these exorcism sessions is truly remarkable. It is not uncommon for the patient to bemoan the rejection he felt upon being weaned as a babe, and a few individuals even see their troubles going back to the traumatic effects of their own birth.

In conclusion, mention must be made of certain practices which have their base in native esthetics but which depend upon the pervasive aversion to the natural body and its functions. There are ritual fasts to make fat people thin and ceremonial feasts to make thin people fat. Still other rites are used to make women's breasts large if they are small, and smaller if they are large. General dissatisfaction with breast shape is symbolized in the fact that the ideal form is virtually outside the range of human variation. A few women afflicted with almost inhuman hypermammary development are so idolized that they make a handsome living by simply going from village to village and permitting the natives to stare at them for a fee.

Reference has already been made to the fact that excretory functions are ritualized, routinized, and relegated to secrecy. Natural reproductive functions are similarly distorted. Intercourse is taboo as a topic and scheduled as an act. Efforts are made to avoid pregnancy by the use of magical materials or by limiting intercourse to certain phases of the moon. Conception is actually very infrequent. When pregnant, women dress so as to hide their condition. Parturition takes place in secret, without friends or relatives to assist, and the majority of women do not nurse their infants.

Our review of the ritual life of the Nacirema has certainly shown them to be a magic-ridden people. It is hard to understand how they have managed to exist so long under the burdens which they have imposed upon themselves. But even such exotic customs as these take on real meaning when they are viewed with the insight provided by Malinowski when he wrote (1948:70):

> Looking from far and above, from our high places of safety in the developed civilization, it is easy to see all the crudity and irrelevance of magic. But without its power and guidance early man could not have mastered his practical difficulties as he has done, nor could man have advanced to the higher stages of civilization.

References

Linton, Ralph. 1936. *The Study of Man.* New York, D. Appleton-Century Co.

Malinowski, Bronislaw. 1948. *Magic, Science, and Religion.* Glencoe, The Free Press.

Murdock, George P. 1949. *Social Structure.* New York, The Macmillan Co.

Critical Thinking

1. What is "Nacirema" spelled backwards? Where are they actually located on a map? Who are they, really?

2. Why do the customs of the Nacirema seem so bizarre when they are written about in anthropological style?

3. Having read the article, do you view American culture any differently than you did before? If so, how?

4. Has this article helped you to view other cultures differently? If so, how?

5. If this article has distorted the picture of American culture, how difficult is it for all of us, anthropologists included, to render objective descriptions of other cultures?

Create Central

www.mhhe.com/createcentral

Internet References

Apologetics Index
www.apologeticsindex.org/site/index-c

Journal of Anthropology of Religion
www.mehtapress.com/social-science-a-humanities/
journal-of-anthropology-of-religion.html

Magic and Religion
http://anthro.palomar.edu/religion/default.htm

Miner, Horace. From *American Anthropologist,* by Horace Miner, June 1956, pp. 503–507.

Unit 7

UNIT

Prepared by: Elvio Angeloni, *Pasadena City College*

Sociocultural Change

The origins of academic anthropology lie in the colonial and imperial ventures of the past five hundred years. During this period, many people of the world were brought into a relationship with Europe and the United States that was usually exploitative and often socially and culturally disruptive. For over a century, anthropologists have witnessed this process and the transformations that have taken place in those social and cultural systems brought under the umbrella of a world economic order. Early anthropological studies—even those widely regarded as pure research—directly or indirectly served colonial interests. Many anthropologists certainly believed that they were extending the benefits of Western technology and society, while preserving the cultural rights of those people whom they studied. But representatives of poor nations challenge this view and are far less generous in describing the past role of the anthropologist. Most contemporary anthropologists, however, have a deep moral commitment to defending the legal, political, and economic rights of the people with whom they work.

When anthropologists discuss social change, they usually mean the change brought about in pre-industrial societies through longstanding interaction with the nation-states of the industrialized world. In early anthropology, contact between the West and the remainder of the world was characterized by the terms *acculturation* and *culture contact.* These terms were used to describe the diffusion of cultural traits between the developed and the less-developed countries. Often this was analyzed as a one-way process, in which cultures of the less-developed world were seen, for better or worse, as receptacles for Western cultural traits. Nowadays, many anthropologists believe that the diffusion of cultural traits across social, political, and economic boundaries was emphasized at the expense of the real issues of dominance, subordination, and dependence that characterized the colonial experience. Just as important, many anthropologists recognize that the present-day forms of cultural, economic, and political interaction between the developed and the so-called underdeveloped world are best characterized as neocolonial. They take the perspective that anthropology should be critical as well as descriptive and they raise questions about cultural contact and subsequent economic and social disruption.

None of this is to say that indigenous peoples can or even should be left entirely alone to live in isolation from the rest of the world. A much more sensible, as well as more practical, approach would involve some degree of self-determination and considerably more respect for their cultures.

Of course, traditional peoples are not the only losers in the process of technological "progress" and cultural destruction. The very same climate change that now seems to be flooding some of the low-lying Pacific islands may also be causing the most highly destructive hurricanes ever to hit the American coasts such as Katrina and Sandy and should be taken as a warning to the rest of us. The more we deprive the traditional stewards (the Indigenous peoples) of their land, the greater the loss in overall biodiversity.

Finally, all of humanity stands to suffer as resources dwindle and as a vast store of human knowledge—embodied in tribal subsistence practices, language, medicine, and folklore—is obliterated, in a manner not unlike the burning of the library of Alexandria 1,600 years ago. We can only hope that it is not too late to save what is left.

Article   Prepared by: Elvio Angeloni, *Pasadena City College*

Ruined

MICHAEL MARSHALL

Learning Outcomes

After reading this article, you will be able to:

- Discuss the relationship between climate change and the decline of civilizations in the past.

- Discuss the prospects of societal collapse as a result of climate change in the modern world.

The most beautiful woman in the world, Helen, is abducted by Paris of Troy. A Greek fleet of more than a thousand ships sets off in pursuit. After a long war, heroes like Achilles lead the Greeks to victory over Troy.

At least, this is the story told by the poet Homer around four centuries later. Yet Homer was not only writing about events long before his time, he was also describing a long-lost civilization. Achilles and his compatriots were part of the first great Greek civilization, a warlike culture centered on the city of Mycenae that thrived from around 1600 BC.

By 1100 BC, not long after the Trojan War, many of its cities and settlements had been destroyed or abandoned. The survivors reverted to a simpler rural lifestyle. Trade ground to a halt, and skills such as writing were lost. The script the Mycenaeans had used, Linear B, was not read again until 1952.

The region slowly recovered after around 800 BC. The Greeks adopted the Phoenician script, and the great city states of Athens and Sparta rose to power. "The collapse was one of the most important events in history, because it gave birth to two major cultures," says anthropologist Brandon Drake. "It's like the phoenix from the ashes." Classical Greece, as this second period of civilization is known, far outshone its predecessor. Its glory days lasted only a couple of centuries, but the ideas of its citizens were immensely influential. Their legacy is still all around us, from the math we learn in school to the idea of democracy.

But what caused the collapse of Mycenaean Greece, and thus had a huge impact on the course of world history? A change in the climate, according to the latest evidence. What's more, Mycenaean Greece is just one of a growing list of civilizations whose fate is being linked to the vagaries of climate. It seems big swings in the climate, handled badly, brought down whole societies, while smaller changes led to unrest and wars.

The notion that climate change toppled entire civilizations has been around for more than a century, but it was only in the 1990s that it gained a firm footing as researchers began to work out exactly how the climate had changed, using clues buried in lake beds or petrified in stalactites. Harvey Weiss of Yale University set the ball rolling with his studies of the collapse of one of the earliest empires: that of the Akkadians.

It began in the Fertile Crescent of the Middle East, a belt of rich farmland where an advanced regional culture had developed over many centuries. In 2334 BC, Sargon was born in the city state of Akkad. He started out as a gardener, was put in charge of clearing irrigation canals, and went on to seize power. Not content with that, he conquered many neighboring city states, too. The empire Sargon founded thrived for nearly a century after his death before it collapsed.

Excavating in what is now Syria, Weiss found dust deposits suggesting that the region's climate suddenly became drier around 2200 BC. The drought would have led to famine, he argued, explaining why major cities were abandoned at this time (*Science*, vol 261, p. 995). A piece of contemporary writing, called *The Curse of Akkad*, does describe a great famine (see end of article).

Weiss's work was influential, but there wasn't much evidence. In 2000, climatologist Peter deMenocal of Columbia University in New York found more. His team showed, based on modern records going back to 1700, that the flow of the region's two great rivers, the Tigris and the Euphrates, is linked to conditions in the north Atlantic: cooler waters reduce rainfall by altering the paths of weather systems. Next, they discovered that the north Atlantic cooled just before the Akkadian empire fell apart (*Science*, vol 288, p 2198). "To our surprise we got this big whopping signal at the time of the Akkadian collapse."

It soon became clear that major changes in the climate coincided with the untimely ends of several other civilizations. Of these, the Maya became the poster child for climate-induced decline. Mayan society arose in Mexico and Central America around 2000 BC. Its farmers grew maize, squashes and beans, and it was the only American civilization to produce a written language. The Maya endured for millennia, reaching a peak between AD 250 and 800, when they built cities and huge stepped pyramids.

Then the Maya civilization collapsed. Many of its incredible structures were swallowed up by the jungle after being abandoned. Not all was lost, though—Mayan people and elements of their culture survive to the present day.

Numerous studies have shown that there were several prolonged droughts around the time of the civilisation's decline. In 2003, Gerald Haug of the Swiss Federal Institute of Technology in Zurich found it was worse than that. His year-by-year reconstruction based on lake sediments shows that rainfall was abundant from 550 to 750, perhaps leading to a rise in population and thus to the peak of monument-building around 721. But over the next century there were not only periods of particularly severe drought, each lasting years, but also less rain than normal in the intervening years (*Science,* vol 299, p 1731). Monument construction ended during this prolonged dry period, around 830, although a few cities continued on for many centuries.

Even as the evidence grew, there was something of a backlash against the idea that changing climates shaped the fate of civilizations. "Many in the archaeological community are really reticent to accept a role of climate in human history," says deMenocal.

Much of this reluctance is for historical reasons. In the 18th and 19th centuries, anthropologists argued that a society's environment shaped its character, an idea known as environmental determinism. They claimed that the warm, predictable climates of the tropics bred indolence, while cold European climates produced intelligence and a strong work ethic. These ideas were often used to justify racism and exploitation.

Understandably, modern anthropologists resist anything resembling environmental determinism. "It's a very delicate issue," says Ulf Büntgen, also at the Swiss Federal Institute of Technology, whose work suggests the decline of the Western Roman Empire was linked to a period of highly variable weather. "The field is evolving really slowly, because people are afraid to make bold statements."

Yet this resistance is not really warranted, deMenocal says. No one today is claiming that climate determines people's characters, only that it sets limits on what is feasible. When the climate becomes less favorable, less food can be grown. Such changes can also cause plagues of locusts or other pests, and epidemics among people weakened by starvation. When it is no longer feasible to maintain a certain population level and way of life, the result can be collapse. "Climate isn't a determinant, but it is an important factor," says Drake, who is at the University of New Mexico in Albuquerque. "It enables or disables."

Some view even this notion as too simplistic. Karl Butzer of the University of Texas at Austin, who has studied the collapse of civilizations, thinks the role of climate has been exaggerated. It is the way societies handle crises that decides their fate, he says. "Things break through institutional failure." When it comes to the Akkadians, for instance, Butzer says not all records support the idea of a megadrought.

In the case of the Maya, though, the evidence is strong. Earlier this year, Eelco Rohling of the University of Southampton, UK, used lake sediments and isotope ratios in stalactites to work out how rainfall had changed. He concluded that annual rainfall fell 40 per cent over the prolonged dry period, drying up open water sources (*Science,* vol 335, p 956). This would

have seriously affected the Maya, he says, because the water table lay far underground and was effectively out of reach.

So after a century of plentiful rain, the Maya were suddenly confronted with a century of low rainfall. It is not clear how they could have avoided famine and population decline in these circumstances. Even today, our ability to defy hostile climes is limited. Saudi Arabia managed to become self-sufficient in wheat by tapping water reservoirs deep beneath its deserts and subsidising farmers, but is now discouraging farming to preserve what is left of the water. In dry regions where plenty of water is available for irrigation, the build-up of salts in the soil is a serious problem, just as it was for some ancient civilisations. And if modern farmers are still at the mercy of the climate despite all our knowledge and technology, what chance did ancient farmers have?

Greek Dark Ages

While many archaeologists remain unconvinced, the list of possible examples continues to grow. The Mycenaeans are the latest addition. The reason for their downfall has been the subject of much debate, with one of the most popular explanations being a series of invasions and attacks by the mysterious "Sea Peoples." In 2010, though, a study of river deposits in Syria suggested there was a prolonged dry period between 1200 and 850 BC—right at the time of the so-called Greek Dark Ages. Earlier this year, Drake analysed several climate records and concluded that there was a cooling of the Mediterranean at this time, reducing evaporation and rainfall over a huge area.

What's more, several other cultures around the Mediterranean, including the Hittite Empire and the "New Kingdom" of Egypt, collapsed around the same time as the Mycenaeans—a phenomenon known as the late Bronze Age collapse. Were all these civilisations unable to cope with the changing climate? Or were the invading Sea Peoples the real problem? The story could be complex: civilisations weakened by hunger may have become much more vulnerable to invaders, who may themselves have been driven to migrate by the changing climate. Or the collapse of one civilisation could have had knock-on effects on its trading partners.

Climate change on an even greater scale might be behind another striking coincidence. Around 900, as the Mayan civilisation was declining in South America, the Tang dynasty began losing its grip on China. At its height, the Tang ruled over 50 million subjects. Woodblock printing meant that written words, particularly poetry, were widely accessible. But the dynasty fell after local governors usurped its authority.

Since the two civilisations were not trading partners, there was clearly no knock-on effect. A study of lake sediments in China by Haug suggests that this region experienced a prolonged dry period at the same time as that in Central America. He thinks a shift in the tropical rain belt was to blame, causing civilisations to fall apart on either side of the Pacific (*Nature,* vol 445, p 74).

Critics, however, point to examples of climate change that did not lead to collapse. "There was a documented drought and even famines during the period of the Aztec Empire," says archaeologist Gary Feinman of the Field Museum in Chicago. "These episodes caused hardships and possibly even famines, but no overall collapse."

Realizing that case studies of collapses were not enough to settle the debate, in 2005 David Zhang of Hong Kong University began to look for larger patterns. He began with the history of the Chinese dynasties. From 2500 BC until the 20th century, a series of powerful empires like the Tang controlled China. All were eventually toppled by civil unrest or invasions.

When Zhang compared climate records for the last 1200 years to the timeline of China's dynastic wars, the match was striking. Most of the dynastic transitions and periods of social unrest took place when temperatures were a few tenths of a degree colder. Warmer periods were more stable and peaceful (*Chinese Science Bulletin,* vol 50, p 137).

The Thirty Years War

Zhang gradually built up a more detailed picture showing that harvests fell when the climate was cold, as did population levels, while wars were more common. Of 15 bouts of warfare he studied, 12 took place in cooler times. He then looked at records of war across Europe, Asia and North Africa between 1400 and 1900. Once again, there were more wars when the temperatures were lower. Cooler periods also saw more deaths and declines in the population.

These studies suggest that the effects of climate on societies can be profound. The problem is proving it. So what if wars and collapses often coincide with shifts in the climate? It doesn't prove one caused the other. "That's always been the beef," says deMenocal. "It's a completely valid point."

Trying to move beyond mere correlations, Zhang began studying the history of Europe from 1500 to 1800 AD. In the mid-1600s, Europe was plunged into the General Crisis, which coincided with a cooler period called the Little Ice Age. The Thirty Years War was fought then, and many other wars. Zhang analysed detailed records covering everything from population and migration to agricultural yields, wars, famines and epidemics in a bid to identify causal relationships. So, for instance, did climate change affect agricultural production and thus food prices? That in turn might lead to famine—revealed by a reduction in the average height of people—epidemics and a decline in population. High food prices might also lead to migration and social unrest, and even wars.

He then did a statistical analysis known as a Granger causality test, which showed that the proposed causes consistently occurred before the proposed effects, and that each cause was followed by the same effect. The Granger test isn't conclusive proof of causality, but short of rerunning history under different climes, it is about the best evidence there can be (*Proceedings of the National Academy of Sciences,* vol 108, p 17296).

The paper hasn't bowled over the critics. Butzer, for instance, claims it is based on unreliable demographic data. Yet others are impressed. "It's a really remarkable study," deMenocal says. "It does seem like they did their homework." He adds

that such a detailed breakdown is only possible for recent history, because older civilizations left fewer records.

So while further studies should reveal much more about how the climate changed in the past, the debate about how great an effect these changes had on societies is going to rumble on for many more decades. Let's assume, though, that changing climates did play a major role. What does that mean for us? On the face of it, things don't look so bad. It was often cooling that hurt past civilizations. What's more, studies of the past century have found little or no link between conflict and climate change. "Industrialized societies have been more robust against changing climatic conditions," says Jürgen Scheffran of the University of Hamburg, who studies the effects of climate change.

On the other hand, we are triggering the most extreme change for millions of years, and what seems to matter is food production rather than temperature. Production is expected to increase at first as the planet warms, but then begin to decline as warming exceeds 3°C. This point may not be that far away—it is possible that global average temperature will rise by 4°C as early as 2060. We've already seen regional food production hit by extreme heat waves like the one in Russia in 2010. Such extreme heat was not expected until much later this century.

And our society's interconnectedness is not always a strength. It can transmit shocks—the 2010 heat wave sent food prices soaring worldwide, and the drought in the US this year is having a similar effect. The growing complexity of modern society may make us more vulnerable to collapse rather than less.

We do have one enormous advantage, though—unlike the Mycenaeans and the Mayas, we know what's coming. We can prepare for what is to come and also slow the rate of change if we act soon. So far, though, we are doing neither.

The Curse of Akkad

'Look on my works, ye mighty, and despair!' All empires fall, but why?

A great drought did occur at the time this tablet was inscribed

For the first time since cities were built and founded,

The great agricultural tracts produced no grain,

The inundated tracts produced no fish,

The irrigated orchards produced neither syrup nor wine,

The gathered clouds did not rain, the masgurum did not grow.

At that time, one shekel's worth of oil was only one-half quart, One shekel's worth of grain was only one-half quart. . . .

These sold at such prices in the markets of all the cities!

He who slept on the roof, died on the roof,

He who slept in the house, had no burial,

People were flailing at themselves from hunger.

Critical Thinking

1. Discuss the causes of the decline of civilizations such as those of the Akkadian Empire and the Maya.

2. Why was there initially a backlash against the idea that changing climates shaped the fate of civilizations? Why is such resistance not warranted?

3. What are some of the specific consequences when the climate becomes less favorable?

4. Why does Karl Butzer view the notion of climate change's impact on civilizations as exaggerated?

5. What is the specific evidence for the impact of climate change on the Maya?

6. What evidence is there that our ability to defy hostile climes is limited even today?

7. Discuss the possible factors for Bronze Age collapse, i.e., the decline of the civilizations of the Mycenaeans (the Greek Dark Ages), the Hittite Empire, and the "New Kingdom" of Egypt.

8. What is the significance of the "striking coincidence" of the simultaneous collapse of the Tang dynasty in China and the Mayan civilization?

9. In what respect are the Aztecs an exception?

10. What do the climate records say about China's dynastic wars and transitions? About wars in Europe, Asia, and North Africa?

11. How was David Zhang able to "move beyond mere correlations" by using the "Granger causality test" with respect to the effects of climate change in Europe?

12. Why does there seem to have been little or no link between conflict and climate change over the past century?

13. Why might we become more vulnerable to collapse rather than less?

14. What is the one "enormous advantage" that we have today?

Create Central

www.mhhe.com/createcentral

Internet References

Murray Research Center
www.radcliffe.edu/murray_redirect/index.php

Small Planet Institute
www.smallplanet.org/food

MICHAEL MARSHALL is an environment reporter for *New Scientist*.

Marshall, Michael. From *New Scientist Magazine*, vol. 215, no. 2876, August 4, 2012, pp. 32–36. Copyright © 2012 by Reed Business Information, Ltd, UK. Reprinted by permission via Tribune Media Services.

Article   Prepared by: Elvio Angeloni, *Pasadena City College*

The Arrow of Disease

When Columbus and his successors invaded the Americas, the most potent weapon they carried was their germs. But why didn't deadly disease flow in the other direction, from the New World to the Old?

JARED DIAMOND

Learning Outcomes

After reading this article, you will be able to:

- Discuss the biological and social circumstances of disease transmission from animals to humans.

- Explain the "one-sidedness" to the disease transmission from Europeans to Native Americans.

The three people talking in the hospital room were already stressed out from having to cope with a mysterious illness, and it didn't help at all that they were having trouble communicating. One of them was the patient, a small, timid man, sick with pneumonia caused by an unidentified microbe and with only a limited command of the English language. The second, acting as translator, was his wife, worried about her husband's condition and frightened by the hospital environment. The third person in the trio was an inexperienced young doctor, trying to figure out what might have brought on the strange illness. Under the stress, the doctor was forgetting everything he had been taught about patient confidentiality. He committed the awful blunder of requesting the woman to ask her husband whether he'd had any sexual experiences that might have caused the infection.

As the young doctor watched, the husband turned red, pulled himself together so that he seemed even smaller, tried to disappear under his bed sheets, and stammered in a barely audible voice. His wife suddenly screamed in rage and drew herself up to tower over him. Before the doctor could stop her, she grabbed a heavy metal bottle, slammed it onto her husband's head, and stormed out of the room. It took a while for the doctor to elicit, through the man's broken English, what he had said to so enrage his wife. The answer slowly emerged: he had admitted to repeated intercourse with sheep on a recent visit to the family farm; perhaps that was how he had contracted the mysterious microbe.

This episode, related to me by a physician friend involved in the case, sounds so bizarrely one of a kind as to be of no possible broader significance. But in fact it illustrates a subject of great importance: human diseases of animal origins. Very few of us may love sheep in the carnal sense. But most of us platonically love our pet animals, like our dogs and cats; and as a society, we certainly appear to have an inordinate fondness for sheep and other livestock, to judge from the vast numbers of them that we keep.

Some of us—most often our children—pick up infectious diseases from our pets. Usually these illnesses remain no more than a nuisance, but a few have evolved into far more. The major killers of humanity throughout our recent history—smallpox, flu, tuberculosis, malaria, plague, measles, and cholera—are all infectious diseases that arose from diseases of animals. Until World War II more victims of war died of microbes than of gunshot or sword wounds. All those military histories glorifying Alexander the Great and Napoleon ignore the ego-deflating truth: the winners of past wars were not necessarily those armies with the best generals and weapons, but those bearing the worst germs with which to smite their enemies.

The grimmest example of the role of germs in history is much on our minds this month, as we recall the European conquest of the Americas that began with Columbus's voyage of 1492. Numerous as the Indian victims of the murderous Spanish conquistadores were, they were dwarfed in number by the victims of murderous Spanish microbes. These formidable conquerors killed an estimated 95 percent of the New World's pre-Columbian Indian population.

Why was the exchange of nasty germs between the Americas and Europe so unequal? Why didn't the reverse happen instead, with Indian diseases decimating the Spanish invaders, spreading back across the Atlantic, and causing a 95 percent decline in *Europe's* human population?

Similar questions arise regarding the decimation of many other native peoples by European germs, and regarding the decimation of would-be European conquistadores in the tropics of Africa and Asia.

Naturally, we're disposed to think about diseases from our own point of view: What can we do to save ourselves and to kill the microbes? Let's stamp out the scoundrels, and never mind what *their* motives are!

In life, though, one has to understand the enemy to beat him. So for a moment, let's consider disease from the microbes' point of view. Let's look beyond our anger at their making us sick in bizarre ways, like giving us genital sores or diarrhea, and ask why it is that they do such things. After all, microbes are as much a product of natural selection as we are, and so their actions must have come about because they confer some evolutionary benefit.

Basically, of course, evolution selects those individuals that are most effective at producing babies and at helping those babies find suitable places to live. Microbes are marvels at this latter requirement. They have evolved diverse ways of spreading from one person to another, and from animals to people. Many of our symptoms of disease actually represent ways in which some clever bug modifies our bodies or our behavior such that we become enlisted to spread bugs.

The most effortless way a bug can spread is by just waiting to be transmitted passively to the next victim. That's the strategy practiced by microbes that wait for one host to be eaten by the next—salmonella bacteria, for example, which we contract by eating already-infected eggs or meat; or the worm responsible for trichinosis, which waits for us to kill a pig and eat it without properly cooking it.

As a slight modification of this strategy; some microbes don't wait for the old host to die but instead hitchhike in the saliva of an insect that bites the old host and then flies to a new one. The free ride may be provided by mosquitoes, fleas, lice, or tsetse flies, which spread malaria, plague, typhus, and sleeping sickness, respectively. The dirtiest of all passive-carriage tricks is perpetrated by microbes that pass from a woman to her fetus—microbes such as the ones responsible for syphilis, rubella (German measles), and AIDS. By their cunning these microbes can already be infecting an infant before the moment of its birth.

Other bugs take matters into their own hands, figuratively speaking. They actively modify the anatomy or habits of their host to accelerate their transmission. From our perspective, the open genital sores caused by venereal diseases such as syphilis are a vile indignity. From the microbes' point of view, however, they're just a useful device to enlist a host's help in inoculating the body cavity of another host with microbes. The skin lesions caused by smallpox similarly spread microbes by direct or indirect body contact (occasionally very indirect, as when U.S. and Australian whites bent on wiping out "belligerent" native peoples sent them gifts of blankets previously used by smallpox patients).

More vigorous yet is the strategy practiced by the influenza, common cold, and pertussis (whooping cough) microbes, which induce the victim to cough or sneeze, thereby broadcasting the bugs toward prospective new hosts. Similarly the cholera bacterium induces a massive diarrhea that spreads bacteria into the water supplies of potential new victims. For modification of a host's behavior, though, nothing matches the rabies virus, which not only gets into the saliva of an infected dog but drives the dog into a frenzy of biting and thereby infects many new victims.

Thus, from our viewpoint, genital sores, diarrhea, and coughing are "symptoms" of disease. From a bug's viewpoint, they're clever evolutionary strategies to broadcast the bug. That's why it's in the bug's interests to make us "sick." But what does it gain by killing us? That seems self-defeating, since a microbe that kills its host kills itself.

Though you may well think it's of little consolation, our death is really just an unintended by-product of host symptoms that promote the efficient transmission of microbes. Yes, an untreated cholera patient may eventually die from producing diarrheal fluid at a rate of several gallons a day. While the patient lasts, though, the cholera bacterium profits from being massively disseminated into the water supplies of its next victims. As long as each victim thereby infects, on average, more than one new victim, the bacteria will spread, even though the first host happens to die.

So much for the dispassionate examination of the bug's interests. Now let's get back to considering our own selfish interests: to stay alive and healthy, best done by killing the damned bugs. One common response to infection is to develop a fever. Again, we consider fever a "symptom" of disease, as if it developed inevitably without serving any function. But regulation of body temperature is under our genetic control, and a fever doesn't just happen by accident. Because some microbes are more sensitive to heat than our own bodies are, by raising our body temperature we in effect try to bake the bugs to death before we get baked ourselves.

We and our pathogens are now locked in an escalating evolutionary contest, with the death of one contestant the price of defeat, and with natural selection playing the role of umpire.

Another common response is to mobilize our immune system. White blood cells and other cells actively seek out and kill foreign microbes. The specific antibodies we gradually build up against a particular microbe make us less likely to get reinfected once we are cured. As we all know there are some illnesses, such as flu and the common cold, to which our resistance is only temporary; we can eventually contract the illness again. Against other illnesses, though—including measles, mumps, rubella, pertussis, and the now-defeated menace of smallpox—antibodies stimulated by one infection confer lifelong immunity. That's the principle behind vaccination—to stimulate our antibody production without our having to go through the actual experience of the disease.

Alas, some clever bugs don't just cave in to our immune defenses. Some have learned to trick us by changing their antigens, those molecular pieces of the microbe that our antibodies recognize. The constant evolution or recycling of new strains of flu, with differing antigens, explains why the flu you got two years ago didn't protect you against the different strain that arrived this year. Sleeping sickness is an even more slippery customer in its ability to change its antigens rapidly.

Among the slipperiest of all is the virus that causes AIDS, which evolves new antigens even as it sits within an individual patient, until it eventually overwhelms the immune system.

Our slowest defensive response is through natural selection, which changes the relative frequency with which a gene appears from generation to generation. For almost any disease some people prove to be genetically more resistant than others. In an epidemic, those people with genes for resistance to that particular microbe are more likely to survive than are people lacking such genes. As a result, over the course of history human populations repeatedly exposed to a particular pathogen tend to be made up of individuals with genes that resist the appropriate microbe just because unfortunate individuals without those genes were less likely to survive to pass their genes on to their children.

Fat consolation, you may be thinking. This evolutionary response is not one that does the genetically susceptible dying individual any good. It does mean, though, that a human population as a whole becomes better protected.

In short, many bugs have had to evolve tricks to let them spread among potential victims. We've evolved counter-tricks, to which the bugs have responded by evolving counter-counter-tricks. We and our pathogens are now locked in an escalating evolutionary contest, with the death of one contestant the price of defeat, and with natural selection playing the role of umpire.

The form that this deadly contest takes varies with the pathogens: for some it is like a guerrilla war, while for others it is a blitzkrieg. With certain diseases, like malaria or hookworm, there's a more or less steady trickle of new cases in an affected area, and they will appear in any month of any year. Epidemic diseases, though, are different: they produce no cases for a long time, then a whole wave of cases, then no more cases again for a while.

Among such epidemic diseases, influenza is the most familiar to Americans, this year having been a particularly bad one for us (but a great year for the influenza virus). Cholera epidemics come at longer intervals, the 1991 Peruvian epidemic being the first one to reach the New World during the twentieth century. Frightening as today's influenza and cholera epidemics are, though, they pale beside the far more terrifying epidemics of the past, before the rise of modern medicine. The greatest single epidemic in human history was the influenza wave that killed 21 million people at the end of the First World War. The black death, or bubonic plague, killed one-quarter of Europe's population between 1346 and 1352, with death tolls up to 70 percent in some cities.

The infectious diseases that visit us as epidemics share several characteristics. First, they spread quickly and efficiently from an infected person to nearby healthy people, with the result that the whole population gets exposed within a short time. Second, they're "acute" illnesses: within a short time, you either die or recover completely. Third, the fortunate ones of us who do recover develop antibodies that leave us immune against a recurrence of the disease for a long time, possibly our entire lives. Finally, these diseases tend to be restricted to humans; the bugs causing them tend not to live in the soil or in other animals. All four of these characteristics apply to what Americans think of as the once more-familiar acute epidemic diseases of childhood, including measles, rubella, mumps, pertussis, and smallpox.

It is easy to understand why the combination of those four characteristics tends to make a disease run in epidemics. The rapid spread of microbes and the rapid course of symptoms mean that everybody in a local human population is soon infected, and thereafter either dead or else recovered and immune. No one is left alive who could still be infected. But since the microbe can't survive except in the bodies of living people, the disease dies out until a new crop of babies reaches the susceptible age—and until an infectious person arrives from the outside to start a new epidemic.

A classic illustration of the process is given by the history of measles on the isolated Faeroe Islands in the North Atlantic. A severe epidemic of the disease reached the Faeroes in 1781, then died out, leaving the islands measles-free until an infected carpenter arrived on a ship from Denmark in 1846. Within three months almost the whole Faeroes population—7,782 people—had gotten measles and then either died or recovered, leaving the measles virus to disappear once again until the next epidemic. Studies show that measles is likely to die out in any human population numbering less than half a million people. Only in larger populations can measles shift from one local area to another, thereby persisting until enough babies have been born in the originally infected area to permit the disease's return.

Rubella in Australia provides a similar example, on a much larger scale. As of 1917 Australia's population was still only 5 million, with most people living in scattered rural areas. The sea voyage to Britain took two months, and land transport within Australia itself was slow. In effect, Australia didn't even consist of a population of 5 million, but of hundreds of much smaller populations. As a result, rubella hit Australia only as occasional epidemics, when an infected person happened to arrive from overseas and stayed in a densely populated area. By 1938, though, the city of Sydney alone had a population of over one million, and people moved frequently and quickly by air between London, Sydney, and other Australian cities. Around then, rubella for the first time was able to establish itself permanently in Australia.

What's true for rubella in Australia is true for most familiar acute infectious diseases throughout the world. To sustain themselves, they need a human population that is sufficiently numerous and densely packed that a new crop of susceptible children is available for infection by the time the disease would otherwise be waning. Hence the measles and other such diseases are also known as "crowd diseases."

Crowd diseases could not sustain themselves in small bands of hunter-gatherers and slash-and-burn farmers. As tragic recent experience with Amazonian Indians and Pacific Islanders confirms, almost an entire tribelet may be wiped out by an epidemic brought by an outside visitor, because no one in the tribelet has any antibodies against the microbe. In addition, measles and some other "childhood" diseases are more likely to kill infected adults than children, and all adults in the tribelet are susceptible. Having killed most of the tribelet, the epidemic then disappears. The small population size explains why tribelets can't sustain epidemics introduced from the outside; at the same time it explains why they could never evolve epidemic diseases of their own to give back to the visitors.

That's not to say that small human populations are free from all infectious diseases. Some of their infections are caused by microbes capable of maintaining themselves in animals or in soil, so the disease remains constantly available to infect people. For example, the yellow fever virus is carried by African wild monkeys and is constantly available to infect rural human populations of Africa. It was also available to be carried to New World monkeys and people by the transAtlantic slave trade.

Other infections of small human populations are chronic diseases, such as leprosy and yaws, that may take a very long time to kill a victim. The victim thus remains alive as a reservoir of microbes to infect other members of the tribelet. Finally, small human populations are susceptible to nonfatal infections against which we don't develop immunity, with the result that the same person can become reinfected after recovering. That's the case with hookworm and many other parasites.

All these types of diseases, characteristic of small, isolated populations, must be the oldest diseases of humanity. They were the ones that we could evolve and sustain through the early millions of years of our evolutionary history, when the total human population was tiny and fragmented. They are also shared with, or are similar to the diseases of, our closest wild relatives, the African great apes. In contrast, the evolution of our crowd diseases could only have occurred with the buildup of large, dense human populations, first made possible by the rise of agriculture about 10,000 years ago, then by the rise of cities several thousand years ago. Indeed, the first attested dates for many familiar infectious diseases are surprisingly recent: around 1600 B.C. for smallpox (as deduced from pockmarks on an Egyptian mummy), 400 B.C. for mumps, 1840 for polio, and 1959 for AIDS.

Agriculture sustains much higher human population densities than do hunting and gathering—on average, 10 to 100 times higher. In addition, hunter-gatherers frequently shift camp, leaving behind their piles of feces with their accumulated microbes and worm larvae. But farmers are sedentary and live amid their own sewage, providing microbes with a quick path from one person's body into another person's drinking water. Farmers also become surrounded by disease-transmitting rodents attracted by stored food.

The explosive increase in world travel by Americans, and in immigration to the United States, is turning us into another melting pot—this time of microbes that we'd dismissed as causing disease in far-off countries.

Some human populations make it even easier for their own bacteria and worms to infect new victims, by intentionally gathering their feces and urine and spreading it as fertilizer on the fields where people work. Irrigation agriculture and fish farming provide ideal living conditions for the snails carrying schistosomes, and for other flukes that burrow through our skin as we wade through the feces-laden water.

If the rise of farming was a boon for our microbes, the rise of cities was a veritable bonanza, as still more densely packed human populations festered under even worse sanitation conditions. (Not until the beginning of the twentieth century did urban populations finally become self-sustaining; until then, constant immigration of healthy peasants from the countryside was necessary to make good the constant deaths of city dwellers from crowd diseases.) Another bonanza was the development of world trade routes, which by late Roman times effectively joined the populations of Europe, Asia, and North Africa into one giant breeding ground for microbes. That's when smallpox finally reached Rome as the "plague of Antonius," which killed millions of Roman citizens between A.D. 165 and 180.

Similarly, bubonic plague first appeared in Europe as the plague of Justinian (A.D. 542–543). But plague didn't begin to hit Europe with full force, as the black death epidemics, until 1346, when new overland trading with China provided rapid transit for flea-infested furs from plague-ridden areas of Central Asia. Today our jet planes have made even the longest intercontinental flights briefer than the duration of any human infectious disease. That's how an Aerolíneas Argentinas airplane, stopping in Lima, Peru, earlier this year, managed to deliver dozens of cholera-infected people the same day to my city of Los Angeles, over 3,000 miles away. The explosive increase in world travel by Americans, and in immigration to the United States, is turning us into another melting pot—this time of microbes that we previously dismissed as just causing exotic diseases in far-off countries.

When the human population became sufficiently large and concentrated, we reached the stage in our history when we could at last sustain crowd diseases confined to our species. But that presents a paradox: such diseases could never have existed before. Instead they had to evolve as new diseases. Where did those new diseases come from?

Evidence emerges from studies of the disease-causing microbes themselves. In many cases molecular biologists have identified the microbe's closest relative. Those relatives also prove to be agents of infectious crowd diseases—but ones confined to various species of domestic animals and pets! Among animals too, epidemic diseases require dense populations, and they're mainly confined to social animals that provide the necessary large populations. Hence when we domesticated social animals such as cows and pigs, they were already afflicted by epidemic diseases just waiting to be transferred to us.

For example, the measles virus is most closely related to the virus causing rinderpest, a nasty epidemic disease of cattle and many wild cud-chewing mammals. Rinderpest doesn't affect humans. Measles, in turn, doesn't affect cattle. The close similarity of the measles and rinderpest viruses suggests that the rinderpest virus transferred from cattle to humans, then became the measles virus by changing its properties to adapt to us. That transfer isn't surprising, considering how closely many peasant farmers live and sleep next to cows and their accompanying feces, urine, breath, sores, and blood. Our intimacy with cattle has been going on for 8,000 years since we domesticated them—ample time for the rinderpest virus to discover us nearby. Other familiar infectious diseases can similarly be traced back to diseases of our animal friends.

Given our proximity to the animals we love, we must constantly be getting bombarded by animal microbes. Those invaders get winnowed by natural selection, and only a few succeed in establishing themselves as human diseases. A quick survey of current diseases lets us trace four stages in the evolution of a specialized human disease from an animal precursor.

In the first stage, we pick up animal-borne microbes that are still at an early stage in their evolution into specialized human pathogens. They don't get transmitted directly from one person to another, and even their transfer from animals to us remains uncommon. There are dozens of diseases like this that we get directly from pets and domestic animals. They include cat scratch fever from cats, leptospirosis from dogs, psittacosis from chickens and parrots, and brucellosis from cattle. We're similarly susceptible to picking up diseases from wild animals, such as the tularemia that hunters occasionally get from skinning wild rabbits.

In the second stage, a former animal pathogen evolves to the point where it does get transmitted directly between people and causes epidemics. However, the epidemic dies out for several reasons—being cured by modern medicine, stopping when everybody has been infected and died, or stopping when everybody has been infected and become immune. For example, a previously unknown disease termed *o'nyong-nyong* fever appeared in East Africa in 1959 and infected several million Africans. It probably arose from a virus of monkeys and was transmitted to humans by mosquitoes. The fact that patients recovered quickly and became immune to further attack helped cause the new disease to die out quickly.

The annals of medicine are full of diseases that sound like no known disease today but that once caused terrifying epidemics before disappearing as mysteriously as they had come. Who alive today remembers the "English sweating sickness" that swept and terrified Europe between 1485 and 1578, or the "Picardy sweats" of eighteenth- and nineteenth-century France?

A third stage in the evolution of our major diseases is represented by former animal pathogens that establish themselves in humans and that do not die out; until they do, the question of whether they will become major killers of humanity remains up for grabs. The future is still very uncertain for Lassa fever, first observed in 1969 in Nigeria and caused by a virus probably derived from rodents. Better established is Lyme disease, caused by a spirochete that we get from the bite of a tick. Although the first known human cases in the United States appeared only as recently as 1962, Lyme disease is already reaching epidemic proportions in the Northeast, on the West Coast, and in the upper Midwest. The future of AIDS, derived from monkey viruses, is even more secure, from the virus's perspective.

The final stage of this evolution is represented by the major, long-established epidemic diseases confined to humans. These diseases must have been the evolutionary survivors of far more pathogens that tried to make the jump to us from animals—and mostly failed.

Diseases represent evolution in progress, as microbes adapt by natural selection to new hosts. Compared with cows' bodies, though, our bodies offer different immune defenses and different chemistry. In that new environment, a microbe must evolve new ways to live and propagate itself.

The best-studied example of microbes evolving these new ways involves myxomatosis, which hit Australian rabbits in 1950. The myxoma virus, native to a wild species of Brazilian rabbit, was known to cause a lethal epidemic in European domestic rabbits, which are a different species. The virus was intentionally introduced to Australia in the hopes of ridding the continent of its plague of European rabbits, foolishly introduced in the nineteenth century. In the first year, myxoma produced a gratifying (to Australian farmers) 99.8 percent mortality in infected rabbits. Fortunately for the rabbits and unfortunately for the farmers, the death rate then dropped in the second year to 90 percent and eventually to 25 percent, frustrating hopes of eradicating rabbits completely from Australia. The problem was that the myxoma virus evolved to serve its own interest, which differed from the farmers' interests and those of the rabbits. The virus changed to kill fewer rabbits and to permit lethally infected ones to live longer before dying. The result was bad for Australian farmers but good for the virus: a less lethal myxoma virus spreads baby viruses to more rabbits than did the original, highly virulent myxoma.

For a similar example in humans, consider the surprising evolution of syphilis. Today we associate syphilis with genital sores and a very slowly developing disease, leading to the death of untreated victims only after many years. However, when syphilis was first definitely recorded in Europe in 1495, its pustules often covered the body from the head to the knees, caused flesh to fall off people's faces, and led to death within a few months. By 1546 syphilis had evolved into the disease with the symptoms known to us today. Apparently, just as with myxomatosis, those syphilis spirochetes evolved to keep their victims alive longer in order to transmit their spirochete offspring into more victims.

How, then, does all this explain the outcome of 1492—that Europeans conquered and depopulated the New World, instead of Native Americans conquering and depopulating Europe?

In the century or two following Columbus's arrival in the New World, the Indian population declined by about 95 percent. The main killers were European germs, to which the Indians had never been exposed.

Part of the answer, of course, goes back to the invaders' technological advantages. European guns and steel swords were more effective weapons than Native American stone axes and wooden clubs. Only Europeans had ships capable of crossing the ocean and horses that could provide a decisive advantage in battle. But that's not the whole answer. Far more Native Americans died in bed than on the battlefield—the victims of germs, not of guns and swords. Those germs undermined Indian resistance by killing most Indians and their leaders and by demoralizing the survivors.

The role of disease in the Spanish conquests of the Aztec and Inca empires is especially well documented. In 1519 Cortés landed on the coast of Mexico with 600 Spaniards to conquer the fiercely militaristic Aztec Empire, which at the time had a population of many millions. That Cortés reached the Aztec capital of Tenochtitlán, escaped with the loss of "only" two-thirds of his force, and managed to fight his way back to the coast demonstrates both Spanish military advantages and the initial naïveté of the Aztecs. But when Cortés's next onslaught came, in 1521, the Aztecs were no longer naïve; they fought street by street with the utmost tenacity.

What gave the Spaniards a decisive advantage this time was smallpox, which reached Mexico in 1520 with the arrival of one infected slave from Spanish Cuba. The resulting epidemic proceeded to kill nearly half the Aztecs. The survivors were demoralized by the mysterious illness that killed Indians and spared Spaniards, as if advertising the Spaniards' invincibility. By 1618 Mexico's initial population of 20 million had plummeted to about 1.6 million.

Pizarro had similarly grim luck when he landed on the coast of Peru in 1531 with about 200 men to conquer the Inca Empire. Fortunately for Pizarro, and unfortunately for the Incas, smallpox had arrived overland around 1524, killing much of the Inca population, including both Emperor Huayna Capac and his son and designated successor, Ninan Cuyoche. Because of the vacant throne, two other sons of Huayna Capac, Atahuallpa and Huáscar, became embroiled in a civil war that Pizarro exploited to conquer the divided Incas.

When we in the United States think of the most populous New World societies existing in 1492, only the Aztecs and Incas come to mind. We forget that North America also supported populous Indian societies in the Mississippi Valley. Sadly, these societies too would disappear. But in this case conquistadores contributed nothing directly to the societies' destruction; the conquistadores' germs, spreading in advance, did everything. When De Soto marched through the Southeast in 1540, he came across Indian towns abandoned two years previously because nearly all the inhabitants had died in epidemics. However, he was still able to see some of the densely populated towns lining the lower Mississippi. By a century and a half later, though, when French settlers returned to the lower Mississippi, almost all those towns had vanished. Their relics are the great mound sites of the Mississippi Valley. Only recently have we come to realize that the mound-building societies were still largely intact when Columbus arrived, and that they collapsed between 1492 and the systematic European exploration of the Mississippi.

When I was a child in school, we were taught that North America had originally been occupied by about one million Indians. That low number helped justify the white conquest of what could then be viewed as an almost empty continent. However, archeological excavations and descriptions left by the first European explorers on our coasts now suggest an initial number of around 20 million. In the century or two following Columbus's arrival in the New World, the Indian population is estimated to have declined by about 95 percent.

The main killers were European germs, to which the Indians had never been exposed and against which they therefore had neither immunologic nor genetic resistance. Smallpox, measles, influenza, and typhus competed for top rank among the killers. As if those were not enough, pertussis, plague, tuberculosis, diphtheria, mumps, malaria, and yellow fever came close behind. In countless cases Europeans were actually there to witness the decimation that occurred when the germs arrived. For example, in 1837 the Mandan Indian tribe, with one of the most elaborate cultures in the Great Plains, contracted smallpox thanks to a steamboat traveling up the Missouri River from St. Louis. The population of one Mandan village crashed from 2,000 to less than 40 within a few weeks.

The one-sided exchange of lethal germs between the Old and New Worlds is among the most striking and consequence-laden facts of recent history. Whereas over a dozen major infectious diseases of Old World origins became established in the New World, not a single major killer reached Europe from the Americas. The sole possible exception is syphilis, whose area of origin still remains controversial.

That one-sidedness is more striking with the knowledge that large, dense human populations are a prerequisite for the evolution of crowd diseases. If recent reappraisals of the pre-Columbian New World population are correct, that population was not far below the contemporaneous population of Eurasia. Some New World cities, like Tenochtitlán, were among the world's most populous cities at the time. Yet Tenochtitlán didn't have awful germs waiting in store for the Spaniards. Why not?

One possible factor is the rise of dense human populations began somewhat later in the New World than in the Old. Another is that the three most populous American centers—the Andes, Mexico, and the Mississippi Valley—were never connected by regular fast trade into one gigantic breeding ground for microbes, in the way that Europe, North Africa, India, and China became connected in late Roman times.

The main reason becomes clear, however, if we ask a simple question: From what microbes could any crowd diseases of the Americas have evolved? We've seen that Eurasian crowd diseases evolved from diseases of domesticated herd animals. Significantly, there were many such animals in Eurasia. But there were only five animals that became domesticated in the Americas: the turkey in Mexico and parts of North America, the guinea pig and llama/alpaca (probably derived from the same original wild species) in the Andes, and Muscovy duck in tropical South America, and the dog throughout the Americas.

That extreme paucity of New World domestic animals reflects the paucity of wild starting material. About 80 percent of the big wild mammals of the Americas became extinct at the end of the last ice age, around 11,000 years ago, at approximately the same time that the first well-attested wave of Indian hunters spread over the Americas. Among the species that disappeared were ones that would have yielded useful domesticates, such as American horses and camels. Debate still rages as to whether those extinctions were due to climate changes or to the impact of Indian hunters on prey that had never seen humans. Whatever the reason, the extinctions removed most of the basis for Native American animal domestication—and for crowd diseases.

The few domesticates that remained were not likely sources of such diseases. Muscovy ducks and turkeys don't live in enormous flocks, and they're not naturally endearing species (like young lambs) with which we have much physical contact. Guinea pigs may have contributed a trypanosome infection like Chagas' disease or leishmaniasis to our catalog of woes, but that's uncertain.

Initially the most surprising absence is of any human disease derived from llamas (or alpacas), which are tempting to consider as the Andean equivalent of Eurasian livestock. However, llamas had three strikes against them as a source of human pathogens: their wild relatives don't occur in big herds as do wild sheep, goats, and pigs; their total numbers were never remotely as large as the Eurasian populations of domestic livestock, since llamas never spread beyond the Andes; and llamas aren't as cuddly as piglets and lambs and aren't kept in such close association with people. (You may not think of piglets as cuddly, but human mothers in the New Guinea highlands often nurse them, and they frequently live right in the huts of peasant farmers.)

The importance of animal-derived diseases for human history extends far beyond the Americas. Eurasian germs played a key role in decimating native peoples in many other parts of the world as well, including the Pacific islands, Australia, and southern Africa. Racist Europeans used to attribute those conquests to their supposedly better brains. But no evidence for such better brains has been forthcoming. Instead, the conquests were made possible by Europeans' nastier germs, and by the technological advances and denser populations that Europeans ultimately acquired by means of their domesticated plants and animals.

So on this 500th anniversary of Columbus's discovery, let's try to regain our sense of perspective about his hotly debated achievements. There's no doubt that Columbus was a great visionary, seaman, and leader. There's also no doubt that he and his successors often behaved as bestial murderers. But those facts alone don't fully explain why it took so few European immigrants to initially conquer and ultimately supplant so much of the native population of the Americas. Without the germs Europeans brought with them—germs that were derived from their animals—such conquests might have been impossible.

Critical Thinking

1. What are the major killers of humanity and where do they come from? How did most victims of war die before World War II? What determined the winners of past wars? What percentage of the pre-Columbian Indian population was killed by Spanish microbes?

2. How might a bug such as salmonella be passively transmitted to its next victim? What examples does the author provide of microbes getting a "free ride" to its next victim? How might they modify the anatomy or habits of their host in order to accelerate their transmission?

3. How does the author, therefore, describe such "symptoms" of disease? Why is it in the bug's interest to make us "sick"? Is it in the bug's interest to kill us? How does the author explain death? How do bacteria survive even though the hosts die?

4. What "common responses" do we use to stay alive?

5. Explain the principle of vaccination. How do the bugs "trick us"? Why is the AIDS virus one of the "slipperiest of all"?

6. What is our slowest defense mechanism? How does the author describe the "escalating evolutionary context"?

7. Explain the difference between pathogens that fight a "guerrilla war," creating a steady trickle of new cases, versus those that conduct a "blitzkrieg" and cause epidemics.

8. What characteristics are shared by infectious diseases that visit us as epidemics?

9. Why does measles die out in populations of less than half a million people but persists in larger population?

10. Why can't such "crowd diseases" sustain themselves in small bands of hunter-gatherers and slash-and-burn farmers?

11. Does this mean that small human populations are free from all infectious diseases? Explain. Why does the author believe these to be the oldest diseases of humanity?

12. When did crowd diseases first develop and what are the various reasons for their increased frequency?

13. What is the paradox regarding these diseases? Where did they come from? Why does the author say we must be constantly bombarded by them?

14. Describe the four stages in the evolution of a specialized human disease from an animal precursor.

15. In what sense do diseases represent evolution in progress? How do the mixoma virus and the Australian rabbits provide an example?

16. How were Europeans technologically superior to Native Americans? What gave Cortez the decisive advantage over the Aztecs? Why were the surviving Aztecs demoralized? What was Pizarro's similar "grim luck"? What happened to the Mound Builders of the Mississippi Valley?

17. What was the author taught in school that originally justified conquest? What do we know now?

18. Why was there "one-sidedness" to the disease transmission in spite of the large Native American populations? Explain the author's reasoning.

Create Central

www.mhhe.com/createcentral

Internet References

Evolution and Medicine Network
http://evmedreview.com

World Health Organization
www.who.int/mental_health/en

JARED DIAMOND is a contributing editor of *Discover,* a professor of physiology at the UCLA School of Medicine, a recipient of a MacArthur genius award, and a research associate in ornithology at the American Museum of Natural History. Expanded versions of many of his *Discover* articles appear in his book *The Third Chimpanzee: The Evolution and Future of the Human Animal,* which won Britain's 1992 COPUS prize for best science book. Not least among his many accomplishments was his rediscovery in 1981 of the long-lost bowerbird of New Guinea. Diamond wrote about pseudo-hermaphrodites for *Discover*'s special June issue on the science of sex.

Article   Prepared by: Elvio Angeloni, *Pasadena City College*

The Americanization of Mental Illness

Ethan Watters

Learning Outcomes

After reading this article, you will be able to:

- Discuss the evidence for the idea that mental illness has never been the same the world over.

- Explain how globalization is undermining local conceptions of self and modes of healing.

Americans, particularly if they are of a certain leftward-leaning, college-educated type, worry about our country's blunders into other cultures. In some circles, it is easy to make friends with a rousing rant about the McDonald's near Tiananmen Square, the Nike factory in Malaysia or the latest blowback from our political or military interventions abroad. For all our self-recrimination, however, we may have yet to face one of the most remarkable effects of American-led globalization. We have for many years been busily engaged in a grand project of Americanizing the world's understanding of mental health and illness. We may indeed be far along in homogenizing the way the world goes mad.

This unnerving possibility springs from recent research by a loose group of anthropologists and cross-cultural psychiatrists. Swimming against the biomedical currents of the time, they have argued that mental illnesses are not discrete entities like the polio virus with their own natural histories. These researchers have amassed an impressive body of evidence suggesting that mental illnesses have never been the same the world over (either in prevalence or in form) but are inevitably sparked and shaped by the ethos of particular times and places. In some Southeast Asian cultures, men have been known to experience what is called amok, an episode of murderous rage followed by amnesia; men in the region also suffer from koro, which is characterized by the debilitating certainty that their genitals are retracting into their bodies. Across the fertile crescent of the Middle East there is zar, a condition related to spirit-possession beliefs that brings forth dissociative episodes of laughing, shouting and singing.

The diversity that can be found across cultures can be seen across time as well. In his book "Mad Travelers," the philosopher Ian Hacking documents the fleeting appearance in the 1890s of a fugue state in which European men would walk in a trance for hundreds of miles with no knowledge of their identities. The hysterical-leg paralysis that afflicted thousands of middle-class women in the late 19th century not only gives us a visceral understanding of the restrictions set on women's social roles at the time but can also be seen from this distance as a social role itself—the troubled unconscious minds of a certain class of women speaking the idiom of distress of their time.

"We might think of the culture as possessing a 'symptom repertoire'—a range of physical symptoms available to the unconscious mind for the physical expression of psychological conflict," Edward Shorter, a medical historian at the University of Toronto, wrote in his book *Paralysis: The Rise and Fall of a 'Hysterical' Symptom.* "In some epochs, convulsions, the sudden inability to speak or terrible leg pain may loom prominently in the repertoire. In other epochs patients may draw chiefly upon such symptoms as abdominal pain, false estimates of body weight and enervating weakness as metaphors for conveying psychic stress."

In any given era, those who minister to the mentally ill—doctors or shamans or priests—inadvertently help to select which symptoms will be recognized as legitimate. Because the troubled mind has been influenced by healers of diverse religious and scientific persuasions, the forms of madness from one place and time often look remarkably different from the forms of madness in another.

That is until recently.

For more than a generation now, we in the West have aggressively spread our modern knowledge of mental illness around the world. We have done this in the name of science, believing that our approaches reveal the biological basis of psychic suffering and dispel prescientific myths and harmful stigma. There is now good evidence to suggest that in the process of teaching the rest of the world to think like us, we've been exporting our Western "symptom repertoire" as well. That is, we've been changing not only the treatments but also the expression of mental illness in other cultures. Indeed, a handful of mental-health disorders—depression, post-traumatic stress disorder and anorexia among them—now appear to be spreading across cultures with the speed of contagious diseases. These symptom clusters are becoming the lingua franca of human suffering, replacing indigenous forms of mental illness.

D
r. Sing Lee, a psychiatrist and researcher at the Chinese University of Hong Kong, watched the Westernization of a mental illness firsthand. In the late 1980s and early 1990s, he was busy documenting a rare and culturally specific form of anorexia nervosa in Hong Kong. Unlike American anorexics, most of his patients did not intentionally diet nor did they express a fear of becoming fat. The complaints of Lee's patients were typically somatic—they complained most frequently of having bloated stomachs. Lee was trying to understand this indigenous form of anorexia and, at the same time, figure out why the disease remained so rare.

As he was in the midst of publishing his finding that food refusal had a particular expression and meaning in Hong Kong, the public's understanding of anorexia suddenly shifted. On Nov. 24, 1994, a teenage anorexic girl named Charlene Hsu Chi-Ying collapsed and died on a busy downtown street in Hong Kong. The death caught the attention of the media and was featured prominently in local papers. "Anorexia Made Her All Skin and Bones: Schoolgirl Falls on Ground Dead," read one headline in a Chinese-language newspaper. "Thinner Than a Yellow Flower, Weight-Loss Book Found in School Bag, Schoolgirl Falls Dead on Street," reported another Chinese-language paper.

In trying to explain what happened to Charlene, local reporters often simply copied out of American diagnostic manuals. The mental-health experts quoted in the Hong Kong papers and magazines confidently reported that anorexia in Hong Kong was the same disorder that appeared in the United States and Europe. In the wake of Charlene's death, the transfer of knowledge about the nature of anorexia (including how and why it was manifested and who was at risk) went only one way: from West to East.

Western ideas did not simply obscure the understanding of anorexia in Hong Kong; they also may have changed the expression of the illness itself. As the general public and the region's mental-health professionals came to understand the American diagnosis of anorexia, the presentation of the illness in Lee's patient population appeared to transform into the more virulent American standard. Lee once saw two or three anorexic patients a year; by the end of the 1990s he was seeing that many new cases each month. That increase sparked another series of media reports. "Children as Young as 10 Starving Themselves as Eating Ailments Rise," announced a headline in one daily newspaper. By the late 1990s, Lee's studies reported that between 3 and 10 percent of young women in Hong Kong showed disordered eating behavior. In contrast to Lee's earlier patients, these women most often cited fat phobia as the single most important reason for their self-starvation. By 2007 about 90 percent of the anorexics Lee treated reported fat phobia. New patients appeared to be increasingly conforming their experience of anorexia to the Western version of the disease.

What is being missed, Lee and others have suggested, is a deep understanding of how the expectations and beliefs of the sufferer shape their suffering. "Culture shapes the way general psychopathology is going to be translated partially or completely into specific psychopathology," Lee says. "When there is a cultural atmosphere in which professionals, the media, schools, doctors, psychologists all recognize and endorse and talk about and publicize eating disorders, then people can be triggered to consciously or unconsciously pick eating-disorder pathology as a way to express that conflict."

The problem becomes especially worrisome in a time of globalization, when symptom repertoires can cross borders with ease. Having been trained in England and the United States, Lee knows better than most the locomotive force behind Western ideas about mental health and illness. Mental-health professionals in the West, and in the United States in particular, create official categories of mental diseases and promote them in a diagnostic manual that has become the worldwide standard. American researchers and institutions run most of the premier scholarly journals and host top conferences in the fields of psychology and psychiatry. Western drug companies dole out large sums for research and spend billions marketing medications for mental illnesses. In addition, Western-trained traumatologists often rush in where war or natural disasters strike to deliver "psychological first aid," bringing with them their assumptions about how the mind becomes broken by horrible events and how it is best healed. Taken together this is a juggernaut that Lee sees little chance of stopping. "As Western categories for diseases have gained dominance, microcultures that shape the illness experiences of individual patients are being discarded," Lee says. "The current has become too strong."

Would anorexia have so quickly become part of Hong Kong's symptom repertoire without the importation of the Western template for the disease? It seems unlikely. Beginning with scattered European cases in the early 19th century, it took more than 50 years for Western mental-health professionals to name, codify and popularize anorexia as a manifestation of hysteria. By contrast, after Charlene fell onto the sidewalk on Wan Chai Road on that late November day in 1994, it was just a matter of hours before the Hong Kong population learned the name of the disease, who was at risk and what it meant.

T
he idea that our Western conception of mental health and illness might be shaping the expression of illnesses in other cultures is rarely discussed in the professional literature. Many modern mental-health practitioners and researchers believe that the scientific standing of our drugs, our illness categories and our theories of the mind have put the field beyond the influence of endlessly shifting cultural trends and beliefs. After all, we now have machines that can literally watch the mind at work. We can change the chemistry of the brain in a variety of interesting ways and we can examine DNA sequences for abnormalities. The assumption is that these remarkable scientific advances have allowed modern-day practitioners to avoid the blind spots and cultural biases of their predecessors.

Modern-day mental-health practitioners often look back at previous generations of psychiatrists and psychologists with a thinly veiled pity, wondering how they could have been so swept away by the cultural currents of their time. The confident pronouncements of Victorian-era doctors regarding the epidemic of hysterical women are now dismissed as cultural artifacts. Similarly, illnesses found only in other cultures are often treated like carnival sideshows. Koro, amok and the like can be found far back in the American diagnostic manual (DSM-IV, Pages 845–849) under the heading "culture-bound syndromes." Given the attention they get, they might as well be labeled "Psychiatric Exotica: Two Bits a Gander."

Western mental-health practitioners often prefer to believe that the 844 pages of the DSM-IV prior to the inclusion of culture-bound syndromes describe real disorders of the mind, illnesses with symptomatology and outcomes relatively unaffected by shifting cultural beliefs. And, it logically follows, if these disorders are unaffected by culture, then they are surely universal to humans everywhere. In this view, the DSM is a field guide to the world's psyche, and applying it around the world represents simply the brave march of scientific knowledge.

Of course, we can become psychologically unhinged for many reasons that are common to all, like personal traumas, social upheavals or biochemical imbalances in our brains. Modern science has begun to reveal these causes. Whatever the trigger, however, the ill individual and those around him invariably rely on cultural beliefs and stories to understand what is happening. Those stories, whether they tell of spirit possession, semen loss or serotonin depletion, predict and shape the course of the illness in dramatic and often counterintuitive ways. In the end, what cross-cultural psychiatrists and anthropologists have to tell us is that all mental illnesses, including depression, P.T.S.D. and even schizophrenia, can be every bit as influenced by cultural beliefs and expectations today as hysterical-leg paralysis or the vapors or zar or any other mental illness ever experienced in the history of human madness. This does not mean that these illnesses and the pain associated with them are not real, or that sufferers deliberately shape their symptoms to fit a certain cultural niche. It means that a mental illness is an illness of the mind and cannot be understood without understanding the ideas, habits and predispositions—the idiosyncratic cultural trappings—of the mind that is its host.

Even when the underlying science is sound and the intentions altruistic, the export of Western biomedical ideas can have frustrating and unexpected consequences. For the last 50-odd years, Western mental-health professionals have been pushing what they call "mental-health literacy" on the rest of the world. Cultures became more "literate" as they adopted Western biomedical conceptions of diseases like depression and schizophrenia. One study published in *The International Journal of Mental Health*, for instance, portrayed those who endorsed the statement that "mental illness is an illness like any other" as having a "knowledgeable, benevolent, supportive orientation toward the mentally ill."

Mental illnesses, it was suggested, should be treated like "brain diseases" over which the patient has little choice or responsibility. This was promoted both as a scientific fact and as a social narrative that would reap great benefits. The logic seemed unassailable: Once people believed that the onset of mental illnesses did not spring from supernatural forces, character flaws, semen loss or some other prescientific notion, the sufferer would be protected from blame and stigma. This idea has been promoted by mental-health providers, drug companies and patient-advocacy groups like the National Alliance on Mental Illness in the United States and SANE in Britain. In a sometimes fractious field, everyone seemed to agree that this modern way of thinking about mental illness would reduce the social isolation and stigma often experienced by those with mental illness. Trampling on indigenous prescientific superstitions about the cause of mental illness seemed a small price to pay to relieve some of the social suffering of the mentally ill.

But does the "brain disease" belief actually reduce stigma?

In 1997, Prof. Sheila Mehta from Auburn University Montgomery in Alabama decided to find out if the "brain disease" narrative had the intended effect. She suspected that the biomedical explanation for mental illness might be influencing our attitudes toward the mentally ill in ways we weren't conscious of, so she thought up a clever experiment.

In her study, test subjects were led to believe that they were participating in a simple learning task with a partner who was, unbeknownst to them, a confederate in the study. Before the experiment started, the partners exchanged some biographical data, and the confederate informed the test subject that he suffered from a mental illness.

The confederate then stated either that the illness occurred because of "the kind of things that happened to me when I was a kid" or that he had "a disease just like any other, which affected my biochemistry." (These were termed the "psychosocial" explanation and the "disease" explanation respectively.) The experiment then called for the test subject to teach the confederate a pattern of button presses. When the confederate pushed the wrong button, the only feedback the test subject could give was a "barely discernible" to "somewhat painful" electrical shock.

Analyzing the data, Mehta found a difference between the group of subjects given the psychosocial explanation for their partner's mental-illness history and those given the brain-disease explanation. Those who believed that their partner suffered a biochemical "disease like any other" increased the severity of the shocks at a faster rate than those who believed they were paired with someone who had a mental disorder caused by an event in the past.

"The results of the current study suggest that we may actually treat people more harshly when their problem is described in disease terms," Mehta wrote. "We say we are being kind, but our actions suggest otherwise." The problem, it appears, is that the biomedical narrative about an illness like schizophrenia carries with it the subtle assumption that a brain made ill through biomedical or genetic abnormalities is more thoroughly broken and permanently abnormal than one made ill though life events. "Viewing those with mental disorders as diseased sets them apart and may lead to our perceiving them as physically distinct. Biochemical aberrations make them almost a different species."

In other words, the belief that was assumed to decrease stigma actually increased it. Was the same true outside the lab in the real world?

The question is important because the Western push for "mental-health literacy" has gained ground. Studies show that much of the world has steadily adopted this medical model of mental illness. Although these changes are most extensive in the United States and Europe, similar shifts have been documented elsewhere. When asked to name the sources of mental illness, people from a variety of cultures are increasingly likely to mention "chemical imbalance" or "brain disease" or "genetic/inherited" factors.

Unfortunately, at the same time that Western mental-health professionals have been convincing the world to think and talk about mental illnesses in biomedical terms, we have been simultaneously losing the war against stigma at home and abroad. Studies of attitudes in the United States from 1950 to 1996 have shown that the perception of dangerousness surrounding people with schizophrenia has steadily increased over this time. Similarly, a study in Germany found that the public's desire to maintain distance from those with a diagnosis of schizophrenia increased from 1990 to 2001.

Researchers hoping to learn what was causing this rise in stigma found the same surprising connection that Mehta discovered in her lab. It turns out that those who adopted biomedical/genetic beliefs about mental disorders were the same people who wanted less contact with the mentally ill and thought of them as more dangerous and unpredictable. This unfortunate relationship has popped up in numerous studies around the world. In a study conducted in Turkey, for example, those who labeled schizophrenic behavior as *akil hastaligi* (illness of the brain or reasoning abilities) were more inclined to assert that schizophrenics were aggressive and should not live freely in the community than those who saw the disorder as *ruhsal hastagi* (a disorder of the spiritual or inner self). Another study, which looked at populations in Germany, Russia and Mongolia, found that "irrespective of place . . . endorsing biological factors as the cause of schizophrenia was associated with a greater desire for social distance."

Even as we have congratulated ourselves for becoming more "benevolent and supportive" of the mentally ill, we have steadily backed away from the sufferers themselves. It appears, in short, that the impact of our worldwide antistigma campaign may have been the exact opposite of what we intended.

Nowhere are the limitations of Western ideas and treatments more evident than in the case of schizophrenia. Researchers have long sought to understand what may be the most perplexing finding in the cross-cultural study of mental illness: people with schizophrenia in developing countries appear to fare better over time than those living in industrialized nations.

This was the startling result of three large international studies carried out by the World Health Organization over the course of 30 years, starting in the early 1970s. The research showed that patients outside the United States and Europe had significantly lower relapse rates—as much as two-thirds lower in one follow-up study. These findings have been widely discussed and debated in part because of their obvious incongruity: the

regions of the world with the most resources to devote to the illness—the best technology, the cutting-edge medicines and the best-financed academic and private-research institutions—had the most troubled and socially marginalized patients.

Trying to unravel this mystery, the anthropologist Juli McGruder from the University of Puget Sound spent years in Zanzibar studying families of schizophrenics. Though the population is predominantly Muslim, Swahili spirit-possession beliefs are still prevalent in the archipelago and commonly evoked to explain the actions of anyone violating social norms—from a sister lashing out at her brother to someone beset by psychotic delusions.

McGruder found that far from being stigmatizing, these beliefs served certain useful functions. The beliefs prescribed a variety of socially accepted interventions and ministrations that kept the ill person bound to the family and kinship group. "Muslim and Swahili spirits are not exorcised in the Christian sense of casting out demons," McGruder determined. "Rather they are coaxed with food and goods, feted with song and dance. They are placated, settled, reduced in malfeasance." McGruder saw this approach in many small acts of kindness. She watched family members use saffron paste to write phrases from the Koran on the rims of drinking bowls so the ill person could literally imbibe the holy words. The spirit-possession beliefs had other unexpected benefits. Critically, the story allowed the person with schizophrenia a cleaner bill of health when the illness went into remission. An ill individual enjoying a time of relative mental health could, at least temporarily, retake his or her responsibilities in the kinship group. Since the illness was seen as the work of outside forces, it was understood as an affliction for the sufferer but not as an identity.

For McGruder, the point was not that these practices or beliefs were effective in curing schizophrenia. Rather, she said she believed that they indirectly helped control the course of the illness. Besides keeping the sick individual in the social group, the religious beliefs in Zanzibar also allowed for a type of calmness and acquiescence in the face of the illness that she had rarely witnessed in the West.

The course of a metastasizing cancer is unlikely to be changed by how we talk about it. With schizophrenia, however, symptoms are inevitably entangled in a person's complex interactions with those around him or her. In fact, researchers have long documented how certain emotional reactions from family members correlate with higher relapse rates for people who have a diagnosis of schizophrenia. Collectively referred to as "high expressed emotion," these reactions include criticism, hostility and emotional overinvolvement (like overprotectiveness or constant intrusiveness in the patient's life). In one study, 67 percent of white American families with a schizophrenic family member were rated as "high EE." (Among British families, 48 percent were high EE; among Mexican families the figure was 41 percent and for Indian families 23 percent.)

Does this high level of "expressed emotion" in the United States mean that we lack sympathy or the desire to care for our mentally ill? Quite the opposite. Relatives who were "high EE" were simply expressing a particularly American view of the self. They tended to believe that individuals are the captains of their own destiny and should be able to overcome their problems by force of personal will. Their critical comments to the mentally ill person didn't mean that these family members were cruel or uncaring; they were simply applying the same assumptions about human nature that they applied to themselves. They were reflecting an "approach to the world that is active, resourceful and that emphasizes personal accountability," Prof. Jill M. Hooley of Harvard University concluded. "Far from high criticism reflecting something negative about the family members of patients with schizophrenia, high criticism (and hence high EE) was associated with a characteristic that is widely regarded as positive."

Widely regarded as positive, that is, in the United States. Many traditional cultures regard the self in different terms—as inseparable from your role in your kinship group, intertwined with the story of your ancestry and permeable to the spirit world. What McGruder found in Zanzibar was that families often drew strength from this more connected and less isolating idea of human nature. Their ability to maintain a low level of expressed emotion relied on these beliefs. And that level of expressed emotion in turn may be key to improving the fortunes of the schizophrenia sufferer.

Of course, to the extent that our modern psychopharmacological drugs can relieve suffering, they should not be denied to the rest of the world. The problem is that our biomedical advances are hard to separate from our particular cultural beliefs. It is difficult to distinguish, for example, the biomedical conception of schizophrenia—the idea that the disease exists within the biochemistry of the brain—from the more inchoate Western assumption that the self resides there as well. "Mental illness is feared and has such a stigma because it represents a reversal of what Western humans . . . have come to value as the essence of human nature," McGruder concludes. "Because our culture so highly values . . . an illusion of self-control and control of circumstance, we become abject when contemplating mentation that seems more changeable, less restrained and less controllable, more open to outside influence, than we imagine our own to be."

Cross-cultural psychiatrists have pointed out that the mental-health ideas we export to the world are rarely unadulterated scientific facts and never culturally neutral. "Western mental-health discourse introduces core components of Western culture, including a theory of human nature, a definition of personhood, a sense of time and memory and a source of moral authority. None of this is universal," Derek Summerfield of the Institute of Psychiatry in London observes. He has also written: "The problem is the overall thrust that comes from being at the heart of the one globalizing culture. It is as if one version of human nature is being presented as definitive, and one set of ideas about pain and suffering. . . . There is no one definitive psychology."

Behind the promotion of Western ideas of mental health and healing lie a variety of cultural assumptions about human nature. Westerners share, for instance, evolving beliefs about what type of life event is likely to make one psychologically traumatized, and we agree that venting emotions by talking is more healthy than stoic silence. We've come to agree that the human mind is rather fragile and that it is best to consider many emotional experiences and mental states as illnesses that require professional intervention. (The National Institute of Mental Health reports that a quarter of Americans have diagnosable mental illnesses each year.) The ideas we export often have at their heart a particularly American brand of hyperintrospection—a penchant for "psychologizing" daily existence. These ideas remain deeply influenced by the Cartesian split between the mind and the body, the Freudian duality between the conscious and unconscious, as well as the many self-help philosophies and schools of therapy that have encouraged Americans to separate the health of the individual from the health of the group. These Western ideas of the mind are proving as seductive to the rest of the world as fast food and rap music, and we are spreading them with speed and vigor.

No one would suggest that we withhold our medical advances from other countries, but it's perhaps past time to admit that even our most remarkable scientific leaps in understanding the brain haven't yet created the sorts of cultural stories from which humans take comfort and meaning. When these scientific advances are translated into popular belief and cultural stories, they are often stripped of the complexity of the science and become comically insubstantial narratives. Take for instance this website text advertising the antidepressant Paxil: "Just as a cake recipe requires you to use flour, sugar and baking powder in the right amounts, your brain needs a fine chemical balance in order to perform at its best." The Western mind, endlessly analyzed by generations of theorists and researchers, has now been reduced to a batter of chemicals we carry around in the mixing bowl of our skulls.

All cultures struggle with intractable mental illnesses with varying degrees of compassion and cruelty, equanimity and fear. Looking at ourselves through the eyes of those living in places where madness and psychological trauma are still embedded in complex religious and cultural narratives, however, we get a glimpse of ourselves as an increasingly insecure and fearful people. Some philosophers and psychiatrists have suggested that we are investing our great wealth in researching and treating mental illness—medicalizing ever larger swaths of human experience—because we have rather suddenly lost older belief systems that once gave meaning and context to mental suffering.

If our rising need for mental-health services does indeed spring from a breakdown of meaning, our insistence that the rest of the world think like us may be all the more problematic. Offering the latest Western mental-health theories, treatments and categories in an attempt to ameliorate the psychological stress sparked by modernization and globalization is not a solution; it may be part of the problem. When we undermine local conceptions of the self and modes of healing, we may be speeding along the disorienting changes that are at the very heart of much of the world's mental distress.

Critical Thinking

1. What evidence is there that mental illness has never been the same the world over?

2. What is meant by the "symptom repertoire" of a culture? How has this been aided by those who minister to the mentally ill?

3. Describe the process by which we in the West have spread our modern knowledge of mental illness along with our "symptom repertoire."

4. How was Dr. Sing Lee able to observe a unique form of anorexia in Hong Kong evolve into a Westernized version of the disease?

5. How has globalization enabled Western symptom repertoires to spread across borders with ease?

6. Why do Western health professionals believe their concepts of mental illness are free of cultural bias? How does the author respond?

7. What is the logic behind seeing mental illness as a "brain disease"? Why does it increase the stigma rather than decrease it?

8. How does the belief that spiritual possession causes schizophrenia illustrate the limitations of Western ideas regarding treatment of the disease? How does this relate to differing concepts of self?

9. How is that "offering the latest Western mental-health theories, treatments and categories in an attempt to ameliorate the psychological stress sparked by modernization and globalization is not a solution; it may be part of the problem"?

Create Central

www.mhhe.com/createcentral

Internet References

Human Rights and Humanitarian Assistance
www.etown.edu/vl/humrts.html

World Health Organization
www.who.int/mental_health/en

ETHAN WATTERS lives in San Francisco. This essay is adapted from his book *Crazy Like Us: The Globalization of the American Psyche.*

Article   Prepared by: Elvio Angeloni, *Pasadena City College*

The Price of Progress

JOHN BODLEY

Learning Outcomes

After reading this article, you will be able to:

- Discuss "economic development" as an ethnocentric Western concept.

- Determine if wealth and power are distributed fairly across the world.

> *In aiming at progress . . . you must let no one suffer by too drastic a measure, nor pay too high a price in upheaval and devastation, for your innovation.*
>
> Maunier, 1949: 725

Until recently, government planners have always considered economic development and progress beneficial goals that all societies should want to strive toward. The social advantage of progress—as defined in terms of increased incomes, higher standards of living, greater security, and better health—are thought to be positive, *universal* goods, to be obtained at any price. Although one may argue that tribal peoples must sacrifice their traditional cultures to obtain these benefits, government planners generally feel that this is a small price to pay for such obvious advantages.

In earlier chapters [in *Victims of Progress,* 3rd ed.], evidence was presented to demonstrate that autonomous tribal peoples have not *chosen* progress to enjoy its advantages, but that governments have *pushed* progress upon them to obtain tribal resources, not primarily to share with the tribal peoples the benefits of progress. It has also been shown that the price of forcing progress on unwilling recipients has involved the deaths of millions of tribal people, as well as their loss of land, political sovereignty, and the right to follow their own life style. This chapter does not attempt to further summarize that aspect of the cost of progress, but instead analyzes the specific effects of the participation of tribal peoples in the world-market economy. In direct opposition to the usual interpretation, it is argued here that the benefits of progress are often both illusory and detrimental to tribal peoples when they have not been allowed to control their own resources and define their relationship to the market economy.

Progress and the Quality of Life

One of the primary difficulties in assessing the benefits of progress and economic development for any culture is that of establishing a meaningful measure of both benefit and detriment. It is widely recognized that *standard of living,* which is the most frequently used measure of progress, is an intrinsically ethnocentric concept relying heavily upon indicators that lack universal cultural relevance. Such factors as GNP, per capita income, capital formation, employment rates, literacy, formal education, consumption of manufactured goods, number of doctors and hospital beds per thousand persons, and the amount of money spent on government welfare and health programs may be irrelevant measures of actual *quality* of life for autonomous or even semiautonomous tribal cultures. In its 1954 report, the Trust Territory government indicated that since the Micronesian population was still largely satisfying its own needs within a cashless subsistence economy, "Money income is not a significant measure of living standards, production, or well-being in this area" (TTR, 1953: 44). Unfortunately, within a short time the government began to rely on an enumeration of certain imported consumer goods as indicators of a higher standard of living in the islands, even though many tradition-oriented islanders felt that these new goods symbolized a lowering of the quality of life.

A more useful measure of the benefits of progress might be based on a formula for evaluating cultures devised by Goldschmidt (1952: 135). According to these less ethnocentric criteria, the important question to ask is: Does progress or economic development increase or decrease a given culture's ability to satisfy the physical and psychological needs of its population, or its stability? This question is a far more direct measure of quality of life than are the standard economic correlates of development, and it is universally relevant. Specific indication of this *standard* of living could be found for any society in the nutritional status and general physical and mental health of its population, the incidence of crime and delinquency, the demographic structure, family stability, and the society's relationship to its natural resource base. A society with high rates of malnutrition and crime, and one degrading its natural environment to the extent of threatening its continued existence, might be described as at a lower standard of living than is another society where these problems did not exist.

Careful examination of the data, which compare, on these specific points, the former condition of self-sufficient tribal peoples with their condition following their incorporation into the world-market economy, leads to the conclusion that their standard of living is *lowered,* not raised, by economic progress—and often to a dramatic degree. This is perhaps the most outstanding and inescapable fact to emerge from the years of research that anthropologists have devoted to the study of culture change and modernization. Despite the best intentions of those who have promoted change and improvement, all too often the results have been poverty, longer working hours, and much greater physical exertion, poor health, social disorder, discontent, discrimination, overpopulation, and environmental deterioration—combined with the destruction of the traditional culture.

Diseases of Development

Perhaps it would be useful for public health specialists to start talking about a new category of diseases. . . . Such diseases could be called the "diseases of development" and would consist of those pathological conditions which are based on the usually unanticipated consequences of the implementation of developmental schemes.

Hughes & Hunter, 1972: 93

Economic development increases the disease rate of affected peoples in at least three ways. First, to the extent that development is successful, it makes developed populations suddenly become vulnerable to all of the diseases suffered almost exclusively by "advanced" peoples. Among these are diabetes, obesity, hypertension, and a variety of circulatory problems. Second, development disturbs traditional environmental balances and may dramatically increase certain bacterial and parasite diseases. Finally, when development goals prove unattainable, an assortment of poverty diseases may appear in association with the crowded conditions of urban slums and the general breakdown in traditional socioeconomic systems.

Outstanding examples of the first situation can be seen in the Pacific, where some of the most successfully developed native peoples are found. In Micronesia, where development has progressed more rapidly than perhaps anywhere else, between 1958 and 1972 the population doubled, but the number of patients treated for heart disease in the local hospitals nearly tripled, mental disorder increased eightfold, and by 1972 hypertension and nutritional deficiencies began to make significant appearances for the first time (TTR, 1959, 1973, statistical tables).

Although some critics argue that the Micronesian figures simply represent better health monitoring due to economic progress, rigorously controlled data from Polynesia show a similar trend. The progressive acquisition of modern degenerative diseases was documented by an eight-member team of New Zealand medical specialists, anthropologists, and nutritionists, whose research was funded by the Medical Research Council of New Zealand and the World Health Organization. These researchers investigated the health status of a genetically related population at various points along a continuum of increasing cash income, modernizing diet, and urbanization. The extremes on this acculturation continuum were represented by the relatively traditional Pukapukans of the Cook Islands and the essentially Europeanized New Zealand Maori, while the busily developing Rarotongans, also of the Cook Islands, occupied the intermediate position. In 1971, after eight years of work, the team's preliminary findings were summarized by Dr. Ian Prior, cardiologist and leader of the research, as follows:

We are beginning to observe that the more an islander takes on the ways of the West, the more prone he is to succumb to our degenerative diseases. In fact, it does not seem too much to say our evidence now shows that the farther the Pacific natives move from the quiet, carefree life of their ancestors, the closer they come to gout, diabetes, atherosclerosis, obesity, and hypertension.

Prior, 1971: 2

In Pukapuka, where progress was limited by the island's small size and its isolated location some 480 kilometers from the nearest port, the annual per capita income was only about thirty-six dollars and the economy remained essentially at a subsistence level. Resources were limited and the area was visited by trading ships only three or four times a year; thus, there was little opportunity for intensive economic development. Predictably, the population of Pukapuka was characterized by relatively low levels of imported sugar and salt intake, and a presumably related low level of heart disease, high blood pressure, and diabetes. In Rarotonga, where economic success was introducing town life, imported food, and motorcycles, sugar and salt intakes nearly tripled, high blood pressure increased approximately ninefold, diabetes two- to threefold, and heart disease doubled for men and more than quadrupled for women, while the number of grossly obese women increased more than tenfold. Among the New Zealand Maori, sugar intake was nearly eight times that of the Pukapukans, gout in men was nearly double its rate on Pukapuka, and diabetes in men was more than fivefold higher, while heart disease in women had increased more than sixfold. The Maori were, in fact, dying of "European" diseases at a greater rate than was the average New Zealand European.

Government development policies designed to bring about changes in local hydrology, vegetation, and settlement patterns and to increase population mobility, and even programs aimed at reducing certain diseases, have frequently led to dramatic increases in disease rates because of the unforeseen effects of disturbing the preexisting order. Hughes and Hunter (1972) published an excellent survey of cases in which development led directly to increased disease rates in Africa. They concluded that hasty development intervention in relatively balanced local cultures and environments resulted in "a drastic deterioration in the social and economic conditions of life."

Traditional populations in general have presumably learned to live with the endemic pathogens of their environments, and in some cases they have evolved genetic adaptations to specific diseases, such as the sickle-cell trait, which provided an immunity to malaria. Unfortunately, however, outside intervention has entirely changed this picture. In the late 1960s, sleeping sickness suddenly increased in many areas of Africa and even spread to areas where it did not formerly occur, due to the building of new roads and migratory labor, both of which caused increased population movement. Large-scale relocation schemes, such as the Zande Scheme, had disastrous results when natives were moved from their traditional disease-free refuges into infected areas. Dams and irrigation developments inadvertently created ideal conditions for the rapid proliferation of snails carrying schistosomiasis (a liver fluke disease), and major epidemics suddenly occurred in areas where this disease had never before been a problem. DDT spraying programs have been temporarily successful in controlling malaria, but there is often a rebound effect that increases the problem when spraying is discontinued, and the malarial mosquitoes are continually evolving resistant strains.

Urbanization is one of the prime measures of development, but it is a mixed blessing for most former tribal peoples. Urban health standards are abysmally poor and generally worse than in rural areas for the detribalized individuals who have crowded into the towns and cities throughout Africa, Asia, and Latin America seeking wage employment out of new economic necessity. Infectious diseases related to crowding and poor sanitation are rampant in urban centers, while greatly increased stress and poor nutrition aggravate a variety of other health problems. Malnutrition and other diet-related conditions are, in fact, one of the characteristic hazards of progress faced by tribal peoples and are discussed in the following sections.

The Hazards of Dietary Change

The traditional diets of tribal peoples are admirably adapted to their nutritional needs and available food resources. Even though these diets may seem bizarre, absurd, and unpalatable to outsiders, they are unlikely to be improved by drastic modifications. Given the delicate balances and complexities involved in any subsistence system, change always involves risks, but for tribal people the effects of dietary change have been catastrophic.

Under normal conditions, food habits are remarkably resistant to change, and indeed people are unlikely to abandon their traditional diets voluntarily in favor of dependence on difficult-to-obtain exotic imports. In some cases it is true that imported foods may be identified with powerful outsiders and are therefore sought as symbols of greater prestige. This may lead to such absurdities as Amazonian Indians choosing to consume imported canned tunafish when abundant high-quality fish is available in their own rivers. Another example of this situation occurs in tribes where mothers prefer to feed their infants expensive nutritionally inadequate canned milk from unsanitary, but *high status,* baby bottles. The high status of these items is often promoted by clever traders and clever advertising campaigns.

Aside from these apparently voluntary changes, it appears that more often dietary changes are forced upon unwilling tribal peoples by circumstances beyond their control. In some areas, new food crops have been introduced by government decree, or as a consequence of forced relocation or other policies designed to end hunting, pastoralism, or shifting cultivation. Food habits have also been modified by massive disruption of the natural environment by outsiders—as when sheepherders transformed the Australian Aborigines' foraging territory or when European invaders destroyed the bison herds that were the primary element in the Plains Indians' subsistence patterns. Perhaps the most frequent cause of diet change occurs when formerly self-sufficient peoples find that wage labor, cash cropping, and other economic development activities that feed tribal resources into the world-market economy must inevitably divert time and energy away from the production of subsistence foods. Many developing peoples suddenly discover that, like it or not, they are unable to secure traditional foods and must spend their newly acquired cash on costly, and often nutritionally inferior, manufactured foods.

Overall, the available data seem to indicate that the dietary changes that are linked to involvement in the world-market economy have tended to *lower* rather than raise the nutritional levels of the affected tribal peoples. Specifically, the vitamin, mineral, and protein components of their diets are often drastically reduced and replaced by enormous increases in starch and carbohydrates, often in the form of white flour and refined sugar.

Any deterioration in the quality of a given population's diet is almost certain to be reflected in an increase in deficiency diseases and a general decline in health status. Indeed, as tribal peoples have shifted to a diet based on imported manufactured or processed foods, there has been a dramatic rise in malnutrition, a massive increase in dental problems, and a variety of other nutritional-related disorders. Nutritional physiology is so complex that even well-meaning dietary changes have had tragic consequences. In many areas of Southeast Asia, government-sponsored protein supplementation programs supplying milk to protein-deficient populations caused unexpected health problems and increased mortality. Officials failed to anticipate that in cultures where adults do not normally drink milk, the enzymes needed to digest it are no longer produced and milk *intolerance* results (Davis & Bolin, 1972). In Brazil, a similar milk distribution program caused an epidemic of permanent blindness by aggravating a preexisting vitamin A deficiency (Bunce, 1972).

Teeth and Progress

There is nothing new in the observation that savages, or peoples living under primitive conditions, have, in general, excellent teeth. . . . Nor is it news that most civilized populations possess wretched teeth which begin to decay almost before they have erupted completely, and that dental caries is likely to be accompanied by periodontal disease with further reaching complications.

Hooton, 1945: xviii

Anthropologists have long recognized that undisturbed tribal peoples are often in excellent physical condition. And it has often been noted specifically that dental caries and the other dental abnormalities that plague industrialized societies are absent or rare among tribal peoples who have retained their traditional diets. The fact that tribal food habits may contribute to the development of sound teeth, whereas modernized diets may do just the opposite, was illustrated as long ago as 1894 in an article in the *Journal of the Royal Anthropological Institute* that described the results of a comparison between the teeth of ten Sioux Indians who were examined when they came to London as members of Buffalo Bill's Wild West Show and were found to be completely free of caries and in possession of all their teeth, even though half of the group were over thirty-nine years of age. Londoners' teeth were conspicuous for both their caries and their steady reduction in number with advancing age. The difference was attributed primarily to the wear and polishing caused by the traditional Indian diet of coarse food and the fact that they chewed their food longer, encouraged by the absence of tableware.

One of the most remarkable studies of the dental conditions of tribal peoples and the impact of dietary change was conducted in the 1930s by Weston Price (1945), an American dentist who was interested in determining what caused normal, healthy teeth. Between 1931 and 1936, Price systematically explored tribal areas throughout the world to locate and examine the most isolated peoples who were still living on traditional foods. His fieldwork covered Alaska, the Canadian Yukon, Hudson Bay, Vancouver Island, Florida, the Andes, the Amazon, Samoa, Tahiti, New Zealand, Australia, New Caledonia, Fiji, the Torres Strait, East Africa, and the Nile. The study demonstrated both the superior quality of aboriginal dentition and the devastation that occurs as modern diets are adopted. In nearly every area where traditional foods were still being eaten, Price found perfect teeth with normal dental arches and virtually no decay, whereas caries and abnormalities increased steadily as new diets were adopted. In many cases the change was sudden and striking. Among Eskimo groups subsisting entirely on traditional food he found caries totally absent, whereas in groups eating a considerable quantity of store-bought food approximately 20 percent of their teeth were decayed. This figure rose to more than 30 percent with Eskimo groups subsisting almost exclusively on purchased or government-supplied food, and reached an incredible 48 percent among the Vancouver Island Indians. Unfortunately for many of these people, modern dental treatment did not accompany the new food, and their suffering was appalling. The loss of teeth was, of course, bad enough in itself, and it certainly undermined the population's resistance to many new diseases, including tuberculosis. But new foods were also accompanied by crowded, misplaced teeth, gum diseases, distortion of the face, and pinching of the nasal cavity. Abnormalities in the dental arch appeared in the new generation following the change in diet, while caries appeared almost immediately even in adults.

Price reported that in many areas the affected peoples were conscious of their own physical deterioration. At a mission school in Africa, the principal asked him to explain to the native schoolchildren why they were not physically as strong as children who had had no contact with schools. On an island in the Torres Strait the natives knew exactly what was causing their problems and resisted—almost to the point of bloodshed—government efforts to establish a store that would make imported food available. The government prevailed, however, and Price was able to establish a relationship between the length of time the government store had been established and the increasing incidence of caries among a population that showed an almost 100 percent immunity to them before the store had been opened.

In New Zealand, the Maori, who in their aboriginal state are often considered to have been among the healthiest, most perfectly developed of people, were found to have "advanced" the furthest. According to Price:

> *Their modernization was demonstrated not only by the high incidence of dental caries but also by the fact that 90 percent of the adults and 100 percent of the children had abnormalities of the dental arches.*

Price, 1945: 206

Malnutrition

Malnutrition, particularly in the form of protein deficiency, has become a critical problem for tribal peoples who must adopt new economic patterns. Population pressures, cash cropping, and government programs all have tended to encourage the replacement of traditional crops and other food sources that were rich in protein with substitutes, high in calories but low in protein. In Africa, for example, protein-rich staples such as millet and sorghum are being replaced systematically by high-yielding manioc and plantains, which have insignificant amounts of protein. The problem is increased for cash croppers and wage laborers whose earnings are too low and unpredictable to allow purchase of adequate amounts of protein. In some rural areas, agricultural laborers have been forced systematically to deprive nonproductive members (principally children) of their households of their minimal nutritional requirements to satisfy the need of the productive members. This process has been documented in northeastern Brazil following the introduction of large-scale sisal plantations (Gross & Underwood, 1971). In urban centers the difficulties of obtaining nutritionally adequate diets are even more serious for tribal immigrants, because costs are higher and poor quality foods are more tempting.

One of the most tragic, and largely overlooked, aspects of chronic malnutrition is that it can lead to abnormally undersized brain development and apparently irreversible brain damage; it has been associated with various forms of mental impairment or retardation. Malnutrition has been linked clinically with mental retardation in both Africa and Latin America (see, for example, Mönckeberg, 1968), and this appears to be a worldwide phenomenon with serious implications (Montagu, 1972).

Optimistic supporters of progress will surely say that all of these new health problems are being overstressed and that the introduction of hospitals, clinics, and the other modern health institutions will overcome or at least compensate for all of these difficulties. However, it appears that uncontrolled population growth and economic impoverishment probably will keep most of these benefits out of reach for many tribal peoples, and the intervention of modern medicine has at least partly contributed to the problem in the first place.

The generalization that civilization frequently has a broad negative impact on tribal health has found broad empirical support (see especially Kroeger & Barbira-Freedman [1982] on Amazonia; Reinhard [1976] on the Arctic; and Wirsing [1985] globally), but these conclusions have not gone unchallenged. Some critics argue that tribal health was often poor before modernization, and they point specifically to tribals' low life expectancy and high infant mortality rates. Demographic statistics on tribal populations are often problematic because precise data are scarce, but they do show a less favorable profile than that enjoyed by many industrial societies. However, it should be remembered that our present life expectancy is a recent phenomenon that has been very costly in terms of medical research and technological advances. Furthermore, the benefits of our health system are not enjoyed equally by all members of our society. High infant mortality could be viewed as a relatively inexpensive and egalitarian tribal public health program that offered the reasonable expectation of a healthy and productive life for those surviving to age fifteen.

Some critics also suggest that certain tribal populations, such as the New Guinea highlanders, were "stunted" by nutritional deficiencies created by tribal culture and are "improved" by "acculturation" and cash cropping (Dennett & Connell, 1988). Although this argument does suggest that the health question requires careful evaluation, it does not invalidate the empirical generalizations already established. Nutritional deficiencies undoubtedly occurred in densely populated zones in the central New Guinea highlands. However, the specific case cited above may not be widely representative of other tribal groups even in New Guinea, and it does not address the facts of outside intrusion or the inequities inherent in the contemporary development process.

Ecocide

"How is it," asked a herdsman . . . "how is it that these hills can no longer give pasture to my cattle? In my father's day they were green and cattle thrived there; today there is no grass and my cattle starve." As one looked one saw that what had once been a green hill had become a raw red rock.

Jones, 1934

Progress not only brings new threats to the health of tribal peoples, but it also imposes new strains on the ecosystems upon which they must depend for their ultimate survival. The introduction of new technology, increased consumption, lowered mortality, and the eradication of all traditional controls have combined to replace what for most tribal peoples was a relatively stable balance between population and natural resources, with a new system that is imbalanced. Economic development

is forcing *ecocide* on peoples who were once careful stewards of their resources. There is already a trend toward widespread environmental deterioration in tribal areas, involving resource depletion, erosion, plant and animal extinction, and a disturbing series of other previously unforeseen changes.

After the initial depopulation suffered by most tribal peoples during their engulfment by frontiers of national expansion, most tribal populations began to experience rapid growth. Authorities generally attribute this growth to the introduction of modern medicine and new health measures and the termination of intertribal warfare, which lowered morality rates, as well as to new technology, which increased food production. Certainly all of these factors played a part, but merely lowering mortality rates would not have produced the rapid population growth that most tribal areas have experienced if traditional birth-spacing mechanisms had not been eliminated at the same time. Regardless of which factors were most important, it is clear that all of the natural and cultural checks on population growth have suddenly been pushed aside by culture change, while tribal lands have been steadily reduced and consumption levels have risen. In many tribal areas, environmental deterioration due to overuse of resources has set in, and in other areas such deterioration is imminent as resources continue to dwindle relative to the expanding population and increased use. Of course, population expansion by tribal peoples may have positive political consequences, because where tribals can retain or regain their status as local majorities they may be in a more favorable position to defend their resources against intruders.

Swidden systems and pastoralism, both highly successful economic systems under traditional conditions, have proved particularly vulnerable to increased population pressures and outside efforts to raise productivity beyond its natural limits. Research in Amazonia demonstrates that population pressures and related resource depletion can be created indirectly by official policies that restrict swidden peoples to smaller territories. Resource depletion itself can then become a powerful means of forcing tribal people into participating in the world-market economy—thus leading to further resource depletion. For example, Bodley and Benson (1979) showed how the Shipibo Indians in Peru were forced to further deplete their forest resources by cash cropping in the forest area to replace the resources that had been destroyed earlier by the intensive cash cropping necessitated by the narrow confines of their reserve. In this case, certain species of palm trees that had provided critical housing materials were destroyed by forest clearing and had to be replaced by costly purchased materials. Research by Gross (1979) and others showed similar processes at work among four tribal groups in central Brazil and demonstrated that the degree of market involvement increases directly with increases in resource depletion.

The settling of nomadic herders and the removal of prior controls on herd size have often led to serious overgrazing and erosion problems where these had not previously occurred. There are indications that the desertification problem in the Sahel region of Africa was aggravated by programs designed to settle nomads. The first sign of imbalance in a swidden system appears when the planting cycles are shortened to the point that garden plots are reused before sufficient forest regrowth can occur. If reclearing and planting continue in the same area, the natural patterns of forest succession may be disturbed irreversibly and the soil can be impaired permanently. An extensive tract of tropical rainforest in the lower Amazon of Brazil was reduced to a semiarid desert in just fifty years through such a process (Ackermann, 1964). The soils in the Azande area are also now seriously threatened with laterization and other problems as a result of the government-promoted cotton development scheme (McNeil, 1972).

The dangers of overdevelopment and the vulnerability of local resource systems have long been recognized by both anthropologists and tribal peoples themselves. But the pressures for change have been overwhelming. In 1948 the Maya villagers of Chan Kom complained to Redfield (1962) about the shortening of their swidden cycles, which they correctly attributed to increasing population pressures. Redfield told them, however, that they had no choice but to go "forward with technology" (Redfield, 1962: 178). In Assam, swidden cycles were shortened from an average of twelve years to only two or three within just twenty years, and anthropologists warned that the limits of swiddening would soon be reached (Burling, 1963: 311–312). In the Pacific, anthropologists warned of population pressures on limited resources as early as the 1930s (Keesing, 1941: 64–65). These warnings seemed fully justified, considering the fact that the crowded Tikopians were prompted by population pressures on their tiny island to suggest that infanticide be legalized. The warnings have been dramatically reinforced since then by the doubling of Micronesia's population in just the fourteen years between 1958 and 1972, from 70,600 to 114,645, while consumption levels have soared. By 1985 Micronesia's population had reached 162,321.

The environmental hazards of economic development and rapid population growth have become generally recognized only since worldwide concerns over environmental issues began in the early 1970s. Unfortunately, there is as yet little indication that the leaders of the new developing nations are sufficiently concerned with environmental limitations. On the contrary, governments are forcing tribal peoples into a self-reinforcing spiral of population growth and intensified resource exploitation, which may be stopped only by environmental disaster or the total impoverishment of the tribals.

The reality of ecocide certainly focuses attention on the fundamental contrasts between tribal and industrial systems in their use of natural resources, who controls them, and how they are managed. Tribal peoples are victimized because they control resources that outsiders demand. The resources exist because tribals managed them conservatively. However, as with the issue of the health consequences of detribalization, some anthropologists minimize the adaptive achievements of tribal groups and seem unwilling to concede that ecocide might be a consequence of cultural change. Critics attack an exaggerated "noble savage" image of tribals living in perfect harmony with nature and having no visible impact on their surroundings. They then show that tribals do in fact modify the environment, and they conclude that there is no significant difference between how tribals and industrial societies treat their environments. For example, Charles Wagley declared that Brazilian Indians such as the Tapirape

are not "natural men." They have human vices just as we do.... They do not live "in tune" with nature any more than I do; in fact, they can often be as destructive of their environment, within their limitations, as some civilized men. The Tapirape are not innocent or childlike in any way.

Wagley, 1977: 302

Anthropologist Terry Rambo demonstrated that the Semang of the Malaysian rain forests have a measurable impact on their environment. In his monograph *Primitive Polluters,* Rambo (1985) reported that the Semang live in smoke-filled houses. They sneeze and spread germs, breathe, and thus emit carbon dioxide. They clear small gardens, contributing "particulate matter" to the air and disturbing the local climate because cleared areas proved measurably warmer and drier than the shady forest. Rambo concluded that his research "demonstrates the essential functional similarity of the environmental interactions of primitive and civilized societies" (1985: 78) in contrast to a "noble savage" view (Bodley, 1983) which, according to Rambo (1985: 2), mistakenly "claims that traditional peoples almost always live in essential harmony with their environment."

This is surely a false issue. To stress, as I do, that tribals tend to manage their resources for sustained yield within relatively self-sufficient subsistence economies is not to make them either innocent children or natural men. Nor is it to deny that tribals "disrupt" their environment and may never be in absolute "balance" with nature.

The ecocide issue is perhaps most dramatically illustrated by two sets of satellite photos taken over the Brazilian rain forests of Rôndonia (Allard & McIntyre, 1988: 780–781). Photos taken in 1973, when Rôndonia was still a tribal domain, show virtually unbroken rain forest. The 1987 satellite photos, taken after just fifteen years of highway construction and "development" by outsiders, show more than 20 percent of the forest destroyed. The surviving Indians were being concentrated by FUNAI (Brazil's national Indian foundation) into what would soon become mere islands of forest in a ravaged landscape. It is irrelevant to quibble about whether tribals are noble, childlike, or innocent, or about the precise meaning of balance with nature, carrying capacity, or adaptation, to recognize that for the past 200 years rapid environmental deterioration on an unprecedented global scale has followed the wresting of control of vast areas of the world from tribal groups by resource-hungry industrial societies.

Deprivation and Discrimination

Contact with European culture has given them a knowledge of great wealth, opportunity and privilege, but only very limited avenues by which to acquire these things.

Crocombe, 1968

Unwittingly, tribal peoples have had the burden of perpetual relative deprivation thrust upon them by acceptance—either by themselves or by the governments administering them—of the standards of socioeconomic progress set for them by industrial civilizations. By comparison with the material wealth of industrial societies, tribal societies become, by definition, impoverished. They are then forced to transform their cultures and work to achieve what many economists now acknowledge to be unattainable goals. Even though in many cases the modest GNP goals set by development planners for the developing nations during the "development decade" of the 1960s were often met, the results were hardly noticeable for most of the tribal people involved. Population growth, environmental limitations, inequitable distribution of wealth, and the continued rapid growth of the industrialized nations have all meant that both the absolute and the relative gap between the rich and poor in the world is steadily widening. The prospect that tribal peoples will actually be able to attain the levels of resource consumption to which they are being encouraged to aspire is remote indeed except for those few groups who have retained effective control over strategic mineral resources.

Tribal peoples feel deprivation not only when the economic goals they have been encouraged to seek fail to materialize, but also when they discover that they are powerless, second-class citizens who are discriminated against and exploited by the dominant society. At the same time, they are denied the satisfactions of their traditional cultures, because these have been sacrificed in the process of modernization. Under the impact of major economic change family life is disrupted, traditional social controls are often lost, and many indicators of social anomie such as alcoholism, crime, delinquency, suicide, emotional disorders, and despair may increase. The inevitable frustration resulting from this continual deprivation finds expression in the cargo cults, revitalization movements, and a variety of other political and religious movements that have been widespread among tribal peoples following their disruption by industrial civilization.

References

Ackermann, F. L. 1964. *Geologia e Fisiografia da Região Bragantina, Estado do Pará.* Manaus, Brazil: Conselho Nacional de Pesquisas, Instituto Nacional de Pesquisas da Amazonia.

Allard, William Albert, and Loren McIntyre. 1988. Rondônia's settlers invade Brazil's imperiled rain forest. *National Geographic* 174(6):772–799.

Bodley, John H. 1970. *Campa Socio-Economic Adaptation.* Ann Arbor: University Microfilms.

———. 1983. *Der Weg der Zerstörung: Stammesvölker und die industrielle Zivilization.* Munich: Trickster-Verlag. (Translation of *Victims of Progress.*)

Bodley, John H., and Foley C. Benson. 1979. Cultural ecology of Amazonian palms. *Reports of Investigations,* no. 56. Pullman: Laboratory of Anthropology, Washington State University.

Bunce, George E. 1972. Aggravation of vitamin A deficiency following distribution of non-fortified skim milk: An example of nutrient interaction. In *The Careless Technology: Ecology and International Development,* ed. M. T. Farvar and John P. Milton, pp. 53–60. Garden City, N.Y.: Natural History Press.

Burling, Robbins. 1963. *Rengsanggri: Family and Kinship in a Garo Village.* Philadelphia: University of Pennsylvania Press.

Davis, A. E., and T. D. Bolin. 1972. Lactose intolerance in Southeast Asia. In *The Careless Technology: Ecology and International Development,* ed. M. T. Farvar and John P. Milton, pp. 61–68. Garden City, N.Y.: Natural History Press.

Dennett, Glenn, and John Connell. 1988. Acculturation and health in the highlands of Papua New Guinea. *Current Anthropology* 29(2):273–299.

Goldschmidt, Walter R. 1972. The interrelations between cultural factors and the acquisition of new technical skills. In *The Progress of Underdeveloped Areas,* ed. Bert F. Hoselitz, pp. 135–151. Chicago: University of Chicago Press.

Gross, Daniel R., et al. 1979. Ecology and acculturation among native peoples of Central Brazil. *Science* 206(4422):1043–1050.

Hughes, Charles C., and John M. Hunter. 1972. The role of technological development in promoting disease in Africa. In *The Careless Technology: Ecology and International Development,* ed. M. T. Farvar and John P. Milton, pp. 69–101. Garden City, N.Y.: Natural History Press.

Keesing, Felix M. 1941. *The South Seas in the Modern World.* Institute of Pacific Relations International Research Series. New York: John Day.

Kroeger, Axel, and François Barbira-Freedman. 1982. *Culture Change and Health: The Case of South American Rainforest Indians.* Frankfurt am Main: Verlag Peter Lang. (Reprinted in Bodley, 1988a:221–236.)

McNeil, Mary. 1972. Lateritic soils in distinct tropical environments: Southern Sudan and Brazil. In *The Careless Technology: Ecology and International Development,* ed. M. T. Farvar and John P. Milton, pp. 591–608. Garden City, N.Y.: Natural History Press.

Mönckeberg, F. 1968. Mental retardation from malnutrition. *Journal of the American Medical Association* 206:30–31.

Montagu, Ashley. 1972. Sociogenic brain damage. *American Anthropologist* 74(5):1045–1061.

Rambo, A. Terry. 1985. *Primitive Polluters: Semang Impact on the Malaysian Tropical Rain Forest Ecosystem.* Anthropological Papers no. 76, Museum of Anthropology, University of Michigan.

Redfield, Robert. 1953. *The Primitive World and Its Transformations.* Ithaca, N.Y.: Cornell University Press.

———. 1962. *A Village That Chose Progress: Chan Kom Revisited.* Chicago: University of Chicago Press, Phoenix Books.

Smith, Wilberforce. 1894. The teeth of ten Sioux Indians. *Journal of the Royal Anthropological Institute* 24:109–116.

TTR: *See under* United States.

United States, Department of the Interior, Office of Territories. 1953. *Report on the Administration of the Trust Territory of the Pacific Islands* (by the United States to the United Nations) for the Period July 1, 1951 to June 30, 1952.

———. 1954. *Annual Report, High Commissioner of the Trust Territory of the Pacific Islands to the Secretary of the Interior* (for 1953).

United States, Department of State. 1955. *Seventh Annual Report to the United Nations on the Administration of the Trust Territory of the Pacific Islands* (July 1, 1953 to June 30, 1954).

———. 1959. *Eleventh Annual Report to the United Nations on the Administration of the Trust Territory of the Pacific Islands* (July 1, 1957 to June 30, 1958).

——. 1964. *Sixteenth Annual Report to the United Nations on the Administration of the Trust Territory of the Pacific Islands* (July 1, 1962 to June 30, 1963).

——. 1973. *Twenty-Fifth Annual Report to the United Nations on the Administration of the Trust Territory of the Pacific Islands* (July 1, 1971 to June 30, 1972).

Critical Thinking

1. Why is "standard of living" an intrinsically ethnocentric concept as a measure of progress? What is a more useful measure and why? What does a careful examination based upon the specific points show?

2. In what ways does economic development increase the disease rate of affected peoples?

3. How does the author answer critics who argue that such figures simply represent better health monitoring? List the examples cited.

4. Explain the effects of government policy on peoples' adaptations to local environmental conditions.

5. Describe the circumstances under which peoples' dietary habits have been changed as a result of outside influences. What has happened to nutritional levels and why?

6. To what was attributed the differences in dental health between the Sioux Indians of Buffalo Bill's Wild West Show and Londoners?

7. What did Weston Price find in his studies?

8. Describe the chain of events that goes from the adoption of new economic patterns to changes in the kinds of crops grown to low wages to nutritional deprivation (principally of children).

9. What is one of the most tragic, and largely overlooked, aspects of chronic malnutrition?

10. What are the prospects that modern health institutions will overcome these problems?

11. How does the author respond to critics who charge that tribal peoples have always had low life expectancies, high infant mortality rates, and nutritional deficiencies?

12. What factors have contributed to population growth?

13. What are the consequences for each of the following:
    • Official policy restricting swidden people to smaller territories?
    • Resource depletion forcing people to participate in the world-market economy?
    • The settling of nomadic herders and the removal of prior controls on herd size?
    • Shortening the planting cycles?

14. How does the reality of ecocide focus attention on the fundamental contrasts between tribal and industrial systems in their use of natural resources? Who controls such resources and how they are managed?

15. What do the critics of the "noble savage" image claim? How does the author respond?

16. In what respects do tribal peoples feel deprivation as a result of "modernization"?

Create Central

www.mhhe.com/createcentral

Internet References

Association for Political and Legal Anthropology
www.aaanet.org/apla/index.htm

Human Rights and Humanitarian Assistance
www.etown.edu/vl/humrts.html

The Indigenous Rights Movement in the Pacific
www.inmotionmagazine.com/pacific.html

Murray Research Center
www.radcliffe.edu/murray_redirect/index.php

WWW Virtual Library: Indigenous Studies
www.cwis.org

Article   Prepared by: Elvio Angeloni, *Pasadena City College*

Ecuador's Paradise Lost

President Correa tried to save the world's most biodiverse forest, but the West ignored his offer.

CHRISTIAN PARENTI

Learning Outcomes

After reading this article, you will be able to:

- Discuss the importance of the Yasuni reserve and the threats to its existence.

- Discuss the relationship between the Yasuni initiative and the problem of global climate change.

- Discuss how important the decision about whether to drill for oil is to Ecuador.

The tapir, dark brown and the size of a small cow, had been shot in the head and floated away dead before the hunters could retrieve it. Now the man at the helm of our outboard skiff, traveling up a muddy Ecuadorean river in the Yasuni National Park with some scientists from the Tiputini Biodiversity Station, has spotted the freshly killed animal.

A couple kilometers further upriver, we pass a hunting party of Indians. They have new clothes; one of the men wears a big watch; a woman in their party has a bright yellow dress; on their canoe sits a big new outboard engine. These are all signs that they are not local subsistence hunters, but outsiders in search of illegal bush meat to sell in the towns. As we glide by, the Indians smirk condescendingly at the worried conservation-minded scientists. This is how jungles die: one tapir at a time, bit by bit, nibbled away by poachers, settlers, and illegal loggers.

Yasuni is scientifically determined to be the most biologically diverse place on earth: researchers here even discovered a fungus that can digest plastic. But Yasuni sits atop a large part of Ecuador's known petroleum reserves and that means this global treasure is under dire threat.

For a time, the effort to save Yasuni appeared to have a real chance. In 2007, at the peak of a recent wave of global concern about anthropogenic climate change, Ecuador's left-wing president, Rafael Correa, promised to keep 20 percent of the country's known petroleum reserves—an estimated 846 million barrels of Yasuni's Ishpingo-Tambococha-Tiputini (ITT) oil field—permanently out of reach . . . *if* the international community would contribute at least half of the revenue that Ecuador could earn by extracting the oil (about $3.5 billion).

Donations were held in a trust fund operated by the United Nations Development Group and used to finance alternative energy projects like wind and solar. The fund needed to raise only $350 million a year for the next 10 years. And the plan was seen as a possible model for other developing economies wishing to escape dependence on oil exports.

But shortly after Correa launched the Yasuni initiative, the global financial crisis of 2008 hit, and the few states—mostly in Europe—that had responded positively dialed back their support. Meanwhile, the largest economies and the worst polluters—including the United States and China—simply ignored the plan. Announcing the end of the Yasuni initiative on August 16, Correa put it bluntly: "The world has failed us."

Like the Keystone XL pipeline, Yasuni is something of a global test case for the climate-activist rallying cry of "Leave the oil in the soil and the coal in the hole." If humanity cannot manage to refrain from drilling for oil beneath the most biologically diverse place on earth, then how can we expect any state or community not to drill for oil beneath barren desert, degraded farmland, or on the ocean floor?

Now the jungle here will likely be destroyed, not necessarily by oil spills but by the larger economic reverberations of petroleum development. First will come the oil prospectors, and with them roads. Upon the roads will come hunters, loggers, miners, drug smugglers, settlers, ranchers, and thus deforestation.

Across the planet, other bad signs are converging. Global emissions continue to increase. The massive fracking-led natural

Yasuni National Park

962K Hectares in size (2.4 million acres)
4,000 Species of vascular plants
2,274 Species of trees and shrubs
593 Species of birds
150 Species of amphibians
120 Species of reptiles
80 Species of bats

gas boom has driven energy prices so low that many wind and solar projects are no longer economically viable. And a recently leaked draft of the Fifth Assessment Report from the Intergovernmental Panel on Climate Change (IPCC) warns that global sea levels could rise more than three feet by the end of the century if emissions continue unabated. As if that wasn't bad enough, many scientists say that the IPCC is once again being too conservative. Michael Mann, director of Pennsylvania State University's Earth System Science Center, told the *Huffington Post* that sea levels could rise six feet by 2100.

The fight for Yasuni is not just about climate and biodiversity; it is also about cultural survival. Most people here are Quechua-speaking Napo Runas, whom historians believe are the descendants of traumatized survivors of the violence of the late-nineteenth-century Amazon rubber boom. But at the heart of Yasuni live the Waorani, about 4,000 people who speak a language unrelated to any other. An estimated 200 to 400 Waorani are "uncontacted"—living in voluntary isolation. They never venture out of the forest, and in 2007 the Ecuadorean government made it illegal for outsiders to go in after them with Bibles or "aid."

The Waorani first met the modern world thanks to oil. In 1937, Shell started prospecting in Waorani territory. But the Indians resisted—killing workers, burning and looting oil camps. For many years, they effectively kept the company out. In 1956, a group of evangelical Christians from the Summer Institute of Linguistics attempted contact, but the Waorani killed them with wooden spears.

By the early 1970s, missionaries had converted some Waorani. Around that time, the Tagaeri clan separated from the rest of the Waorani and fled deep into the jungle. In 1987, two Catholic missionaries working with local oil firms, Monsignor Alejandro Labaka and Sister Ines Arango, tried to meet the Tagaeri and convince them to allow oil company personnel to enter their territory. The missionaries were found dead, full of spears. In 1993, two adventure tourists disappeared in the same area.

There is still occasional trouble. In 2008, an illegal logger was speared to death while stealing trees, and there were unconfirmed rumors of a massacre of anywhere from 5 to 15 Waorani.

Closer to the research station, along a road built by the Spanish oil company Repsol, are Waorani who, after being contacted in the 1970s, now live in settled communities and survive by a mix of farming, hunting, and day labor for the oil company. Far from being the noble savages of Western fantasy, the Waorani along the Repsol road range from hard-working mothers to young, progressive college kids (I met one who wanted to go study in Cuba), to angry old quasi-bandits who resent the scientists as much as the oil company.

Diego Mosquera, manager of the Tiputini Biodiversity Station, knows these people well. Part of his job involves a weekly trip bringing the station's garbage out and its supplies in. Frequently, a group of Waorani men associated with a tough old warrior named Nambea stop Mosquera on the road and demand tribute.

"Sometimes their demands are pretty outrageous, like 'Give me a million dollars,'" Mosquera explained. "I say, 'I don't have it.' So they say, 'OK, give me a mattress and a watermelon.'"

On one trip, they stopped Mosquera and gave him a detailed list of financial demands in formally written Spanish: "Dear Diego, this is to remind you of your obligation to pay us. If you should fail to pay, we will burn down your research station, kill all your monkeys and kill you. Thank you, and have a nice day."

We can read in the Waorani's threats a measure of the real stakes involved. Though Ecuador's oil is not massively important to the world—it produces some 500,000 barrels a day, about the same as Australia or Thailand—the oil is important to Ecuador. The country only has a "B" credit rating and thus pays high interest rates. This is partly the result of a "selective default" on $3.2 billion in foreign debts, which Correa declared "illegitimate" in 2008. Against this backdrop, financing development with oil revenues is all the more alluring.

Meanwhile, 27 percent of Ecuadoreans live in poverty, with many of them going hungry; as the World Bank puts it, they are unable to "meet their nutritional requirements even if they spend everything they have on food." Many of the Ecuadorean poor are well organized and militant, and they protest vigorously with mass marches and roadblocks. This puts heavy pressure on Correa from the left to deliver services and thus increase state spending, though the same forces tend to oppose exploitation in Yasuni.

The Ecuadorean economy needs a more equitable distribution of wealth, but it also needs investment and jobs. The state needs revenue to fund its expanding experiment in poverty reduction and tropical social democracy. Under such conditions, it is hard not to drill for oil. The country's proven oil reserves of 6.5 billion barrels could underwrite all manner of future development schemes. As OilPrice.com puts it: "Oil brings in a dependable cash flow and prices remain near historic highs. If Ecuador can return to its previous, higher levels of oil production, it would be an easy guaranteed growth opportunity." No wonder the Chinese are set to help finance a $12.5 billion oil refinery in Ecuador.

Unlike the Waorani on the Repsol road who threatened to "burn down" the research station and "kill all your monkeys," the government of Ecuador asked politely and argued reasonably. Yet the rich nations ignored the Yasuni initiative— and if they continue to fail to mitigate carbon emissions and build out a new carbon-free energy economy, it's not hard to imagine a scenario in which the world does essentially "burn down," killing all of the monkeys—even the very clever ones in business suits.

Critical Thinking

1. Discuss the importance of the Yasuni reserve and the threats to its existence.
2. Why was the Yasuni initiative a gobal test case in combating climate change and why did it fail?
3. Discuss the likelihood that the jungle will be destroyed.
4. What are the other "bad signs" across the globe that climate change is occurring?
5. Why is the fight for Yasuni also about cultural survival?
6. What are the stakes involved for Ecuador when deciding whether to drill for oil?

Create Central

www.mhhe.com/createcentral

Internet References

Association for Political and Legal Anthropology
www.aaanet.org/apla/index.htm
WWW Virtual Library: Indigenous Studies
www.cwis.org

CHRISTIAN PARENTI, a professor at the School for International Training Graduate Institute, is the author of *Tropic of Chaos: Climate Change and the New Geography of Violence.*

Article   Prepared by: Elvio Angeloni, *Pasadena City College*

Saving Our Identity: an Uphill Battle for the Tuva of China

Yuxin Hou

Learning Outcomes

After reading this article, you will be able to:

- Discuss the ways in which economic development has impacted traditional Tuva culture.

- Discuss the impact of the Cultural Revolution and government neglect upon Tuva health and social problems.

The Tuva are ancient hunters and nomadic peoples whose lineage can be traced back more than a 1000 years to the Tang dynasty. Described in the Tang dynasty-era book *Tongdian* as "skiing hunters" and during the Yuan dynasty as "forest people," they lived a free, mobile life around the Yenisei River and the Altai and Sayan Mountains. According to Chinese historical records, the Tuva were hunters and nomads until the Qing dynasty, which lasted from the mid-1600s to the early twentieth century. They declared independence from China in 1912, directly following the Chinese revolution of the year before, and in 1944 were incorporated into the USSR as an autonomous oblast (administrative region). Today, the Tuva are scattered across Xinjiang (China), outer Mongolia, and Russia. Chinese Tuva mainly live in the three villages of Kanas, Hemu, and Baihaba, with a total population of around 2,500.

As the Chinese government endeavors to push economic development and continues to establish itself as a major world power, groups like the Chinese Tuva are especially vulnerable to mental, physical, social, and cultural suffering. Tuva elder Mengboer has witnessed the great cultural shifts of the last half century. In his words, "Before the Cultural Revolution, we could freely conduct hunting and nomadic life in the forest and grasslands; shamanism, natural worship, and hunting taboos had endowed us with ecological wisdom. However,

with the rapid development of national assimilation, forced settlement, tourism, and the implementation of hunting prohibition, we were drawn into a strange and crazy world that is full of utilitarianism, demoralization, anthropocentrism, and economic centrism."

This rapid transformation has hugely impacted the Chinese Tuvas' traditional culture, livelihood, survival concepts, natural environment, and naturalistic values. Since the Cultural Revolution, they have also endured the loss of their own pluralistic medicine traditions and now face the dilemma of a modern medical system. The small, simple clinics in Chinese Tuva villages are short on both medicine and doctors, so ailments like the common cold or fevers sometimes prove fatal due to expired medicine or misdiagnosis. As a result, increasing numbers of Tuva refuse to see a doctor. However, they can no longer seek out traditional folk healers, such as shamans or the family sage—they have all but vanished.

Crises of Culture, Identity, and Language

The Tuva are defined as a cross-national ethnic group separated by national borders (China, Mongolia, and Russia), though for the purposes of national identification the Chinese government classifies them as Mongolian. Wuyun, an elder Tuva who runs several small businesses in the community, explains the difficulty of being classified this way: "We should be identified as a separate Tuva ethnic minority instead of belonging to Mongolia due to our unique language and the historical relation with the Tuva people of China. Most Tuva live outside of China, so we were afraid that once we were classified as Mongolian people, gradually we would be assimilated into Mongolia and lose our own language and culture," she says.

Chinese Tuva were identified as Mongolian as a result of state power and the consideration of border security and stability, but the ensuing identity crisis has challenged their collective psychological and cultural identity. In daily life, Chinese Tuva used the Tuva language as their family language and the Kazak language as an inter-ethnic language. The Mongolian language was rarely used, and most Chinese Tuva cannot speak it fluently. However, many can speak fluent Mandarin due to the influence of institutionalized education and practical consideration.

The Tuva language has been called "the live fossil of old Turkish language" without the written system. As Tuva elder Aeruna, a retired primary school teacher, explains, "In the beginning of the establishment of People's Republic of China, we endeavored to establish the Tuva language school. But, we could never fulfill it. It became impossible after we were identified as a Mongolian ethnic group." With the rapid development of modern education and urbanization, increasing numbers of young Tuva are denied the chance to use the Tuva language. As a result, Tuva has become an endangered language. Suder, a herdsman in the community, offers another perspective; he has two children who are currently being educated in a Han Chinese school. "Although I know our language is at risk, we still hope our children will have a good grasp of Mandarin, which could bring them more opportunities and better future," he says.

Population On the Brink

Following the Cultural Revolution, most Chinese Tuva who lived through it later suffered from mental illness. Depression and mental illness also afflicts young Chinese Tuva within national assimilation projects, most likely due to forced settlement and hunting prohibition. These blows to their traditional ways of life, along with the government's social neglect, have led to feelings of resentment and desperation that are frequently accompanied by alcohol abuse, crime, and even suicide. Melingsha is a Tuva housewife who lost her husband to complications from alcohol abuse. "During the long winter," she said, "we could not continue our own traditional life of hunting and gradually fell into alcoholism. Alcoholics included youngsters, old people, pregnant women, and even minors. The alcoholism also created a series of social problems such as divorce, violence, crime, and suicide," which have all contributed to population decline.

The number of pregnant women who are alcoholics, in concert with poor delivery conditions, has worsened the population decline. According to Mengkerqia, a knowledgeable local elite, "From 2007–2008, the death number and birth number of Chinese Tuva were 42 and 12, respectively. In 2009–2010, the numbers were 38 and 9. Additionally, Chinese Tuva women have been increasingly intermarrying with Han (Chinese), Kazak, and Hui Peoples. They have had to make such decisions as a result of the large number of male alcoholics in our native population." The official point of view is that the main factor of population decline is inbreeding. Tala, an elder Tuva housewife, refutes this: "Historically, consanguineous marriage never happened in our society. Because we belonged to different tribes, we strictly followed the marriage taboo of no marriage within seven generations," she says.

In actual fact, the Tuvas' population declined as a dual result of forced settlement during the Cultural Revolution and modern day tourism; in a vicious cycle, the difficulties faced by Tuva men in particular exacerbated the rate of alcoholism, and alcoholism has worsened the marriage problem. In addition to the overt causes of national assimilation projects, forced settlements, and hunting prohibitions, there are more problems lurking behind the scenes: sedentary centrism, economic centrism, and anthropocentrism have pushed the current Chinese nomadic people and other small ethnic groups to the brink. But, the future is not written yet. If given a chance, it is possible that the ecologism, environmentalism, and naturalism practiced by these once nomadic people could bring much enlightenment to modern civilization.

Critical Thinking

1. Discuss the ways in which economic development has impacted traditional Tuva culture.

2. Discuss the Tuva's identity crisis.

3. How have the Cultural Revolution and government neglect led to health and social problems among the Tuva?

4. Discuss the official explanation for the Tuva population decline and the real reasons for it.

Create Central

www.mhhe.com/createcentral

Internet References

Human Rights and Humanitarian Assistance
www.etown.edu/vl/humrts.html

WWW Virtual Library: Indigenous Studies
www.cwis.org

YUXIN HOU is a postdoctoral research fellow at NGO Research Center, School of Public Policy and Management, Tsinghua University, Beijing, China.

Article   Prepared by: Elvio Angeloni, *Pasadena City College*

Blood in the Jungle

SCOTT WALLACE

Learning Outcomes

After reading this article, you will be able to:

- Discuss the ways in which Brazil has become the most dangerous country in the world in which to work as an environmentalist.
- Discuss the global economy as the underlying cause of the violence against environmentalists.

On the edge of a lonely dirt road that winds through farmland and forest in the eastern Amazon Basin of Brazil stands a simple marble slab. It's a memorial to a local rainforest defender who was gunned down on his motorcycle, together with his wife, on the site on the morning of May 24, 2011.

Nearly two years later, I stand on the road by a swollen brook, trying to reconstruct the chain of events that led to the brutal deaths of José "Zé Cláudio" Ribeiro da Silva and Maria do Espirito Santo. The afternoon is muggy and overcast, with low-hanging, leaden clouds threatening more rain, raising the prospect of getting stuck out here in the middle of nowhere.

"The gunmen were hiding in the brush over there," says Maria's brother-in-law José Maria Gomes Sampaio, who has accompanied me on a bouncy two-hour ride in a 4×4 across flooded plains and fields dotted with dilapidated ranchos and herds of white, hump-backed steers. A wiry man with pleading dark eyes and an Adam's apple that bobs when he speaks, Sampaio, 49, walked past this very spot only a half-hour before the ambush. "They were already here when I went by," he says, pointing into the shadows beyond the washed-out bridge that forced the victims to slow their dirt bike to a crawl, putting the couple directly in their gunsight.

The killers evidently knew when the couple would be traveling. In the predawn darkness, they took up positions behind a blind of thicket close by the decrepit bridge. It was a time of day when there would likely be no witnesses. And the shotgun with its spray of buckshot would confound efforts to identify a murder weapon. It was a well-planned operation. Not likely the work of two illiterate, down-and-out men in their early 30s. Certainly not acting on their own, anyway.

From this vantage point at the bottom of a gentle slope, I get an uncanny sense of straddling the very edge of Brazil's most violent frontier. On the one side of the road, electric-green cattle pastures roll away into the distance, as far as the eye can see. On the other side, colossal castanha and andiroba trees, draped in thick lianas, soar to neck-craning heights, the remnants of a virgin rainforest Zé Cláudio and Maria died trying to defend from the chain saws that had already leveled much of the forest in this part of the Amazon Basin.

Somewhere in the treetops, a toucan yelps. I turn back to inspect the memorial more closely. "They want to do the same thing to me they did to Chico Mendes and Sister Dorothy," it reads. Prophetic words, spoken by Zé Cláudio at a public gathering six months before he and Maria were gunned down. The inscription is mostly intact, but it's been vandalized by the impact of two bullets, leaving it fractured.

It has been 25 years since the assassination of Chico Mendes, the rubber tapper who made defense of the Amazon rainforest an international cause célèbre after he was shot dead by the son of a rancher. And it has been nine years since Ohio-born nun Dorothy Stang was killed in similar circumstances. The shattered plaque offers a grim testament to how risky it still is to stand up for the rainforest. Environmental activists in Brazil and around the world continue to pay the ultimate price for their convictions. And their numbers are mounting.

Zé Cláudio and Maria, both in their early 50s at the time of their deaths, had been married for nearly 30 years. For even longer they'd been fighting to protect their lush forestland from illegal loggers, ranchers, and the operators of clandestine charcoal pits that reduced magnificent, centuries-old trees to sacks of briquettes. In 1997, they helped succeed in petitioning the federal government to create the Praia Alta-Piranheira agro-forestry settlement, 84 square miles of public land to provide themselves and other family farmers a sustainable living while keeping the forest intact. Its purpose stood in stark contrast to other pursuits that had turned so much of southern Pará, a state in Brazil, into an epicenter of violence and devastation.

But the boundaries of the reserve could hold back neither the bloodletting nor the pillage. Fourteen years after Zé Cláudio and Maria helped found the settlement, its forest cover had shrunk from 80 percent to 20 percent. Speculators snatched up parcels and sold off the timber. They flipped the land to cattlemen and wheeler-dealers looking for a quick buck. They imposed their own brand of frontier justice, tapping when necessary into an abundant pool of underemployed enforcers, or jagunços, from the rough-and-tumble slums of Marabá, Pará's fourth-largest city, which boasts one of the highest murder rates in Brazil.

Evidently, it was to this reservoir of talent that the enemies of Zé Cláudio and Maria turned in the spring of 2011. Nearly two years later, two out-of-work day laborers—Alberto Lopes do Nascimento, 30, and Lindoiy onson Silva Rocha, 31—sat in prison blues in a Marabá courtroom, charged with carrying out the murders with coldblooded calculation. Silva Rocha, named in honor of the 36th president of the United States, happened to be the brother of José Rodrigues Moreira, a rancher whose efforts to acquire land inside the reserve had been repeatedly frustrated by Zé Cláudio and Maria. Moreira, a tightly wound and fervently religious man of 43 with short-cropped auburn hair and pinched brow, was also on trial, accused of ordering the killings.

Violence unleashed against green activists is on the rise. London-based rights group Global Witness says more than 700 environmentalists were murdered in the decade that began in 2001. Either because documentation of such crimes is more thorough in Brazil than elsewhere or because its frontier is the most violent—perhaps both—more than half of the global death toll was recorded within its borders. In any event, Brazil is considered the most dangerous country in which to work as an environmentalist today.

Many of the victims of environmentally motivated violence are not your typical placard-waving rabble-rousers, but rather are grass-roots leaders who stand up for their communities when threatened by environmental calamity. "Often these people become involved because they're fighting for what's being taken away from them and their communities," says Jane Cohen, an expert in environmental health at Human Rights Watch in New York City. "They're especially vulnerable because they usually don't have a support network, and things can really escalate before their stories get on the national or international radar."

Worldwide, the most violent years were 2010, when 96 activists were killed, and 2011, the most recent year assessed, when 106 were slain. At that rate, chances are that someone will be killed somewhere on the planet this week for investigating toxic runoff from a gold mine, protesting a mega-dam that will flood communal farmland or trying to shield endangered wildlife from well-armed poachers. Rights advocates warn the upward trend is likely to continue. And because of the spotty quality of reporting, the overall number of killings is likely to be a good bit higher.

"We may be seeing just the tip of a much larger iceberg," says Bill Kovarik, a communications professor at Radford University in Virginia who tracks cases of abuse perpetrated on green activists. "The world needs to be aware of the people who are dying to save what's left of the natural environment."

The underlying cause of the violence appears to be the expanding reach of the global economy into hitherto inaccessible hinterlands. These are regions where governance is shakiest and where traditional, subsistence-oriented communities find themselves up against much more powerful, profit-hungry players.

"It is a well-known Parádox that many of the world's poorest countries are home to the resources that drive the global economy," reads a 2012 Global Witness report. "Now, as the race to secure access to these resources intensifies, it is poor people and activists who increasingly find themselves in the firing line."

A Laotian community organizer named Sombath Somphone, 60, vanished from a police checkpoint outside the capital of Vientiane in 2012. His disappearance came after he spoke up for victims of a land-grab scheme that saw village rice fields bulldozed to make way for a foreign-owned rubber plantation.

Francisco Canayong, 64, was president of a Philippine farmers association when he was stabbed to death in 2012. Two months earlier, he had rallied villagers to block a China-bound shipment of chromite ore from an illegal mine that was poisoning local water sources. He and two other activists had also testified that they'd overheard the mine's boss making plans to kill the trio if they succeeded in shutting down the operation.

In the oak forests of southwestern Mexico, communities are under siege from illegal loggers backed by drug cartels seeking to expand their acreage of opium poppies and marijuana. Entire towns have risen up to torch logging trucks and expel corrupt officials, arming themselves against traffickers and timber poachers. But resistance comes at a high price: Several villagers have been murdered while out collecting mushrooms and firewood in what remains of the forest.

Mexico may be an extreme case, but experts say it points to the connection between the consumption of goods in the rich, industrialized nations, and the environmental and human toll in poor nations. Protesters at an Australian-owned mine in Indonesia are threatened and brutalized by government troops. Park guards in Central Africa are ambushed by poachers who slaughter wildlife for tusks and body parts that will ultimately sell as high-priced aphrodisiacs in Asian markets. An uncontacted tribe in Peru faces deadly peril from the encroachment of men and machines exploring for oil that will end up in the pumps of an American gas station. In the eastern Amazon where Zé Cláudio and Maria lived and died, charcoal from illegally cut trees is used to smelt pig iron, a key ingredient in the steel assemblies of cars sold in the United States and Europe.

"There's a resource that someone wants," Kovarik says, describing the pattern of events that puts environmental advocates at risk of harm. "People are displaced to get it. They organize and speak up, and their leaders are killed. It's happening all around the world, and it needs to be investigated."

The cases are by nature difficult to investigate. Local authorities are often in the pockets of those who have a vested interest in covering up the crime. And the assassinations are likely to involve complicated conspiracies, with instigators distancing themselves through a series of middlemen from the "kill team"—often two men on a fast-moving dirt bike, one driving, the other with a finger on the trigger.

Like the murders of Chico Mendes and Dorothy Stang, the deaths of Zé Cláudio and Maria provoked such widespread revulsion that Brazilian officials were forced to act. Bringing the killers to justice came to be seen as an early test of President Dilma Rousseff's commitment to the rule of law. It also posed a serious challenge to one of her core tenets—that Brazil can remain a bastion of biological and cultural diversity even while exploiting the riches of the Amazon Basin with massive development projects. She dispatched federal agents to investigate.

They had a lot of work to do. After all, José Rodrigues Moreira was but the latest in a long list of people Zé Cláudio and Maria had crossed paths with over the years. As the reserve's forest cover shrank, the couple had denounced illegal land clearing, unauthorized logging, the illicit buying and selling of parcels, and the charcoal pits that not only devastated woodlands but also employed slave labor to do it. And many families on the settlement had turned to ranching themselves after failing to secure credit for more eco-friendly activities such as extracting oils and salves from rainforest nuts and fruits. They came to resent what they saw as the couple's purist hectoring.

"There was an internal ideological war underway within the settlement," says Claudelice Silva dos Santos, 31, Zé Cláudio's youngest sister. I've just arrived at the slain couple's former home, a simple cabin set back in the woods, a few miles from the scene of the crime. Claudelice and several sisters and brothers-in-law are lounging on the front porch, drinking coffee, and smoking cigarettes. "The association was divided between those who sought a sustainable alternative to cutting down the forest and those who were willing to partner with outside interests." The outside interests, she says, are mostly ranchers seeking to extend their pasturelands into the settlement.

The government detectives narrowed their focus in the end to a single line of inquiry, and Moreira and the two alleged triggermen were taken into custody and charged with murder. Oddly, prosecutors did not present what appeared to be evidence of a larger conspiracy. A federal police wiretap recorded Moreira, in hiding after hearing reports that linked him to the murders. In the phone call, he instructed a relative to tell a pair of fellow ranchers to hire an attorney for his defense. Otherwise, he threatened, he would "deliver them all" to authorities. Moreira got his lawyers. The wiretap was not introduced as evidence. The other ranchers were never charged.

The jury in Marabá eventually returned a verdict that astounded everyone in the packed courtroom. The hit men were found guilty; Moreira was absolved and set free. Lawyers on both sides called it "schizophrenic," contradictory. Without a prime mover—an "intellectual author," in legal terms—the murders made no sense; neither of the killers had any known connection to the victims, except through Moreira. By the jury's logic, it was a crime without motive.

The decision left the families of Zé Cláudio and Maria stunned and fearful. Not only were the apparent co-conspirators who Moreira threatened to expose in the wiretapped conversation still on the loose; now Moreira himself was as well. "Sure, we're afraid," says Claudelice, her darting eyes probing the nearby forest. The memorial has been shot up, and gunfire has been heard close to the house as well. It's an intimidation tactic that dates back to the years when Zé Cláudio and Maria were still alive. Back then, she says, Zé Cláudio often maintained a nighttime vigil from the crook of a tree to counter shadowy figures who took potshots at the house that she believes were intended to kill her brother. "Thank God they didn't succeed . . ." Claudelice starts to say, then catches herself in mid-sentence at the unintended irony. They did, in fact, succeed all too well. Quickly shifting gears, she adds: "But my brother and his wife fought till the end for an ideal. Who are we if we don't show the same courage? It was our blood, not just theirs, that was spilled here."

She and a brother-in-law, Luiz, take me on a short hike back through the woods. Despite the pastureland pressing in from all sides, the 50-acre property feels like a small reserve in its own right, practically all of it intact, virgin rainforest. The decaying leaf litter exudes a spongy dankness underfoot. In 10 minutes, we reach a towering castanha—a Brazil-nut tree—so wide that it would take at least eight people joined hand to hand to encircle its base. Zé Cláudio had estimated the colossus to be about 600 years old—older than the discovery of the New World itself. Hundreds of similar behemoths inside the reserve have already been toppled to make way for cattle and charcoal.

Rights activists fear the verdict will feed a culture of impunity that reigns in southern Pará and throughout the Brazilian Amazon. Of more than 914 cases of land-related killings over the past 30 years, all but a dozen gunmen have gone scot-free. Only six intellectual authors have served time in prison, amounting to a conviction rate below 2 percent.

With receding hairline and bookish eyeglasses, José Batista Gonçalves Afonso, a Catholic Church lawyer who advised the prosecution in the case against Moreira and conspirators, looks more like the priest he studied to be in his youth than the rainforest and human rights crusader he has become, a man who has received multiple death threats. He has helped file an appeal in the case, hoping to bring a new trial against Moreira. "Convicting the boss would have a squelching effect," he says. "They'll have to think twice before contracting killers to do their work."

That's unlikely to happen any time soon, in Afonso's view. Brazil has set itself on a course that will see more land conflict, not less, as it seeks to boost commodity exports—minerals, beef and soy—to pay for massive public-works projects and social programs. It could be the government applying eminent domain over indigenous lands to dam a river. Or a rancher illegally clearing land for cattle. Wherever the challenge comes from, there will be push-back from traditional communities. "We see the greatest number of conflicts where the frontier is expanding into the Amazon," says Afonso, who pledges to stand behind those who resist. "We're going to confront the loggers, the cattle breeders, the ranchers. We will impede their advance." It's a fight he almost seems to welcome. In any case, it's a fight that's far from over.

Critical Thinking

1. Discuss the circumstances of the deaths of environmental advocates trying to protect the Amazon rainforest.

2. In what respects is Brazil the most dangerous country in which to work as an environmentalist?

3. What have often been the motivations of the environmentalists? Why are they especially vulnerable?

4. What have been some of the typical reasons for the murders?

5. Discuss the global economy as the underlying cause of the violence and the specific circumstances that have preceded it in various places in the world.

6. Why are such murder cases difficult to investigate? What happened in the murder case of Zé Cláudio and Maria and why?

7. In what sense is there a "culture of impunity" with respect to the murders of rights activists?

8. Why is it likely that there will be more conflict, not less, in Brazil?

Create Central

www.mhhe.com/createcentral

Internet References

Association for Political and Legal Anthropology
www.aaanet.org/apla/index.htm
Human Rights and Humanitarian Assistance
www.etown.edu/vl/humrts.html

SCOTT WALLACE is the author of *The Unconquered: In Search of the Amazon's Last Uncontacted Tribes.*

Article   Prepared by: Elvio Angeloni, *Pasadena City College*

Being Indigenous in the 21st Century

With a shared sense of history and a growing set of tools, the world's Indigenous Peoples are moving into a future of their own making without losing sight of who they are and where they come from.

WILMA MANKILLER

Learning Outcomes

After reading this article, you will be able to:

- Discuss the values Indigenous People share about the natural world.

- Explain why we should care about the loss of human cultures.

There are more than 300 million Indigenous People, in virtually every region of the world, including the Sámi peoples of Scandinavia, the Maya of Guatemala, numerous tribal groups in the Amazonian rainforest, the Dalits in the mountains of Southern India, the San and Kwei of Southern Africa, Aboriginal people in Australia, and, of course the hundreds of Indigenous Peoples in Mexico, Central and South America, as well as here in what is now known as North America.

There is enormous diversity among communities of Indigenous Peoples, each of which has its own distinct culture, language, history, and unique way of life. Despite these differences, Indigenous Peoples across the globe share some common values derived in part from an understanding that their lives are part of and inseparable from the natural world.

Onondaga Faith Keeper Oren Lyons once said, "Our knowledge is profound and comes from living in one place for untold generations. It comes from watching the sun rise in the east and set in the west from the same place over great sections of time. We are as familiar with the lands, rivers, and great seas that surround us as we are with the faces of our mothers. Indeed, we call the earth Etenoha, our mother from whence all life springs."

Indigenous people are not the only people who understand the interconnectedness of all living things. There are many thousands of people from different ethnic groups who care deeply about the environment and fight every day to protect the earth. The difference is that Indigenous People have the benefit of being regularly reminded of their responsibilities to the land by stories and ceremonies. They remain close to the land, not only in the way they live, but in their hearts and in the way they view the world. Protecting the environment is not an intellectual exercise; it is a sacred duty. When women like Pauline Whitesinger, an elder at Big Mountain, and Carrie Dann, a Western Shoshone land rights activist, speak of preserving the land for future generations, they are not just talking about future generations of humans. They are talking about future generations of plants, animals, water, and all living things. Pauline and Carrie understand the relative insignificance of human beings in the totality of the planet.

Aside from a different view of their relationship to the natural world, many of the world's Indigenous Peoples also share a fragmented but still-present sense of responsibility for one another. Cooperation always has been necessary for the survival of tribal people, and even today cooperation takes precedence over competition in more traditional communities. It is really quite miraculous that a sense of sharing and reciprocity continues into the 21st century given the staggering amount of adversity Indigenous Peoples have faced. In many communities, the most respected people are not those who have amassed great material wealth or achieved great personal success. The greatest respect is reserved for those who help other people, those who understand that their lives play themselves out within a set of reciprocal relationships.

There is evidence of this sense of reciprocity in Cherokee communities. My husband, Charlie Soap, leads a widespread self-help movement among the Cherokee in which low-income volunteers work together to build walking trails, community centers, sports complexes, water lines, and houses. The self-help movement taps into the traditional Cherokee value of cooperation for the sake of the common good. The projects also build a sense of self-efficacy among the people.

Besides values, the world's Indigenous Peoples are also bound by the common experience of being "discovered" and subjected to colonial expansion into their territories that has led to the loss of an incalculable number of lives and millions and millions of acres of land and resources. The most basic rights of Indigenous Peoples were disregarded, and they were subjected to a series of policies that were designed to dispossess them of their land and resources and assimilate them into colonial society and culture. Too often the policies resulted in poverty, high infant mortality, rampant unemployment, and substance abuse, with all its attendant problems.

The stories are shockingly similar all over the world. When I read Chinua Achebe's *Things Fall Apart,* which chronicled the systematic destruction of an African tribe's social, cultural, and economic structure, it sounded all too familiar: take the land, discredit the leaders, ridicule the traditional healers, and send the children off to distant boarding schools.

And I was sickened by the Stolen Generation report about Aboriginal children in Australia who were forcibly removed from their families and placed in boarding schools far away from their families and communities. My own father and my Aunt Sally were taken from my grandfather by the U.S. government and placed in a government boarding school when they were very young. There is a connection between us. Indigenous Peoples everywhere are connected both by our values and by our oppression.

When contemplating the contemporary challenges and problems faced by Indigenous Peoples worldwide, it is important to remember that the roots of many social, economic, and political problems can be found in colonial policies. And these policies continue today across the globe.

Several years ago Charlie and I visited an indigenous community along the Rio Negro in the Brazilian rainforest. Some of the leaders expressed concern that some environmentalists, who should be natural allies, focus almost exclusively on the land and appear not to see or hear the people at all. One leader pointed out that a few years ago it was popular for famous musicians to wear T-shirts emblazoned with the slogan "Save the Rainforests," but no one ever wore a T-shirt with the slogan "Save the People of the Rainforest," though the people of the forest possess the best knowledge about how to live with and sustain the forests.

With so little accurate information about Indigenous Peoples available in educational institutions, in literature, films, or popular culture, it is not surprising that many people are not even conscious of Indigenous Peoples.

The battle to protect the human and land rights of Indigenous Peoples is made immeasurably more difficult by the fact that so few people know much about either the history or contemporary lives of our people. And without any kind of history or cultural context, it is almost impossible for outsiders to understand the issues and challenges faced by Indigenous Peoples.

This lack of accurate information leaves a void that is often filled with nonsensical stereotypes, which either vilify Indigenous Peoples as troubled descendants of savage peoples, or romanticize them as innocent children of nature, spiritual but incapable of higher thought.

Public perceptions will change in the future as indigenous leaders more fully understand that there is a direct link between public perception and public policies. Indigenous Peoples must frame their own issues, because if they don't frame the issues for themselves, their opponents most certainly will. In the future, as more indigenous people become filmmakers, writers, historians, museum curators, and journalists, they will be able to use a dazzling array of technological tools to tell their own stories, in their own voice, in their own way.

Once, a journalist asked me whether people in the United States had trouble accepting the government of the Cherokee Nation during my tenure as principal chief. I was a little surprised by the question. The government of the Cherokee Nation predated the government of the United States and had treaties with other countries before it executed a treaty with one of the first U.S. colonies.

Cherokee and other tribal leaders sent delegations to meet with the English, Spanish, and French in an effort to protect their lands and people. Traveling to foreign lands with a trusted interpreter, tribal ambassadors took maps that had been painstakingly drawn by hand to show their lands to heads of other governments. They also took along gifts, letters, and proclamations. Though tribal leaders thought they were being dealt with as heads of state and as equals, historical records indicate they were often objects of curiosity, and that there was a great deal of disdain and ridicule of these earnest delegates.

Tribal governments in the United States today exercise a range of sovereign rights. Many tribal governments have their own judicial systems, operate their own police force, run their own schools, administer their own clinics and hospitals, and operate a wide range of business enterprises. There are now more than two dozen tribally controlled community colleges. All these advancements benefit everyone in the community, not just tribal people. The history, contemporary lives, and future of tribal governments is intertwined with that of their neighbors.

One of the most common misperceptions about Indigenous Peoples is that they are all the same. There is not only great diversity among Indigenous Peoples, there is great diversity within each tribal community, just as there is in the larger society. Members of the Cherokee Nation are socially, economically, and culturally stratified. Several thousand Cherokee continue to speak the Cherokee language and live in Cherokee communities in rural northeastern Oklahoma. At the other end of the spectrum, there are enrolled tribal members who have never been to even visit the Cherokee Nation. Intermarriage has created an enrolled Cherokee membership that includes people with Hispanic, Asian, Caucasian, and African American heritage.

So what does the future hold for Indigenous Peoples across the globe? What challenges will they face moving further into the 21st century?

To see the future, one needs only to look at the past. If, as peoples, we have been able to survive a staggering loss of land, of rights, of resources, of lives, and we are still standing in the early 21st century, how can I not be optimistic that we will survive whatever challenges lie ahead, that 100 or 500 years from now we will still have viable indigenous communities? Without question, the combined efforts of government and various religious groups to eradicate traditional knowledge systems has had a profoundly negative impact on the culture as well as the social and economic systems of Indigenous Peoples. But if we have been able to hold onto our sense of community, our languages, culture, and ceremonies, despite everything, how can I not be optimistic about the future?

And though some of our original languages, medicines, and ceremonies have been irretrievably lost, the ceremonial fires of many Indigenous Peoples across the globe have survived all the upheaval. Sometimes indigenous communities have almost had to reinvent themselves as a people but they have never given up their sense of responsibility to one another and to the land. It is this sense of interdependence that has sustained tribal people thus far and I believe it will help sustain them well into the future.

Indigenous Peoples know about change and have proven time and time again they can adapt to change. No matter where they go in the world, they hold onto a strong sense of tribal identity while fully interacting with and participating in the larger society around them. In my state of Oklahoma alone, we have produced an indigenous astronaut, two United States congressmen, a Pulitzer Prize-winning novelist, and countless others who have made great contributions to their people, the state, and the world.

One of the great challenges for Indigenous Peoples in the 21st century will be to develop practical models to capture, maintain, and pass on traditional knowledge systems and values to future generations. Nothing can replace the sense of continuity that a genuine understanding of traditional tribal knowledge brings. Many communities are working on discrete aspects of culture, such as language or medicine, but it is the entire system of knowledge that needs to be maintained, not just for Indigenous Peoples but for the world at large.

Regrettably, in the future the battle for human and land rights will continue. But the future does look somewhat better for tribal people. Last year, after 30 years of advocacy by Indigenous Peoples, the United Nations finally passed a declaration supporting their distinct human rights. The challenge will be to make sure the provisions of the declaration are honored and that the rights of Indigenous Peoples all over the world are protected.

Indigenous Peoples simply do better when they have control of their own lives. In the case of my own people, after we were forcibly removed by the United States military from the southeastern part of the United States to Indian Territory, now Oklahoma, we picked ourselves up and rebuilt our nation, despite the fact that approximately 4,000 Cherokee lives were lost during the forced removal. We started some of the first schools west of the Mississippi, Indian or non-Indian, and built schools for the higher education of women. We printed our own newspapers in Cherokee and English and were more literate than our neighbors in adjoining states. Then, in the early 20th century, the federal government almost abolished the Cherokee Nation, and within two decades, our educational attainment levels dropped dramatically and many of our people were living without the most basic amenities. But our people never gave up the dream of rebuilding the Cherokee Nation. In my grandfather's time, Cherokee men rode horses from house to house to collect dimes in a mason jar so they could send representatives to Washington to remind the government to honor its treaties with the Cherokee people.

Over the past 35 years, we have revitalized the Cherokee Nation and once again run our own school, and we have an extensive array of successful education programs. The youth at our Sequoyah High School recently won the state trigonometry contest, and several are Gates Millennium Scholars. We simply do better when we have control over our own destiny.

Critical Thinking

1. What do the 300 million Indigenous People of the world have in common? Where does such knowledge come from?

2. In what ways do Indigenous People differ from others who care about the environment?

3. In what respects is there a "shared sense of responsibility for one another" among Indigenous People?

4. Describe the Indigenous People's common experience of "being discovered" and "being subjected to colonial expansion."

5. Why is it important to not just "save the rainforests," but also to "save the people"?

6. How is the battle to protect the human and land rights of Indigenous Peoples made immeasurably more difficult? How does the author suggest that such public perceptions be changed?

7. In what respects were tribal groups, such as the Cherokee, independent entities at one time?

8. In what respects do tribal governments in the United States still exercise a range of sovereign rights?

9. Why is the author optimistic about the future survival of indigenous communities?

10. What challenges lie ahead for Indigenous Peoples and how does the author suggest that they are meeting these challenges?

11. How have the Cherokee shown that "Indigenous Peoples simply do better when they have control over their own lives"?

Create Central

www.mhhe.com/createcentral

Internet References

Association for Political and Legal Anthropology
www.aaanet.org/apla/index.htm

Human Rights and Humanitarian Assistance
www.etown.edu/vl/humrts.html

The Indigenous Rights Movement in the Pacific
www.inmotionmagazine.com/pacific.html

Murray Research Center
www.radcliffe.edu/murray_redirect/index.php

Small Planet Institute
www.smallplanet.org/food

WWW Virtual Library: Indigenous Studies
www.cwis.org

Article   Prepared by: Elvio Angeloni, *Pasadena City College*

Population Seven Billion

By 2045 global population is projected to reach nine billion. Can the planet take the strain? As we reach the milestone of seven billion people this year, it's time to take stock. In the coming decades, despite falling birthrates, the population will continue to grow—mostly in poor countries. If the billions of people who want to boost themselves out of poverty follow the path blazed by those in wealthy countries, they too will step hard on the planet's resources. How big will the population actually grow? What will the planet look like in 2045? Throughout the year we'll offer an in-depth series exploring those questions. The answers will depend on the decisions each of us makes.

ROBERT KUNZIG

Learning Outcomes

After reading this article, you will be able to:

- Define what is meant by the *demographic transition* and discuss the role it has played in world population growth.

- Discuss whether we should be alarmed by population growth, the environment, or both.

One day in Delft in the fall of 1677, Antoni van Leeuwenhoek, a cloth merchant who is said to have been the long-haired model for two paintings by Johannes Vermeer—"The Astronomer" and "The Geographer"—abruptly stopped what he was doing with his wife and rushed to his worktable. Cloth was Leeuwenhoek's business but microscopy his passion. He'd had five children already by his first wife (though four had died in infancy), and fatherhood was not on his mind. "Before six beats of the pulse had intervened," as he later wrote to the Royal Society of London, Leeuwenhoek was examining his perishable sample through a tiny magnifying glass. Its lens, no bigger than a small raindrop, magnified objects hundreds of times. Leeuwenhoek had made it himself; nobody else had one so powerful. The learned men in London were still trying to verify Leeuwenhoek's earlier claims that unseen "animalcules" lived by the millions in a single drop of lake water and even in French wine. Now he had something more delicate to report: Human semen contained animalcules too. "Sometimes more than a thousand," he wrote, "in an amount of material the size of a grain of sand." Pressing the glass to his eye like a jeweler, Leeuwenhoek watched his own animalcules swim about, lashing their long tails. One imagines sunlight falling through leaded windows on a face lost in contemplation, as in the Vermeers. One feels for his wife.

Leeuwenhoek became a bit obsessed after that. Though his tiny peephole gave him privileged access to a never-before-seen microscopic universe, he spent an enormous amount of time looking at spermatozoa, as they're now called. Oddly enough, it was the milt he squeezed from a cod one day that inspired him to estimate, almost casually, just how many people might live on Earth.

Nobody then really had any idea; there were few censuses. Leeuwenhoek started with an estimate that around a million people lived in Holland. Using maps and a little spherical geometry, he calculated that the inhabited land area of the planet was 13,385 times as large as Holland. It was hard to imagine the whole planet being as densely peopled as Holland, which seemed crowded even then. Thus, Leeuwenhoek concluded triumphantly, there couldn't be more than 13.385 billion people on Earth—a small number indeed compared with the 150 billion sperm cells of a single codfish! This cheerful little calculation, writes population biologist Joel Cohen in his book *How Many People Can the Earth Support?*, may have been the first attempt to give a quantitative answer to a question that has become far more pressing now than it was in the 17th century. Most answers these days are far from cheerful.

Historians now estimate that in Leeuwenhoek's day there were only half a billion or so humans on Earth. After rising very slowly for millennia, the number was just starting to take off. A century and a half later, when another scientist reported the discovery of human egg cells, the world's population had doubled to more than a billion. A century after that, around 1930, it had doubled again to two billion. The acceleration since then has been astounding. Before the 20th century, no human had lived through a doubling of the human population, but there are people alive today who have seen it triple. Sometime in late 2011, according to the UN Population Division, there will be seven billion of us.

And the explosion, though it is slowing, is far from over. Not only are people living longer, but so many women across the world are now in their childbearing years—1.8 billion—that the global population will keep growing for another few decades at least, even though each woman is having fewer children than she would have had a generation ago. By 2050 the total number could reach 10.5 billion, or it could stop at eight billion—the difference is about one child per woman. UN demographers consider the middle road their best estimate: They now project that the population may reach nine billion before 2050—in 2045. The eventual tally will depend on the choices individual couples make when they engage in that most intimate of human acts, the one Leeuwenhoek interrupted so carelessly for the sake of science.

With the population still growing by about 80 million each year, it's hard not to be alarmed. Right now on Earth, water tables are falling, soil is eroding, glaciers are melting, and fish stocks are vanishing. Close to a billion people go hungry each day. Decades from now, there will likely be two billion more mouths to feed, mostly in poor countries. There will be billions more people wanting and deserving to boost themselves out of poverty. If they follow the path blazed by wealthy countries—clearing forests, burning coal and oil, freely scattering fertilizers and pesticides—they too will be stepping hard on the planet's natural resources. How exactly is this going to work?

There may be some comfort in knowing that people have long been alarmed about population. From the beginning, says French demographer Hervé Le Bras, demography has been steeped in talk of the apocalypse. Some of the field's founding papers were written just a few years after Leeuwenhoek's discovery by Sir William Petty, a founder of the Royal Society. He estimated that world population would double six times by the Last Judgment, which was expected in about 2,000 years. At that point it would exceed 20 billion people—more, Petty thought, than the planet could feed. "And then, according to the prediction of the Scriptures, there must be wars, and great slaughter, &c.," he wrote.

As religious forecasts of the world's end receded, Le Bras argues, population growth itself provided an ersatz mechanism of apocalypse. "It crystallized the ancient fear, and perhaps the ancient hope, of the end of days," he writes. In 1798 Thomas Malthus, an English priest and economist, enunciated his general law of population: that it necessarily grows faster than the food supply, until war, disease, and famine arrive to reduce the number of people. As it turned out, the last plagues great enough to put a dent in global population had already happened when Malthus wrote. World population hasn't fallen, historians think, since the Black Death of the 14th century.

In the two centuries after Malthus declared that population couldn't continue to soar, that's exactly what it did. The process started in what we now call the developed countries, which were then still developing. The spread of New World crops like corn and the potato, along with the discovery of chemical fertilizers, helped banish starvation in Europe. Growing cities remained cesspools of disease at first, but from the mid-19th century on, sewers began to channel human waste away from drinking water, which was then filtered and chlorinated; that dramatically reduced the spread of cholera and typhus.

Moreover in 1798, the same year that Malthus published his dyspeptic tract, his compatriot Edward Jenner described a vaccine for smallpox—the first and most important in a series of vaccines and antibiotics that, along with better nutrition and

sanitation, would double life expectancy in the industrializing countries, from 35 years to 77 today. It would take a cranky person to see that trend as gloomy: "The development of medical science was the straw that broke the camel's back," wrote Stanford population biologist Paul Ehrlich in 1968.

Ehrlich's book, *The Population Bomb,* made him the most famous of modern Malthusians. In the 1970s, Ehrlich predicted, "hundreds of millions of people are going to starve to death," and it was too late to do anything about it. "The cancer of population growth . . . must be cut out," Ehrlich wrote, "by compulsion if voluntary methods fail." The very future of the United States was at risk. In spite or perhaps because of such language, the book was a best seller, as Malthus's had been. And this time too the bomb proved a dud. The green revolution—a combination of high-yield seeds, irrigation, pesticides, and fertilizers that enabled grain production to double—was already under way. Today many people are undernourished, but mass starvation is rare.

Ehrlich was right, though, that population would surge as medical science spared many lives. After World War II the developing countries got a sudden transfusion of preventive care, with the help of institutions like the World Health Organization and UNICEF. Penicillin, the smallpox vaccine, DDT (which, though later controversial, saved millions from dying of malaria)—all arrived at once. In India life expectancy went from 38 years in 1952 to 64 today; in China, from 41 to 73. Millions of people in developing countries who would have died in childhood survived to have children themselves. That's why the population explosion spread around the planet: because a great many people were saved from dying.

And because, for a time, women kept giving birth at a high rate. In 18th-century Europe or early 20th-century Asia, when the average woman had six children, she was doing what it took to replace herself and her mate, because most of those children never reached adulthood. When child mortality declines, couples eventually have fewer children—but that transition usually takes a generation at the very least. Today in developed countries, an average of 2.1 births per woman would maintain a steady population; in the developing world, "replacement fertility" is somewhat higher. In the time it takes for the birthrate to settle into that new balance with the death rate, population explodes.

When child mortality declines, couples eventually have fewer children—but that transition takes a generation.

Demographers call this evolution the demographic transition. All countries go through it in their own time. It's a hallmark of human progress: In a country that has completed the transition, people have wrested from nature at least some control over death and birth. The global population explosion is an inevitable side effect, a huge one that some people are not sure our civilization can survive. But the growth rate was actually at its peak just as Ehrlich was sounding his alarm. By the early 1970s, fertility rates around the world had begun dropping faster than anyone had anticipated. Since then, the population growth rate has fallen by more than 40 percent.

The fertility decline that is now sweeping the planet started at different times in different countries. France was one of the first. By the early 18th century, noblewomen at the French court were knowing carnal pleasures without bearing more than two children. They often relied on the same method Leeuwenhoek used for his studies: withdrawal, or coitus interruptus. Village parish records show the trend had spread to the peasantry by the late 18th century; by the end of the 19th, fertility in France had fallen to three children per woman—without the help of modern contraceptives. The key innovation was conceptual, not contraceptive, says Gilles Pison of the National Institute for Demographic Studies in Paris. Until the Enlightenment, "the number of children you had, it was God who decided. People couldn't fathom that it might be up to them."

Other countries in the West eventually followed France's lead. By the onset of World War II, fertility had fallen close to the replacement level in parts of Europe and the U.S. Then, after the surprising blip known as the baby boom, came the bust, again catching demographers off guard. They assumed some instinct would lead women to keep having enough children to ensure the survival of the species. Instead, in country after developed country, the fertility rate fell below replacement level. In the late 1990s in Europe it fell to 1.4. "The evidence I'm familiar with, which is anecdotal, is that women couldn't care less about replacing the species," Joel Cohen says.

The end of a baby boom can have two big economic effects on a country. The first is the "demographic dividend"—a blissful few decades when the boomers swell the labor force and the number of young and old dependents is relatively small, and there is thus a lot of money for other things. Then the second effect kicks in: The boomers start to retire. What had been considered the enduring demographic order is revealed to be a party that has to end. The sharpening American debate over Social Security and last year's strikes in France over increasing the retirement age are responses to a problem that exists throughout the developed world: how to support an aging population. "In 2050 will there be enough people working to pay for pensions?" asks Frans Willekens, director of the Netherlands Interdisciplinary Demographic Institute in The Hague. "The answer is no."

In industrialized countries it took generations for fertility to fall to the replacement level or below. As that same transition takes place in the rest of the world, what has astonished demographers is how much faster it is happening there. Though its population continues to grow, China, home to a fifth of the world's people, is already below replacement fertility and has been for nearly 20 years, thanks in part to the coercive one-child policy implemented in 1979; Chinese women, who were bearing an average of six children each as recently as 1965, are now having around 1.5. In Iran, with the support of the Islamic regime, fertility has fallen more than 70 percent since the early '80s. In Catholic and democratic Brazil, women have reduced their fertility rate by half over the same quarter century. "We still don't understand why fertility has gone down so fast in so many societies, so many cultures and religions. It's just mind-boggling," says Hania Zlotnik, director of the UN Population Division.

"At this moment, much as I want to say there's still a problem of high fertility rates, it's only about 16 percent of the world population, mostly in Africa," says Zlotnik. South of the Sahara, fertility is still five children per woman; in Niger it is seven. But then, 17 of the countries in the region still have life expectancies of 50 or less; they have just begun the demographic transition. In most of the world, however, family size has shrunk dramatically. The UN projects that the world will reach replacement fertility by 2030. "The population as a whole is on a path toward nonexplosion—which is good news," Zlotnik says.

The bad news is that 2030 is two decades away and that the largest generation of adolescents in history will then be entering their childbearing years. Even if each of those women has only two children, population will coast upward under its own momentum for another quarter century. Is a train wreck in the offing, or will people then be able to live humanely and in a way that doesn't destroy their environment? One thing is certain: Close to one in six of them will live in India.

I have understood the population explosion intellectually for a long time. I came to understand it emotionally one stinking hot night in Delhi a couple of years ago. . . . The temperature was well over 100, and the air was a haze of dust and smoke. The streets seemed alive with people. People eating, people washing, people sleeping. People visiting, arguing, and screaming. People thrusting their hands through the taxi window, begging. People defecating and urinating. People clinging to buses. People herding animals. People, people, people, people.

—Paul Ehrlich

In 1966, when Ehrlich took that taxi ride, there were around half a billion Indians. There are 1.2 billion now. Delhi's population has increased even faster, to around 22 million, as people have flooded in from small towns and villages and crowded into sprawling shantytowns. Early last June in the stinking hot city, the summer monsoon had not yet arrived to wash the dust from the innumerable construction sites, which only added to the dust that blows in from the deserts of Rajasthan. On the new divided highways that funnel people into the unplanned city, oxcarts were heading the wrong way in the fast lane. Families of four cruised on motorbikes, the women's scarves flapping like vivid pennants, toddlers dangling from their arms. Families of a dozen or more sardined themselves into buzzing, bumblebee-colored auto rickshaws designed for two passengers. In the stalled traffic, amputees and wasted little children cried for alms. Delhi today is boomingly different from the city Ehrlich visited, and it is also very much the same.

At Lok Nayak Hospital, on the edge of the chaotic and densely peopled nest of lanes that is Old Delhi, a human tide flows through the entrance gate every morning and crowds inside on the lobby floor. "Who could see this and not be worried about the population of India?" a surgeon named Chandan Bortamuly asked one afternoon as he made his way toward his vasectomy clinic. "Population is our biggest problem." Removing the padlock from the clinic door, Bortamuly stepped into a small operating room. Inside, two men lay stretched out on examination tables, their testicles poking up through holes in the green sheets. A ceiling fan pushed cool air from two window units around the room.

Bortamuly is on the front lines of a battle that has been going on in India for nearly 60 years. In 1952, just five years after it gained independence from Britain, India became the first country to establish a policy for population control. Since then the government has repeatedly set ambitious goals—and repeatedly missed them by a mile. A national policy adopted in 2000 called for the country to reach the replacement fertility of 2.1 by 2010. That won't happen for at least another decade. In the UN's medium projection, India's population will rise to just over 1.6 billion people by 2050. "What's inevitable is that India is going to exceed the population of China by 2030," says A. R. Nanda, former head of the Population Foundation of India, an advocacy group. "Nothing less than a huge catastrophe, nuclear or otherwise, can change that."

China is already below replacement fertility, thanks in part to its coercive one-child policy.

Sterilization is the dominant form of birth control in India today, and the vast majority of the procedures are performed on women. The government is trying to change that; a no-scalpel vasectomy costs far less and is easier on a man than a tubal ligation is on a woman. In the operating theater Bortamuly worked quickly. "They say the needle pricks like an ant bite," he explained, when the first patient flinched at the local anesthetic. "After that it's basically painless, bloodless surgery." Using the pointed tip of a forceps, Bortamuly made a tiny hole in the skin of the scrotum and pulled out an oxbow of white, stringy vas deferens—the sperm conduit from the patient's right testicle. He tied off both ends of the oxbow with fine black thread, snipped them, and pushed them back under the skin. In less than seven minutes—a nurse timed him—the patient was walking out without so much as a Band-Aid. The government will pay him an incentive fee of 1,100 rupees (around $25), a week's wages for a laborer.

The Indian government tried once before to push vasectomies, in the 1970s, when anxiety about the population bomb was at its height. Prime Minister Indira Gandhi and her son Sanjay used state-of-emergency powers to force a dramatic increase in sterilizations. From 1976 to 1977 the number of operations tripled, to more than eight million. Over six million of those were vasectomies. Family planning workers were pressured to meet quotas; in a few states, sterilization became a condition for receiving new housing or other government benefits. In some cases the police simply rounded up poor people and hauled them to sterilization camps.

The excesses gave the whole concept of family planning a bad name. "Successive governments refused to touch the subject," says Shailaja Chandra, former head of the National

Population Stabilisation Fund (NPSF). Yet fertility in India has dropped anyway, though not as fast as in China, where it was nose-diving even before the draconian one-child policy took effect. The national average in India is now 2.6 children per woman, less than half what it was when Ehrlich visited. The southern half of the country and a few states in the northern half are already at replacement fertility or below.

In Kerala, on the southwest coast, investments in health and education helped fertility fall to 1.7. The key, demographers there say, is the female literacy rate: At around 90 percent, it's easily the highest in India. Girls who go to school start having children later than ones who don't. They are more open to contraception and more likely to understand their options.

So far this approach, held up as a model internationally, has not caught on in the poor states of northern India—in the "Hindi belt" that stretches across the country just south of Delhi. Nearly half of India's population growth is occurring in Rajasthan, Madhya Pradesh, Bihar, and Uttar Pradesh, where fertility rates still hover between three and four children per woman. More than half the women in the Hindi belt are illiterate, and many marry well before reaching the legal age of 18. They gain social status by bearing children—and usually don't stop until they have at least one son.

As an alternative to the Kerala model, some point to the southern state of Andhra Pradesh, where sterilization "camps"—temporary operating rooms often set up in schools—were introduced during the '70s and where sterilization rates have remained high as improved hospitals have replaced the camps. In a single decade beginning in the early 1990s, the fertility rate fell from around three to less than two. Unlike in Kerala, half of all women in Andhra Pradesh remain illiterate.

Amarjit Singh, the current executive director of the NPSF, calculates that if the four biggest states of the Hindi belt had followed the Andhra Pradesh model, they would have avoided 40 million births—and considerable suffering. "Because 40 million were born, 2.5 million children died," Singh says. He thinks if all India were to adopt high-quality programs to encourage sterilizations, in hospitals rather than camps, it could have 1.4 billion people in 2050 instead of 1.6 billion.

Critics of the Andhra Pradesh model, such as the Population Foundation's Nanda, say Indians need better health care, particularly in rural areas. They are against numerical targets that pressure government workers to sterilize people or cash incentives that distort a couple's choice of family size. "It's a private decision," Nanda says.

In Indian cities today, many couples are making the same choice as their counterparts in Europe or America. Sonalde Desai, a senior fellow at New Delhi's National Council of Applied Economic Research, introduced me to five working women in Delhi who were spending most of their salaries on private-school fees and after-school tutors; each had one or two children and was not planning to have more. In a nationwide survey of 41,554 households, Desai's team identified a small but growing vanguard of urban one-child families. "We were totally blown away at the emphasis parents were placing on their children," she says. "It suddenly makes you understand—that is why fertility is going down." Indian children on average are much better educated than their parents.

That's less true in the countryside. With Desai's team I went to Palanpur, a village in Uttar Pradesh—a Hindi-belt state with as many people as Brazil. Walking into the village we passed a cell phone tower but also rivulets of raw sewage running along the lanes of small brick houses. Under a mango tree, the keeper of the grove said he saw no reason to educate his three daughters. Under a neem tree in the center of the village, I asked a dozen farmers what would improve their lives most. "If we could get a little money, that would be wonderful," one joked.

The goal in India should not be reducing fertility or population, Almas Ali of the Population Foundation told me when I spoke to him a few days later. "The goal should be to make the villages livable," he said. "Whenever we talk of population in India, even today, what comes to our mind is the increasing numbers. And the numbers are looked at with fright. This phobia has penetrated the mind-set so much that all the focus is on reducing the number. The focus on people has been pushed to the background."

It was a four-hour drive back to Delhi from Palanpur, through the gathering night of a Sunday. We sat in traffic in one market town after another, each one hopping with activity that sometimes engulfed the car. As we came down a viaduct into Moradabad, I saw a man pushing a cart up the steep hill, piled with a load so large it blocked his view. I thought of Ehrlich's epiphany on his cab ride all those decades ago. People, people, people, people—yes. But also an overwhelming sense of energy, of striving, of aspiration.

The annual meeting of the Population Association of America (PAA) is one of the premier gatherings of the world's demographers. Last April the global population explosion was not on the agenda. "The problem has become a bit passé," Hervé Le Bras says. Demographers are generally confident that by the second half of this century we will be ending one unique era in history—the population explosion—and entering another, in which population will level out or even fall.

But will there be too many of us? At the PAA meeting, in the Dallas Hyatt Regency, I learned that the current population of the planet could fit into the state of Texas, if Texas were settled as densely as New York City. The comparison made me start thinking like Leeuwenhoek. If in 2045 there are nine billion people living on the six habitable continents, the world population density will be a little more than half that of France today. France is not usually considered a hellish place. Will the world be hellish then?

Some parts of it may well be; some parts of it are hellish today. There are now 21 cities with populations larger than ten million, and by 2050 there will be many more. Delhi adds hundreds of thousands of migrants each year, and those people arrive to find that "no plans have been made for water, sewage, or habitation," says Shailaja Chandra. Dhaka in Bangladesh and Kinshasa in the Democratic Republic of the Congo are 40 times larger today than they were in 1950. Their slums are filled with desperately poor people who have fled worse poverty in the countryside.

Whole countries today face population pressures that seem as insurmountable to us as India's did to Ehrlich in 1966. Bangladesh is among the most densely populated countries in the world and one of the most immediately threatened by climate change; rising seas could displace tens of millions of Bangladeshis. Rwanda is an equally alarming case. In his book *Collapse,* Jared Diamond argued that the genocidal massacre of some 800,000 Rwandans in 1994 was the result of several factors, not only ethnic hatred but also overpopulation—too many farmers dividing the same amount of land into increasingly small pieces that became inadequate to support a farmer's family. "Malthus's worst-case scenario may sometimes be realized," Diamond concluded.

Many people are justifiably worried that Malthus will finally be proved right on a global scale—that the planet won't be able to feed nine billion people. Lester Brown, founder of Worldwatch Institute and now head of the Earth Policy Institute in Washington, believes food shortages could cause a collapse of global civilization. Human beings are living off natural capital, Brown argues, eroding soil and depleting groundwater faster than they can be replenished. All of that will soon be cramping food production. Brown's Plan B to save civilization would put the whole world on a wartime footing, like the U.S. after Pearl Harbor, to stabilize climate and repair the ecological damage. "Filling the family planning gap may be the most urgent item on the global agenda," he writes, so if we don't hold the world's population to eight billion by reducing fertility, the death rate may increase instead.

Eight billion corresponds to the UN's lowest projection for 2050. In that optimistic scenario, Bangladesh has a fertility rate of 1.35 in 2050, but it still has 25 million more people than it does today. Rwanda's fertility rate also falls below the replacement level, but its population still rises to well over twice what it was before the genocide. If that's the optimistic scenario, one might argue, the future is indeed bleak.

But one can also draw a different conclusion—that fixating on population numbers is not the best way to confront the future. People packed into slums need help, but the problem that needs solving is poverty and lack of infrastructure, not overpopulation. Giving every woman access to family planning services is a good idea—"the one strategy that can make the biggest difference to women's lives," Chandra calls it. But the most aggressive population control program imaginable will not save Bangladesh from sea level rise, Rwanda from another genocide, or all of us from our enormous environmental problems.

People packed into slums need help, but the problem that needs solving is poverty, not overpopulation.

Global warming is a good example. Carbon emissions from fossil fuels are growing fastest in China, thanks to its prolonged economic boom, but fertility there is already below replacement; not much more can be done to control population. Where population is growing fastest, in sub-Saharan Africa, emissions per person are only a few percent of what they are in the U.S.—so population control would have little effect on climate. Brian O'Neill of the National Center for Atmospheric Research has calculated that if the population were to reach 7.4 billion in 2050 instead of 8.9 billion, it would reduce emissions by 15 percent. "Those who say the whole problem is population are wrong," Joel Cohen says. "It's not even the dominant factor." To stop global warming we'll have to switch from fossil fuels to alternative energy—regardless of how big the population gets.

The number of people does matter, of course. But how people consume resources matters a lot more. Some of us leave much bigger footprints than others. The central challenge for the future of people and the planet is how to raise more of us out of poverty—the slum dwellers in Delhi, the subsistence farmers in Rwanda—while reducing the impact each of us has on the planet.

The World Bank has predicted that by 2030 more than a billion people in the developing world will belong to the "global middle class," up from just 400 million in 2005. That's a good thing. But it will be a hard thing for the planet if those people are eating meat and driving gasoline-powered cars at the same rate as Americans now do. It's too late to keep the new middle class of 2030 from being born; it's not too late to change how they and the rest of us will produce and consume food and energy. "Eating less meat seems more reasonable to me than saying, 'Have fewer children!'" Le Bras says.

It's too late to keep the new middle class of 2030 from being born. But it's not too late to change the ways we all consume.

How many people can the Earth support? Cohen spent years reviewing all the research, from Leeuwenhoek on. "I wrote the book thinking I would answer the question," he says. "I found out it's unanswerable in the present state of knowledge." What he found instead was an enormous range of "political numbers, intended to persuade people" one way or the other.

For centuries population pessimists have hurled apocalyptic warnings at the congenital optimists, who believe in their bones that humanity will find ways to cope and even improve its lot. History, on the whole, has so far favored the optimists, but history is no certain guide to the future. Neither is science. It cannot predict the outcome of *People* v. *Planet,* because all the facts of the case—how many of us there will be and how we will live—depend on choices we have yet to make and ideas we have yet to have. We may, for example, says Cohen, "see to it that all children are nourished well enough to learn in school and are educated well enough to solve the problems they will face as adults." That would change the future significantly.

The debate was present at the creation of population alarmism, in the person of Rev. Thomas Malthus himself. Toward the end of the book in which he formulated the iron law by which unchecked population growth leads to famine, he declared that law a good thing: It gets us off our duffs. It leads us to conquer the world. Man, Malthus wrote, and he must have meant woman too, is "inert, sluggish, and averse from labour, unless compelled by necessity." But necessity, he added, gives hope:

"The exertions that men find it necessary to make, in order to support themselves or families, frequently awaken faculties that might otherwise have lain for ever dormant, and it has been commonly remarked that new and extraordinary situations generally create minds adequate to grapple with the difficulties in which they are involved."

Seven billion of us soon, nine billion in 2045. Let's hope that Malthus was right about our ingenuity.

Critical Thinking

1. Why should we be alarmed about continued world population growth?

2. How did Thomas Malthus explain world growth?

3. Discuss the "demographic transition" as an explanation for population growth.

4. How has medical science aided population growth?

5. What is meant by "replacement fertility"? Why do populations continue to expand for a period after reaching replacement fertility?

6. In what parts of the world has fertility fallen significantly? What was the "demographic dividend" and what did it mean for the United States? Where do we still find high fertility rates?

7. What have been some of the key factors in reducing fertility in such places as China and India?

8. Why do critics say is it more important to focus on health, education, and the personal decisions people make regarding fertility rather than on "numerical targets"?

9. Why are many people justifiably worried that Malthus will finally be proved right on a global scale?

10. In what respects do some say the focus on population rather than the environment is wrong? What matters more than simply the number of people, according to the author?

11. In what sense did Malthus express hope?

Create Central

www.mhhe.com/createcentral

Internet References

Murray Research Center
www.radcliffe.edu/murray_redirect/index.php

Small Planet Institute
www.smallplanet.org/food

ROBERT KUNZIG is *National Geographic*'s senior editor for the environment.

Kunzig, Robert. From *National Geographic*, January 2011, pp. 40, 42–43, 45, 48–49, 60–63. Copyright © 2011 by National Geographic Society. Reprinted by permission.